1 HABIT FOR ENTREPRENEURIAL SUCCESS

---

300 LIFE-CHANGING HABITS TO TURBO-CHARGE YOUR BUSINESS

STEVEN SAMBLIS

FORBES RILEY

Foreword by
LES BROWN

EST HAB1T 2019
PRESS
A VOICE FOR BRILLIANT MINDS

From Steven Samblis

To my Daughters Lindsay and Kaitlyn. To Forbes Riley for being the best business partner ever. Lastly to Mattie for your support and incredible artistic talent.

From Forbes Riley

With deep love, admiration and sincere appreciation, I am grateful to my family, students, and friends that have made this journey, the trip of a lifetime. I'm humbled by your honesty, willingness to play full out, and strive to support a cause greater than ourselves.

To Ryker and Makenna, my twins, you are the wind beneath mommy's wings, and your love has allowed us all to fly!

A huge thank you to Steve Samblis, who created magic, a concept of Habits everyone needs to embrace, and a professional partnership that is second to none!

This book is dedicated to YOU, whoever you are and wherever you are. I am YOU. A dreamer, a schemer, and TEAMER - We are in this together, and our rising tides shall lift all boats.

CONTENTS

INTRODUCTION

- Watch your thoughts; they become your words.
- Watch your words; they become your actions.
- Watch your actions; they become your Habits.
- Watch your Habits; they become your character.
- Watch your character; it becomes your destiny.

When Steve Samblis and I first met over the phone, little did we realize that we would have created a best-selling book enrolling more than 130 top entrepreneurs sharing their top Habits within a month.

What made this possible is based on the above quote. Both Steve and I, throughout our careers, have carved out strong work ethics, a tenacity to get it done (whatever it is), and the Habit of believing that anything IS possible.

Another Habit I have followed is maintaining friendships, for it is said, "Connect with someone when you don't need them, so they are there... when you do."

I grew up ironically as a rather awkward, ugly little girl with a broken nose, eight years of braces, overweight, and hair so frizzy from the back I looked like I had a black triangle sitting on my head. I was shy, had very few friends, and spent most of my time, when not getting straight As in school... at home watching tv and movies.

It wasn't until I was well into my 20's that I began to understand and embrace the notion of teamwork and friendships. I had to shatter my limiting beliefs that people couldn't be trusted and only wanted to use you. Sad, but that was part of the fabric of my youth. Today, thanks to so many amazing people believing in me, allowing me to be vulnerable and to trust (like I teach so many others) that we are perfectly imperfect and more than enough.

I feel beyond blessed to be working with Steve Samblis, one of the few souls I have met that leads with his heart but does EVERYTHING and MORE he says and truly delivers.

I am very proud of my friends and students who embraced this idea and helped me launch the book within 24 hours and finish it less than four weeks later -- THAT is unheard of -- unless you have a partner as outrageous as I do!

Forbes Riley

Co-Author

FOREWORD BY LES BROWN

Les Brown and Co-Author Forbes Riley

I am continually looking for ways to improve myself. Every day I'm reading or listening to something and seeking to discover more about myself. That's a Habit that I have maintained for years. Good Habits have been the foundation of how I live my life. That is why it is a pleasure to write the foreword for "I Habit for Entrepreneurial Success."

Habits, to me, are rituals that you engage in regularly. When I wake up in the morning, I have a Habit of saying, "All things work together for good for those who love God and for those who are called according to His purpose." I have this affirmation that I repeat all day. "Lord, whatever I face today, together, you and I can handle it."

You could spend the next four decades searching for Habits that will best serve you, and through trial and error, you may eventually find ones that work. Forbes Riley and Steven Samblis transform those decades into days by bringing together an incredible group of Entrepreneurs, each with unique Habits that have made them successful. They have done the heavy lifting for you. All you have to do is pick your 1st Habit and make it part of who you are.

The only difference between you and the highly successful people in this book is that they decided to embrace Habits that steadied them on the path towards success.

I love how this book was written because they not only tell you the Habits, but they give you the big "Whys." Why the Habits work, and a guide on how to implement them into your life.

As a professional speaker, I have spoken to more than seven million people around the world. I have published countless books that have been published in multiple languages. I know, if you move through life with a strong foundation of good Habits, there is no limit to who you can become.

Do yourself a favor and let that hunger inside of you make you reach higher every day.

Every day, ask yourself, "what do you want out of life" what do you want out of the job, career, relationship, what will make you happy. You have to ask yourself questions. How will you know when you got it. Be specific; don't be vague by saying, "I just want to be happy."

Once you begin to determine what you want, write down. Reading it three times a day, that is morning, noon, and night. It will cause you to focus. When the negative thoughts tell you that you can't do it, that will make you focus. It will discipline your thinking. You are going to become so creative, ideas will pop up. Reading it every day gives you imaginative thoughts that will lead you towards your main goal.

Entrepreneurs reading this book will truly understand nothing is impossible with good Habits. I have been a personal friend and fan of Forbes Riley for many years, and I encourage you to embrace this book and truly learn to manifest your best life.

That's my story, and I'm sticking to it.

Warmly,

Les Brown

Motivational Speaker, Author, Former Radio DJ, Former Television Host

THE CREATION OF THE 1 HABIT™ MOVEMENT

My name is Steven Samblis, and it is my honor to present to you "1 Habit For Entrepreneurial Success." I hope this book will have a profound effect on your life.

To help you to get the most out of this book, I feel it is essential that I share with you how the 1 Habit™ Movement was created, and more importantly, why it was created.

I say the following with absolute certainty. Taking ownership of just one of the Habits in this book will have a profound effect on your life. I know this because when I learned about the power of Habits and instilled the first one into who I was, my life changed forever. I know the same can happen to you, and here is where it gets exciting. Add on another Habit and another after that, and you will find your life taking off on automatic pilot to the greatness that you were born to achieve.

The Beginning

From the time I was a young man, brand new to business, I knew the way to be successful was to find successful people that came before me and do the things they did. I was a stockbroker at the time. I would find the most successful stockbrokers, study what they did, and do the same thing. I would start my day at the same time. I went to lunch at the same time. I ate dinner at the same time. I went home at the same time. I made calls when they were making calls and studied the market when they did. After the end of doing this for six months, I was mentally and physically fried. Something was missing.

One of my heroes at this point in my life was a stockbroker named Al Glover. Al worked with me at a Dean Witter in Cocoa Beach, Florida. It was the early 80's. Cocoa Beach was a sleepy town where you could buy a charming home for under $50,000.00. Al was making a few million a year in commissions.

Al's office was right across from mine, so I every once in a while I would pop in his doorway and ask him how he became so successful, hoping to find the key. On one particular day, Al told me to sit down, watch, and listen. As he stood behind his desk, he picked up the phone and called a client, whom he later told me was a huge client but somewhat challenging to deal with. She always over-analyzed his recommendations, and by the time she was ready to pull the trigger, it was usually too late. "Mrs. Rooney, we have a terrific tax free bond yielding 8%, and I thought you would be interested." Al delivered the words and waited. It felt like an eternity went by as he sat silently on the phone, waiting for her response. "I have worked with you for many years, and during that time, you have missed out on incredible opportunities, which would have made you a great deal of money. This will be one of those. You have the money sitting in your Money Market, making a few points taxable. If you do not take this position, I am not doing my job and will no longer be able to be your Financial Advisor. I will pass your account on to somebody else." Al then stopped talking and waited. Another eternity went by until Al said. "Great, we will buy $200,000.00. I will place the order for you in the morning. Great decision. Talk to you soon."

I looked at Al stunned. "You were willing to throw away one of your biggest clients if she had said no?" Al went on to tell me that he had created a nightly Habit. Every evening at 6 pm, he looked at his book of 2000 clients and picked the five most difficult ones. He then called each one and gave them one shot to turn the relationship around, or he would dump them. He told me that this 1 Habit gave him a tremendous sense of peace. As it turned out, most clients just needed a little nudge to understand what a good position they were in having him manage their money. From that day forward, their attitudes and how they worked with him was dramatically improved.

As I left Al's office, I was inspired. I was motivated and worked hard, but motivation is just the thing that gets you started. It is Habits like Al's 6 pm calls that keep you going and drive you down the pathway to success.

Habits, once a part of you, are automatic. They don't drain your energy. They guide you along the right path to the life you want to live.

I went to my office, sat on my chair, and bounced up and went right back to Al's office. "Al, this is an amazing Habit, the 6 pm calls. However, I don't have 2000 clients. What one Habit could I make part of me that would get me to that 2000 client number?" Al took a moment and told me in a very matter of fact way. "Every night before you go home, map out your next day. If you have clients or prospects you will want to call tomorrow, make a list before you go home. If you have a trade ticket that you need to place in the morning, write it out before. Set yourself up for success every day by preparing the night before."

Wow. He was so right! I started with that 1 Habit, and it was a game-changer. I eventually instilled other Habits. This, in turn, led me to my goal. Within five years, I was managing over 2000 clients.

Fast forward to 2 years ago. I was filming interviews at Greg Reid's Secret Knock. This incredible gathering was attended by some of the highest achievers on the planet. As we prepared to roll the interviews, a thought of my friend Al came to me. "Habits." I was about to talk to very high achievers, let's roll the dice and see if these incredibly successful people had unique Habits that guided them to success. I decided to ask each person the same question. One question and one question only. "If you could instantly instill in a child, one Habit, what would it be and why?" The first answer was perfect. The second one was great. As I listened to each answer, I thought to myself,

"What would my life be like if these Habits were a part of who I am?" I also notice that many of these successful people from many different walks of life had the same Habits.

Although I realized my videos were good, I knew there was something more. As a book, the reader could skim through it and land on a Habit and say, "That is a Habit I want to make a part of me." They could instill the Habit, and once it is part of them, they can flip through the pages and find the next one.

With the idea in hand, I set out to find 100 extremely high achievers from many walks of life to contribute to our first book. I was amazed by the extraordinary people that were willing to work with me and offer their Habits. I still have such gratitude for them, believing in me enough help me make this dream a reality.

The 1 Habit Movement

After we published the first book, I watched as the incredible contributors to the book began telling stories about how they became a part of the book. They talked about how excited they were about its extraordinary potential. One contributor emailed me and said, "Steve, what you have created is more than a book. It has become a movement."

The Power of Collaboration

One of the most exciting parts of creating the first 1 Habit book was spending each day talking with some of the most inspiring people on the planet. Even more exciting, we were receiving more Habits, then we could fit into one book.

I began to see groupings of Habits that fit for particular demographics. It was at that time that I decided 1 Habit would become a book series. I would take the processes I used to create the first book and replicate it for each book going forward.

If I were to create a book series, the bottleneck would be finding people for each book. I found the solution. I would team up with a co-author for each new book in the series. It would be their responsibility to bring in contributors to the book they were working on.

Each co-author is an expert in a particular field. Co-authors find the Contributors and then organize their submissions.

As of this writing, we have twenty new 1 Habit books in process with twenty incredible co-authors. My goal is to publish once a month, each for particular groups of people.

Steven Samblis – Co-Author and Creator of the 1 Habit™ Book Series.

a

HOW TO MAKE A HABIT YOUR OWN

The Cycle of a Habit

All Habits follow a specific path

By Steven Semblis Creator of 1 Habit

The Habit

The trigger that
ignites the Habit

The reward - All
Habits have
rewards attached

Before we get into how to make a Habit your own, it is important to understand the cycle of a Habit. With this simple understanding, you will find it easier to make a Habit your own.

There is a cycle to all Habits. The cycle has three steps.

1st step: The Habit. It is the behavior you want to change, add, or remove.

2nd Step: The Reward. It is the payoff you get from the Habit.

3rd Step: The Trigger. It is the thing that makes you perform the Habit.

Keep this simple cycle in mind as you begin laying out your road map to making a Habit your own.

If you've ever tried to create a new Habit and have felt overwhelmed in the process of making even the slightest change, know that you're not alone. It's normal for emotions to come up when you're doing something new. It's also normal to want to QUIT and go back to your comfort zone, despite knowing those old Habits don't support your highest vision. As humans, we crave certainty. It makes us feel safe.

But safety doesn't always lead to success, and sometimes, risk is the best thing we can do to reap the rewards of leaning in and doing something different.

Realize that your hands are in the air mentality when it comes to change won't serve you. Despite what you might think based on your old patterns or society's conditioning, you are capable of achieving anything you desire, and it starts with *choosing yourself first* and creating NEW Habits to fuel you forward, no matter what.

The Habits in all of our 1 Habit™ books have been carefully sourced by some of the most successful people to help you upgrade all areas of your life. The steps outlined below, as well as the inspiration laid out for you throughout these pages, *work if you work them.* So before you toss this book aside and let it collect dust, understand that this is not your typical "ra-ra" book. This is a book to challenge your beliefs, show you that what you want is on the other side of your fear (inaction) and that anything's possible when you commit to the process of change/up-leveling.

If you think about your day to day routine, it's made up of Habits, right? And yes, some are better than others. That's okay! Change is possible, and you are more than capable. All of your current Habits, including the way you think, were created based on consistency - by YOU! So if you're feeling frustrated and wishing you could just (insert desire here), I am here to tell you that you absolutely can, and this book will help you get there... *faster.*

At this point, you might be evaluating what your current Habits are, and if you're not, I'm certain you will be by the end of this book. An important characteristic of a Habit is that it's automatic - you don't even think about it - so changing them takes conscious effort. Having awareness around how you spend your time and energy can be humbling, but it's necessary if you want to step into something greater. The truth is, we waste so much of our precious resources on things that don't move the needle forward because we've gotten so used to doing things a certain way.

The good news is, you have the power to change that at any time!

So how do you create new Habits that *stick?* Well, I've compiled a list of 30 steps that are not only proven to help you get started but also beneficial in supporting your long-term success. Before you read on, though, please understand that I am not asking you to do all of these things at once. I'm not crazy (and neither are you!). What I am inviting you to consider is that the way you're doing things right now isn't working (or you wouldn't be reading this book!). And more importantly, you can make positive changes in a short amount of time, starting small and gradually upgrading your daily Habits as they become a natural part of your routine.

After all, your morning coffee... your bath before bed... your need to answer every email as soon as it hits your inbox... the lack of time set aside for your workouts... even the route you take to and from work... all of these *Habits* were created *by you*, which means that only YOU have the power to change them.

Are you ready? Good! Let's get started.

1. **Set yourself up to win.** How many times have you told yourself you'd "start tomorrow" only to have tomorrow never come? I get it! Instead, focus on creating time and space and understand what needs to be present for you to achieve the goal you've set for yourself.

2. **Practice compassion.** You are not perfect, and you never will be. That's a beautiful thing! So if things don't go exactly the way you envision, understand that there's a lesson there and honor

where you're at, while acknowledging where you still have room to grow.

3. Be clear on your WHY. One of the biggest mistakes and reasons for failure is a lack of clarity around *why* you want to make the change in the first place. When your *why* is big enough, nothing can stop you - not even YOU!

4. Choose curiosity over judgment. Ugh, the infamous "judgment". Let's be honest; how well does that work for you? Instead, when you mess up (because you're human!), get curious. How could you have done it differently? How could you have shown up better? Who could you have asked for help? What needs to change to have a more positive result next time? Then rework your plan to support this new information.

5. Choose gratitude. *Gratitude turns what we have into enough.* Ever heard that saying? It's true! With everything and everyone that comes into your experience, give thanks for the opportunity to learn, grow, expand yourself. Remember to say "THANK YOU" for it all, and that includes having gratitude for yourself.

6. Stay consistent. The statement, *never skip a Monday,* could not be truer! When creating new Habits, it's important to keep your eye on the prize. If you want to get back to a regular workout routine, commit to moving your body *every single day* for 30 days. Skipping days while trying to create a new Habit will only make it harder to stick to. You'll notice that once you've completed those 30 days, your mind will be wired for movement (or whatever Habit you're implementing), and just like that, it's now part of your routine.

7. Find an accountability buddy. Everything is better with friends, right? Habits are no different, especially if it's a Habit that you want to create, but that feels reaaallllly hard to make happen. Grab your bestie and set up a check-in schedule, and make it fun!

8. Use visualization. Did you know there are now brain studies that show the power of our thoughts? In fact, it's been shown that our minds are capable of producing the same mental instructions as our actions.[1] Yea, how's that for some serious motivation! What we think, we become so think good thoughts and visualize them in the present moment as if they've already come to fruition. Add to that: *action,* and you'll be unstoppable.

9. Have a mantra. No, these aren't just for yogis. Think back to the *"Why"* you decided on (the reason you want to make this new Habit a reality). Create a statement or come up with a word that embodies the result you're working towards, or the way you want to feel in the process of instilling this new Habit. This can be an I AM statement (I AM capable... worthy... unstoppable...) or like I said, a single word like, HEALTHY. Whatever resonates for you, choose that. There is no right or wrong here.

10. Notice your self-talk. Every time a thought comes into your head that doesn't feel extra supportive, ask yourself: would I say this to my spouse... my child... my parents... my friends? If the answer is no, it's time to flip the script and create a more loving internal dialogue.

11. Ask for support. This might feel vulnerable. But just remember that people intrinsically want to help. If this is uncomfortable for you, even better. Creating new Habits isn't meant to be easy; it's meant to challenge you and show you what you're made of, which is far more than you may realize.

12. Identify your triggers. Oh yes, the things that set us off and have us grabbing for the ice cream, or blowing our budget on a new pair of shoes! What (or who) are they? Write these down.

13. Come up with positive responses to your triggers. Now that you know what (or who) they are, how can you set yourself up to win if (when) they show up?

14. Start small. Small changes over time can make a massive impact. If you haven't worked out in years, saying you're going to run a marathon in a month probably isn't a great idea. Instead, can you commit to walking for at least 20 minutes each day and gradually increasing your time and intensity until you get where you want to go, physically? Decide what that looks like. Write it down.

15. Choose ONE Habit to implement at a time. I have a feeling you're ambitious, and you probably have a laundry list of things you want to achieve. Good for you! But instead of trying to do all the things immediately, choose ONE thing. Getting a win under your belt releases dopamine in the brain (that feel-good chemical) and will inspire you to keep going!

16. Celebrate your wins. So now that you've got that dopamine swirling around CELEBRATE!! You did it, and that is amazing... YOU are amazing!

17. Keep a journal. It's okay if you're not a writer, the point of keeping track is to look back and see how far you've come. Writing down the emotions throughout the process can be an interesting gauge, and can provide a really beautiful space for growth and healing.

18. Be specific. Do you want to lose weight, or do you want to lose 10 pounds? The more specific you can get, the easier it will be to create a plan to set yourself up to win - and be able to recognize when success happens.

19. Create a plan. How are you going to achieve this? Who can help keep you on track? What needs to change so you can replace an old Habit with this new, more supportive one? Write it down.

20. Have a reward in mind for when you succeed! Have you been putting something on hold just waiting "until"? Now is the perfect time to allow yourself permission to indulge in the reward you've been pawning over. *"After I workout for 30 days in a row, I'm going to get myself those new shoes I've been eyeing to celebrate!"* Or maybe it's a trip you've wanted to take, or whatever it may be... let this be your permission slip to reward yourself for your hard work and celebrate the new Habit you just implemented into your life.

21. Believe that it's possible. Because it is! And you are far more capable than you may realize. *Whether you think you can or you think you can't, you're right. - Henry Ford*

22. Be so committed that nothing can stop you. Eye. On. The. Prize. That new Habit is not going to happen on its own! How bad do you want it? I hope you said something like, *more than anything.* What is not doing this costing you, your family, your life?

23. Record your affirmations (and use them!). Use the voice memo on your phone to record your mantra, an I AM statement, your "Why," something that PUMPS YOU UP and encourages you to stay the course. Listen as often as you need to in order to keep pushing, even when the going gets tough.

24. Share with a loved one. This is different than having someone do the work with you to reach your goal (that new Habit!). Simply stating your intention and plan to make it happen and asking others to support you in your efforts keeps the fire burning a little hotter. As humans, we want to know that people care and that they're proud of us. Letting your spouse or kids know that you're going to be making some changes can inspire the entire family to get on board. Pay it forward!

25. Get plenty of rest. We all know that feeling tired doesn't exactly lend well to motivation. Commit to getting uninterrupted sleep each night.

26. Drink a ton of water. Maybe don't drink a gallon of water before bed, but nourishing your cells with proper hydration not only helps you sleep better, it helps you stay energized and fueled during your day while helping to transport nutrients to your cells and wherever else they're needed. Water is the ultimate brainpower! And healthy brains make better decisions.

27. Nourish your mind, body, and soul. Surround yourself with people that will encourage and uplift you. These are the real angels on earth. We become the five people we spend the most time with, so make sure your circle supports the Habits you're looking to cultivate.

28. Avoid situations that would tempt you to "cheat" on yourself. If you know that joining everyone for a Happy Hour on Friday is going to cause you to indulge when you're committed to "clean eating without alcohol," do yourself a favor and skip it! There will be plenty more opportunities to partake in these things once you've gotten your Habits in check.

29. If you mess up, find the lesson, and keep moving forward. You are human, and you will mess up. Totally okay! Beating yourself up, harsh self-criticism, and unwarranted negative self-judgment are not supportive, and just don't feel good. Let it go! And commit to doing better next time. Now, if you find that you use this mentality as an excuse to keep repeating mistakes, that's a different story. This is meant to forward you, not sabotage your progress.

30. Don't start without a plan. If you were driving cross-country, you'd probably pull out a map, right? The same goes for creating Habits. If you want to get from point A to point B with ease, see step 1 and set yourself up for success! Fail to plan, plan to fail. It's that simple.

So there you have it! Thirty steps to help you not only upgrade your Habits *but make them stick!* If you are serious about living your best life, your Habits are imperative to your success. Our intention for the 1 Habit™ series is to make this as easy as possible for you in the way of motivation, empowerment, and support.

You're an intelligent person, so I am confident you are fully aware that, as much as we'd love to make these changes for you, it's not possible. But our hope is that by laying out the foundation for you, you will not only begin to see how simple it can be - but also be inspired to get to work!

On behalf of myself and all of our contributors, WE BELIEVE IN YOU! Now get out there, create some new Habits, and achieve your dreams.

Resources:

https://www.psychologytoday.com/us/blog/flourish/200912/seeing-is-believing-the-power-visualization[1]

DEFINITION OF HABIT

Habit: A behavior pattern acquired by frequent repetition or physiologic exposure that shows itself in regularity or increased facility of performance.

- Merriam-Webster Dictionary

IMPORTANT NOTE - HOW TO USE THIS BOOK

DO NOT PICK THIS BOOK UP AND READ IT FROM COVER TO COVER.

1 Habit books are created to help you to find and instill new Habits that will change your life forever. The best way to use this book is as follows...

1. After you have read "How to Make a Habit Your Own", flip through the pages and let a Habit find you.
2. Decide if the Habit will enhance your life. If the answer is "Yes," go to step 3. (If not go back to step 1)
3. Follow the steps in the chapter "How to Make a Habit Your Own."
4. Once you have done so, and the Habit is a part of who you are, go back to step 1 and repeat.

Continue these steps, 1 Habit at a time, and you may change your life forever!

1

PREPARE FOR TOMORROW'S SUCCESS TONIGHT

STEVEN SAMBLIS

Why: When working from home, you need to be organized, or else you will lose the divide between home and work life. This Habit will help you to organize and give you peace of mind at night to enjoy your home life.

This Habit is also very fast to instill but will result in a substantial positive impact on your life.

I learned this Habit when I was a brand new stockbroker.

Here is how it works...

Every night before you go home, map out your next day. If you have clients or prospects you will want to call tomorrow, make a list with their names and numbers. If you have a trade ticket that you need to place in the morning, write it out the night before. No matter what it is you are doing tomorrow, there is an opportunity to prepare the night before. It is even a great idea to set out clothes for the next day.

Make this the evening Habit that you do in a couple of parts. When you finish your workday, take a moment to plan tomorrow's workday. This lets you close out each workday with a calm, organized spirit.

When you are ready to retire for the evening, take a moment and plan out your wardrobe for the morning.

Doing these things puts you at peace and lets you even get a better night's sleep. This simple 1 Habit can be a massive game-changer in your life.

THE UN-HABIT: STOP LISTENING TO YOUR WELL-MEANING FRIENDS

Why: When you work from home, you will probably interact more with family and friends than business associates. This can be good and bad, depending on who those people are.

This is a Habit that was given to me by Queen Latifa, while I was interviewing her and Dolly Parton together for a movie called Joyful Noise.

I have interviewed over 1000 of the top actors in the world on camera for a show called Cinema Buzz. One day I realized that I was sitting across from the most successful people on the planet, why not tap into that and learn more from them than just who they played in their movies.

As I sat across from Queen and Dolly, I asked them... "You are two of the most successful women in not just Hollywood, but in business in general. I have two daughters. What would you tell them is the key to your success?"

What Queen Latifa said to me stuck with me maybe more than anyone else I spoke to. She told me that when she was growing up and told her well-meaning friends that she wanted to be a singer, a rapper, an actor, they told her, "Don't be silly. You will never do that. Stick to what you know."

She realized that those well-meaning friends and family members could very well be the biggest obstacles to her getting out of her situation and becoming what she dreamed of.

Sometimes we surround ourselves with people that will enable laziness. That will allow you not to try. To give up. To not dream. A lot of times, those people are family and friends that we grew up with.

I know this is a difficult one, but this is a Habit that you need to change, and it could be a pretty painful move.

These family and friends that will give you the comfort to be Ok in your mediocrity do so from a loving place but also a place of fear.

There is a story about Crab fishermen. As they bring up the cages, they throw the crabs into a bucket with no lid. The reason they can do this is that if one of the crabs tries to get out, the others will grab him and pull him back in.

Sit back and look at the people you surround yourself with. Are they pulling you back in, or are they lifting you up? As painful as it may be, once you have the answer, you must either help them to change, or you need to make a change.

About Steven: I am the creator of the bestselling 1 Habit book series, published by 1 Habit press, a vertically integrated media company focusing on the development of human potential.

2

PITCH DAILY

FORBES RILEY

Why: As kids, we learn quickly to pitch for what we want. A baby cries to get the attention of their mom, a toddler smiles sweetly to get a treat, and a teenager assures you how much they love you before asking for your credit card. All these are forms of pitches.

As adults, we begin to associate pitching with selling, and suddenly it's "hard" to do. Let me shatter that notion and show you that the "Art of Pitching" is about exciting, engaging, enrolling, and ultimately getting a yes.

In my career, I've become known as the "Queen of Pitch." I got hired by "Body by Jake" to launch the cable network, Fit-Tv, where I created and filmed the pitches for over 1500 different health and fitness products that aired for 5 years. Together we revolutionized the way products were pitched on TV, and Jake sold our network to FOX for 500 million dollars. I went on to host 189 infomercials, won Best Female Presenter 9 times, and grossed more than 2.5 Billion dollars in product sales... all through the Power of the Pitch.

But the pitch is not something that happens solely when you have a product to sell. Pitching is all around us. It's how you get someone to say yes, and you unconsciously do it all day, every day without realizing it. You pitch your friends or family to go to your choice of movie, restaurant, date, etc.

The secret to my success was I became more aware of it, consciously practice it, and reap the benefits of making a sale or closing a customer.

I parlayed my pitching skills as a spokesperson for major companies and generated millions on HSN and QVC for more than 28 years. I have a motto that says, "Dream It, Believe It, Achieve It."

Every day, I strive to pitch health, wealth, and happiness.

Mastering the art of pitching is essential for articulating what you do and why you do it. Let the frustration of getting tongue-tied and not feeling you have the authority to ask for what you want go away. The freedom and confidence this skill creates will help you effectively get your message out to the world with the results you desire. When YOU make it a Habit to "pitch" something every day, whether it's your product, your service, your ideas, or your dreams... they have a knack for coming true!

HAB1T™

The Un-Habit: Stop Waiting for Permission

Why: What is Permission? You can ask for it, receive it, grant it, and even deny it, but somehow it controls and limits us.

Let me tell you the story of 4 strangers who wanted a "heart," a "brain," "courage," and to "go home" willing to endure a life-threatening journey because they believed the Great Wizard of Oz could grant their wishes.

It turns out the wizard had no special powers, for he was just a man. However, they DID get a heart, brain, courage, and go home. How? He gave them Permission to understand they already possessed those qualities.

The Wizard of Oz shines a light to illuminate how hard we are on ourselves and how easily we give up our power. When in doubt, look within for the answer. It turns out you're more powerful than you think, and often enough, you don't need to ask anyone for Permission.

It seems the notion of Permission begins as a child. Did you know the average toddler hears "no" almost 400 times a day? That's when you start to understand that there are "rules" and that pushing boundaries has negative consequences.

As an adult, there are laws to obey, social parameters to adhere to, and internal guidelines all steering us to what we have and do not have "Permission." But who ultimately makes THAT decision?

Do you need to be granted Permission to leave an abusive relationship, lose those last 30 pounds, or quit your corporate job to follow an entrepreneurial dream?

I often hear people share what they can't do or have a fear of. They don't grant themselves Permission to strive outside the box they have built for themselves. It turns out it is just a bad Habit to focus on the negative and self-enforce limiting beliefs. IT'S NOT REAL!

Question? Is there something you want or lack, but seems unattainable?

My 3 step system:

1. Ask yourself what YOU want
2. Examine WHY you want it
3. Determine how HORRIBLE your life will be if you don't attain it.
4. Decide that this is something worth fighting for and believing in!
5. Say THESE words in the mirror "I hereby GRANT you PERMISSION to _____(fill in the blank)_____"

So, are YOU waiting for Permission to move forward and take action?

For the past 20 years, I've witnessed how glorious someone's life becomes when they shatter limiting beliefs and grant themselves Permission to understand they are enough. This has become my life's purpose; I call it Forbes Factor Breakthru. I've designed exercises that unleash your full potential and serve to shatter what has been holding you back. Truly learning to harness the positive power of granting yourself Permission to manifest your dream life is my goal. I've given myself

Permission to help others live their best lives; what will you grant yourself Permission for?

About Forbes: Forbes Riley mesmerizes audiences with her authentic, inspirational style that is second to none. Often referred to as Oprah meets Tony Robbins she transports, transforms and transfixes audiences from 100 to 10,000. As one of the pioneers behind the As Seen on TV infomercial phenomenon, Forbes Riley has hosted 180+ infomercials and guested on QVC/HSN generating more than $2.5 billion in global sales including Jack Lalanne Juicer, Montel Williams Healthmaster and her signature fitness product, SpinGym. As a health and fitness expert, Forbes was inducted into the National Fitness Hall of Fame and is the creator and CEO of the fitness phenomenon, SpinGym. SpinGym has sold more than 2 million units and she has a team of worldwide Brand

Ambassadors promoting workplace wellness to major corporations. She is the co-creator of the 1 Habit book for entrepreneurial success and is proud that her 17 year old twins, Ryker and Makenna, are contributors to the book. Forbes cherishes her successes, but most important to her is her family and helping others live up to their true potential.

3

LOOK BIG, ACT BIG, BECOME BIG

ALEC STERN

Why: "Looking Big, Acting Big, Becoming Big" is all about perspective and perception. Entrepreneurs often project smallness and make unnecessary excuses for being small.

Naturally, not everyone is out to become a behemoth like Amazon or Google. So, what I mean by looking big is looking capable, credible, experienced, proven, etc. It's about putting your best foot forward. But I routinely see entrepreneurs fail to put their best foot forward in some fundamental ways when engaging in important meetings and communications. For example, your email address alone says something about you. If your business email address ends in @gmail, @hotmail, @yahoo, it says small. Think about it. How seriously will a prospective customer or partner take you if you do not invest the few dollars required to obtain a branded email address tied to your domain address? i.e., you@yourdomain.com. Putting your brand forward and amplifying it at every turn helps you look big.

Another way to look big, not to mention organized and prepared, is to create a branded, brief slide presentation. Imagine you're meeting with a prospective customer, partner, investor, mentor, etc. What if you had five slides like the following:

1. Who you are?
2. What you do?
3. What makes you unique?
4. What your customers are saying about you?
5. How you might work with the person or company to whom you are speaking?

When you kick off the call or meeting, ask if you can share a few slides. They will always say yes. Then, guess what? You lead and own the meeting. As a follow-up, save these slides as a PDF document and email it to them. By doing so, you have just enabled this person to review your information again and share it with other would-be decision-makers. You've put your best foot forward and enabled the person to advocate for you. When you are asked to meet with a larger team, introduce these same five slides and own the meeting, again, by acting and looking big.

What about your website and social media channels? These are the "front doors" through which your important audiences will enter. Choose your social platforms carefully, be consistent, be branded, and be active. Ensure your posts are current and engage with your fans and followers to show others you are serious about your business. Make "Look Big, Act Big," your mantra, and you will "Become Big."

The Un-Habit: Get out of "Stealth Mode" when working on your idea, product, or service

Why: All too often, I speak to entrepreneurs who want to keep their idea close to the vest or stay in "Stealth Mode." Stealth mode is when you avoid sharing or talking to anyone about what you're working on. Sometimes this is done out of fear that someone will steal your idea. In reality, you can share a lot of information without giving away your "Secret Sauce." Other times companies stay in stealth mode because they feel their idea, product, or service is unfinished and not quite ready to share.

I've heard entrepreneurs say I don't need to talk to my target market because I am my target market. Coming from the target market is often how entrepreneurs come up with their start-up ideas. But it is not a question of knowledge; it's a question of perspective. One of the unbreakable rules is you never stop talking to your target market to get current feedback.

Feedback is a gift. With the ever-changing market landscape and needs of your target market, you should be getting feedback early and often. This feedback will help validate your idea, confirming you are headed in the right direction, or you may learn some great ways to enhance or advance your idea. When you get feedback, avoid going to those closest to you, like family or people you have done business with. Instead, go to qualified people you don't know to get truly brutal, honest feedback.

When you seek feedback from your target market, first get a thorough understanding of their goals and objectives.

(Hint): Just ask.

Once you understand this, ask yourself if your idea or offering is going to help them achieve their goals. Are you saving them time, money, or gaining more revenue, customers, etc.? Then share your idea and set the stage for them to provide feedback, potentially become a customer, or refer you to others to talk to.

About Alec: Alec Stern has more than 25 years of experience as a founder, mentor, investor, and hyper-growth agent for companies across various industries. He's been a co-founder or founding team member of 8 start-ups with five exits - two IPOs and three acquisitions.

As a primary member of Constant Contact's founding team, Alec was one of the original three who started the company in an attic. Alec was with the company for 18 years from start-up, to IPO, to a $1.1 Billion-Dollar acquisition. Alec has also been a Co-Founder or founding team of several other successful start-ups, including VMark (IPO & acquisition), Reacher Grasper Cane, and MOST Cardio.

4

SOLVE A PROBLEM OR SERVE A NEED

SHARON LECHTER

W**hy:** Successful businesses do one of two things. Solve a problem or Serve a need.

When I work with my clients, I have them focus on the Personal Success Equation, from my book Three Feet from Gold. It helps them determine the best way to Solve the problem or Serve the Need in a focused and scalable way. Too many of us think we have to do everything on our own (SOURCE www.personalsuccesseuqation.com)

[(P + T) x A x A] + F

[(Passion + Talent) x Association x Action] + Faith

When you focus on the problem you solve and the need you serve as you create your personal success equation, you speed your way to success.

. . .

PASSION AND TALENT

You start by combining your passion (Your Why or Purpose) and Your Talent (Education and Experience). Most of us think that is all we need. We believe we can become an expert in everything we need to create our own success.

Power of Association

Truly successful people understand the importance of the Power of Association. Surrounding yourself with the right people is essential to creating a successful and sustainable business. You have heard the saying, "If you are the smartest person in the room, you are in trouble." You want to hire people who are strong where you are weak. Seek to have the right people on your team, people who will challenge you, and support you. And most importantly, find a mentor who will guide you on your journey.

Taking Action

Also, you have to take Action. So often we know what we need to do...but just don't do it. We choose to procrastinate or get mired in analysis paralysis. Having a mentor will help keep you accountable to take action towards your goals.

Having Faith in Yourself

Of equal importance is having Faith in yourself. Having faith that what you are doing is needed and necessary...and faith that you will succeed.

Since the most successful businesses do one of two things: Solve a Problem or Serve a Need. Remind yourself of what problem you are solving or what need you are serving every day. It will help you get through the tough times and take your mind off "you," reminding you to focus on serving the greater good.

During these times of uncertainty, keeping your focus on the service you provide to others provides the motivation and inspiration to keep moving forward. You are adding value to other peoples' lives.

The Un-Habit: WRITE IT DOWN NOW --- NOT LATER!

Why: As a general proposition, you will have 20% raving fans, 20% of people who have no interest or are negative towards you (naysayers), and the middle 60% of your audience will be ambivalent or just unaware of you. It represents the bell curve of your customer base. Too many entrepreneurs spend a lot of their time on the 20% of those who don't like them trying to CONVERT them into fans. It can be very hard work. STOP IT.

That being said, I am not saying to ignore them completely. Create a response program that "listens to your negative customers or fans," so they feel "heard." Seek information about their complaints to see if you need to make adjustments in how you do business. Resolve any issue that you can through establishing a process and team for future customer complaints but do not get emotionally involved in the problems.

The Law of Attraction is in action here. When you focus on negativity...you attract more negativity. Instead of focusing on the people who do not like you, and do not want you to succeed, focus on the people who love you. You will see by focusing on these positive people...you will attract more positive people into your world. And the bonus is that you will have a lot more fun while you do it!

As an Entrepreneur, your focus needs to be on the future of your business and growing your happy customer base.

Focus your energy on the 20% of your audience, who are your raving fans, turning them into your greatest assets. They will become viral marketing machines for you, and soon their efforts will start converting the 60% in the middle into following you. Arm your fans with the tools to spread the word about how fabulous you and your business are. Establish a way for them to provide reviews for you and provide social media posts that they can share to spread the word. Just remember to have a nurturing campaign ready to receive your new fans, and you will see the 20% of your raving fan base grow exponentially.

Remember what problem you are solving, or what need you are serving and allow your satisfied customers to spread the word.

ABOUT SHARON: Sharon Lechter is recognized globally as an expert on the topics of financial education and entrepreneurship. She is an New York Times Bestselling author and international keynote speaker, an award winning entrepreneur, philanthropist and a licensed CGMA. As founder and CEO of Pay Your Family First, a financial education organization, Sharon has served as a Presidential Adviser to Presidents Bush and Obama on the topic.

In 2009, Sharon was appointed to the National CPA Financial Literacy Commission as a national spokesperson on financial literacy and was reappointed in 2014. Sharon is also a Founding Chancellor for Junior Achievement University of Success and was Arizona Chairman for the 2020 Women on Boards initiative.

5

FEED THE MACHINE

PAUL LOGAN

Why: This Habit encompasses all of the Habits of my life, big or small. I think of this Habit as a table with three legs. The legs are the Body, the Mind, and the Spirit.

I feed each of those legs every day. I do something physical with my body; I've been training martial arts since I was 13. I practice this daily, which for me not only enriches my body but my mind and spirit as well. I lift weights to train and sculpt my body. I do other physical activities like hiking, sports, archery, biking, etc. to help keep my body healthy. I also am very careful with my nutrition and what I put into my body, strengthening it from the inside, getting rest, all to keep me camera ready.

For my Mind, I try to learn from everybody that I meet every day. Knowledge is power. Whether it's in-person learning, reading a book, taking a course, listening to a podcast, watching a movie, just thinking about things, I'm a sponge for knowledge. Every interaction that I have, I try to learn either what to do and emulate it, or maybe more importantly, what not to do, and try not to do that. It's very valuable to observe something in other people or their behavior and realize it's what we don't want for ourselves because sometimes it's easier to see bad Habits in others rather than in the mirror. If you can do this and learn from that, you may break or avoid bad Habits.

For the Spiritual leg, no matter what you believe in, whether it's God, or the Universe, or anything larger than us, I feed that facet of my life every day.

> One of the ways I do it is to be grateful, thankful for what I have.

Every morning, I wake up saying, "Thank you for allowing me to live this day." And every night before I go to sleep, I say, "Thank you for giving me the gifts that you gave me in this life." Whether they were "good gifts" or were challenges or obstacles that helped me sharpen my blades, get stronger, and overcome them, which ultimately strengthened me, would feed the machine.

If any of the three legs are lacking, the table will not stand straight, and you'll feel a little bit off. If you concentrate too much on one leg and the others fall behind, it will grow out of proportion, and the table will also not stand straight. You need to maintain a balance, keeping the legs as uniform as you can. So feed the machine.

HABIT™

THE UN-HABIT: DO IT NOW. STOP PROCRASTINATING

WHY: If you put things off until the due date and get that unexpected occurrence in your life where you have to choose to do what is thrown at you or what you have been procrastinating about and putting off, both results will suffer. Giving yourself time lets you make the best decisions possible, and that is a game-changer.

I was a procrastinator for a long time. To beat this, I started to slide up deadlines on my own. If someone says, "Paul, I need this done by the 30th." I will slide my deadline up to the 15th. I give myself an extra two weeks if that's possible. Sometimes people say, "Oh, hey, this is due the next day." Then you have to drop whatever you are doing and hit it hard, just to get it done.

Also, I start things almost immediately. I might not finish them right away, but if someone says, "Okay, I need you to do X, Y, and Z." maybe I'll take out a notebook, and I'll plan it out, outline it, brainstorm. Or perhaps I'll make a couple of phone calls or do some research. So at least I started the process right away.

I think my procrastination came because I excelled at school naturally. I never studied throughout grade school or high school or just barely and got straight A's. College was the same thing. I used to cram last minute, the night before the exam. My buddies were studying weeks before, and I was like, "Nah." and still, I got A's and B's. I was just fine.

When I got to chiropractic school, I was hit with a harsh dose of reality. It was a frying pan to the face. In my first anatomy class, people were studying for three, four weeks. I'm like, "Eh. I'm good" A couple of days before, I'm looking at some flashcards reading a bit. Then that test hit me that morning. I was like, "What?!!" And yeah, so it was definitely a reality check. I was like, "All right, this procrastination thing is over." Which is why I don't procrastinate anymore and am able to accomplish my goals and live life to its fullest.

About Paul: Paul Logan, an accomplished actor, martial artist, writer, and producer. He is one of the stars in the galaxy of action cinema. He was raised in Valley Cottage, New York. He graduated from SUNY Purchase College as a biochemistry major then moved to California to attend the Los Angeles College of Chiropractic.

For 2 1/2 years, PAUL LOGAN played Glen Reiber on NBC's Days Of Our Lives. Paul's Television credits also include

FRIENDS, ANGEL, SMITH and many films for SYFY Channel. He has starred in many action films and has just written, produced, and starred in the Action/Horror film THE HORDE, which was nominated for Action Film Of The Year.

Paul holds a black belt in Okinawan Go Ju Ryu Karate. He has been training MMA for the past 15 years. He doesn't drink, smoke, or do any drugs. After losing his dad very suddenly in 1993, Paul lives every day as if it were his last.

6

WORK HARD TO STAY IN THE NOW

MARLA GIBBS

Why: I believe that remaining present throughout our lives may seem like an easily enforceable Habit, but the truth is that many of us struggle to stay off auto-pilot for an entire day at work or school. Through Habitual practice, I've realized that careful consideration of our surroundings will amplify the value we may derive from our experiences. This holds true for both ourselves and the people we've shared those experiences with throughout. Because there is no other time.

It's important to set aside time during the day to be mindful and conscious of my environment. Throughout my journey to remain "present", I've strengthened my confidence and enjoyed life more because of it. Especially in today's environment, there can be a lot of stress in our lives, and taking time to meditate or simply breathe can reduce this.

We can gain a lot of value in our individual lives by taking notice of the beautiful things that surround each of us. They say you should believe none of what you hear and half of what you see because we rely on our minds to tell us what we're looking at, but sometimes our perception is off. We are always looking to the future or trying to recall the past. This takes us away from God and the NOW. It takes a lot of work and determination to stay in the NOW because our minds are so busy. Our minds are so powerful, but; the mind is not who we are. We think of the mind as crucial and relevant to our identity. Throughout our lives, our minds are speaking in a formulation of scenarios; little movies in our heads that look real, but only to us. Our minds make judgments that are often-times totally off, but there is so much attention given to the mind that this concentration of our energy makes us view the mind as ourselves. Within the mind is where we, as human beings, hold our worries, fears, interests, and judgments. We are one with God and everyone else.

THE UN-HABIT: JUDGING OTHERS

Why: For us to focus our attention on improving ourselves, we need to focus our focus on casting judgments on others. To judge someone, we consider another individual's actions in contrast to our perception of the situation. Still, in doing so, we are wasting energy living a life that we are not the centerpiece of.

Holistically speaking, we, as human beings, feel our best when we support others instead of judging them. Think about it, the Judgements we make about others are often-times the flaws we see in ourselves. Still, if we continuously identify these flaws as external, then we will never correct the internal issues that drive us to formulate judgments in the first place. Judging separates us, and at the same time, restricts us from evolving into our highest selves.

Negative judgments often come from our wounds whose origins we must identify, confront, and unpack, and only then can we begin to correct our flaws. We cannot solve every individual's internal struggle, but we can collectively encourage and uplift each other. But first, we must know, it's an inside job. As they say, "you spot it, you got it.

At the end of our journey through life, we do not receive a list of complaints made against us or believe that somewhere there is a grand list with people who have been judged by us. I think that the end of our journey is weighed, what matters is how we served. Did we take advantage of the NOW moment? Did we uplift someone? Did we stand for something? Ultimately, we must all strive to be remembered for the love we gave, not the judgments we rendered. Instead of judging and punishment being encouraged throughout society, we should be attempting to teach empathy and compassion. History has shown that throughout hard times, humanity is resilient. Regardless of our race or religious beliefs, our pain, and our joys, our families' desires connect us. In the end, We must accept that We are all one, and judging others is judging ourselves.

About Ms. Gibbs: Marla Gibbs is a five-time Emmy-nominated actress, known for her memorable role as the feisty maid Florence, on the 70's CBS hit comedy, "The Jeffersons'. Marla later starred in her own sitcom, "227", which she helped to produce and develop. The show introduced audiences to two loving parents raising their daughter and dealing with real issues.

Marla received eight NAACP Image Awards and an Essence Magazine's "Woman of the Year." Marla has performed in numerous tv and movie projects such as "ER," "Cold Case," "Scandal," "The First Family," "NCIS," "Breaking Bad," "The Dave Chappelle Show," "One Fine Christmas" and "Love Jacked." She also received a daytime Emmy nomination for "Passions."

7

ACKNOWLEDGE THE PEOPLE AROUND YOU

DR. CINDY CORK

Why: Everyone likes to be acknowledged by the people around them. We all want to be seen by others, for them to acknowledge that we are alive. To be recognized for the space that we take upon the planet. To feel that we are valued.

My parents taught me always to acknowledge the people around me, no matter their station in life. They taught me that I was not better than anyone else; we are all human beings, and we all deserve to be treated with dignity and respect.

Early in life, I was taught that we all contributed to society, and the CEO of a company was no more important than the custodian. They both play critical roles in the company. As Antoine de Sainte - Exupery said, "One man may hit the mark, another blunder, but heed not these distinctions. Only from the alliance of the one, working with and through the other, are great things born."

It doesn't take any significant effort to smile and acknowledge the presence of someone in your path.

And don't underestimate the power of that gesture. You never know how that encounter can affect the other person. You may have prevented someone from taking their own life because they felt unloved and invisible. You may have given someone the confidence to face a challenging situation.

What you have done with that small gesture is to let that person know that they are essential, that they are worthy. That creates a ripple effect, and that person now models your behavior and goes on to affect the lives of others.

In our digital age, I feel this Habit is in desperate need of cultivation. We are so attached to our devices that we forget common courtesies. We use our phones as an excuse to avoid looking at other people in the eye because *gasp* we might have to interact with a real person!

But human interaction is important! This is how we learn to communicate effectively and persuasively. This is how we connect emotionally with each other. This is how we learn and grow mentally and spiritually.

Here's a secret: when those around you feel important and appreciated, they root for your success. They are loyal. They edify you to others. They go out of their way to help you in any way they can.

When you make it a Habit to acknowledge the people around you, you will soon notice that others will begin acknowledging you for your contributions.

THE UN-HABIT: COMPARING YOURSELF TO OTHERS.

Why: Teddy Roosevelt said, "comparison is the thief of joy," and these words are so true.

We learn at an early age the comparison game. Our parents compare us to our siblings, "why can't you be as smart/talented/behaved as your brother/sister?"

Our teachers compare our schoolmates' academic abilities and deem us gifted, average, or "learning-disabled."

At recess or PE class, our athletic abilities are compared, and based on those; we get picked first for a team or last.

As teenagers, we begin comparing ourselves to our peers. Are we as good looking? As popular? Or nerdy and ugly?

Tragically, this occurs during our formative years, because it sets the stage for our insecurities and complexes that plague us throughout our adult lives.

How many of us have pursued careers that we didn't love just because we felt the pressure that it was expected of us?

How many of us gave up a dream because we were told that we "didn't have what it takes"?

As adults, we compare our lives to those of our friends, colleagues, and contemporaries. We define our success by weighing our material assets against theirs. Do we have a fancier car, a bigger house, more expensive clothes?

Thus begins the cycle of "Keeping up with the Joneses." We wear ourselves out chasing the almighty dollar to show that we are just as successful.

We fail to realize that appearances can be deceiving and that the person we are busy comparing ourselves to is hiding behind a facade.

They may have expensive things but be hundreds of thousands of dollars in debt. They may be very wealthy but have superficial relationships.

You don't know what challenges they may have faced getting to where they are.

Your happiness can only be found from within. Do what makes you sing inside because that joy will propel you to success and keep you successful. When you aren't happy, no amount of money or material things will create that feeling for you long term.

Redefine success to match your achievements. Be proud of the hard work that got you to where you are now.

Remember, your greatest achievement was being conceived - one sperm out of millions managed to fertilize that egg to create you.

Everything that you've done since is just icing on the cake!

About Dr. Cindy: As a pharmaceutical chemist , Dr. Cindy quickly learned that medications were not the path to true health when she was diagnosed with an "incurable" disorder that she overcame with the use of alternative therapies. She changed focus and went on to study the eye, and she has been helping people to transform the way they see the world for 23 years as an Optometric Physician. In addition to her Doctorate, she is certified in several powerful healing modalities and uses a unique combination of modern day medicine, holistic pathways and cutting-edge tools for accelerating human change to care for her clients.

8

ALWAYS GET BACK UP

COCOVINNY ZALDIVAR

Why: The saying is simple, "Every setback is a setup for a comeback." This means that every time we fail or get knocked off of our path, it's important to see it as a temporary setback, a full-on setup for the comeback. It's taken me years to realize that to make it, we all need to have this balanced approach to life, using optimism and gratitude for the challenges that we are presented with.

One of my first challenges was at an early age of 15 years old. My father was incarcerated, and I became the head of the household with my mother, Marilyn. We struggled and almost ended up homeless with my little sister Erica.

After working two full-time jobs and finishing high school, I realized that starting my own business and being my own boss was the only option if we were going to make it. Luckily, we worked hard as a team and made it through. I was able to purchase my first house at 18 in Las Vegas, where my mom and Erica lived for many years.

Many other stories like this have proven to me that if we were meant for mediocrity, we wouldn't be faced with such amazing feats or challenges. So consider yourself blessed and honored to run with the torch.

If it were easy, everyone would be doing it, and if it weren't hard, you wouldn't be able to learn to grow and eventually share the wisdom you were destined to acquire.

Always remember to stay calm, because cool heads will prevail. Some of the best tools I've used when facing tough times is to have thick skin, short term memory, and a positive attitude.

It's taken over 25 years of trial and error in numerous ventures to gain the wisdom to know what is right for me and my purpose. Without a deep connection to your cause or purpose, it is much harder to stay focused and do what it takes to reach your goal and destination.

No matter where you are in your journey, always remember to respect your creators, stay grounded, humble, and never let anyone talk you out of your dreams. Whatever you think, speak, believe, and take action towards daily will become your reality. The Un-Habit: Quitting every time it gets hard, or you face temporary defeat.

THE UN-HABIT: QUITTING EVERY TIME IT GETS HARD, OR YOU
FACE TEMPORARY DEFEAT

Why: It's important to stop asking for permission from others. This is one of the reasons many people quit and never make it to the next level. For example, Marcus Lemois and a team of patent experts said that I would never get my patent issued for my Coco Taps invention. As of April 2020, just months after their doubts, I can proudly say that my invention is now a fully issued patent, and it feels better than you can imagine defying all the odds. If you break the Habit of giving up when things get hard or when others deem them impossible, you will go far.

Being uncomfortable is part of breaking through to your true potential and making a real impact on your life.

We all have been given gifts to share with the world, and part of the process of life is to discover your own "why" and how you are meant to share it with the world. People make plans and set goals all the time, but the difference between the ones that reach their goals and see the plans come to fruition is action and the discipline to power on and continue even when it's hard and may seem impossible in some moments. Just because people don't believe or have faith in you doesn't mean you have to lose hope. Keep going! Everyone told me it was impossible to get my father out of prison. The top lawyers and so-called experts said I had no chance on his release and that he was guilty beyond a shadow of a doubt. In my eyes, the punishment didn't fit the crime, so I ended up lobbying the entire Nevada Supreme Court and, after eight years, was able to receive a full pardon for his sentence and he was released.

Finding your truth and reason for living will take lots of time, energy, and exploration. Don't be afraid when you are lost. Just keep on keeping on because anything worth doing is worth overdoing. Only you know what it's going to take to reach true fulfillment and enlightenment for your life. Listen to your inner calling and voices of intuition. My inner voice has led me to help people and the planet by solving problems with zero waste and circular economic designed products. They say you have to go within, or you'll always go without. My wish for you is that you learn how to always listen to that inner voice, and may it lead you to Health Wealth CocoLove and Happiness. Always follow the sunshine and the Coconuts.

About CocoVinny: CocoVinny has been called the Elon Musk of the coconut industry. Now, as an accomplished Eco-Inventor and Zero Waste Educator and Speaker, CocoVinny has taken his idea into the market and has received the first awarded ZeroWaste certified business in Las Vegas. Having been seen by millions on TV, CocoVinny was featured on TheProfit on

CNBC, and ABC hit TV Show Shark Tank. He is an accomplished two-time finisher of a 70.3 IronMan race in Kona, Hawaii, as well as a full LA marathon. CocoVinny also spends his free time playing music on the Ukulele and Piano. A born philanthropist, CocoVinny donates his time to help inspire youth in the community and participates in many fundraising initiatives for numerous non-profit organizations. Miracle Flights, New Life Beginnings, and the JDRF are just a few of the many organizations he regularly supports.

9

VISUALIZE YOUR SUCCESS

PATRICK K. PORTER, PHD

Why: This Habit is important because you set a plan consciously, and subconsciously, you put powerful inner forces to work, creating the Habits of success.

It's been clinically shown that you can interrupt old patterns of belief that, in the past, prevent success by hardwiring new patterns in the early morning that stimulate problem-solving and creative it's.

Our brains, just like our behaviors, get stuck in patterns once you unlock the underlying fear of success and step out first mentally preparing for success, it is natural to create the physical world changes.

Your subconscious, which runs 95% of your life if left to regulate itself, programs your future based on past behavior, good or bad. The breakthrough entrepreneur knows that true success starts first In their thoughts. Then becomes the success they see in the world around them.

Using the principle of digital coffee, you can switch your brain frequency and learn to relax and train your brain to wake up to the

Infinite possibilities that exist in the world around you.

Armed with this daily Inspiration, your first step each day can be shaped to form the future you desire. It's is your beliefs that fuel your behaviors and trigger the life experiences you need to

Accomplish your life goals.

This is also a powerful process to keep your work-life balance, so you live the life you want without sacrificing personal life.

This is also a powerful process to keep your work-life balance, so you are living the life you want without the sacrifice of a personal life.

This is also a powerful process to keep your work-life balance, so you are living the life you want without the sacrifice of a personal life.

THE UN-HABIT: ELIMINATE PESSIMISTIC THINKING AND CLAIM YOUR RIGHT TO A POSITIVE OPTIMISTIC LIFESTYLE

Why: It's important to balance negative thinking so that you stay focused on the field of possibilities. In the law of quantum physics, it is known that if a person focuses on only one outcome. Let's say a negative one, the field of possibility collapses on that one thought. To retrain this part of the brain, we have to look at Hebb's Law, "Neurons that fire together wire together."

This means that the brain builds networks of thoughts, positive or negative. With the daily practice of 10 powerful minutes, you change the wiring in the brain so that new circuits are born. Circuits that are those of creativity and problem-solving.

When used over time, these new circuits, like the 21-day rule of change, create new, more powerful patterns that create positive change in your life.

I have found, like in martial arts, you can't fight force with force. This 10 minute works like tia chi for the mind. Science also shows the thoughts we think about being the life we bring about. So the focus is to change your daily thoughts to change the trajectory of your life from fear, stress, and frustration to excitement, calm, and creativity.

The best part of this 10-minute performance mindfulness strategy is you can prove this to your self. With a calm breath and 10 minutes, you will begin to feel and notice these changes immediately. And the brain circuits get stronger with time. Like building a muscle at the gym, your mental muscles get stronger conditioning you against the physical stress and pain that negative thinking can cause.

At first, this practice can be done just before getting out of bed. But if you are like most, you will quickly shift the practice to sitting in a comfortable chair and conducting your daily board meeting in your mind.

The power to produce results resides within you. This one simple process could be the spark that sets fire to your dreams.

About Dr. Porter: Patrick K. Porter, Ph.D., is an award-winning author, educator, consultant, entrepreneur, and speaker. With 30 years of experience operating the largest self-help franchise, he has become a highly sought-after expert within the personal improvement industry. He has sold over 7 million of his self-help products worldwide.

He has been on the cutting edge of brainwave entrainment technology for 31 years. He was a co-developer of the MC2, the first personal light & sound brain training machine, voted "Best New Gadget of the Year" at the 1989 Consumer Electronics Show.

10

ALWAYS BE PUNCTUAL

TERESA CUNDIFF

W hy: Creating the Habit of punctuality will change your life for the better and is so important for EVERYTHING you do! When you become a punctual person, it means you have pulled your life together and respect yourself. You are planning ahead to make it to your appointments, to your events and to your rendezvous! But more importantly, you are demonstrating respect for the other person's time and your own! This is so important! Not only should you be on time, you should be early! There is a saying, "To be early, is to be on time. To be on time, is to be late!" Punctuality makes it clear to the person you are meeting that he or she is important and that you appreciate and understand the value of his or her time.

A person who is punctual must become a planner of sorts and a clock watcher. If you say to yourself, "I'm always late," it's because you just aren't thinking far enough into your day to see what requires your attention and when. If you are distracted by things, eliminate them. If your lose track of time, set the timer on your phone and use it to aid you. Becoming a punctual person will bring order to the chaos in your life with just this one Habit change, but I submit to you that it's more than just a Habit change. It's a lifestyle change!

When you bring order to your life by being on time to work and your meetings, etc. everything else will just click into place!

Your colleagues will notice the change in you; you will feel your own degree of professionalism begin to rise and the sense of pride in yourself will take hold, and you will feel like a new person. You do not have to settle and just live with the, "I'm always late," mentality! You are stronger and better than label you have placed on yourself! Make the change now! If you are going to hit your snooze button twice and you know that, set your alarm 20 minutes earlier! If you struggle picking out what to wear in the mornings, take time the night before and sort it out and then stick to that choice in the morning! If you are going to drive thru somewhere for breakfast, factor that into your drive time. Being punctual just requires some critical thinking about your day and planning ahead. You can turn yourself into the person with the reputation for always being the first one at the meeting! I believe in you!

THE UN-HABIT: LEARNING THAT LIFE ISN'T FAIR

Why: Our house on Charlemagne Blvd was the gathering place for the neighborhood. We had a slick finished concrete screened in patio that was really big, so all the kids would come to our house to roller skate. My mom was a stay-at-home mom then, and we would have nights when the kids would bring their bikes over, and she would bust out the tools, and everybody would work on their bikes. The rules were that if you were going to play at our house, you had to play fair! Very body knew them; everybody followed them. It was the late 1960's.

One day my mom had gone over to the neighbor's house across the street when one kid had committed some egregious offense. I was 5 years old, and I wasn't going to stand for that! I marched my little self out of the patio, down the driveway and just as I stepped into the street, I was struck by a car. My undaunted sense of right and wrong had put me right in the path of real life. You see, I had never been told to look both ways before I crossed the street! Why? Because I was so little that it had never occurred to my parents that I would ever even attempt such a thing without one of them beside me. Even to this day, I still want things to be black and white, but I have learned that life isn't fair! So, let me share the secret with you right here, it's all about managing your expectations! Read that again! This is a principle that you can apply to all of life's situations.

I'm an honest person; therefore, I expect other people to be honest with me. That is a dangerous expectation. But, if I manage that expectation going in and know that even though my conscience is clear and that I am dealing honestly, the other person may not be. So, here life may not be fair, but I don't have to be hurt by it because I am managing my expectations about the other person. I am in control of my thoughts.

This principle is something I wish someone had talked to me about when I was in my 20's. Take what I'm saying here to heart and never forget it. You will be well served by knowing that life isn't fair.

About Teresa: As someone who has always loved words and the English language, Teresa Cundiff has now hung out her shingle as a Professional Proofreader. Her tag line is, "I know where the commas go!" Everything that is written needs to be proofed, and even professional writers need a second set of eyes to proof their copies. Technology makes the transmission of documents easier than ever before! Teresa will ease your mind so you can write! Get your ideas on the page! She will put the commas where they go!

11

CREATE LOVE IN YOUR LIFE

ANN LANDSTROM

W hy: Self Love is EVERYTHING. How do you love other people and love what you do if you can't love yourself?

It wasn't until my fifties where I could look in the mirror and say I love you to myself. Women, especially always are our worse self critics, and we focus on putting ourselves down in the mirror and then in life.

After walking out of a mentally and verbally abusive marriage where my self-worth had been broken down, I started to go through a lot of self-development books and courses. I learned how to start loving myself and let go of the past and move forward to success. Slowly day by day I stood in the mirror and told myself that I am okay just the way I am, I am beautiful, I am a success, I am worth abundance and love. After years of telling myself that I loved myself and could do anything, I set my mind to things that started to shift. My photography work went to a whole different level, and all of a sudden, I began to meet and photograph the people I had admired and received help from by reading their books and taking their seminars. The law of attraction had made a full circle in my life. The vision boards that I had put together also helped me move forward and attract and achieve my dreams. Writing notes to yourself and posting them all over where you can see them daily also helped me, and I kept repeating the words repeatedly until they felt real, and I believed them.

THE UN-HABIT: I DON'T LIKE WHAT I SEE IN THE MIRROR

Why: When you feel good, you look good, and when you look good, you feel good. Beating yourself up regularly in the mirror and what you say to you received in your thoughts are very abusive to yourself. Think about if another person told you daily what you say to yourself in the mirror and your mind. Changing your mindset will change your mind and free you to fulfill your dreams and goals.

Start with reading books like "The four agreements" and understand that your life will never be the same when you follow those agreements. Understand when you wake up in the morning that you choose how you want your day to go. If you start with gratitude and write down or say out loud 3-5 things you are grateful for, then go to the mirror and start telling yourself that you forgive yourself, you love yourself, and that you believe in yourself and that you are capable of doing anything you want to do.

Do this every day for 30 days, and you will see a change in your mood and self-esteem. Also, take a selfie a day and say something nice about your image that is looking back at you. Example: I have beautiful eyes. I love my lips; I love my smile.

Practice this exercise for 30 days as well, and you will see a shift in your self-esteem and self-love. Once you have build-up, self-value, and self-love, it's time to start building and walking towards your dreams and desires.

Ask yourself what do you want in your life then start taking baby step actions to get there. Remember, if Apple and Google were born in a garage, your dreams and inspirations can blossom as well if you believe and implement the right steps to get there and have a will and determination, it WILL happen.

ABOUT ANN: As a result of having a photo session with Ann Photography, you will have magazine quality images of the best version of yourself representing you and your business. You will have legacy portraits to leave behind for your children and grandchildren since you can't frame your selfies on your phone. Represent yourself and your brand with the best image you have ever seen of yourself and attract your perfect client and fall in love with the image looking back at you from my lens. You only get ONE first impression. Let Ann Photography help you with yours.

12

DREAM BIG

JILL LIBERMAN

Why: Everything starts with a dream, so dream big. No goal is too big if you believe in yourself. Put in the passion and effort to turn your dream into a reality. It is essential always to have a goal because to get what you want; you must first know what you want. Dreams inspire. They give you hope, purpose, and something to work towards. When you focus on getting what you want, everything changes. No one will chase your dreams for you. It is up to you to live the life of your dreams. Dreams do not need to remain dreams. They become a reality. Dreaming big is exciting. It opens doors. It sparks a fire in your soul. It helps you find your purpose, push your limits, and pursue your passion. It is so essential to create a Habit of dreaming big because it can truly change your life.

Once you understand the only limitations are the ones in your mind, the possibilities are endless. You can do anything. When you believe there is no need to settle, you won't. Get in the Habit of choosing to think big and believing you can do anything. Taking action is easy when you have the mindset that nothing can stop you. Dreaming big applies to all areas of your life, not just your career. Have a dream for your home, health, material things, etc. Develop daily Habits to help you work towards and reach these goals. Your dream is your mission statement. Set the bar high. It's your life. You deserve to be happy.

THE UN-HABIT: ELIMINATE NEGATIVE WORDS

Why: Your thoughts are very powerful. Thoughts become words that translate into actions. It is important to limit or eliminate negative words such as can't, never, and don't. When you can successfully filter out negative words and substitute positive choices, you retrain your brain. This is a great way to help develop a positive mindset and attitude, which changes everything. Eliminating words such as can't, don't, and never is a simple way to be more productive. It is critical for living a positive, healthy, and successful life. Using positive words can also motivate you. Positive language is a way of being kind to yourself. When you use positive word choices, you are supporting and encouraging yourself. When you use negative words, you are setting yourself up for self-defeat.

The wrong words can limit you and stand in the way of your success. If you say don't believe you can accomplish something, you are right; you won't. You limit yourself and your chances of succeeding when you say you can't do something. You encourage yourself when you tell yourself you can, and you will succeed. When you say something, you begin to believe it. If you tell yourself something is too difficult for you before you try, you are sabotaging your actions. Because words can shape your beliefs, use them to improve your life. State your words in a way that presents moving forward.

Allow your words to fuel your confidence and help create opportunities. Your words can lift you or tear you down. Thoughts become things. Allow your thoughts and words to encourage you, not create limiting beliefs. You can do anything if you believe you can. Use your words to help you reach your potential rather than allowing them to limit your actions. Your words are a reflection of what you are thinking, and what you are thinking is your reality.

Choose wisely.

About Jill: Jill Liberman founded Choose Happy to spread the powerful message happiness is a choice. People connected with the message so strongly that she speaks to sold out audiences all over the world on the importance of happiness. In addition to her book Choose Happy: Your Go-To-Guide to living a happier life, and Jill's motivational speeches, the Choose Happy lifestyle brand has now extended to an inspirational apparel line. When you're happy, you can do anything.

13

EXPRESS GRATITUDE DAILY

LOUIS AGIUS

Why: My life has been filled with drama and challenges for the longest time, from having a low, middle-class upbringing, where money was scarce and always feeling I didn't have enough to eventually feeling like I wasn't enough, to growing up being a workaholic and slaving away 80 hour work weeks to make sure my kids end up having everything I didn't growing up, which resulted in not spending enough time with them which let into a divorce.

I was also made redundant a couple of times while living abroad, almost ending up homeless on numerous occasions. I was barely making rent, unable to pay the bills, having debts piling up, and debt collectors sending me warnings and calling me every other day. I know what it's like to barely have enough money to put food on the table.

I can honestly say I had hit my rock bottom and the one thing I can attribute that saved me from my funk when I came across A

Gratitude Prayer by Napoleon Hill while reading "Think and Grow Rich". The prayer states the following:

"I ask not, for Divine providence for more riches but more wisdom with which to accept and use wisely the riches I received at birth in the form of the power to control and direct my mind to whatever ends I desire."

Napoleon Hill suggests:

1. Procure a neat pocket-sized notebook.
2. On page 1, write down a clear description of You Most Desire in Life.
3. On page 2, write down a clear statement of what you intend to Give in Return.
4. Memorize both statements.
5. Repeat a dozen times daily.
6. State the Expression of Gratitude as listed above

This Habit alone has completely transformed my life and that of my loved ones in unimaginable ways. In summary, when you are grateful for what you have, it doesn't leave room for feeling sad or frustrated with what you don't have.

You cannot feel two opposing emotions simultaneously; you cannot feel happy and angry at the same time. So by choosing gratitude, you're choosing an emotion that serves you instead of dragging you down.

When you accept what is and look at the glass half full, you start seeing opportunities amidst the challenges. Once you pass that breakthrough, the reward is far greater than the obstacle you had to overcome.

So next time you're faced with a challenge, start listing down things you are grateful for both in general and reasons to be grateful for this specific challenge.

THE UN-HABIT: STOP SEEKING VALIDATION FROM OTHERS

Why: We all seek validation at some level; we want to feel loved and appreciated by our loved ones, our parents, our partners, our kids, our teachers, our friends, and extended family, our co-workers, business partners, social circles, etc..

Human beings are social creatures and not too far off from our mammal friends most of us like to form packs; this inherently creates an environment where we always end up looking up to someone and seeking their validation.

Although there's nothing inherently wrong with that, it can be detrimental to your success, regardless of what success means to you right now as you read this.

Why is that you ask?

I can give you two reasons:

1. By seeking validation from others, you're subconsciously saying, "I'm not good enough," and you're permitting someone else to tell you what you should be or what you should do.

The pursuit of success requires a level of drive that is fueled by a burning desire of wanting to be and do more and confidence that already are that person in the making. Feeling like you need someone else permission nullifies this confidence by making you feel non-worthy.

2. It makes you play small. You need first to understand this: The majority of people are not successful because they are not willing to do what successful people do. This means that to be successful, you are likely to go against the grain, and people are likely to judge you because of it.

If you're afraid of being criticized because of this, you will likely play small and choose to blend in instead of standing out. Please don't do this, play big always, you have been given a gift, and you must share it.

Remember these two things next time you feel like you don't want to do something out of being judged.

1. Most people are too absorbed with what is going on in their lives to even pay any notice to what you're up to.

2. Other people's opinions of you are not going to pay your bills and provide you and your loved ones the lifestyle you deserve. So at the end of the day, their opinions are worth squat because I can't buy to eat with opinions, but I can book a vacation with the money I earned playing big.

ABOUT LOUIS: Louis Agius hosts an annual digital marketing event called 'The Digital Profits Summit' bringing world class speakers from all across the globe and like minded entrepreneurs together under one roof and teaches them over 3 days how to grow, scale and automate their business online to 6,7,8 figures.

Louis has been teaching his clients how to leverage digital tools and resources that anyone can use irrespective of their experience how to earn a full time income even in their sleep. With his system, your business does not become solely depended on you, you can stop trading time for money and have peace of mind that you business stays thriving while you're on vacation.

14

IGNORING NAYSAYERS

ROBERT J MOORE

Why: If you're a successful entrepreneur, you likely lost more relationships than they have gained. Why? The path narrows when climbing to the top. The more successful you've become, the more people shoot arrows of jealousy and naysaying in your direction.

Want to know a secret to help you keep things in perspective? Most of the time, naysayers act out because they're afraid. That's right: naysayers project their fears and doubts onto you. Or they're afraid you'll change for the better and leave them behind, or they (and wrongfully) believe that everyone is as afraid as they are of leaving their comfort zone.

Remember that people who are too weak to follow their dreams will usually try to discourage yours. You're not going to build success overnight, so proving them wrong is going to take time.

Allow people in your life who keep you positive and motivated. Rid yourself of the ones who drag you down. You can't bring negative people up to your level; they will drag you down to theirs. Doing what you love has a high price to pay, sacrifices must be made.

However, I've also encountered my fair share of naysayers. Those people who drain every ounce of motivation out of you. Yeah. Once you've removed those negative influences, or least put some distance between you and them, create a support system of people who assist you and put a smile on your face and know your worth and don't let anyone tear you down.

You will mostly become who you surround yourself with. If you only associate with negative people, you'll likely be a negative person as well. If you surround yourself with people who are going after their dreams, overcoming their fears, and developing their talents, you will do the same.

If someone is telling you how to be better, listen. If someone is telling you why you will never be worthy, walk away.

THE UN-HABIT: AVOIDING PROCRASTINATION

Why: Entrepreneurship and procrastination: not an ideal combination. Procrastination is a Habit – a deeply ingrained pattern of behaviour. This means that you will not break it overnight. Habits only stop being Habits when you avoid practicing them, and procrastination is a trap that many of us fall into.

Procrastination usually involves ignoring an unpleasant, but likely more important task, in favor of more enjoyable or more manageable tasks. Once you're in the Habit of procrastinating, it can be hard to see a way out. If you're already swimming in overdue projects, how can you ever get ahead?

The first step to overcoming procrastination is to recognize that you're doing it. Then, identify the reasons behind your behaviour and use appropriate strategies to manage and overcome it.

Procrastination isn't a weakness or a problem you have. It's perfectly normal to procrastinate. We all do it, even successful people. The difference is that the latter knows how to avoid the root cause of procrastination.

To stop procrastinating, you need to have a clear goal that motivates you into action and thinking smart. Think of the outcome for you and your business, as this will be the first step to overcoming procrastination.

You often procrastinate because you don't have a clear business objective that you are working towards. Your mind becomes sidetracked onto other more interesting tasks.

You need to create a clear outcome, break it down into smaller tasks, and plan them out. This will help create clear deliverables and objectives to achieve during the day. Not only does this help keep you focused, but it also enables you to progress even faster towards your goals.

Ensure that you state when you are going to finish your tasks and make them public to the team. To further increase your accountability, share the aims you have on your social media.

About Robert: Robert J Moore positively shows that the hard times only make you more persuasive if you face them. He has built a foundation that allows entrepreneurs to become up-branded and become more recognized throughout the world. By collaborating in one of his many Magnetic Entrepreneur books series, or receiving high-end coaching, you too will be able to achieve any goal you desire to achieve. All possibilities are endless when you remove the roadblocks; that's why we became a Guinness World Record holder and a highly successful business.

15

NEVER STOP LEARNING

DOMINGO SILVAS III

Why: Our ability to learn as an entrepreneur helps us see what is possible and learn how to get it done. If you look at the definition of "to learn" you get: gain or acquire knowledge of or skill in (something) by study, experience, or being taught.

Knowledge is one of the most important outcomes of learning. To gain knowledge is to experience new skills, value, and help dreams come true.

When you start your journey as an entrepreneur, we seek guidance and some direction on what to do next. We know we are going to encounter difficult situations and are going to have to decide on a matter that we don't know of. At this point, we research, ask mentors for guidance, or make a gut decision. Either way, you choose to go, a determination is made, and a new experience has begun. These situations can lead to success or a negative outcome, but either way, you have just gained knowledge and learn a unique experience.

This is why I genuinely believe "learning" is a key Habit to have. Now, there are other ways to gain knowledge. You can set aside time to read a book, listen to a new podcast, and watch a video on YouTube. We live in a generation that allows us to seek guidance and knowledge from many other forms, and you will find one that suits your lifestyle.

"TELL ME, AND I FORGET. TEACH ME, AND I REMEMBER. INVOLVE ME, AND I LEARN." –BENJAMIN FRANKLIN

Learning is a crucial Habit and affects not just you but those in your life. To live your best life and make the most of it, keep your eyes and heart open to make the most of it.

THE UN-HABIT: NEVER STOP DREAMING

Why: Something we all do as entrepreneurs is "DREAM."

Our dreams can be exciting, be concerning, and even sometimes just weird. As an entrepreneur, our dreams give are very much goals to achieve.

We dream of a better lifestyle, a better car, a rental property on a beautiful island, or can be about building a 6 or 7 figure company that leads to all of those outcomes.

Over the past 20 years as an entrepreneur, my dreams have shifted and sometimes became more complicated. The reason is that as I got closer to obtaining my dream, I realized that I could go more in-depth and wider on my dreams. There are four tips I used to make this happen.

#1 Be relentless in your pursuit. Dreams can feel a million miles away, but they get closer the most relentless you are heading toward them.

#2 Get Focused. During our journey towards your dreams, don't get distracted. Our journey will throw things in our path, but stay focused and remember your dream is obtainable.

#3 Celebrate all the way. While you work your way towards your dream, celebrate all the winners. It makes the journey so much fun.

#4 Be clear on your dream by creating a vision board. Vision boards help you visualize your dream. Spend time every year to update your vision board and add to it and celebrate the ones you obtain during your journey. Vision boards are essential and helpful. Create one now.

"You see things; and you say, 'Why?' But I dream things that never were; and I say, 'Why not?'"

– George Bernard Shaw

Never stop chasing your dream as an entrepreneur. As we obtain them, we give those who are watching our journey get excited about obtaining theirs. Dreams are contagious.

ABOUT DOMINGO: After creating 6 7-figure companies, Domingo created the blueprint to success for entrepreneurs. With this method, you will be able to create a 90-day success plan that you and your team can use to start & scale your business. This method will help eliminate the guessing and allow you and your team to focus on what is needed. To your success!

16

KEEPING A MORNING ROUTINE

STEVE "THE HURRICANE" WEISS

Why: I believe that most problems and issues individuals have day to day come from being stressed out and worrying. This is where a routine is everything. Each of us has a mind, body, heart (emotions), and soul. We all must spend time satisfying the needs they have before we can effectively serve others. It begins with prayer and meditation to appreciate and show gratitude for what we have. This centers us spiritually. Reading, allows the mind to become stimulated and get cognitive function optimal. Next comes physical movement. Going for a walk, taking a boot camp class, hitting the weights all elevate the heart rate and get the juices flowing. Lastly, spending time with those we love fills the need for interaction, leading to emotional stability.

My morning routine is my secret Habit because it allows me to focus on my work and clients better. I begin each day hours before ever thinking about my business. I start with prayer, scripture, and meditation. I read a passage to reflect and stimulate my mind, pray, and express gratitude for my life and all the blessings in it. After, I go for a long walk with my wife, and then I have a workout session. This gives me time with the most important person in my world whom I committed to spending the rest of my life with, and then focus on my health so that I feel energized and healthy. When cleaning myself up, I eat breakfast and spend time with my children. I'll learn about their thoughts, dreams, and plans for the day. These moments are so unique as I know one day they will grow up and live their lives away from me, so I cherish and make the most of it while they last. Finally, I connect with my parents, siblings, and friends; before heading into my office. This way, my emotions and anything I could be worried about have been put at ease. Now that all is good in my world, I can easily focus on supporting my staff, helping our customers, and being the best entrepreneur I can be.

The Un-Habit: Complaining while doing nothing to change it!

Why: When people continuously complain, this leads to so many unhealthy Habits—overeating, drinking, addictions, depression, anxiety, bad relationships, financial hardships, etc. The list goes on and on. It is ok to complain during the process of searching for a solution, but complaining and doing nothing is toxic! No matter what the complaint is about, it can be broken through some fundamental problem-solving skills.

First, Identify truly what the problem is. This is harder than it sounds, as often we complain about things because we don't truly understand. Take health, for example. People often complain about being tired. To solve this issue, we need to identify what's causing this problem in the first place. Is it sleep Habits, too much work, stress, real health issues (disease, etc.), overeating before bed, nighttime routine, watching something stimulating, and so on.

Second, once you've identified the issue, you have to research your possible solutions. I say solutions because no one solution fits everyone, so you'll want to have multiple options to try. Staying with being tired and saying it's bedtime routine as the issue, research solutions others (both friends/family and experts) have been attempting to help them with this issue. Maybe it's taking a warm bath and reading before bed. Could be having a warm cup of decaffeinated tea with honey. Perhaps making sure your last meal is at least 2 hours before trying to start to fall asleep. By having multiple solutions, you have a high probability for success.

Third, experiment. Try one of your possible solutions out. Give it a few attempts to see if it solves your problem. Collect and record data. If it works, great, if not, try another solution. This could take a few days, weeks, months, or even years, depending on what it is.

Finally, determine your solution. Once you have figured it out, enjoy the victory. Let others know about your triumph. Be willing to lend advice and support to those who struggled as you did prior.

This is one of the healthiest good Habits to have.

About Steve: Steve "The Hurricane" has created a simple, yet powerful program to launch your business into the stratosphere! The Small Business Success System is your 7-Figure Business Playbook. Everything you need to scale your business: lead generation, conversions, mastering funnels, and so much more. This fool proof program will help you dominate your marketplace, generating more sales, helping more customers, and making your dreams a reality. Become a force of nature! Are you ready to blow away the competition?

17

PRACTICE YOUR PIVOT

ASHLEY CHEEKS

Why: Savvy people know that clarifying a goal and mapping a plan to achieve it is the key to success. However, where most plans fail is their lack of attention to the one big obstacle that will inevitably appear. That obstacle is the surprise pivot you will need to make. You may not know when it will come, but you will come to that pivot point eventually.

Throughout hundreds of business plans, I've written for entrepreneurs, clarifying the "goal" is often difficult for many new business founders. However, the harder part appears when a new challenge tries to change your path towards that goal. In the face of that challenge, you have to get comfortable pivoting away from your original plan and be ready to execute a new one.

My husband and I failed at this miserably in one of our businesses. We learned the hard way that being open to a pivot will make or break your success. We opened a car wash in Houston, a great success that was carefully planned and well executed. Soon, the pivot point showed up - a competitor moved into our territory, and it was clear that the business was going to be severely impacted. Customer counts dropped, we entered a price war to beat the competition, and overall, things took a turn for the worst. Looking back, there were several pivot points. These pivot points were easy to see but not easy to accept because they weren't part of the original plan. Had we accepted it, we could have made smaller pivots towards that new goal and executed a new plan. But we weren't great at pivoting, not back then. We were great at planning, but not at pivoting.

Studies show that failure to pivot is among the top 20 reasons entrepreneurs experience failure according to CB Insights. Every entrepreneur will face a pivot point. It may not be easy or comfortable, but it will come and will be less painful if you prepare for it now. By beginning each day with a lot of goals, you are creating a plan to maximize your time. At the end of that goal list, add "pivot TBD." By the end of the day, if you haven't figured out where the pivot was, you need to reflect. Was there a moment where you should have changed your course but decided to "stick to the plan" because it was easier? The more you can find these moments and focus on practicing your pivot, the more you allow yourself to take the most successful path - even if unplanned - in your entrepreneurial journey.

THE UN-HABIT: STOP LIVING BY "SHOULDS..."

Why: Some entrepreneurs live and die by the "shoulds" in their life. These can be in the past, like "I should have gone to college." It can be in the future, like "I should start exercising." Saying "I should" is like wearing a weighted backpack. It gets heavy fast and doesn't support you on your journey. It isn't filled with helpful supplies; it is just dead weight.

Entrepreneurs get into the Habit of saying "I should" and following it with a responsibility, a chore, a task, or a wish. This depletes power and energy and takes your power away by weighing you within actionable thoughts. When you transform "I should" into definite terms, like "I will" or "I will not," it lightens the pack. It frees your mind to create an action. Instead of saying, "I should post a new job for our team," make it a real decision. Will you post that job today? Will you delegate it to a team member or handle it some other way?

Instead of saying, "I should spend more time with my family," transform it into action. "I will spend more time with my family by giving them 30 minutes of focused time every day." If every entrepreneur stopped saying "I should" and empowered themselves to do or not do those things that come to mind, they can use their energy in more impactful ways and reach their goals sooner.

With negative "shoulds," like "I should have gotten a college degree," those are regrets that need to be reframed. You either decide to go back to school in your future or accept that path as one that you decided not to take. There is no "should"; there is just did or didn't. Will or won't.

I challenge you to be more powerful and more amazing by removing the phrase "I should." Anytime you say it, out loud or in your mind, replace it with an action statement. "I will," or "I won't." "I did" or "I didn't," If there is regret or guilt associated, journal out how that was ultimately an important thing in your journey. Accept and release, and unburden yourself from your "shoulds."

About Ashley: The founder of Written Success, an agency that creates professional business plans and pitching documents for entrepreneur fundraising. Ashley developed a unique approach to writing business plans that is simpler and more powerful than traditional methods. With her style, start-ups have found great success in securing bank loans, investor funding, and achieving the key milestone of first-year survival. With an exceptional mix of market research and careful launch strategy, she has helped start-ups raise over $550M in funding and is the resident pitch consultant for several investor networks.

18

TRUSTING THAT LIFE HAPPENS FOR YOU

DR. MANON BOLLIGER

Why: Healing is not a future-orientated process. Healing always happens in the present moment. Just like life itself, we live and are present in the moment, and we can't separate life from what's happening around us. In the same way, healing is a present moment process that integrates everything happening around us and to us...actually for us...into how we are responding to it. One cannot separate healing from what's happening. Healing is inherent in life itself. It is dealing with and working through conflict, discordance, loss, and the unexpected at the moment, rather than waiting for the body to express this through symptoms such as discomfort and pain.

In business, if you're ignoring all the negative comments coming in and you're wiping them off your screen, you're likely doing that the same with the symptoms that are accumulating in your body, compromising your health. If you are ignoring your inbox on your computer - you are likely ignoring your body's inbox as well.

The old paradigm of treating symptoms with big bandages is coming to an end. Getting to the root of any illness is about dealing with the stressors life confronts us with at the moment. It's about our ability to dance with what life presents us, which keeps our minds, hearts, and bodies initiated in the healing process. Regrets, just like procrastination, is an energy drain. Giving our attention to the past and what one "should have" or "could have" takes our attention away from what can be done right now.

Likewise, focusing on what might happen and avoiding eventualities detracts us from the focus necessary to the only time that truly matters...the present. Being present to this is actually what prevention in health is all about. Taking a step, or an action every day based on creating the life you love that supports you in every way.

This is the perfect moment to live your best day ever. Consider being grateful for all that you have, your team, all the people in your life you love, and all of whom YOU are being. Nourish your body and your soul. Focus on making this planet a reflection of how you live. Treat your inner "ecology" like the ecology of this planet.

Treat your symptoms or dis-ease like your customers. Get to the root of the problem and course correct. How you Live is How you Heal because How you do Anything is How you do Everything.

THE UN-HABIT: INABILITY TO BE WITH STILLNESS IN THE FACE OF THE UNKNOWN

Why: The inability to be with stillness in the face of the unknown is the number one Habit to break. Learning to be in stillness, in acceptance without resistance to the unknown, is where the creative process' begins.

It is the step that allows for our deepest intuition to emerge and frees us for downloads to happen. It is where we surrender to our emerging creativity.

In the face of life challenges, whether they be with your health, business, or the pivots required because of the pandemic, there are three steps to connect with our deepest knowing and inner peace: The three I's to living an inspired life.

The first is Information Gathering. The second is Insight and Reflection, and the Third is Intuition, or as they call it in business "acumen".

Most people look for answers to come from the outside. They rely on business coaches, health experts or authorities to show them the way. The third step, developing and fostering intuition, is often forgotten.

In the first step, Information Gathering, it is important to proceed with an inquisitive "child's mind". Look at the evidence, check the facts, notice the trends, and speed up your learning curve by learning from mentors that have forged ahead of you in the general direction you want to go. Be aware of confirmation bias. Confirmation bias usually pops up when something resonates with you. This can be very misleading as it often is based on unquestioned assumptions and beliefs.

In step two, Insight and Reflection, are the steps in which you test the information you have decided to follow. It is only through experience and feedback that you will be able to assess whether the strategy works individually. This is where you have a chance to course-correct, pivot, and gather feedback. This is the same process both in life and in health.

Through this process, one gets clarity on the underpinning beliefs, and it allows us to align ourselves to our inner knowing that resonates with our deepest profound intuition. Insight is the necessary step to train your intuition to guide us in the direction most aligned with our vision.

Though the third step, Intuition is born out of Insight and Information; stillness is where we go beyond what we think and believe. That is where all the magic happens. That's where the real opportunity lies. It is where your very own voice and purpose is born.

ABOUT DR. MANON: With a deep personal connection to health advocacy, Dr. Manon Bolliger, a Naturopathic Medical Doctor, CEO and Founder of an International training center called Bowen College, is dedicated to consciousness in the healing process. Devoted to a "Healer in Every Household," her unique methodology guides both the practitioner and the health advocate on a path to physical, emotional, and spiritual wellness. It all starts with our body's innate wisdom and its capacity to heal itself. As author of several books and keynote speaker Dr. Manon reminds us of our choices in health and in life.

19

START EACH DAY WITH AN INSPIRATION
CRISTIAN HAUSER

Why: Without motivation to get up and do what you need every day to achieve your goal, nothing will get done. I like to wake up every morning, and the first thing I see is a big motivational poster that says, "Remember your Why," and that gets me up and running faster than my coffee. It fuels my ambition and reminds me that every day is a chance to accomplish my goals.

While in the car, I put a good podcast instead of the same old songs playing again and again. Listen to audiobooks as I drive long distances or go on a flight.

Suppose you start with small baby steps, something as simple as one motivational video a day in the morning as you enjoy breakfast. That one action will make all the difference in your life, that one action will help you grow, keep you motivated, and fuel that part of your soul screaming to be more.

We all have the potential to be great, to be anything our heart desires. But it takes work. It takes courage, ambition, mindset. Your mindset will help you achieve your goals, feed it every morning with something that inspires you, something that motivates you. That makes your heart sing!

THE UN-HABIT: DON'T SLEEP THE DAY AWAY

Why: It's your day off, and the alarm rings, and you hit the snooze button for the 5th time. It's now past 10 am, and you are still in bed. You finally had enough and decided to wake up to get your self a cup of coffee. You feel sluggish and tired. You look at your clock and wonder where did the day goes.

Yes, you are not alone; many people wake up this way. They live their average lives, and do their average things, can't wait for the weekend to go and party, or their day off to sleep all day.

That's the average life that most people live every day, and it should scare you. Because deep inside you, you know you have more to offer, you know you are great, you know that you were not put on this earth to be average. No, you are more, you can feel it in your heart, that there is more to you than people know.

What's keeping you from reaching that greatness, that sense of real purpose, is your Habits. Bad Habits to be precise. They are keeping you in your comfort zone. And no one wants to leave the comfort zone because it requires work. And no matter how much you go and tell yourself, you will do the work to be better; you don't.

The mission in your equation is MOTIVATION. Yes, I will repeat it, Motivation! Motivation is the spark of life that gets you up and running, which fuels your body with ambition and sets you in the right mindset to accomplish great things. Suppose you don't have the time to be motivated. In that case, the solution is simple, wake up 30 minutes earlier than what you set your alarm for every day and listen to a motivational video every day. Go and find yourself a BIG motivational poster with a phrase that speaks to you, which motivates you and puts it right in front of your bed. So that the moment you wake up, it's the very first thing you see. Follow these steps every day, and you will recognize the old you because now your mindset is set on GREATNESS!

About Cristian: I am the creator of LiveGreatness.com, a motivational apparel and art website inspired by my mentor Forbes Riley. Live Greatness's goal is not to change the world but to empower and dress the people that will.

20

LEARN MORE AND NEVER SETTLE

JOSHUA SELF

Why: I'm passionate about learning, and I've made it a Habit to continue to study, grow, and expand my mind on a variety of topics. In college, it was from film making and 3d motion graphics. Out of college, I moved onto fitness and nutrition. What ignited my brain waves was learning about biomechanics and how the body operates to build muscle efficiently and safely. I became so obsessed with the concepts that when I applied them to myself, within a year, I won the most prominent bodybuilding show in the world, "The Arnold Classic," and started competing around the world.

When it comes to weight training, most people learned to lift from their dad or their high school coach, as I did, but it turns out there is a specific science that makes the process more efficient and much more effective. Understanding ideas such as resistance and strength curves mixed with the model of "time under tension". Most people engage in movements that may be quite harmful in the long run, like doing the overhead presses and dips.

I have taken the techniques that I have learned and mastered and not only applied them to my own body but train others, created courses, and even teach via Zoom.

Concerning nutrition, we have all been fed lies. Especially when it comes to protein, it was eye-opening to me after being mentored by a doctor who focuses on blood, and he inspired me to give up red meat and chicken. In my last world championship, I won as a vegetarian.

I am committed to learning and improving and researching to find answers that help me succeed in life. When I'm not in the gym, I'm in the tv studio doing production or in front of the computer building animation that is mind-bending. Being passionate, never settling, and always growing both in body, mind, and spirit is central to all that I do, and what I believe everyone should be doing. We all have ONE life, continue to grow in every aspect of it, and don't let anything stop you from achieving your goals.

THE UN-HABIT: STOP BEING YOUR WORST CRITIC

Why: We are our worst enemies when it comes to our potential. You never know who you until you push your limits.

Human beings have this incredible ability to limit ourselves. Why do people do this? You do this to limit the possibility that you will fail - but more growth comes from failure.

I'm a huge fan of MJ, and he said. "I've missed more than 9,000 shots in my career. Lost almost 300 games. Twenty-six times, I've been trusted to take the game-winning shot and missed. I've failed over and over and over again in my life." But I don't give up.

This year for the first time in my life, I felt physically paralyzed. I had to stop what I've been working so hard for over eight years to be. On Jan 2, 2020, my world changed when a kid in a car slammed into me while driving my motorcycle. Shattered my body and my dreams. I was in the hospital, ICU, surgery. Destroyed my Talus (ankle) bone and four broken ribs. I spent six months in bed and a wheelchair. I went through so much nerve pain; it's hard to describe the feeling. I felt like someone erased my painting my life working so hard on. I lost almost 20 pounds of muscle. I felt embarrassed by the way I looked, even though I knew it wasn't my fault.

This, mixed with the COVID Quarantine, played havoc on my spirit. As the months loomed on, the questions filled my mind... can I get back up? Should I get back up... But on Jun 1, I decided to get back into the gym. I have a teenage son and daughter and a woman I love so very much. At 43, I have a long life ahead of me, so I set out to rebuild. -- With my knowledge of weight training, I knew I could reconstruct my body by performing many of my exercises sitting down. Once I started, I haven't stopped. Now, three months later, I'm feeling almost back to normal. Not my foot yet, but my muscles. I walk with a cane now, but I'm coming along nicely. My goal is to compete again at the Arnold in March of 2021. I won't let anything get in my way if I can help it. I refuse to give up my body and my mind.

Remember, if it is to be, it's up to me!

About Joshua: Joshua Self has always aspired to greatness, and unparalleled drive is reflected in his strict dedication and commitment to training. Twice he's won the Arnold Classic, the Cutler, and Pro World Champ. He is a student of exercise physiology and biomechanics. Joshua also expresses himself creatively as a 3D designer and rendering artist. A former Chippendale, Joshua has also been an actor in a variety of tv and movie projects.

21

CONSISTENT ACTION

JENNIFER JERALD

Why: In a world of constant change and uncertain outcomes, it can become challenging to keep moving forward. The Habit of consistent action has become a saving grace in all of my attempts to be successful. The only times I have failed in my journey to success are when I stopped taking consistent action, froze up in the face of adversity, and stopped dead in my tracks in the confines of fear.

Every day will pose different challenges, or opportunities, and equally various successes or triumphs. With each day posing these two dialectical sides to success, it is important to remain consistent in the action you are taking. Consistent Action may not determine specific outcomes; however, it will ensure that a positive outcome is just around the corner.

Consistent action may include small action, or it may consist of HUGE action. No matter what size your action is, consistency is the key. Doing something every day that is aligned with the ultimate outcome will be both rewarding and progressive.

Taking the time to make sure my action plan consists of daily action steps to support my goals has created more positive outcomes, connections, and success than anything else I have ever done as an entrepreneur. Whether I have made a couple of phone calls to potential clients, added a chapter to my book, completed another course in my certifications, or recorded another podcast, to name a few - every consistent action has brought different levels of reward and success.

To be consistent means, "... fully dedicate yourself completely to a task, activity, or goal. It means to stay engaged without distraction fully. To be consistent requires a commitment on your part. It requires that you commit yourself to a sustained effort of action over the long-term.", according to... blog.iq-matrix.com › consistency-in-action.

I have learned through consistent action that more success than not happens and often shows up in ways unexpected. It usually comes more quickly than I ever imagined, as well.

As a Director with Tupperware I have learned that consistent action taken today would show up as results in as little as three weeks. This little gem has carried me through many journeys and to where I am today.

A TIP:

Create a journal or a jar titled "CONSISTENCY IN ACTION."

Each day write down 1-5 things you did for your goals, tasks, or activities. At the end of the year, you will see your success and know exactly why you have it as you review your "Consistency In Action" entries from the year!

Enjoy the journey!

THE UN-HABIT: FREEZING IN FACE OF FEAR

Why: Freezing in the face of fear is an entrepreneur's death sentence for success. Everyone will face challenges, adversity, roadblocks, and brick walls along the way to entrepreneurial success. The difference between those that make it and those that don't is whether they freeze in the moment of resistance.

Hundreds, if not thousands, have referred to fear as F.E.A.R., or False Evidence Appearing Real. We have learned through this acronym that F.E.A.R. is the illusion of danger, failure, or loss. I, for one, have suffered from F.E.A.R. for most of my life and have shriveled behind it's paralyzing qualities. This has cost me dearly in my journey to success, until now.

Today, I can share that breaking the Habit of "Freezing in the Face of Fear" is becoming a reality. Don't get me wrong; I still have my moments. However, they are much farther apart and last for much shorter periods. Learning to break this Habit is the fundamental basis for my success and can be for yours.

F.E.A.R. is the sum of life experiences, environments, and the words we have conditioned throughout our lives. F.E.A.R is the strongest evidence of existing limiting beliefs and the quickest way to STOP any progress towards our goals and, ultimately, our success. F.E.A.R. almost stopped me from making this entry today. I'll share how I overcame that in a moment.

Recently I learned from Dr. Joseph McClendon III that we could "Face Emotion And Replace it!" - YES!!! I have found this to be a more productive use of F.E.A.R.

As fear comes at us today, instead of freezing completely, may we each just S.T.O.P. for a MOMENT, and then move through it.

My steps for pushing through are

1. Stabilize
2. Think it through
3. Overcome the objection(s)
4. Press forward with confidence.

The key for overcoming fear and learning to control it instead of it controlling me is to remove it altogether. Learning how to go THROUGH it instead of under it or over it allows me to break the wall down. By breaking through and destroying that wall, I can never hide behind THAT ONE ever again. Never leave a hiding place for success by skirting fear. Face it and Replace it! Destroy it! And Live your Best Life!

ABOUT JENNIFER: Jennifer Jerald developed a platform strategy to help parents, especially moms, work from home and earn a full-time living while only working part-time hours. Jennifer helps mothers increase their time at home to be present with their families while leveling up their income and creating a life of their dreams. She does this one piece, one party, one session and one day at a time by helping people save time, space, taste, and waste as your Tupperware Lady for Life! Jennifer is also your personal one-on-one coach focused on helping you overcome challenges in life by improving confidence, increasing success and accelerating personal growth.

22

MEDITATE DAILY TO GET INSPIRED

DENISE MILLETT-BURKHARDT

Why: I was overworked and over-stressed and forgetting to take time for myself. As a result, I had high anxiety and even weight issues. I was building an empire without a reflection of any kind. The lack of imagination blocked my perception of all that I could achieve. I was not receptive to additional inspiration outside of my daily work environment. The answer to relieving stress and anxiety from a very noisy world took time to reveal itself. Meditation is the source of all imagination and deep-seated soul searching. When we meditate, we open up our line of communication to our higher power, and we are filled with inspirations that can lead us to the greatness that we are. Taking time to meditate daily is a purposeful daily practice that assists us in creating a daily pattern for success in business and our personal life. Taking a moment to meditate and feel about what we are seeking will give us the answers from inside. When we are quiet in such a busy world, we can tap into the river of knowledge.

There are several forms of meditation to assist you in your journey, and everyone has their style. For some, this means daily prayer, which might include a declaration of gratitude and inquiry for knowledge. For others taking the time to go for a walk to clear their minds can also bring answers because you are getting the sunlight and exercise that your body needs to get clarity. There is also relaxation meditation, which could include a long bath or soak in a hot tub, yoga, or other methods to wind down. Or simply sitting on your front porch listening to nature as it gives you its wisdom.

Taking purposeful action to add meditation daily will increase your productivity exponentially as you take time to seek the answers instead of blindly relying on your thought process alone. When you allow yourself to meditate and take in instead of always giving out, you are open to higher frequencies. So, take the time to cook in silence or garden outside, play soft music on an instrument, write, or say your prayers at night and talk to God. Sometimes the answers will just come to you. The moments of silence that we capture in our noisy existence will give you the freedom to find inspiration rather than to react to a busy lifestyle. When we take the time to renew ourselves, we are giving space to realize our potential.

THE UN-HABIT: FORGETTING TO MOVE

Why: Taking action is the only step that can be taken for success. Taking action means movement. For some, the thinking process comes very quickly, and movement is not as desirable. For others, moving around to motivate the brain can be the method needed. I am here to tell you that we all have things we can work on.

I am not a runner, and I do not go to the gym or work out daily. In all things, we create a daily Habit by taking the time to do something repetitively to change our lifestyle. Not everyone has the money or ability to go to the gym and get a traditional amount of exercise as we were taught in gym classes 20 years ago. The key is finding a passion for something and sticking to it.

It doesn't take money to get in shape, and we could easily use that for an excuse. The truth in the matter is that there are hundreds of ways to change our physical appearance and well-being, which could include something that we love. Trying different methods to take the action that is required to love something is all that is needed. Don't go in with the mindset of personal appearance but instead well-being.

To get moving, you could go outside, walk around your yard, pick a few weeds, or start your day just tidying up after your meditation. The SpinGym by Forbes Riley is a very simple tool with a method that works. What about an evening walk every night when the air cools, or following an exercise show and doing a daily routine? Taking small steps to increase your activity will help you get motivated to do the work that needs to be done. Remember, there are so many forms of exercise. Take time to be purposeful. This is the answer. Make time, even if it is only ten minutes a day. You will find your tolerance grows, and you give it more than you believed you would. Every action you take daily, including movement, can increase your productivity to a whole different level.

About Denise: Born and raised in Brooklyn, New York, Denise Millet Burkhardt was a prodigy and exemplary student. At the tender age of 21 she was already working on Wall Street until the Sub-prime Banks closed.

Immediately she made a transition into the television industry and charity concerts for veterans. Soon after finding success in these arenas, she was recognized as owning one of the first OTT networks amongst the youngest of women in these ranks. Now the owner of 14 television networks of all PG-14 programming she stands in harmony for the Entertainment Industry with music, entertainment, health, nutrition, education and information to create positive reinforcement globally. Some of her achievements include a 2019 Telly Award, and a congressional award for invaluable service to the community.

23

CALENDAR YOUR PRIORITIES

MICHELE MALO

Why: I genuinely believe what you prioritize gets done. The best way to ensure success is to actively control your calendar with activities that will bring you closer to your health, love, and business goals.

The first step is to establish concrete goals that can be measured and quantified.

The biggest mistake that people make is not making these goals realistic. Don't get me wrong; you need to push yourself, but make sure you believe you can do it. For example, do not say you are going to work out every day at 5 am for two hours, when the last time you were up at 5 am you were getting home from the bar. Start with three days a week and get up and hour earlier than you usually do, and once this becomes second nature, add a day, etc. You get it, the Habit of working out has now become a priority in your life. It is a scheduled part of your day.

Once those top three priorities are finished, everything else completed on your to-do list is a bonus for the day. Celebrate how much you have accomplished, and then make sure you sit down and write down your next top three priorities. The key is consistency. If you struggle with consistency, find an accountability buddy, especially in the beginning. This can be a friend, but if you want to have some real skin in the game, put your money where your dreams are, hire a personal trainer, a business coach, and any professional to help you achieve your goals.

Once the infrastructure is in place, make sure a timeline and quantifiable goals are written down. I have found that if I have a big goal such as running a marathon, I can break that huge undertaking into smaller goals such as completing a 5K, then 10K, half marathon, and then the marathon. Knowing what and when you need to get things done will help you achieve your ultimate goal.

Once you start knocking down your initial goals, you will be amazed at how you are crushing life one priority at a time.

THE UN-HABIT: STOP LETTING YOUR BAD HABITS SNEAK BACK INTO YOUR LIFE

Why: This Un-Habit has been something that I have struggled with personally my whole life. I call myself the restoration specialist because I believe people do not need to reinvent themselves. They need to restore their beauty and brilliance that has always been there but needs to be polished and brought back to the surface. The biggest enemy of a complete and long-lasting restoration are recurring bad Habits.

The struggle is real because once your beautiful brilliance is shinning, you have to continue to work at it and not allow old Habits and self-doubts to tarnish your sparkle.

An excellent example of a bad Habit I struggle with, especially when times are tough, is what I call the Flip or Flop Syndrome. It can be very serious, sucking time right out from under you and taking away your happiness of completing your top three priorities. If you don't treat the syndrome, you will have long term consequences, such as low self-esteem, financial issues, and crushed dreams. How do you recognize the symptoms? The first sign is that your tv automatically turns itself on to HGTV. Then it begins, you slowly lose yourself as you start to watch a house being flipped and all the problems they encounter, well then you have to see how the project turned out. This cycle continues and the next thing you know four hours have gone by and nothing has been accomplished, and somehow you are exhausted. The problem is this continues to happen, and a week goes by, and you have not gained any momentum with any of your important goals.

You must guard against allowing these bad Habits from creeping back into your life. You miss one workout, then it's a week. This becomes the new pattern. As we go through difficult times, bad Habits come creeping back as we are establishing our new take on life, family, and doing business. The time is now to live life like your hair is on fire with urgency, strategy, and passion.

About Michele: I deliver an appetite for sanity to entrepreneurs and corporate go getters needing to make a change in their lives. I offer up the success menus that will allow my clients to pick their desired result off the menu. It usually begins with the mindset menu. Diving deep into what is holding them back and why they continue to do the same things over and over expecting a different result – Insanity.

24

BE INTENSELY GOAL ORIENTED

SHERONTELLE DIRSKELL

W hy: Choosing the Habit to be intensely goal-oriented will be necessary to setting goals and achieving them. Creating this Habit will bring value to not only you but those around you and can make life better.

"I am the happiest when I am in control of my life." I have discovered that what may seem to be immense, impossible feats will pivot our direction through courage.

I became successful in my field of work by being intensely goal-oriented. What appeared to me as obstacles were really only opportunities to move to the next level in life. Sometimes when we immerse ourselves in our daily routines, it can give this perception that we are being productive. Being goal-oriented brings your vision to life.

You will start to notice that when you start setting goals, you will have energy, clarity, enthusiasm, the will power to be successful, relentless, stability, courage, feeling the ability to let go of procrastination, and knowing life can evolve.

We are the manifestation of our ideas. Having goals can set the tone for the future, show dedication, discipline, perseverance, & a direction to where we want our business & personal lives to go. If you have trouble with procrastination, you can set a goal to overcome to push past the debilitating fear you may have.

You can execute more of your goals when you can find ways of managing your time. Every move that you make in your life is calculated. This discipline says that there is no shortcut to excellence. You have to be great at your craft to be successful. Being intensely goal-oriented will help identify your purpose, it creates a timeline for your mission for you & your company, and then you are ready to unleash the potential from your insane focused thinking. There is a huge gap between who we are today and who we need to become to execute our goals and put them into action.

THE UN-HABIT: SAYING THAT I DON'T HAVE TIME TO SET GOALS

Why: Saying that I don't have time to set goals is like saying I don't have time to live. When I was an adolescent, some Habits were forming that I couldn't comprehend then. I was active in the cross-country sport yet, I never was great at it, thinking back, I believe it was because I never set any goals to reach success. Taking the time to set goals later in my life became the force to balancing my life and becoming a valuable asset. Decisions give birth to consequences. Nothing happens until you get it done, so I had to un-Habit that I don't have the time and clarify how to prioritize it.

I began to think about how important it is to make time to set one personal goal I wanted to achieve. You have to be willing to be uncomfortable to prepare to live beyond the Habit formed of not creating goals. No longer did I want to be stuck in the system to accommodate what wasn't working in my life professionally & personally because it became my every day. We all have the potential of enormous success, but you have to build a system of good forming Habits so that you can be a successful individual, CEO, Founder, Leader, and whatever title you would like to add.

Your power is in the Habits that you create on a day to day basis. It is paramount to take a leap and do something that you have never done before because that is how your development change. Use these steps one day at a time, first be willing to challenge yourself. Set daily goals, have a vision, write it down, and execute towards it daily. It is in the completion of a goal is where you will receive your greatest reward. Our mind is the control tower for our entire life. You can have all the money in the world if you don't set worthy goals with intention, I can only hope that you soon realize that good health, good relationships, peace, joy, love, or happiness come through our daily routine.

About Sherontelle: Sherontelle Dirskell has created a mission to inspire men, women, & children to live beyond their fears, pursue their dreams, and step into their greatness. As a Motivational Speaker, she has created workshops, online blogging & Live Instagram Conversations teaching others how to unlock their fears & release their fullest potential. Sherontelle also does freelancing in the entertainment industry as a Celebrity Music Publicist being a liaison between music artists, labels, media outlets, through PR campaign building, music release promotions, media training, and social media campaigns.

25

FILL THE GAP

EDIT B KISS

W hy: Fill the GAP is the way how we reach our dreams. I have always been a dreamer, and I always find a way to achieve them by filling the GAP.

First, I set my dream; then, I started to analyze the situation: What do I lack to reach that goal? I connect with people, ask them around, read books and news, and search on the net. When I find what I need to get there, I start to implement the actions or learning the skills.

Growing up in a communist country not having all the abundance, I always looked for a way to earn money and travel the world. My dream was to work on a cruise ship. I was 19 years old, and I was looking at advertisements in the newspaper, and I found a German river cruise where I could work as a maid. That time I was speaking fluently in German besides my Hungarian. The only thing they asked is to have 1.5

months' experience in a hotel as a cleaner. A week later, I started working in the 5 star Marriott hotel cleaning 18 rooms a day. After 1.5 months, I said to them I am ready.

They informed me that they change the requirements and I need to speak English too. At that time, I was learning English from a nice lady once a week for a couple of months; I was far from speaking English. But I knew what I had to do, I applied an au-pair program to the UK, and I sold my violin and piano and headed to London on a night coach within two months. After half a year, I was speaking pretty well and returned to my country, but this time I was aiming to work on a Caribbean cruise, not a river cruise in Germany anymore. After finishing the first year of the University, I asked for a break and flew to Miami, where I started a fantastic Caribbean adventure.

When I was at the University and wanted to have an Internship in Mexico, I started to work for the exchange office for free to be close to the fire. I also started to have Spanish lessons, and because it wasn't available in our engineering faculty, I went to the lawyers to learn Spanish. One Mexican internship landed at our University, and I was the one taking it that summer. As I started my spiritual practices, strengthen my six senses, the GAPs began to fill themselves.

The Un-Habit: Thinking negative thoughts

Why: Negative thinking, such as "I am not good enough," " I can not do this," " I am too stupid," "it is too hard" will hold you back from achieving your goals and also lower your vibration and make you more vulnerable to think more negative thoughts. Everything is energy, and the words also have energy.

We attract what we think. That is why I am always telling my Reiki clients that it is not enough that I am raising their vibration; they need to keep it high with positive thinking. If they continue to think negatively, they ruin the results of the healing, and they go back to square one.

Negative talk is also blocking the chakras. The chakras are the centers of our energy body completely aligned with our endocrine glands. If, for example, we think that we are not good enough and we are unworthy, our Solar plexus chakra will be blocked, and we could have physical illnesses in our stomach or liver. That is why the people who drink too much alcohol and poisoning their liver also have self-esteem issues.

The bad news is that we get into a cycle where we are having these negative emotions, and blocking our chakras more, we will have more negative thinking due to our conditions. So we need to realize our bad Habit and unlearn it and overwrite it with a positive talk by repetition in our subconscious mind.

Using positive affirmations and practicing gratitude daily is a great way to create the change and rewrite your future. Suppose your negative thinking is rooted in emotional traumas from your childhood. In that case, it can only be released from the unconscious mind by source memory healing when the brain reaches the Delta brainwave through transcendental meditation.

Transcendental meditation also activates the pineal gland, which starts to produce serotonin and melatonin, and the Hippocampus will begin to grow new neurons. The Pituitary gland will release Human Growth Hormones and Oxytocin. So the body, by receiving an extra amount of these calming and bonding hormones, will be more likely to act and think positively.

About Edit: Edit B Kiss is a powerful spiritual healer and transformation life coach. Her program helps people to get cleaned from blockages, healing them from hidden emotional traumas through the use of source memory healing, Karma Healing and Reiki.

She has healed people of long-lasting pains, blockages, ancestor defects and emotional traumas so they could live fulfilled and joyful lives. She has clients from all over the world, including the United States, New Zealand, the United Kingdom, Hungary, and Nigeria; these range from millionaire traders to influencers to artists.

26

MAKE YOUR BED WHEN YOU WAKE UP
LAURIEANN CAMPBELL

Why: When you make your bed, you are telling yourself that the day has begun. It motivates you to complete your daily tasks knowing at the end of your achievements, you can cozy back into it, but it is prepared for you. Imagine going to a hotel, and the housekeepers don't make your bed, and you come back to your room in shambles as you left it. Your life should reflect the desire in the morning to create an environment that invites you to a bed that shows appreciation for work well done.

I make my bed every day, knowing it's inviting me back in from order I created in the morning to order that I mess up again during the night. The comfy sheets in disarray until the morning comes, and it beckons me to put the order back to proceed with my day that way – with order.

I then go to my list. I never overwhelm myself. I have a four list rule for both work and home.

And I truly believe if one on the list can wait until tomorrow and I have put in my eight to twelve hours in, I don't feel guilty. I write it into the next day.

Exercise is also a daily Habit, and I give credit to my dogs for that. They make sure I get my walks. I also have my spin gym that I carry around. It's a workout I can do even when in a ZOOM meeting. Fun fact - Most people won't even notice I am working out while at the meeting!

THE UN-HABIT: STOP LETTING PEOPLE BULLY YOU!

Why: When I was young, I was told I was too nice. Because I was "too nice," I allowed myself to be bullied. I was also tall, so I was perceived as fat because my weight was so much more than my petite friends. I was also different. I liked being on my own and yet with people. However, when I was with people, I enjoyed entertaining them.

When you are someone like me, bullying can affect you because you don't want to fight back. But you have to learn it isn't about you. It's about THEM. Later in life, one of the bullies told me she was jealous because I always looked good. To that, my mother would not allow me to wear jeans to school. It was another reason I was different. At the time in my life, she was bullying me. I didn't see her jealousy, only the cruelty. I just thought I deserved it.

NO ONE deserves to be bullied. My daughter went through it too, and she didn't want to tell me. I never told my parents either. Why stop allowing it to hurt you? Because it's not healthy for your mindset

About LaurieAnn: I am a Masters Certified Handwriting Analyst and Grapho Therapist and Podcaster who makes sure you become the best you can be through the neuroscience of handwriting and perfecting not only your character, but your signature to assist in making you a success. And then I interview you on my Podcast. :)

27

FIND THE JOY & KEEP MOVING FORWARD

SONIA CLARK

Why: Finding joy is more than just being happy. There is joy in just about everything we can do, even doing the dishes! It's your perspective, no matter the obstacles and tasks. We all must run some gauntlets in life; it's how we run them that matters. This perspective and application will make you more resilient, take on challenges with positivity, move forward with positivity, and spread positivity.

One person alone can find it difficult to make huge impacts, but when we pull together, all paying-it-forward with positivity, the impacts make a difference. Find the joy, and keep moving forward.

This saying helps us personally and professionally. We cannot live in the past but only learn from it. We live right now, but that "right now" is very fleeting. The very next minute is our near future, so we need to live in this one minute and the near future being the very next minute. We then realize we can have more power over our future with choices, attitudes, and applications. We can then think about how we will approach our near few minutes and so on with joy, which is infectious. We owe it to ourselves, our loved ones, our communities, our countries, and the planet.

Overcoming my obstacles and reflectively learning the lessons, I've been helping others do the same for many years, both personally and professionally. I've truly enjoyed the journey so far. Now spreading the message globally through my programs and interviewing formidable leaders, I know I'm not alone, and neither are you.

We can only but move forward into the future. We cannot go back and live in the past. We all fall over here and there, so we need to get better skilled at not falling over and getting back up and stronger in picking up others along the way. Becoming skilled is from education, application, on-teaching, and then experience.

Only YOU can do it. When you've practiced it and have helped pick up others along the way, you get stronger. You demonstrated leadership and on-taught something to someone. When there is a lot of "YOU's," then you become "WE." This is the tipping point; you become stronger when there are more of you. Strengthen the group of like-mindedness with lots of positivity. Find the joy and spread the joy and keep moving forward. These actions are leverage, and together we can make the world a better place and positively impact our future generations. These are my lessons for all Entrepreneurs.

THE UN-HABIT: OMIT THE WORD"BUT" FROM YOUR VOCABULARY.

Why: We all need to stop using the word "but." Why? The word "but" negates everything you said before it. Society is programmed to think on a conscious and unconscious level that as soon as you say the word "but" you're not as believable, you're untrustworthy and negative. You've just lost some credibility. It takes a lot of building up of credibility to be influential when communicating with another person or a group. When you're communicating with others, it's because you want to influence others with what you mean, your opinion, your message, your "why," your product, your service, why you, and why this way, and the list goes on.

From the communication research of Professor Emeritus of Psychology Albert Mehrabian, 55% of communication is non-verbal (body language), 38% is tonality (tone of your voice and intent), leaving you 7% for verbal (words). What this means is that we must choose our words carefully and leverage every percentage of communication as much as possible. It doesn't mean we have to use big fancy words to articulate ourselves, as it's best to be simplified to ensure our message is clear. It's precisely that. We need to be truly clear and reasonably concise.

So you might be asking yourself, "well, what do I say then?" When you're communicating, think about saying your message in short bullet point sentences. To omit the word "but," you'll often need to rearrange your sentences. This will also force you to be more positive as well as factual with your message. In turn, this will lower the chances of miscommunication and angry clients. The word "but" is often a Habit of our communication preferences, and like learning any new language, it will take practice and time to use your words and message in different ways.

When we use the word "but" regularly with our internal thoughts, we are often thinking more negative. You might want to ask yourself if you're unintentionally setting yourself up for more failure than success? Small improvements can make big changes in your success. Lets' set you up for success and prosperity, come join me in my programs.

About Sonia: Sonia Clark is a Prosperity Entre-Leadership Business Strategist, Trainer, and Coach providing professional and personal development programs and projects for Business Owners & Staff across the globe with the ethos of paying-it-forward.

28

DO WHAT MAKES YOU FEEL UNCOMFORTABLE

TODD SU

Why: This Habit moves incredible mountains. It prevents you from being satisfied. Sometimes it is the things that you don't want to do that make the most differences in life and business. Especially in business, the email that you need to send to help damage control of the client. The person you want to connect with that you are afraid to meet or talk to. The follow-up email to see if that person is interested. The call with that customer that you haven't reached out to in a while. As you manifest what you want, these people and tasks will gravitate toward your goals. You will begin to see relationships starting to flow to your life and business. Planning time off or with your family becomes easier because you are held to something you have written down or committed to. These items sometimes take the most brainpower. Our instinct is to do what is easiest. We find the funniest way and save the most time doing things. These items may not and usually isn't the most productive thing to do.

You start to plan things better by now prioritizing what the biggest pain is. Now your day flows smoother. You don't have that burden hanging over your head, which creates better flow and a better state of mind. It's that one percent better you feel after the arduous task is done that lifts your spirit. For the same reason going up the mountain is tough; you enjoy the trip down the mountain. I hated making my bed, but just that simple task cleared my mind and made me much more productive. I started to think about how life should be organized the same, and there should be more time to reflect on things and, therefore, clean my desk, so my mind is clear. Then it was my car which made me look more professional although it was an older car at the time. Little steps of what is tough make the biggest difference.

The Un-Habit: Stop Negative thoughts

Why: This is defeatist behavior. Don't let a broken nail or some burnt toast make you feel like the day is done. In everyone's daily lives, there are always going to be hurdles. But out of those hurdles, some champions are developed. There was a time when I had promised to be an event, and it was raining, and I was only five people that showed up. We were supposed to network with a bunch of cool speakers and guests, but no one showed up because it was outdoor, and it was cold, windy, dirty, and rainy. I decided to show up, and there were no speakers there, and they were cleaning up. I ended up offering to help clean up, and it turned out to be the organizer of the event.

As we cleaned up and chatted, he shared incredible golden nuggets. After cleaning up and going out to dinner, we talked until 2:00 am. He introduced me to some incredible people, including Frank Shankwitz, Les Brown, the founder of Priceline. Some pretty cool cats. Some of them became my mentors and friends. Negative thoughts hijack our mindset. We hear that a deal may fall through, and we expect it instead of becoming problem solvers. One client ended up saying how they thought that they made a mistake buying the home. If I had been negative, I would have given up. Instead, I asked them why did they feel that way and had empathy for them. I no longer wanted to sell a home but to help them fix their problem. It turned out they were worried about living far from their in-laws. I ended up finding them a house that had another home next door. Instead of 0 sales, I ended up with two homes I put up for sale and sold and found them two homes next to each other. The negative mindset is a Habit you want to be rid of.

About Todd: Todd Su is President and CEO of Advantage Homes & Realty World Todd Su and Company. He specializes in Modular Housing, Hotels and Real Estate. As a Philanthropist and Entrepreneur, he is passionate about giving back. Contributing financially to donation of homes to those in need, orphanages as well as Veterans for down-payment assistance. Annual give back events include Free Easter events and donated 10's of thousands of backpacks each year. He started his first company in 1996 to establish an affordable housing solution to that of traditional site built homes. Todd and Cindy completed a 120 unit project recently in San Luis Obispo in 2020. With 1000's of units built and sold including 25 years of experience in the industry and having been a board member of many Associations. With 13 offices in the state, they have the become the largest Modular company in California.

29

PRACTICE ACTIVE LISTENING

DR. KIM MARTIN

W hy: As a result of my 23 years as a medical practitioner, I have found that the following form of "Active Listening has been the basis of my practice and can be applied to any interpersonal relationship.

Miscommunications are common in life but when it's about the subject of healthcare these misunderstandings can lead to serious issues. Here are the steps that anyone may follow in order to practice active listening!

1. Building a Trusting Network

As a medical practitioner, I often consider this step-in term of the patient and physician relationship. In order to effectively treat my patients' aliments, an exact diagnosis is essential. However, to reach a correct diagnosis both parties must have the willingness and trust in the other to continue moving forward. Medicine is not always immediate because it takes time to see the effects, but over time we become stronger and recover. Active listening is the same way since it requires trust from all participants modeled in the same way as the doctor and patient relationship. We build trust through being vulnerable which sounds scary, but once you've built a cohesive network, you'll wonder how you survived so long without trust.

2. Learn to Speak Last

Typically, when people hear of "active listening" they claim it's simple and easy to do, yet this appears in contrast to our reality. We experience people shouting their opinions from the rooftops or on social media in a new generation of communication. This is why is can be challenging to learn to hear others. We have so much excitement and noise carrying around us, that in we can become triggered by a small aspect and lose track of the entire task. If we apply from this step, the notion of being the last to speak in a conversation, then we've set ourselves up for more open and transparent conversations. We allow our companions and friends to express their ideas or emotions before weighing-in with our own concerns. Instead of wondering when it'll be our chance to speak next, we simply continue to listen without the prospect of interrupting or shifting the topic of focus.

3. Be Authentic

Active listening requires a lot of energy and attention to detail, but once you've practiced it will come easily. More important than paying attention to the information we're receiving, is to project an honest response. As previously said, active listening can be tiring, especially if one of the participants isn't being truthful. This creates a flawed dynamic for future encounters and exchanges with this individual which will ultimately put stress on the relationship; professional, romantic, or otherwise.

THE UN-HABIT: "I DON'T HAVE TIME"

Why: The Habit with the highest priority to "break" is revealed in the words, "I don't have enough time."

Everyone has the same amount of time; the issue is how we intend to spend it. By saying, "I don't have enough time" our intention is clear: I will procrastinate.

As a chiropractor advising on exercise, home therapy, or a change in dietary Habits, I have heard this repeatedly.

When they have returned for their next visit, I inquire about whether they had followed my advice and in-response they say that *time* got away from them. Sometimes, I'll ask if they managed to catch a game on TV this past week or hang out with friends.

Invariably, they respond with, "Yes, I did." To one of my questions concerning where their time went. After all, they have the same amount as you and I, so consider how we spend it.

I have to admit, for many years, I too was guilty of saying this. Why? Because it works in most instances to get the other person to let you off the hook.

The universe works in an amazingly simple manner: whatever you say, the universe hears and responds, "okay, here is more of that." For example, if we say we want a new car, the universe seems to give us an even greater sense of "wanting" rather than the actual automobile.

Instead, I've found it's better to phrase these situations differently. If we were to say: "I am ready for a new car, or my new car is on its way," then the universe will provide it. Then we must be alert for the opportunities that will arise to get a new car.

Therefore, we must learn to take the proper actions on a consistent and prompt basis once we have made a clear statement of our future goals and desires.

Therefore, when we have a desire or a task, it is best to be clear about what we want in a positive tone and use of language. In this respect, we can see how positivity will improve our interactions with others, but more internally our mood will shift as well. Positive energy is often rewarded by the universe, I don't know how but it works!

So, my best advice is three-fold:

1. Follow the original three steps described above to improve Active Listening
2. Limit or stop saying, and thus believing that you don't have enough time.
3. Finally, phrase all of your intentions the way you want the outcome to present itself in the future.

About Dr. Martin: As a natural health care provider with over 23 years in private practice, Dr Kim Martin has found that the most important thing that people want is to be heard especially about their health. she has designed a 1:1 online platform that is customized and addresses areas like auto-immune, blood sugar, anxiety, stress, thyroid, and gut issues. " Health is not taken seriously until sickness show up"

30

LOOK AT THE BRIGHT SIDE

CHRISTINA KUMAR

Why: Looking at the bright side of things gives you hope, and with hope comes solutions. With everything, good or bad, a lesson can come from it. If you look at the bright side and think positively, you can also create the energy and inspiration to do more than you would have if you didn't. Looking at the bright side also calms you, which can be so beneficial to health and wellness, especially now. Also, it makes you feel good, which is a great reason to practice it. Having a positive outlook can also help you get through many situations and thrive.

Having a positive mindset can also help you to build courage. When you look at the positive outcomes of a problematic situation, you realize that it was a problematic situation that helped you become stronger. When looking at the bright side of things, we can become more resilient and bounce back much faster. As an athlete, the more we use our "bright side" muscles, the easier it will be to call on. As an entrepreneur, this can be an essential skill to use in the day-to-day.

When we look at the bright side, we have the strength to try again. Many of those who have created mind-blowing things had the power to try again when it didn't work the first time, sometimes even hundreds of times! This shows that looking at the bright side can give you the strength you need to succeed.

THE UN-HABIT: PESSIMISM

Why: This Habit is important to break because it can hold back important ideas and solutions. Entrepreneurs need important ideas and solutions to solve problems. This is why we need to be supportive of new things to improve the status quo. When we are optimistic, we have a higher capacity to make things happen; with pessimism, we stop this flow.

When we look for coaches and mentors, we don't gravitate towards pessimistic ones for a reason. We go to the ones that look at the brighter side of situations and events that help us see things in a new and inspirational way, which then motivates us as well as gives us greater confidence.

Most people like to be around others who make them feel good about themselves. When we look at our most important relationships, they usually include those we can trust to help us through difficult situations with a positive outlook and those that care enough to help us look at the bright side. These people are not only feeding into your life love and encouragement, but hope for tomorrow, which is why we need to be these people as well for others.

When we turn to optimism and seeing the bright side, we give ourselves a chance. A chance at our future, a chance at our dreams, as well as a better tomorrow. What more can we ask for than having a better tomorrow? Try giving it a chance; think of a situation you find yourself pessimistic over and from now on instead, think of the bright side of the situation. You may be surprised by your results!

About Christina: Christina Kumar is the founder of Christina Kumar PR which connects established businesses and public figures to the press which is needed to expand their reach. With experience in obtaining media such as television interviews, live speaking engagements, radio, and online media for Grammy award-winning musicians, Olympic medalists, as well as international businesses; there is a variety of media opportunities that can be enlisted.

31

JOURNALING AND SCHEDULING YOUR TIME DAILY

MELODY JOHNSON

Why: Journaling allows you to write your thoughts and reflect on how to change your thoughts. Since your thoughts dictate everything, it also dictates your schedule.

If you are journaling things that are negative, look at your schedule. Is it filled with activities that will press you towards your goal? Are your activities supporting the time you are investing in that goal? Are you scheduling adequate time for that goal? Journaling also allows you to recall ideas you may have had and use them to propel you to goals you can place on your schedule. It also changes your way of thinking.

Journaling gives you creative ideas to use later and allows you to express yourself. Ideas from journaling can be placed into the schedule into smaller goals/tasks on your schedule.

Journaling gives yourself a peek into your feelings, challenges you encounter, and how to change your thoughts.

Listen, if you don't write the goal down--no matter how awesome that idea is-, then it never happened. And don't say you will write it later cause everyone always forgets to write it down. It has even happened to me. When you write those goals on your schedule, you promise to commit your time and energy to make that goal come true.

Scheduling also holds you accountable if you are wasting time. If you see you are spending more time binge-watching your favorite show or are on Instagram or Facebook more than usual, think how you make your time productive? Did you try your best to accomplish that goal? When you see your schedule and how it was spent, you may feel that twinge of regret or disappointment, especially if you see large blocks of wasted time.

It will make you rethink how you use your time and who is using your time. Taking a course on pitching with Forbes Riley might help or read an additional book on maximizing your time and activities might help you. Scheduling helps you to reflect on why goals are not being accomplished and allow you to think about how to improve that area of your life.

Always take the time to journal because it allows you to help reach your goals!

THE UN-HABIT: WRITE IT DOWN NOW --- NOT LATER!

Why: When my husband and I had our first son in New York, we were in a cramped, one-bedroom apartment with our oldest son, who was less than one. At that time, we had little money-- But we did have an imagination and had a schedule. We journaled, wrote down everything we wanted, and had a schedule to plan for the things to help us meet the goal we wanted-- which was to move from New York to Georgia.

From writing down those goals and using our schedule, almost like a checklist, we were able to meet that goal!

When we finally got to Georgia-- and a year later, got the home we wanted along with the jobs. But, there was something I stopped doing. I did not journal consistently. I also stopped scheduling things consistently. I used some journaling techniques and scheduling --but only to complete graduating from college and to advance at work. Sadly, even then, it was not consistent. What I missed out on were opportunities we could have expanded upon to help others.

What ended up happening? Well, I ended up just--drifting.

I wanted things but became complacent. Complacency is dangerous. If you feel satisfied now, then there is a close chance you might not want to continue to improve in the one area you can thrive! One day it hit me. I realized that I had not used my true potential and needed to shake off complacency. I was ticking off boxes in my career and education, but nothing in the area of my passion, which left me feeling void. The realization came to me that journaling and scheduling is the key to success. Many great leaders make writing a daily activity. Writing is the key to freedom. Writing allows you to do the things you always wanted to do and open you to new opportunities.

So, learn from my lesson and journal and schedule your activities daily! Don't just drift and cruise through life! Or worse, hope to do it...later. Because later never comes. It just goes on and on. By journaling, you allow yourself to think freely and let your ideas flow into goals you can apply to your schedule.

About: As an educational reading and behavior specialist for over ten years, I developed a company called, Loving Literacy, that supports students with reading challenges, eliminates frustration for parents, and boosts the love for reading. Reading eliminates the every day struggles and allows kids to expand their imagination. Want to eliminate tears and fears and replace them with smiles? Need a break from working remotely and being the teacher? Tired of looking endlessly for worksheets that are boring?

32

LIVE POSITIVELY AND CELEBRATE LIFE
AMANDA HUDES

Why: Thinking positively is one thing, but LIVING positively is quite another. When living with such intention to be happy and create happiness around you, it becomes part of your entire lifestyle. You aren't just saying, "I CAN do this," but instead, "I can be AMAZING at this and I WILL," pushing any negative thoughts out the window.

Living positively is taking thinking positively to the next level. It's celebrating the small moments and the large ones. It's listening to your gut and believing that you can do anything you set your mind to. It's believing that you can, even if you're not 100% sure, even if you believe at an 80% level, you know it's possible. You know there is a chance, and there is a good chance if you keep taking actions that give you the confidence to believe you can do anything. Being your own biggest advocate by speaking up and by surrounding yourself with other ambitious, intelligent, supportive people who cheer you on will help you want to share your wins and continue achieving goal after goal. Being able to conceptualize reaching your success points, because we all have those points in our lives that hit the check mark (Done! Success!) will help to make them real. When you believe, you can achieve. Every single step is leading you on the path to success in your eyes. And with every achievement, and every flutter of excitement, celebrate in a big way because you deserve it! Appreciate your hard work, become truly proud of the work you have done, and believe in yourself because YOU WILL, YOU CAN, AND YOU ARE AMAZING.

It's so easy to get caught up with what isn't working well in your life, even joining forces with friends and family to have complaint sessions about it, or what turns into them. But isn't it more productive and just more enjoyable to talk about what is going well in your life and what you're excited about?! When we surround ourselves with people who have that same desire to be happy and take action steps towards that goal, it's so much easier to challenge ourselves to let go of fear and walk towards all of the good in this world.

Celebrating life means appreciating and being grateful for the small moments. We lost power from a tropical storm this week, and believe me; it was not a productive few days. But when the power suddenly came on and the lights shined above us, my toddler yelled out, "Whoo-hoo! Let's have a dance party!" Let's celebrate life. Let's dance in the rain with smiles on our faces. When you create the Habit of living positively and celebrating life, every day will become happier and more freeing.

THE UN-HABIT: CARING WHAT PEOPLE THINK

Why: We are trained to do things that "make people like us." But what is the point if at the end of our lives we look back and realize we didn't live our actual lives at all but instead someone else's? Often we follow the route we believe, or are told, others want us to follow, from our career path to becoming a parent to making friends with people we don't have anything in common with. We do what society deems as "successful," we work towards goals that make us seem hardworking, and we display an appearance of "living our best life."

But in the end, what kind of life is it if it isn't the one that excites you? Why don't we say "yes" to more events, activities, and choices that make us feel great and "no" to people and actions that make us feel bad and less like ourselves?

Someone doesn't like the mole on your cheek, so you're thinking about getting it removed? Do YOU like it? Why do you value someone else's opinion higher than you value your own? Why is their opinion of what is beautiful more accurate than what you believe is beautiful? Imagine if Cindy Crawford had cared. What makes each of us unique is what makes us beautiful, inside and out.

There is such freedom in living authentically. Of course, we want people to like us, that's natural. But don't we want people to like us for who we truly are, not just what we portray? What a deeper relationship we can form with others when we allow them to see us! We have a choice every single day to wake up and be who we were born to be. You know who that is, whether you know deep inside or very clearly. Wasting one more day being who we think others want us to be is no way to celebrate life, and wow, what a great life it could be! No one can be a better you than you, so why are we all trying to become each other? What makes each of us special is that we are all different! What makes you unique? Give us more of that! Be YOU, and do it with a smile.

About Amanda: Amanda Hudes is the Founder of Smiling Through Chaos, helping women and couples smile more, stress less, and look and feel their best during their event planning experience. As an Event Planner and Wellness Coach, as well as an Amazon Bestseller of "Smiling Through The Chaos Of Wedding Planning," her mission is to help people celebrate life. Everything she does is customized to the client, using her creativity and diverse background to create the best experience possible.

33

BECOME CONSCIOUS OF YOUR THOUGHTS

LISA LONG

W hy: You create your life by the energy of your thoughts, feelings, and emotions. The energy you vibrate brings you similar energies by the Law of Attraction. You get what you put out. Like attracts like. Old thoughts are old Habits. Change them.

The more you become CONSCIOUS of your thoughts, the more you can change them to something you prefer to attract. When you feel a low-level emotion, ask yourself, "What was that thought?"

That is becoming conscious. You can then turn that thought around to something more positive. You take back your power.

If you stay in that low-level emotion agreeing with that old low-level thought, it feels disempowering. You create and attract disempowering energy into your future. The universe gives you what you ask for, not from your words, but from the energy you vibrate. If you feel heavy, you are vibrating at a low level. Wake up!

Ask yourself, "what am I thinking? What is under that? Where did I get that? Do I want to believe it or let it go?" Then choose.

Tell yourself, "I disagree with that. That was my dad's, or mom's, or whoever. Not mine. Release." Then turn your attention away from it.

Sometimes it is not easy to change a thought to something better because you have thought about it a lot. If that is the case, distract yourself. Do something else, like take a bath, a nature walk or listen to beautiful music. Break the pattern of that old thought, and it will eventually go away. But you have to become conscious of the way you are feeling first. Then aware of the thoughts. When empowered, you change the energy, thought, and vibration. You become a conscious creator!

Many of our thoughts were instilled in us when we were little. They do not serve us. So let them go. You are a master, you can do this, or you would not be here at this great time of awakening on this planet.

THE UN-HABIT: UNCONSCIOUSNESS, FALLING ASLEEP

Why: We are experiencing "The Great Awakening." People have been unconscious and asleep for thousands of years. They had no idea that they create their reality through their thoughts, energy, and vibration. They blamed others, and that disempowered them.

Low-level emotions feel heavy. High-level thoughts and emotions feel wonderful. Your higher self, Source, Guidance, whatever you choose to call it stays in the highest vibration and calls you to reach higher. The more you find appreciation and laughter, the higher your vibration moves.

Maintain a positive attitude as much as possible. Make it a Habit to be appreciative and be happy. Remember, "Like attracts Like." Enjoy life, and it will become easier to enjoy and live in Joy!

Many are waking up now. This can be a very challenging time as people become confused. Many need help and awakened people to lead the way.

But this is tricky as we are all waking up at different stages. You can help. We can help. But you have to walk the path yourself, first.

At first, waking up is not as easy because you have old Habits and patterns of thought that try to maintain their control. They do not want you to take back your power. So you have to decide that this is something YOU are choosing. You take back your power.

You make it a Habit to reach for better feeling thoughts. You are worthy. You can do this!

The more you move your MIND and thoughts to a higher level, the easier your life gets, and you hold more Light in your body.

You are becoming happier, healthier, and more prosperous. You HOLD that energy for others to reach it also. You become the leader you were born to be. Consciousness is a choice. Choose it, get happy, and blessings will flow to you.

About Lisa: A master who chose an abusive childhood, Lisa transcended unconsciousness levels. She vowed to make it easier for others, so they would not have to undergo the years of suffering she experienced.

Lisa Long works remotely with clients in the White House Press Room, United Nations, Air Force Two. She helps A-list celebrities, lawyers, executives, FBI, police, and has healed doctors. Her mission is to bring awakening concepts to the world thru her extensive work. She shares 25 years of multidimensional awareness thru her books and classes to transform how people see themselves. Lisa teaches Enlightenment, Longevity, and Prosperity.

34

BUILD A COMMUNITY

AMY J. MORRISON

Why: Due to being an only child, doing things by myself was a Habit. It came naturally to me. Friends would say to me," Amy, why don't you ask for help?" I needed to create a new Habit of building a community around me so that I wouldn't be alone. And also for me to allow people to contribute to me while I get to contribute to them too.

The Habit of being alone affected many areas of my life negatively. One of them was through my business.

Being a SoloPrenuer had its advantages and disadvantage. For the advantages, there wasn't any drama, no worrying about anybody canceling last minute, no arguments & confrontations, or the scare of someone stealing or taking clients from me.

I could have my schedule; I could do what I wanted, and when I wanted to do it. And I could take a vacation when I wanted to.

There wasn't as much responsibility as I felt as there would be from having employees or subcontractors.

The disadvantages took a toll on my stress level that I didn't know would happen. I realized that I still would have a problem as if an employee canceled at the last minute, except it was even more challenging. When I was sick or an emergency would happen, the client would still be without having help that day. There was nobody else to fill that spot, and I wouldn't be able to tell the client, "I will make sure you have help by such and such date."

What I learned was that I realized that being on my own without a team created more challenges, and by being alone, I didn't have the help that was needed for budgeting business details. Things that I necessarily wasn't good at. Which took a lot of time to figure out on my own that also created costly mistakes.

By opening myself to allowing people into my life, I was able to breathe and have my life back. While also giving a way for others to contribute, and have an employment or subcontractor opportunity, so they too wouldn't be by themselves.

The Un-Habit: Keeping Unhealthy Relationships

Why: Does it ever happen to you where you realize you may be doing things that may not benefit you from something that happened in your childhood?

From things that happened to me in my childhood, it created me into being a codependent people pleaser, which led to keeping relationships that weighed me down. Friendships, work relationships, and romantic relationships.

I wasn't aware that I was doing this until I became divorced and had someone tell me that's what they were noticing, and I still really didn't know quite yet because I hadn't learned what was needed. I didn't know what I didn't know, so that Habit kept happening.

The main area I noticed this was happening was in romantic relationships. I was repeating the same Habit of it not working out. Through me just sheer wanting it to stop happening, I researched how to break the Habit. I would hear things like, you need to let those that are weighing you down go, so you can be open to what will lift you. When I broke the unknown healthy Habit of choosing to be in relationships that weren't healthy, a whole new kind of relationship popped up that I didn't realize I needed to let go of.

What I learned is that some of my friendships were also weighing me down. They had me stuck in limiting beliefs like, I wish I had what they had, I'm not good enough because I don't have what they have. The relationships were dead weight. They were keeping me from being me. Letting relationships go isn't easy at all. We see the best of what could happen. We can still love them, it's learning to love them from afar. It is an act of loving you first.

After I let go of friendships that I noticed were keeping me held back from what I wanted and needed to do, I was able to focus and had the required time. When we let go of what isn't serving us anymore, it gives us time to learn about things we have wanted to do. To complete the vision, we have and give room for partners to come alongside us, through you creating that space of being open to new relationships.

About Amy: Amy Morrison was a Single Mother who raised two phenomenal children that are now adults. She is so proud to me their Mother and loves to see them use their wings to fly into their own greatness. She lives in the Pacific Northwest area of Washington state, on a cliff where she can see both whales & Sunsets .

35

DISCOVER NEW HABITS

PAUL CAPOZIO

Why: This is especially effective for those who have difficulty starting new routines and sticking to them.

As an example, Coffee time is my daydreaming time. Adding 15 minutes to my morning coffee Habit allows me to see the big picture.

It was always difficult to break until I realized it was meditation, not a waste of time. Now it is the most powerful part of my day. It's allowed me to create my reality for my day and my entire life.

The more time you can spend in self-realization and mindfulness, is more time in a calmer place. Those battles that occur in your mind cloud your ability to see the right decisions.

Judgment, fear, Jealousy, they all keep you from becoming the real you. Focusing on the nuts and bolts, the how, is less important. We do not have the drive to sustain what's coming next. The struggles, financial issues, and false starts will all happen; it is designed that way.

The WHY, on the other hand, is the gas in the tank. Your why is the strength from within, and if you don't have one, get one quick. Great ideas are abundant. Funding if you manifest it is readily available. But with no gas in the tank with no burn in your belly, you will fail. Without a why you build on sand, and people can smell it a mile away.

WHY will have people wondering what you're doing, not struggling to get off that pitch call. Why will Nourish you?

Personally, my why is based on my family issues. The ability to care for loved ones well past my ability to earn for them. Saying when I'm dead, they still need my help.

Focus on sustaining focus on your long-range goals. The day-to-day is automatic. Deadlines are done for us already.

The Un-Habit: Negative self-talk

Why: It is the number one reason people don't leap. It is the reason for the lack of happiness. Everything begins in the mind. Mind your mind.

We find so many creative ways to talk ourselves out of things because of fear, because of the negative reactions of friends and family. Suddenly, the opinion of your brother-in-law who sits on the couch eating chili with his fingers becomes a significant opinion? When you heard that great idea or even better thought of it yourself or someone you always wanted to partner with is willing to partner with you, what are you going to do about it?

I promise your thoughts will try to creep into your brain like an earwig. Limiting beliefs will Reveal themselves to you. One you didn't even know you had. That is when you leap, not because you can fail because you can win.

Sure, do your homework dot your I's and cross your T's then move at 100 miles an hour. Know that you know that, you know. Sometimes 10% of a team is way more valuable than going alone. Know your strengths and know your weaknesses. But never let those weaknesses prevent you from achieving.

That is your business plan. Eliminate the weaknesses by any means necessary. This Habit is so critical to break because it fosters overthinking or, worse yet, multiple projects.

Pick your one golden idea and forget the rest. They may be great ideas, but you made a decision, and your choice of the rest is just a major distraction. More mind games that your fears are playing with yourself. If you keep worrying about what you don't know, you won't even have confidence in what you do know. There's a phrase I keep repeating to myself over and over, and that is "I Got This"!

ABOUT PAUL: Paul Capozio was Born in Hoboken NJ way before it became SoHo West, the greatest claims it has was the birthplace of baseball and Frank Sinatra.

A street kid I felt college was just a four year delay into the real world and the ability to earn an income. I started a contracting company at 20. bankruptcy at 24 and then President of sales and marketing for a $1.5 billion dollar company in New York City at 40. Yes there were many stops from 24 to 40 but those all were my "education"

36

SERVE SOMETHING LARGER THAN YOU

CHINEME NOKE

Why: I am a firm believer that the route to real success and happiness in any endeavor, including our entrepreneurial lives, is to live a life full of flow and meaning.

Some support for my belief is found in a TED talk in 2004, where Martin Seligman identified three types of "Happy Lives."

The first was what he termed a "Pleasant Life," which involved the pursuit of as much pleasure as possible. However, he found that there were three drawbacks to this endeavor:

1. the behavior was not modifiable and could be passed on
2. it could quickly become a non-fulfilling Habit
3. it could become extremely difficult to adapt

The second type of perceived happiness was what he termed as the "Good Life" where there is forced engagement, a could-not-care-less attitude, an underlying loss of feeling, being apathetic - showing or feeling no interest, enthusiasm, or concern for those with whom one is interacting.

The third type of "Happy Life" is what Seligman termed the "Meaningful Life" which is where we learn what our highest strengths are and use them in the Habitual service of, and the belonging to, something larger than we are - for our own lives, entrepreneurial success, and the common good.

Once such Habits are formed, studies show that it will ensure a fulfilled, meaningful, happy life that will transcend into all of our entrepreneurial endeavors. Studies have shown that altruism lasts, while mere fun is transitory, according to Yale University in "The Science of Well Being."

The strongest life (including entrepreneurial) satisfaction comes from Meaningfulness. Engagement is okay, but purely pleasure provides no satisfaction or lasting success whatsoever.

To achieve life and entrepreneurial success, we need to form intentional, effortful activities and Habits based on our particular strengths. These are what determine our overall happiness, agrees Sonja Lyubomirsky in "The How of Happiness."

The application of these strengths can then be applied in the service of something larger than ourselves, such as in our entrepreneurial endeavors, to ensure success and lasting happiness within positive institutions and social purposes. The application of this principle Habit led me to abandon the structured corporate world and begin to apply my principal strengths of Engagement and Accomplishment to a life of entrepreneurial service of inspiring and assisting the success of others by facilitating the necessary changes and Habits.

THE UN-HABIT: STOP INVESTING IN "AWESOME STUFF."

Why: I have found that the general norm of people investing in what I've come to know as "awesome stuff" (AS) needs rethinking.

Examples of AS are things such as clothes, shoes, cars, the next hot shiny new object, etc. It's usually the case that we believe that these things will fulfill us and make us happy. However, the reality is that we soon get used to them and they have no lasting meaning. Therefore, we soon need to repeat the investment, over and over and over again, thus maintaining the AS Habit.

We should instead invest in stuff that doesn't stick around, such as experiences! This type of stuff will create wonderful memories for us because there's no time to get used to them and begin taking them for granted.

In Yale University's ground-breaking course, The Science of Well-Being, the psychology of wellness was studied, and they found that we are unaware of what makes us happy for the most part. So we tend to fall into the recurring trap of seeking and acquiring AS instead of other, life-enhancing experiences. We then wonder why many of us are so miserable.

Our intuition is to seek out AS, but according to Yale's study, our intuition is wrong!

Wonderful experiences linger in our memories. We get to share them time and time again with a whole host of other people and audiences. Telling others of our experiences to involve them, and they begin to resonate with our stories. Also, experiences are less susceptible to social comparisons - they tend to be pretty unique and tend to make the listeners happy.

I'm smiling as I recalled my first zip-lining experience a few years ago. I suffer from vertigo and have long had zip-lining on my bucket list, but whenever the opportunity presented itself, I would shy away from it. However, on that occasion, I bit the bullet and went for it. My fear was eventually overcome, and the memory will always stay with me.

Whenever I tell people about my wonderful zip-lining experience, it's as if they are there, along with me on that amazing ride. The Yale study also found that the Habit of acquiring "things" (AS) tends to make other people feel envious when compared to hearing about meaningful experiences. Consequently, were we to rethink the former, potentially, everybody would benefit from the latter.

ABOUT CHINEME: Chineme Noke has a long career as a Lawyer, Success Coach, International Award-Winning Author of Special Hidden Talents and Online Entrepreneur. Her expertise is in all-round Obstacle and Challenge obliteration - with ease. She does this by dealing effectively with what she calls the mountains and molehills that success seekers encounter in their daily lives by following her seven-step action plan. She is the founder of the Unstoppable Bizpreneurship program and the Unstoppable Shepreneurs private group, as well as the author of the soon to be published - Unstoppable Shepreneurs: Become An Emboldened and Empowered Woman, Live An Exceptional Life and Leave Your Legacy.

37

TRACK MONEY DAILY

ELENI ANASTOS

Why: Money loves attention!

Money impacts all of us, on a daily basis and touches every aspect of a business, yet many people feel disempowered, often avoiding the topic altogether. Countless entrepreneurs under-earn, over-deliver and settle for a lifestyle that is less than they desire.

If you want a rich and rewarding relationship with your spouse, your children, your friends or your clients, don't you have to pay attention to them? So, how can you expect to have a rich and rewarding relationship with money, if you don't pay proper attention to it?

What you believe about money does impact your life. Do your beliefs support your life goals, the life you want to have going forward? Or, have they been serving as roadblocks holding you back?

Yes, money has tremendous value and can serve powerful purposes, but it does not have to have power over you. I first learned this valuable lesson from my entrepreneurial grandfather. He taught me to pay attention to the numbers and record the amount coming in daily.

Yes, money has tremendous value and can serve powerful purposes, but it does not have to have power over you. I first learned this valuable lesson from my entrepreneurial grandfather, who was a restaurant owner. Every evening he brought home the daily receipts. We then sat together at the dining room table, carefully added them up, and entered the totals into the book. It was there, that my grandfather taught me to pay attention to the numbers and record the amount coming in daily.

It is a simple, yet effective Habit you can employ immediately to deepen your connection with money.

Create an electronic tracking sheet or simply use a notebook (one page for the entire month, with individual dates listed). Write your desired monthly income goal at the top. Each day, record the amount of money that comes in from all business sources (deposit for services, product sales, recurring payments from clients, etc.) before any deductions, expenses, taxes, etc. What we focus on expands and it is important to focus on money coming in!

If nothing comes in, record the zero and deal with the emotions that may come up, rather than avoiding the issue. Do not wait until you have money coming in regularly to start tracking. When you initiate the attention with money, you are in control. The reality, "you are the cause, money is the effect" and when you learn to wield that power, your life can change significantly. Review your sheet for the month and look for patterns to gain insight. Once you see patterns, you can make new decisions and take new actions to produce desired results.

Money will always get your attention, positively or negatively, so put yourself in the driver's seat by tracking.

The Un-Habit: Letting Other People Rent Space in Your Head

Why: Henry Ford stated, "Whether you think you can or think you can't, you're right."

Our beliefs dictate our thoughts, which lead to our actions. The important question to ask, "whose beliefs are leading you"?

Have you ever been excited about starting something new, whether it be a project or business venture, only to have other people "rain on your parade?"

I recall a conversation with a wonderfully enthusiastic entrepreneur who was excited about launching her new business. Linda had this dream for a couple of years and knew it was time to execute. She had developed a business plan, identified her niche and was excited about connecting with people to be of service. Linda had a true entrepreneurial spirit and was anxious to launch and start making money. She had no doubts that this was the path for her.

Linda shared her vision with some friends and relatives who immediately began poking holes in her dream.

"That's not a viable idea." "It will be hard for you to find clients." "Can you really make money doing that?" "This isn't a good time to start a business."

You could see Linda visibly shrink down when sharing this information with me. Her enthusiasm for launching quickly faded and she began questioning herself. "Can I really do this?" "Is it viable?" "How am I going to make it happen?"

It is perfectly acceptable for people to not believe in your dreams. Most likely they are projecting their own limiting beliefs onto you. However, if those beliefs continue to impact you, even after the people are gone, you have let them rent space in your head.

Be protective of your dreams, like you would anything of value to you. Not all dreams are meant to be shared with everyone. Be mindful of whose beliefs are dictating your thoughts and actions. It is your dream, your choice, your life.

Your yes, has to be bigger than, their no!

ABOUT ELENI: Eleni Anastos is a Prosperity Coach and Business Strategist who helps entrepreneurs and executives make more money. She created a virtual prosperity program to assist her clients to increase income, have greater impact, and live the lifestyle they desire. Through Eleni's proprietary assessments and proven techniques, you will bust through money and mindset blocks. Wasting no time in getting results, Eleni helps leverage your abilities and opens the gateway to abundance in all areas of your life and business. Think of her as Tony Robbins meets Suze Orman, with a little no-nonsense Detroit sass thrown into the mix.

38

WORK TO STAY RELEVANT

MAKENNA RILEY

Why: My Habit is to do daily research, keep up with trends, and stoke the fires of youthful curiosity that keep me thinking outside the box.

I've been exposed to the entrepreneurial world my entire life because my Mom, Forbes Riley, a business and television mogul who has sold over $2 billion, insisted on taking me everywhere. She spent many years on HSN with me backstage, watching vividly. I recall being 6 yrs old when my mother was selling her fitness product SpinGym live; I took notes and offered viable feedback about her presentation, the models, her co-host, and even telling her to make the call to action more direct. This essentially led to an unbreakable bond between us. I became her Secret Weapon. In 2011, I sat in on a SpinGym meeting, keep in mind I was 8 yrs old, and suggested a tweak to the product offer, resulting in a $48,000 savings! I remember being baffled that no one else seemed to notice this slight but impactful change. Then it hit me; my Mom valued my input because it was based on imagination, thinking outside the box and not being confined by adult logic.

Making money outside of having a 9 - 5 job has always intrigued me, and I started my first business at age 12. 2008 was when no one knew what e-commerce, dropping shipping, funnels, etc. existed. As one of the first in the industry, it allowed me to access some of the biggest players and propelled me into an "overnight success" and was determined to keep innovating, learning, and staying relevant. Recently these vital skills have allowed me to turn a $19 product into a $100,000 month.

What I am trying to bring to your attention is that you need to know what's relevant in the world outside of you and your business. It's crucial to your success to see what is happening beyond just the nightly news and social media gossip. My grasp of this concept has allowed me to leapfrog over many people who seem to wait. My hope for you is always to stay young at heart and curious. If you need help staying relevant, just reach out... while I'm still young enough to help!

THE UN-HABIT: BREAK THE HABIT THAT ONLY YOUNG PEOPLE KNOW HOW TO MASTER THE INTERNET

Why: I find it hard to believe that at 17 I've been making money and working on the internet for almost 6 years. The confusing part is that I talk to capable adults about this, and they look at me like I have two heads. I get the same question over and over, "How could you possibly make money online?" News flash, the internet isn't only meant to answer emails or post on social media. There are never-ending opportunities to make money online, but there IS one slight caveat. Systems are always changing, growing, and improving, which is intimidating and causes many individuals not born in the technology age, to give up before even trying. My generation does have one advantage, which is we are still open to learning. After you leave school, many believe that the learning phase in their life is over. I cannot express how detrimental this mindset will be to you and your business. You must always be learning and growing, fighting to stay relevant in a world that is shifting daily.

I had the pleasure of meeting the creator of a digital platform that changed my life and many others for the better. He created one of the most effective funnel building systems on the market. I made it a point to explain my issues with elements of his software that landed me on his podcast and resulted in a friendship. He mentioned me at a conference in front of 10,000 people!

Enroll your kids into your business. This concept brought my mother and me closer than ever because we became this unstoppable duo. That's why I took it upon myself to stay current, involve myself in Facebook groups, and help others navigate the internet successfully. I created the program, Marketing with Makenna, where I essentially become your lifeline to the internet. The future is here. We are never going back to the old way of life, so you can either grow with us or be left behind. We are a society that is only ever moving forward, so if you are looking to move your business online... The time to start is today. Feel free to contact me as I can make this process easy and enjoyable!

About Makenna: Makenna Riley is a young award-winning digital marketer who has grossed more than $250,000 as a teenage CEO by the age of 17. She started her first company at the tender age of 12. She began interviewing and learning from some of the biggest names in motivational speaking and business, Clickfunnels Russell Brunson, Sharon Lechter, Les Brown, Adrian Morrison, Shark Tank's Kevin Harrington, and more. Her first product, Rant Calls, launched live via Facebook and grossed $12,000 in just the first 15 minutes. At age 14, she got her boating license and launched a campaign to help unprivileged kids go out on the water in Florida. She quickly raised $10,000 needed to complete her mission. Everything Makenna touches turns to gold. She has built online brands for celebrities, created marketing funnels, and captured the attention of worldwide podcasts and magazines like Entrepreneur and Inc.

39

LEARN AT LEAST ONE NEW THING EVERYDAY

RYKER RILEY

Why: This is a Habit I learned from my parents, both successful entrepreneurs with very different skill sets. I learned a lot of maintenance work from my dad, like using tools, fixing appliances, running rentals, managing costs, and turning that into a business. From my mom, Forbes Riley, I learned digital marketing, how to create courses, talk to large crowds, and the secret to giving a professional pitch. I remember saying to my mom a long time ago, "Why am I not super good at any one thing but average at a variety of things." She replied with "you will have more success as an adult if you don't focus on just one thing but become a master of many." So I set out on a path, at just 17 years old, to become the best version of myself by learning at least one thing every day.

So how does this relate to you? I find that if you try to learn at least one new thing every day, it promotes growth, change, and in essence, creates success. By having more 'value' assigned to you, you expand your potential opportunities down the road. Having a little bit of knowledge over a wide variety of topics makes it very easy to start a career in any area you would like to pursue. What is essential to remember is that knowledge is power.

My biggest growth opportunities have sprung up from what I have learned on the internet. My earliest leadership skills and strategy tactics came from video games (ironically, which most parents don't want their kids to engage in). Now I focus on learning sales funnels, eCommerce, and digital marketing. The best part about learning these new things is they are easy to monetize, and I get to work with my twin sister Makenna, helping adults who haven't learned new things every day.

The Un-Habit: Expecting Perfection the first time

As my father always said, "Don't let the perfect ruin the good." As a middle schooler, I would always find myself frustrated and discouraged when I could not complete a task perfectly. Of course, it would've been nice; however, there is much more learning to be done when you give yourself a break and have the patience to fail. The best lessons I have ever learned were from not perfecting my projects for the first time. You should define Perfection for yourself and know that you will learn something even more valuable that you can use down the road if you don't achieve it.

I created a course with my sister, Makenna Riley, about three months ago. Our goal was to make a perfect course. We set a launch date and were determined to release it with a bang. As hard as we worked to build the course and marketing strategy, it was never perfect, but we made a plan to launch on a certain date. We ended up releasing it anyways, and it was by far one of the best decisions we had ever made. This lack of Perfection within the course allowed us to better bond with our audience and grow with them. It was a great learning point for us because we found out what worked and what needed to be changed in real-time. Ultimately our final product was better than anything we could have dreamed of.

The greatest feeling and learning points come from a failed experience. Nothing is stopping you except for the fear within this thought that everything must be perfect. Life is full of imperfections, which is what makes it interesting. Learn to embrace the flaws and grow from them. This will ultimately help you reach even further success in your career down the road.

About Ryker: Ryker Riley is an upcoming leader with big dreams. He is a 17 year old who has always been a competitive spirit, scholastically and athletically. An award winning chess player at the age of 8 and took his middle school baseball team to State. He is a strong believer in trying as many new experiences as possible leading him to competitive swimming, bowling, golf, skiing, inline skating, and slalom water skiing. In high school, as a freshman, he became the starting Varsity Quarterback for the Green Devils and a county wrestling champion. While excelling in a variety of sports was fun and challenging, Ryker has devoted a lot of his time to academic excellence. And his focus has driven him to achieve all A's throughout his time in the elite 'International Bachelorette' (IB) program of his high-school. With eyes now towards picking a college, Ryker continues to build out his portfolio of expertise.

40

FOCUS ON INCHES BECAUSE THEY LEAD TO RICHES

ALBERT COREY

Why: I have always had goals that were larger than life. Every time I was trying to hit the home run on the first swing. When I would strike out, I would get upset and quit. Never to go forward and always failing, never going anywhere. Ever-changing and going down on different days.

One day I had the light bulb go off about why I never finished. To Achieve greatness in one life, we have to go down a path. I realized that my goals had to be so big that it is almost impossible to finish. And to reach them, I needed to work every day, taking one baby step at a time. As you start to feel that you are making progress, It will keep you motivated and bring you into tomorrow excited that you will reach your goal. All this is happening one baby step at a time.

You have to realize that miss-steps are always going to happen. With tiny steps, it's easy to retrace and figure out why it went wrong. More straightforward to go back and fix and get back on the path and moving forward.

It is easier to get help with small steps. Mentor or peers can break down what you're doing and solve this issue quicker without having started over.

Taking small steps could be as simple as listing to a podcast or YouTube for 15 minutes a day. It can also be reading a book or blog post. Joining Facebook Groups is another right way to get to the tops. You could post your issue, and some can assist you. It could also inspire you when you answer someone else post.

Your end game is finding ways for you to keep climbing the mountain. Taking one step at a time is your key to success.

The Un-Habit: Using Social Media Wrong

Why: Using Social Media Wrong is wasting your time and life. There is so much good that could one could find when you use the internet.

Most will not learn to inspire to communicate with like-minded people. They tend to worry about what happened to a friend they knew almost 20 years ago when they were in high school. It could lead to cheating on their boyfriend or even worse breaking up your marriage.

Others will try to live their life like who they see on social media. Like if a famous person is wearing designer closes, They have to go out and buy that same style. Did they ever think that the star hates the design? The only reason is a brand is paying them an endorsement fee to get the pubic excited so that they can increase their profits.

YouTube a site that could take most of your time for mindless Videos. Spend this educate you when you are stuck and solve your problem Most will use it to watch the crazy mindless videos. They are funny, but how much wasted and utilized to empower themselves.

Some will post videos so they can prevent insight violence. One type of person could find that video and use it to cause harm and destruction of property.

Cyberbullying is how social media used to cause terror in people's life. Children are the ones that are getting hurt. In some cases, it leads to suicide. Making you feel bad about the body is how it also could be bad for you. You are looking at pictures of Superstars and think that person is perfect online. Little did you know that they have professional Photoshop artists making them perfect. In real life, they could look just like you.

ABOUT ALBERT: Over the last four decades, I have seen business owners leave millions of hard-earned money on the table. This really bothered me because I knew in my heart there was a way to fix the problem. After years of research, I created and implemented a process that has saved over 16,000 of my business clients millions of dollars. I knew what I created can work for anyone, so I packaged it into a system called "Ninja Profit Secrets." In less than 30 minutes a day, anyone using my system can discover hidden riches that was always theirs and put it right back into their pockets.

41

PREPARE YOURSELF FOR TAKE OFF

ERIC J. ZULEY

W hy: Broadening our minds is key to building knowledge for greater success in the marketplace and corporate world. This can be thought of as exercising the brain. As we need daily movement and exercise to our health, we also need growth and exercise to access and use the library in our heads.

I have found that if I take a half-hour to an hour a day to learn something new, I exponentially broaden my horizons. This could be an online course in something to add to your expertise, reading a book, listening to a podcast, playing an instrument, learning a language, getting a new certification, or even getting a degree online. Anything that you might find a passion for could increase your IQ and give you abilities to improve your services and workload. Also, learn ways to organize yourself, or about nutrition can support you in daily choices that you make. Just know that everything you do to create a regular practice for learning will always help you achieve your goals on a higher level. Each step you take is a leap to the future.

I have spent countless hours online in courses, on YouTube, and other learning methods to become the man that I am today. Everything that I learn stimulates me to create something that can benefit all my clients. With a passion for increasing eZWay Family members' reach in the world, I learned that new tools give me more resources to share with others. I become more valuable. When I learn, my clients get new ways to win. When you learn, the knowledge increase will only magnificently serve your clients. It will broaden their horizons as it has yours. Every tool you can share for a resource to your clients will be an added value to you as an entrepreneur. Never underestimate the value of education, even on a short term, daily basis.

THE UN-HABIT: JUMPSTARTING WITHOUT PREPARATION

Why: In the past, I have had the unfortunate Habit of jumping out of bed and hitting workload full force. This didn't allow for any self-care as I just kept the momentum going until my energy was depleted. The inner source was drained for lack of meeting my other needs. We all need a certain amount of rest, nutrition, and brain stimulation. Without these, we will experience a real burnout for what needs to be accomplished.

Creating an intentional morning routine will help us start in the right way. Get up, meditate, or pray and have a nutritional breakfast. Maybe even add a little exercise to jumpstart your metabolism. Ceremoniously taking action for self-care in the morning will activate your ability to endure and accomplish what needs to be done to build your success. Do not forget to take care of yourself. Do not delay in taking action first to nourish your body and mind. The only thing holding you back could be the one daily Habit that would nurture you.

In the same sense, you might find that purposeful action at night to get relaxation to prepare for a good night's sleep could be an asset to you. This is an excellent way to get the REM that your mind needs to be productive in itself.

Self-care is essential to our well-being. Take a moment and replenish yourself to build your stamina for success.

Self-care is essential to our well-being. Take a moment and replenish yourself to build your stamina for success. You must add air to the tire to keep it from going flat, just as you need to nourish your well-being. Creating Habits to do self-care will give you the energy needed to support your clients in the best possible way. Do not neglect yourself. Be your number one priority.

ABOUT ERIC: Eric Zuley is recognized as an award winning top ten social media influencer in the world a Multimedia Marketing Mogul that has mastered the art of monetizing media. He created the nationally and internationally recognized movement #eZWay endorsed by over 500 celebrities, influencers, CEO's and change makers. This movement has its own social network directory similar to Facebook, Amazon, Yelp, Netflix and the Hollywood Walk of Fame all rolled into one.

42

VISUALIZATION AND GRATITUDE

DR. DANTÉ SEARS

Why: My 1 Habit is to Create My Life through manifestation, using visualization, faith, and gratitude together in a straightforward exercise.

I envision the world as I want it to be - the things I want to happen and show up in my life - and I thank God/Universe for it in the affirmative; aloud in prayer.

Example: "Thank You for my gorgeous dream house, fulfilling friendships, and infinite success in all of my endeavors. Thank you for my (insert thing you want)."

I say this with utmost gratitude while envisioning it as if it already happened. When I say 'thank you', I feel that it is already mine and experience gratitude on a full-body level that is palpable; it creates a new reality. This is the most important part of the Habit and is backed up by quantum mechanics and many other spiritual practices, including the bible, wherein

Jesus thanked the Father for his gifts in advance and acted in faith as if it were so, therefore bringing the imagined into reality.

Many people miss this part, and when they pray, it is to ask or beg for what they want, but this will not result in the same powerful results because they are not harnessing their God-Given powers to create.

When I do this daily, I find that the things I want to show up, effortlessly. My only job is to accept them when they come.

I say thank you to the Universe (Spirit) from the very seat of my soul.

This Habit makes life easier; it transforms your vibration from wanting and 'needy' to successful and 'receiving'. It's the number one secret to living life on your terms.

When you ask with gratitude, you invest faith in the world around you, believing that what you want will happen. This strengthens the energetic system of support within and around you, causing a magnetic frequency that draws what you want towards you.

When you own your thoughts and express gratitude for the things, you want <as if> it is already yours, your mindset will transform to attraction, your words will draw others in, your genuinely infectious joy will inspire others to give you what you want; knowing they will receive what they want in return.

Combined with a well-thought intention, this exercise brings you to your wildest dreams in light-speed. You can go as fast and as far as your faith, vision, and sincerest gratitude will take you. The sky isn't the limit. You are.

The Un-Habit: Fear is (False Evidence Appearing Real) Destroying Your Future

Why: Fear is the seed of doubt, of lack, or nothingness. It creates nothing, gives nothing, and produces nothing... except more fear, lack, and loss.

Fear is not real. Fear is imaginary. Fear keeps you from making that follow-up call to get the 'Yes'. Fear brings anxiety, which is the result of living in the future instead of enjoying the present. Fear is the result of imagined danger. Are you on a burning ship - or sitting at home, imagining the danger? Of course, you believe that if you were in <actual danger>, you'd be too busy fighting for your life to read this!

Fear keeps you up at night. It causes you to settle for things that aren't right for you. Fear keeps you from your best possible outcome. It closes off opportunities before you've had the chance to explore them.

HUGE SECRET: The universe doesn't sort out what you want from what you fear - it gives you whatever you focus your ENERGY on! Just like driving - your vehicle goes to where your attention is focused. The same is true for energy and manifestation. Wherever you place, your focus is where you'll end up. This is true for those fearing an untimely demise and those determined to achieve their dreams. Both will receive what they 'want' (that which they focus on).

EXERCISE: Bring your focus to this moment, wherever you are, and realize that you are safe. Now that you are here, you can see clearly that you are in control at this very moment and have every ability to steer your life and your path in any direction you desire.

Instead of avoiding situations that are not best for you - steer directly to what you want by focusing clearly upon it.

Now, travel into the future and see yourself receiving everything you want. Feel the feelings of what it's like to have it all; experience the joy, relief, exhilaration, and power to achieve your dreams. Now come back to now and walk towards it with focus, knowing You will make it happen.

All things of value are energetic. You are energy; money is energy (currency), health is energy (feelings); love is energy. When you work with Energy in Gratitude (Grat-itude=Great Attitude), life becomes effortless. Envision with Gratitude and Watch the Universe Transform before your very eyes.

ABOUT DR. SEARS: Dr. Danté Sears, DM.,DoD., TTRS, MNLP, RMP, CHt, is the "The Global SOULutionist"; a ten-times certified Metaphysical Doctor and a Doctor of Divinity. Dr. Dantè creates miraculous outcomes for your mind, body, and business (MB3). She is the founder of Wealth XO, World Wealth Bank, SEARS X, and World Prosperity Network, a charity dedicated to transforming the world.

43

STRETCH EVERY MORNING
SUSAN LEVIN

Why: With all the advancements in technology that make our lives "easier," it is creating more harm to our bodies than it is good. We spend too many hours a day looking down at our phones, sitting at our computers, driving in cars, and watching our smart televisions. The excessive amount of time we give our screens is causing an increase in the numbers of people with physical discomfort and chronic pain. The flexibility of our spine and joints is becoming out of alignment, causing muscles to strain with tension. When the body is not balanced and aligned, it is more vulnerable to injuries, aches, and pain.

Since we must rely on this type of communication through our screens, everyone must start tuning in to their body by listening to the stress signs and becoming aware.

This is why taking the first step toward improving your health begins in the morning.

Creating an every day Habit of doing essential morning stretches in bed improves the body's ability to start the day with natural energy. These extra 5 minutes in bed, wake up the body faster than a cup of coffee and a shower.

Understand that your body is active during the night, but at a slow resting state, so it is important to awaken your system naturally. By setting your alarm 5 minutes early, allows special time for Self Care, before opening your eyes, before getting out of bed, before checking your phone and especially before taking care of others.

Begin each day with a few cleansing breaths, creating a positive mindset, and doing a few simple essential stretches. This becomes a morning routine, a healthy Habit that will connect your mind to your body by slowly activating the muscles. These strategic stretches will stimulate digestion, increase blood flow, and start the day feeling strong with positive energy and better posture.

THE UN-HABIT: ACCEPTING NEGATIVE CHATTER IN YOUR MIND

Why: It is amazing how many times a day, negative words or thoughts come into our minds about our behaviors, looks, and attitudes. We tend to criticize ourselves to the point that we get in our way.

Unfortunately, this negative chatter increases when we are trying to be exceptionally strong and confident. I realized this when I was going through a difficult divorce, and it was so easy for me to cut myself down.

Of course, I did not hear or notice the damage this inner voice was causing until I became emotionally and physically broken. At that point, I was unable to pull myself out of this downward spiral alone.

With much difficulty, professional help and the introduction of yoga, I became stronger. To become aware of the negativity in YOUR mind, and un-Habit this unhealthy Habit, play a game with a friend or on your own. Spend the day together and write down any negative words, either one of you says. Continue this game for a week, writing down all the negative chatter. By the end of the week, you will begin to notice the decrease in the amount of times per day of the negativity until one day; you reach zero.

- It takes a lot of work to un-Habit the negative chatter in the mind, but it is worth it.
- Take the mind challenge to notice the words you repeat to yourself, good or bad.
- Stop the brain from the poor self-talk and learn to use only positive words.
- Naturally, a few bad words may slip into the mind but create the ability to notice them immediately.
- You speak to yourself more than you speak to anyone else, be positive, and be kind.

About Susan: Susan Levin is the creator of Personal Priorities Yoga and Nutrition and has been in the wellness community for over 30 years. As a Certified Yoga Instructor with a degree in Nutrition, Susan's passion is helping men and women take control of their health by naturally strengthening the body through stretching, simple movement, proper breathing, and adding whole foods daily.

Understanding the many challenges of LIFE and the concept of NO TIME for Self-care, Susan designed a proven online program that takes 11 minutes a day to become the strongest and healthiest version of yourself. If you complain of lower back pain, body aches, or just overwhelmed and stressed, you will love this simple course that offers practical solutions and professional guidance to live a long and healthy life. You only have ONE body and ONE life, make it the BEST!

44

LEARN TO WAKE WITHOUT AN ALARM

YNGE LJUNG, NMD

Why: All my life, I have told myself what time I wanted to wake up, and I never use an alarm clock, so I wake up by myself and feel fresh and ready for the day! I feel that I slept enough and have no need to go back to sleep! No snooze button! I stay in bed for a few minutes to give grace for waking up, and then plan my day, going through what I wrote in my planner the night before!

To be able to go to sleep without an alarm makes you feel that you got enough sleep! Waking up by a sound disturbs your sleep, and you feel tired and want to hit the snooze button! When you decide to wake up at a certain time - even if you went to bed late - makes you feel like you have enough sleep.

To be able to wake up by yourself also gives you the time to meditate in bed, to prepare yourself mentally for the day, without the need or want to fall back to sleep. You save so much time, and when your feet hit the floor, you are ready to go, ready to do your exercises, and ready for the day - because you already went through it in your head!

When I do the planning, I go through every moment. If I am going to play golf, for example, I go through every stroke, from tee off! This Habit is also great when you go to sleep at night and cannot fall asleep! If you think about a task you have to do, go through every detail, every movement, where you are going to be, people you are going to meet, and what you are going to say to them. Go through exactly what you want to accomplish! The funny thing is that often things happen the way you planned it! You will fall asleep easily, and you will be ready to continue your meditation when you wake up to reinforce your intentions and goals further!

So what you will accomplish with this Habit is that not using an alarm clock is better to sleep, feeling happy when you wake up and more time for planning!

THE UN-HABIT: STOP LETTING YOUR MIND SPEND SO MUCH TIME THINKING THAT YOU CAN NEVER MAKE A DECISION

Why: I have taken many courses and seminars in my life - too many! I have spent 10s of thousands of dollars to learn more, understand more, and be better!

And what did this do to me? I am sure I learned a lot - but did I take more actions?

No - I always thought I needed to know and learn something more!

I love learning, don't take me wrong, but - did I need that $1000 course in management of some sort or other, but felt I didn't know more than when I started, and to learn it well enough to be able to run your business, you need the next course that will cost you 15K, and then there is the year-long coaching you NEED, for another 50K!

Wow! What are you going to do? You took this first course because you know you need to know more about running a business - but - where will I get all this money?

So, there are two Habits you have to undo! The first is the Habit of believing you don't know enough - maybe you think you are a fraud, and it is necessary to have more certificates to hang on your wall, and you take one course or class after another to learn your skills. You also think it's better to know many things and serve your clients better because you're a specialist in this or that!

Well, get over that! Do one thing and do it well, then you can add to your toolbox!

The other is to way your options! Do you need all these courses on how to run a business? Wouldn't it be better to hire a person who already knows all about it? By hiring someone who knows, you start paying them a salary, not a whole year upfront! And getting a really good person who knows the advertising and everything you were going to pay for expensive courses, your business makes more money quicker, and you can relax, and don't need to try to learn something that takes a professional business manager years to learn!

About Dr Ynge: I am Dr Ynge, yes Ynge with a Y - the creator of The Allergy Kit; the first and only DIY kit, to treat your allergies naturally, without shots or drugs, and that can be used for the whole family!

45

ESTABLISH A MORNING ROUTINE

JULIE MICHELSON

Why: For years, I had heard that creating a morning routine was essential for success. I had an idea in my head that the routine needed to be long and complicated. Because of that, I resisted. I promise you that an impactful morning routine does not need to take up too much of your day or be challenging to implement.

Starting your day with some dedicated time for yourself sets you up for success on many levels. It is less about what you include in your routine and more about creating time to ground yourself before you begin receiving input from the world.

Some of the activities that are often included in a morning routine are meditation, breathing exercises, journaling, gratitude journaling, reading, hobbies, and exercise. All of those activities should not be included in one routine. That would take all day! When creating a routine from scratch, I recommend starting small. Incorporating one thing at a time, only for a few minutes in the beginning, and building from there.

Having a committed morning routine benefits all areas of life. It will improve your work in unexpected ways. You will find that you are more effective and efficient and will receive the time back in your day twofold. Perhaps no less important, you will also be a better partner, parent, friend, etc. You will be well equipped to handle the stressors that are thrown at you during the day. A morning routine doubles as a stress management routine, reducing the impact of stress on your body. It will reduce inflammation, increase energy levels, improve mood, improve sleep, and reduce chronic pain.

I encourage you to create a morning routine beginning tomorrow. Remember to start small. Ask yourself what one thing would benefit you most and commit to doing it every morning.

THE UN-HABIT: SACRIFICING SLEEP IN THE NAME OF PRODUCTIVITY

Why: Most entrepreneurs burn the candle at both ends. While this approach may work in the short term, it will decrease long term productivity and lead to health challenges.

There never seems to be enough time in the day. The inbox is always full. It is particularly common for entrepreneurs to steal some time from their sleep to create more hours. Some even wear it as a badge of honor. We take pride in accomplishing and achieving, and often feel like time spent sleeping is a waste of time. That means that we aren't giving our bodies time to rest and repair. We aren't recharging. We are running on empty. We are weakening our immune systems. We are becoming less patient and less than the best versions of ourselves. Our decision-making processes suffer, and our effectiveness as leaders can decline in the process.

While we feel like we aren't losing anything by sneaking some time out of our sleep to increase our productivity, we may be losing more than we bargained for. It may feel like skipping a few hours of sleep to get more done or spend more time with family is that way to go. Again, short term, that may be the case. But long term, it comes at a cost. Often a high price. Our health, business, and relationships can all be negatively affected by shorting our sleep. It is time to get realistic about just how much sleep you truly need (likely much more than four hours) and start to make some changes in priorities.

I challenge you to take stock of your current sleep Habits and notice if they serve your higher interests and long term goals. Are you sneaking time from restorative sleep to compensate for the time you are spending in other areas? Take steps today to prioritize your sleep!

ABOUT JULIE: Julie Michelson helps people with chronic inflammation create the lifestyle changes necessary to reduce their inflammation and reverse their symptoms. She is an international speaker, and a National Board-Certified Functional Medicine Health Coach, who specializes in inflammation and autoimmunity. After going from more than a decade of health decline to living her best life, Julie uses her experience and training to help others create lasting change to reverse their autoimmune symptoms. Julie created Inspired Living with Autoimmunity® to aid others in achieving total wellness.

46

3 BREATHS, 3 GRATITUDES, 3 X A DAY

TSAO-LIN MOY

Why: It is important to focus on three deep breaths in the morning, midday, and before bed, combined with gratitude thoughts.

We often wake up and have racing thoughts, worry, and anxiety, which can cause us to be in a state of fight or flight and survival mode. This happens because, during sleep, we process much of what occurred during the day. Often people will think about what did not work or what went wrong and what they will need to do the next day. That is what instructs your brain to "think" about during sleep, so when we wake up, it can cause panic and anxiety. If those racing thoughts are given energy, they will cause the entire day to start in panic mode, also known as sympathetic.

Gratitude has shown to shift brain chemistry to feelings of well being and combined with breathing; it is an anchor to set a new Habit in the nervous system.

When we are in that sympathetic dominance, it is hard to be positive; stress hormones repress the brain, so less creativity or ability to receive information can lead to greater opportunity and wellness.

Taking 3 deep breaths with positive thoughts, we can set our intention and the nervous system to calm and heal, rest, and digest by tapping into the vagus nerve. This is a mind-body practice so that we can be in alignment with our thoughts, action, and brain chemistry. Breathing deeply, we can send oxygenated blood to our whole body and relieve inflammation.

By doing this practice first thing in the morning, we can develop this Habit of recognizing that we can calm ourselves and have resources within that we can always tap into.

3 deep breaths midday, with gratitude, remind us that we don't let circumstances dictate our nervous system or our mind, that we can pause and reset.

3 deep breaths before bed with gratitude. Clearing out the worries and pressures from the day, 3 deep breaths, and connect with the intention of rest and digest will help to get deeper and restorative sleep. Directing thoughts of gratitude and breathing, you will wake up refreshed, optimistic, creative, and motivated.

The Un-Habit: I'm not good enough

Why: Many people chase success based on feelings of not good enough, which translates into never feeling satisfied or fulfilled. If you are telling yourself that you are not good enough, then it means you are making a comparison to someone or some standard that is not you. This is judgment. No matter how successful, you can feel like an imposter because of not appreciating who you are, your uniqueness. People pursue careers because they are trying to be good enough. We see a lot of perfectionism in the I'm not good enough Habit, and it's destructive. On social media, everyone is posting about their "success," always smiling faces and pictures of dream vacations and ideal family scenes. The fake you is seeking happiness in a faked life with other people that are also displaying a "fake" life.

Unfortunately, not good enough Habit happens at a young age when we are forming our identity and following what our parents have imbued as values. Whether parents realized it or not, we model behaviors for our children.

What will change in their life if they break this Habit of not good enough is that they will see the gift that they are as a human being with a purpose They will be able to appreciate their wins, and step out of judgment and the all or nothing, win or lose paradigm. Their children will get to experience a parent that modeling confidence, independent thinking, and possibility.

They will be free from comparing themselves to others or something that is not real, and they can pursue something that they love.

The not good enough Habit silenced will allow creativity in and permit us to explore gifts and talents and, ultimately, their purpose. When someone is doing what their purpose is, they can experience fulfillment and connection within themselves and out in the world.

This will impact their family, and if they have children, it will model self-love values and the importance of what it is to have a purpose.

About Tsao-Lin: Tsao-Lin Moy helps women struggling with infertility heal underlying health issues naturally, so that they can get pregnant in 6 months or less. Her signature system uses step by step processes that are simple to follow and work. It takes them from feeling their body has failed them, hopeless and ashamed to feeling whole and complete and that getting pregnant is possible. Using deep knowledge and principles of alternative and Chinese Medicine, and integrating both Eastern and Western healing modalities in her treatments, women experience powerful alignment in body, mind and soul. Resulting in a happy, healthy and smiling baby.

47

30-60 MINUTES DAILY IN SELF-EDUCATION

SHERRI LEOPOLD

Why: Learning something new every day will grow your business and impact your paycheck!

If you aren't learning and growing, you are dying. Perhaps not in the literal sense, but your brain thrives on the stimulation of learning. I do this self-development most of the time while I am walking to get my daily exercise in. You can listen to thousands of books on tape, YouTube videos. Thousands of podcasts are entirely free at any time of the day. I recommend John Maxwell, Sharon Lechter, Kelly Roach, Or Gary V if you need a starting point. Committing this time to develop your mind will build your business. Not only will it impact your business, but it will also grow your paycheck.

Many people today tend not to venture into learning things unless they can be an expert at it. However, true joy comes from the process, not mastering something. I have seen it through my last 22 years in direct sales and network marketing. People think successful salespeople fall out of the womb that way. We have spent thousands of dollars and thousands of hours studying and implementing what we've learned to become better at our craft. The point is that you never arrive! You will always be learning from someone. If you feel you can't learn anything, you may need an ego check.

I learned this lesson from my Mom. She was a high school graduate but did not attend college. She worked in restaurants as a waitress or hostess most of her adult life. She was always the highest top earner in any place she worked. She tells the most fascinating story of having attended a corporate waitress training where the other waitresses who attended didn't pay attention. She implemented everything she earned. The other wait staff were annoyed when people who came to eat always asked for her specifically. When my Mom shares this story, she always says they could have learned the same information she did, but they were too lazy. If you want to be a powerful entrepreneur and business owner, you will invest your time in learning and growing every day. I repeat, your commitment to educating yourself daily will show up in your paycheck.

Learning isn't about becoming an expert. It's about growing who you are, developing yourself as a person, and expanding your mind to impact your business! If you want to show up more powerfully in your life, commit to learning something new every day. Stimulate your mind and set your brain on fire with new information as a daily exercise. Learning IS the exercise for the mind. Coincidently, you will be more enjoyable and exciting to be around as well!

THE UN-HABIT: SELF-DEPRECATING HUMOR IS SELF-BULLYING!

WHY: One Habit I find alarming is that people frequently degrade themselves in the name of humor. I am acutely aware of this behavior as I have worked very hard to overcome this. Women are exceptionally prone to this behavior as it relates to our physical appearance. We tend to couch our insults in humor, and when someone else laughs and agrees, we feel marginally better. I would go so far as to say they even feel comforted. An example would be when people say things like," If I wore a bikini on the beach, people would run screaming!". Women feel camaraderie in saying, "Oh, me too!"

This troubled me so much that I wrote a book on self-bullying. I feel profoundly driven to help our young people grow up loving who they are exactly as they are today! The amount of suicides today is alarming.

Join me in standing up powerfully for who you are today- no qualifiers! Life will not be great when you lose 20 pounds, make more money, or meet the right person. Life will be magical and wonderful when you realize you are an unrepeatable miracle exactly as you are at this moment!

ABOUT SHERRI: As a child who grew up around domestic violence, Sherri was almost 12 years old before she understood she had a powerful voice. Sherri learned she could create her own destiny and teach others to do the same through the power of thought. As the Leader of the Stop Self-Bullying Movement, and a highly successful network marketer, Sherri mentors' people through a series of techniques that curbs destructive self-talk. Reducing this behavior creates space for greater self-love. She teaches people to stand up in their own personal power and live as the unrepeatable miracle that they were born to be.

48

A HABIT OF HOURLY MOVEMENT

ERIC STUERKEN

Why: The early morning routine is the key foundation for a focused, productive day - SIMPLE. It holds you accountable for your previous night's action. Did you stay up too late? Did you eat/drink too much?

When getting into the 5 am routine, you'll start asking yourself these questions and say, "Was that extra scoop of ice cream worth it?" To get into the AM routine and to make it easier, in the beginning, wake up every day for the first week 15 minutes earlier than the day before until you hit 5 am time

Now that you are there and you can enjoy this time and do precisely the same routine every day. It is critical to stick with it. Write it down and tape it to your mirror "Get up at 5 am". It takes typically around 21 days to love it. The peace of the am is life-changing.

Ok, now to the next part of the daily Habit, movement, and exercise. A few years ago, scientists discovered that sitting all day causes a cascade of harmful metabolic changes that increase your odds of meeting an early end. Sitting has become a public health enemy number one. Let's call it the "Chair disease." Sitting all day is like smoking a pack of cigarettes.

You have 1440 minutes in your day. Nine of those minutes should be used to keep you moving, grooving, and smiling for the other 1431 minutes of your day. Start each morning with nine minutes of movement. Do push-ups, jumping jacks, or just dance for nine minutes each morning, and you have programmed success into the rest of your day!

The Un-Habit: I'll get to that tomorrow

Why: Get it done. If you say it, do it. We've all heard that before - but why? Because once it's done, it's done and off the ever-growing plate of the entrepreneur.

Better yet, it's a feeling of accomplishment, and that's so important for daily momentum and success. It frees the mind to say, "On to the next urgent thing that needs to be done. You also become ready for the next daily critical opportunity or fire to be extinguished.

I'm a firm believer in response time speed. How fast do you respond to an inquiry in your business? How on POINT are you as they say? As a start-up or entrepreneur, it's hugely important to be fast. Today, potential clients want a super-fast response more than anything.

It's also supercritical at the beginning of a new relationship. First impressions today in this world of "no patience" can make or break a deal. As crazy as it seems, it's the way it is.

The only time speed of response should be slowed when it's needed in negotiation. There are times when no response or delayed response can open opportunity. But for most of the daily activity of entrepreneurship, it's much more imperative to be fast than strategic.

You might not be the one with all the answers, but you can get them. Always remember what you lack in skill you can make up with speed of response.

Paying attention to urgent tasks with speed and not doing it tomorrow or procrastinating also makes you have a more precise plan for tomorrow.

If you're getting it done, your mind moves on and doesn't keep thinking about what you didn't accomplish. That little negative thought will affect your nightly sleep. Not sleeping well is a recipe for AM disaster, especially with your new routine. It is a bad way to start your 1440 minutes of your daily success. So everything plays into each other. Get a few things out of the way early in the AM, and see how great and accomplished you feel.

ABOUT ERIC: Eric Stuerken is an avid sports adventurer and has been playing sports since the age of 2. His first love of sports was skiing and anything outdoors. His younger year of playing all sports paved the way for his love of winning, completion, teamwork, and hate of losing.

Because of that love and understanding of what it feels like to be an athlete, Eric has always tried to instill that in others. It starts with movement and feeling muscles you didn't know existed. That leads to mindset and success. With that in mind and to assist in daily movements, Eric developed the "one minute before" wellness platform to move the 85% of the population that doesn't workout or get enough exercise outdoors.

49

DELIBERATELY SET YOUR DIAL TO JOY

DONNA SPARACO MEADOR

W**hy:** I was always a happy kid.

My father had a thunderous voice. My mother balanced that out perfectly with her soft-spoken ways of getting her point across. At that time, I just thought she was naive but I quickly learned I was witnessing wisdom in action. My grandparents on both sides were hard-working people. Dad's side of the family had jobs while mom's side had businesses, even before they stepped off the boat in 1904.

Dad was a salesman throughout my teenage years until he started his own company and mom, a woman before her time, opened up a Health Food Store in 1977.

In 2007 I fell in love. My new husband and I would start a business of installing furniture in Corporate America. We were small and well respected, but even that could not help us as we walked straight into The Great Recession of 2008. We eventually bounced back, but in 2016 I would face the unthinkable: The passing of my husband.

As you can imagine, my heart was crushed. As President of our furniture company, I decided to close it down that same year to focus entirely on my other company which generated residual income and I could more easily operate by myself.

I believe it's when times are tough, we get to find out what we're made of. As I moved through the days and weeks ahead, I kept my finger on the pulse of how I was feeling. This is how I monitored my choices and direction. I had just been through enough heartache to last a lifetime. If I needed to shift direction to feel even the slightest better, I did. If you go off course, even the slightest, you'll end up in a place you don't want to be and when you're already operating at half speed, you have to pay even closer attention. If something doesn't feel right, it probably isn't. Seeking joy is literally how I kept myself on track and my business going.

By day, as a new widow, I was explaining to people how, I would have gotten shortchanged by an insurance contract if it weren't for having this legal plan. I would have never thought it would save me thousands. Now it's my mission to educate and spread the word about the benefits of having one!

By night, my podcast "Daily Dose A Donna" was gaining traction. I didn't even realize people were mimicking my message to "Set your dial to JOY" and were watching from around the world, as I deliberately did my best to set my own dial, crying when I needed to, and laughing when I could.

Since living in despair was not an option, setting my dial to joy became a deliberate Habitual intention.

Today I am a happily remarried spokeswoman offering continued love, support and hope for all those wondering if it's okay to love again.

As a wife and entrepreneur, my life is more enriched because I continually look for joy where it is and not where it's not.

THE UN-HABIT: STOP FOCUSING ON THE VERY THING YOU SAY YOU DON'T WANT

Why: The world is full of people with good intentions who complain about the very things they say they don't want. The laws as I understand it will bring forth that which we think or speak about. The power of life and death is in the tongue. Through the years we have read over and over these lessons from the likes of *Think and Grow Rich*, *The Power of Positive Thinking* and *The Bible* to name a few. If this is all true, why would anyone then, speak about anything they didn't want?

I was always a curious child. I knew there had to be more to life than a white picket fence, so I asked my mother, who then brought me to various respected people in their field. Off we went to meet Priests, Rabbis, Psychics and the like, but it wasn't until my husband passed away that I dug deeper into the vibrational universe and The Laws of Attraction.

Back in the 90's I suffered with chronic fatigue and I can remember the very moment I decided to get better. Now, with my broken heart and feelings of anguish, I thought I should be able to heal my heart in the same manner. Making that decision was the first step. Then set my intentions and be deliberate about setting my dial to joy. This means not only paying attention to social media, but taking action as to who and what you're watching and listening to. We are constantly bombarded with quick snippets of often negative and victim formed messages. The language seeps into our subconscious and easily goes undetected knocking down our own walls of self-love, confidence and personal growth. Gossip is an energy sucker and path deterrent. How we do one thing, is how we do everything which means any time spent complaining or bellyaching about situations you can't or aren't going to take action to control, will only drive you away from your own goals and dreams.

I miss my late husband, but I walk in the understanding that life is perfect even if we may not be able to see it at times. We have the world at our fingertips. Most of our self-talk can be unlearned, but awareness is key. Mindset is everything and a great way to start, is to set your own inner dial to JOY.

ABOUT DONNA: As a widow who would have gotten screwed over by insurance when my claim got denied, I reaped the benefit of working with a company that gets you access to attorneys for less than $50 a month. I would have never dreamed that having this legal plan would save me thousands. So now I'm on a mission to spread the word all over the US and Canada about my legal app. I simply show you how to weave powerful, simple, affordable legal services into your personal and professional life, saving time, effort and money.

50

JUST DO IT!

EVAN TRAD

Why: "Just Do It" is the famous phrase we have heard millions of times, it's famous from the Nike ads, and we may have even said it to ourselves before starting or doing something that will take courage. As entrepreneurs, we do things daily that require us to live without fear and take actions that others wouldn't dream of doing in a million years. When we "just do it," we are taking that consistent action that leads to our success. Consistent action is the work we do when we are just starting our journey as entrepreneurs and working late nights or early mornings to get things done. Consistent action is what closes our clients, and what drives our paychecks. It's what pays our staff, what builds our credibility and makes us memorable. When we "just do it," we live beyond fear and thrive in a constant state of taking action. When you "just do it," you send that email to the celebrity for an interview like I recently did. You make a phone call to that high profile influencer to star in your marketing materials, knowing that the worst they can say is "no." You "just do it" anyway! They could also say yes, and if we don't "just do it," then we will never know, and we live with regret forever!

When we "just do it," our chances of it working 100% of the time are rare. Although it might not always end upright, it's those times that we can learn from what happened when it didn't work out. From that learning, we work harder to do it better! By "just doing it," your life changes dramatically because you are no longer living in a state of fear but living in a state of consistent action! YOU are a BOSS! The combination of having no fear and consistent action is the foundational building blocks of being a successful entrepreneur.

The Un-Habit: Waiting for the stars to align

Another phrase we have heard throughout our lives over and over again is "waiting for the stars to align, "which means waiting to take action until everything is just right! When we wait for all of the stars to align, we wait to take that necessary action to move our lives and our businesses toward that success we have been seeking. Often, we want to wait to take action, but because we are fearful of making a mistake, making the wrong decision, or fearful of doing something wrong, we do nothing. I am going to be very blunt. The stars will NEVER be fully aligned in a way that will feel perfect for you to want to take action. Therefore, when we wait for the stars to align, we will be waiting until we are dead. Someone who wasn't afraid will take your place.

It is perfectly acceptable to make mistakes. It is ok not to know the answers, as long as you can learn and grow. It is that learning that leads to growth and also your personal development. Growth, in turn, leads to success. To change your Habit of waiting for the stars to align, you must step up, take a big deep breath, say to yourself "Just Do It" and take action. If it doesn't work the first time correctly, don't get discouraged! Instead, learn and evaluate how you can do it better next time and then step up and "Just Do It" again! Practice is what gets you closer to winning. When you take that step forward rather than waiting, you work to create that perfect combination of living without fear and taking consistent action that leads to the success you are seeking. You have reached success when you can say, "The stars weren't aligned for me, but because I overcame my fear of perfection, and just did it -" I AM SUCCESSFUL!!"

ABOUT EVAN: Evan Trad is a distinguished educator from Chicago, Illinois. Evan is passionate about helping people with disabilities succeed in school and in life. Evan was the founding special educator at a new charter school in Chicago for nearly ten years. He built the special education program from the ground floor. The experiences with his students inspired Evan to create Team EVAN. Team EVAN empowers people with disabilities and limitations to be more than and stronger than their limitations to become successful entrepreneurs. Through workshops, mentoring, and individualized business planning support and services, Team EVAN empowers these individuals to become successful entrepreneurs.

51

RESET YOUR MINDSET FOR SUCCESS

WENDY MUSCH

Why: Do you ever wonder why things aren't going the way you want them? Why don't you have success in your business? What are you doing wrong? The answer is easy, even if unpleasant. Your thoughts are not aligned with your desires and goals. The issue is your mindset. It isn't where it needs to be for you to succeed in any area of your life, including business.

For you to succeed in business, you must think in terms of what you want rather than what you don't have.

Most people focus entirely on the tangibles of business. They spend massive amounts of money on business development and coaching, tools, systems, and advertising. They buy courses from the gurus, follow their directions, buy what they say to buy, and do what they do all to no avail. They look back and see they have nothing to show for it except an empty bank account and a failing business. They blame everyone and everything for their failure except what they should be blaming...their mindset.

When you endeavor to transform your thinking from what you don't have or what isn't happening to what you want to happen, you will start seeing positive changes. I bet you are thinking, yeah, right. What does she know? I do know because I have done it.

Now you are probably asking, how do I even do that? The solution is simple, but I won't tell you it's easy. If it were that easy, you would have done it by now.

To have success, start spending time thinking about and seeing what you want. Over time, your unconscious mind will believe that you are or have what you see for yourself. The unconscious mind doesn't know the difference between the present and the future. It only knows what is happening now. Therefore, the more you focus on what you want, the more your unconscious mind will believe it to be true. When it only has positive things to focus on, those are the only things your subconscious can bring. The opposite is also true. When you continuously focus on negative things, it will bring you more of those things.

This is just one way to change your mindset to facilitate success. There are many others that I can teach you that in tandem will make success happen even faster.

THE UN-HABIT: STINKIN' THINKIN'

STINKIN' Thinkin' is also known as negative thinking. Negative thinking is all around us, particularly as a result of the media, politicians, and often even history. As a result, it permeates our minds and our way of life without us even being aware of it. So, then what's wrong with negative thinking? It is very insidious and damaging to our well-being and success.

It is damaging to your business because when you focus on all the bad things happening, it makes more bad things happen. When your focus is on the problem rather than the solution, it just makes the problem worse as you get what you think about.

A tangible example of this is worrying about money. Perhaps you can remember a time when you didn't have enough money to pay the bills. You found yourself constantly worrying about how you were going to pay them. The next thing you knew, your car broke down, a storm hit and damaged your home, and unexpected medical issues arose that created more bills. Your negative thinking and constant worrying forced your mind to create a "when it rains, it pours" scenario to occur compounding the issue of not having enough money.

Our minds have incredible control over things in and outside our bodies and, as a result, give us what we think about and focus on. Let's look at people who seem miraculously healed or cured of an illness or a disease. More often than not, it's a result of their focus on the solution and their desired result of recovery rather than the problem. They refuse to consider the negative alternative and focus on what life will be like when the problem is gone. Similarly, people have been known to worry themselves sick over things. It's the same principle.

Negativity begets negativity, so it isn't necessarily your fault especially when it's all around us. However, it is your responsibility to change it, particularly if you want to succeed in your business. It's a simple process, but it isn't an easy process, and it can take a long time to do it. It can take more time for some than others, but everyone CAN do it.

I know from personal experience. It took me quite a while to transform my thinking, but I can help you do it much faster and easier.

About Wendy: Wendy Musch is a best-selling contributing author, speaker, podcaster, mentor, and mindset reset strategist. She helps women who have lost their voice and power break through and reclaim their identities that may been have lost due to abusive relationships, demanding families, empty nests, or major career/business setbacks. Wendy has suffered from many of these issues herself.

Additionally, she has cofounded Empower Her Power, an online platform on Facebook that provides hope and healing to abused women through encouragement, education, mentorship, and mindset strategies.

52

COMMIT TO A RANDOM ACTS OF KINDNESS

JOSE ELIZONDO

Why: When I was younger and living in Mexico, I became familiar with a group of indigenous people called the Tarahumara. Every year they would come down from the mountains, where they lived, sell the baskets they weaved out of yucca leaves to the people of our town. My Mom never hesitated to offer them a room in the house for shelter. In the morning she would make them a meal and prepare them some food to take with them when they left. It might not sound like a lot to some, but considering my Mom was a single mother supporting and raising ten children, this was a significant sacrifice. However, she never viewed it that way. For my Mom, she could help them, so she did.

By committing to kindness, you are changing the script of daily life. You create feelings of abundance within yourself and others. Of course, this practice doesn't mean you have to open up your home to strangers. Anything that you could think of that would make someone else's day a little better would be enough. For example, we've heard of people buying the person next to them in line's groceries or paying for the order behind them in the drive-thru. These acts of kindness cause ripples, but don't feel limited to financial kindness either! Touching other's lives in simple, basic ways like sharing encouraging words or giving a hug, heck even just a pat on the back opens up channels of happiness and gratitude. The practice of kindness focuses your attention from yourself to others and helps you feel connected to them.

Even just witnessing acts of kindness can turn your day around and give you a lasting smile. Sometimes people need to be reminded that simple things bring joy and that they are cared for. It's such a beautiful thing when people help each other.

THE UN-HABIT: JUDGING OTHERS IS COUNTERPRODUCTIVE

Why: One of the most crucial aspects of breaking a bad Habit is recognizing it and acknowledging you have a bad Habit. I've been guilty of a few that need to be broken. Taking a look at myself, I find that I tend rather quickly to make assumptions about others. This is a great place to start. When you find yourself in new conversational territory, do you immediately get turned off when whoever is talking to has views seemingly opposed to yours? I certainly do, and then I will find myself blocking out anything else that they might say because I judge them. I think, "If they don't agree with me, then obviously, they are..." fill in the blank with whatever judgment I have made that day.

Taking a step back and listening to them with an open mind, I find I can start to see where their life experiences validate their reasoning. Often our values completely line up, but when I am passing judgment, I sometimes can't even hear what it is they are also saying. Noticing this, I find that the judgments I am making are usually coming out of a place that I judge myself for. Paying more attention to others without judgment allows room for people with alternative points of view to share their knowledge and experience with you. They could have spent years developing the growth they are sharing with me that day, and because of my bad Habit, I did not give them a chance. Not only do I shut them out when I do this, but I also hurt myself and deny myself the benefit they could bring to my life.

The good thing about a bad Habit is that it can be broken! It is better late than never to break a bad Habit.

ABOUT JOSE: Jose is the founder of Fastlane Marketing and a Marketing Systems Expert who teaches entrepreneurs unique new ways to increase sales predictably and profitably.

53

SCHEDULE YOUR GOALS

ANGEL TUCCY

Why: They say, "if you want to get something done, give it to a busy person." How is it possible that someone who is already busy can handle even more than someone without much to do? I believe it's by design. Busy people design their lives to be full and accomplish as much as they can. To be productive versus busy, you have to take control of how you schedule your day.

Years ago, I fell in love with the Franklin Planner™ system – and carried my black book around with me everywhere I went. After the invention of the Google calendar, the black book was replaced, but the Franklin Habit remained: if it's important, don't just write it down, schedule it.

Every goal requires daily, weekly, and monthly activities and milestones. Without scheduling those activities, the time tends to fly by, along with your goals.

How do you create the Habit of using your calendar to achieve your goals?

Commitments – Before saying yes to anything, check your calendar for availability and ensure that your activities match your goals. This keeps you from becoming distracted by every shiny squirrel.

To-Do Lists – Instead of adding tasks to your to-do list, schedule them.

Goals – Schedule the big goals first, then add the smaller goals around them. I focus my big goals around the four F's.

- Faith
- Finances
- Family
- Fitness

Master Calendar – Keep one master calendar for both work and home. I color code my family calendar from my work calendar.

Symbol Coding System – Use symbols to see at-a-glance what your week looks like.

$ - Revenue Generating Activities

- Sales Calls
- Speaking

@ - High Priority Meeting with:

- Marketing Partners
- VIP Clients
- Influencers

- High Priority Milestones

- Achievement Markers
- Media Features

% - High Priority Tasks

- Podcast/Media Interviews
- Press Releases
- Publishing Books & Online Publications
- Creating courses, webinars, sales funnels.

As a bonus, your calendar can serve as a Journal, an official record for taxes, and my favorite track of all your media features in a Rockstar List.

By reviewing your calendar at the end of each day, you're better prepared for the morning. Once you get in the Habit of using your calendar to schedule your goals, you'll have a permanent tool to keep you on track.

The Un-Habit: Stop making a To-Do List

I'm an avid list-maker. In fact, the first 2 books I published were about making lists. I believe lists keep me organized and help me to keep track of all the many things I accomplish. Yet, the reason my to-do lists work is because I schedule the most important items in my calendar and I only use the to-do list to support the appointments.

Having longs to-do lists aren't the goal – they are the guide. Use your to-do lists to support your appointments, to keep you on track.

Use your to-do lists to determine what you can Do, Dump or Delegate.

Do –Ask yourself, does this generate revenue, or is this something only I can do?

Dump – if it's never going to be added as an appointment to your day, ask yourself: Does it really belong on my list?

Delegate – Most of the items on your lists can probably be outsourced to a team or family member, freeing you up to be more productive with your day. Ask yourself: Just because I can do this, should I be doing this?

I use symbols to keep my lists moving forward, and I check off items versus crossing off, just in case I need to review a phone number or an important detail later.

- Checkmark – Item is complete
- X Mark – Item is deleted or canceled
- Dot Mark – Item is in process

Initials with a circle around it – Item has been delegated to person. Be sure to follow up with a checkmark once the item is complete.

I love lists –but I recognize their value is when I take the time to schedule the most important tasks and assess whether or not I can delegate or dump the items that distract me from my goals. Use the to-do list as your guide, not as your goal.

About Angel: Angel Tuccy is one of the country's top trainers on media and publicity. Using media exposure, Angel Tuccy went from being a stay-at-home mom to being recognized and awarded Most Influential Woman of the Year. Angel is a best-selling author, award-winning talk show host, and national speaker. Angel transforms the way audiences think about media and publicity, based on the top lessons she learned from hosting over 2,000 broadcasts and interviewing over 5,000 guests, such as Sharon Lechter, Michael Gerber, Seth Godin, Forbes Riley, Bill Walsh, and Les Brown. Angel's Media Matchmaker site helps you find guests and get booked.

54

RELAX FOR RESULTS

DK WARINNER

Why: "Dream... and Achieve!" – R. Gary Diaz, former CTO, Navistar Corporation

Do your dreams ever seem too big for you? How many of your important tasks remain undone because you feel overwhelmed?

I was in an accident at just 2 years of age, that could have killed me, and (for decades) after that I could hardly get into a car without having a full blown panic attack. Imagine a professional and father of 8, riding panicked in the back seat with 3 European colleagues?

Imagine the base level of stress that was always there for me... how about you? I'm sure you don't have that level of stress in your life... or do you?

Whatever you want to accomplish, adds MORE stress to the equation.

I found a solution, my "One Habit," that not only freed me from that chronic anxiety, but also empowered me to develop a second revenue stream. It's relaxation. Sounds too easy, doesn't it?

Well... do you do that?

Most don't, and I didn't. I was rushing around so much that, though I achieved a lot, I was burning myself out. And I didn't OWN any of it. It was just... production.

By taking just a moment and RELAXING, first:

- Before dreaming.
- Before planning.
- Before doing.
- As we're achieving.
- Before celebrating.

We gain calmness. Centeredness. Clarity. We enter "the zone." Being in that place, releases us to achieve more results!

How would your life change if YOU achieved more, and realized more of YOUR dreams?

Here's what I do.

As you're moving toward doing something (or confused about why you're hesitating) – in your mind, step back to center and check your emotional state. Are you calm, collected, clear? Or are you feeling a little bit agitated, off balance?

Apply your focus to your "gut" and, with your direct intention, lead your emotional center a couple of levels toward calmness, the still pond at sunset, quiet stillness.

Note that I don't say to achieve quiet stillness which might be beyond your reach right now.

Just a couple levels closer.

You will be amazed at how easy it is, and how much more you'll enjoy the doing that follows.

One Habit that will multiply your results!

There is, of course, a lot more to how this Method works...

THE UN-HABIT: DO EVERYTHING YOURSELF

Entrepreneurs go it alone, right? Isn't that what most people think? But there's no faster way to burn out and be part of that 90+% of new venture failures, than going it alone. Why?

Perspective.

We all tend to understand our world, and how our new venture fits in it, based on our own experience. Our own 24-7-365 timeframe. But there's only so much we can pack into our own experience.

Then there's our biases, the mechanisms we apply automatically to "simplify" our life process.

Finally our powerful self-critic which condemns our efforts and ridicules us for trying.

But if I collaborate with others on my venture, won't I lose my identity, my individual style, my credibility as the founder and sole proprietor, even my stake, my ownership of the business? Nope.

Everyone has a burning bridge to take care of somewhere – chances are, it's not yours. If they are genuinely willing to help you, they probably won't have the extra time to take all of those steps you have already taken to build out your offering. Instead, they might even promote you! We haven't even talked about the best part yet.

Perspective.

As in, THEIR perspective, applied to YOUR opportunity! I met with a friend who I've shared my anxiety and stress elimination process with. At the time, I was definitely "going it alone." Burnout and self-doubt had crept in. She saw it. After pausing for a moment, she looked at me intently, and said, "People don't know how to do, what you do! You need to share this." I don't go it alone, anymore.

How do you start shifting away from this bad Habit?

One of the easiest, and least threatening, methods is to give free help, promotion, and advice to others getting their offers off the ground. Social media is a super easy way to do this – get out of your shell, go online, and invest a few minutes in the content someone out there is sharing. Develop an insight, and leave a comment!

An insight can be as simple as celebrating something about their offer that you really like. Guess what happens after that? You might feel just a little bit more comfortable asking for their advice. Or, at the very least, sharing YOUR content in the same forum to invite THEIR comments!

ABOUT **DK:** DK Warinner, despite suffering from chronic anxiety from an early age, developed achievement Habits that led to 3 college degrees in engineering and business (including an MBA from Chicago Booth). DK found his zone of genius in systems engineering, leading to accomplishments in vehicle design, invention (4 patents), manufacturing process optimization, and sales and operations strategy.

DK has more than 2 decades of professional experience at both Fortune 500 companies and small / medium size businesses. DK enjoys long term collaborations as well as consulting, speaking, and training opportunities.

55

FIND JOY IN HARD WORK

KEVIN SORBO

Why: When people think of Hercules, they imagine a hero with superhuman strength and powers beyond mere mortals. When I think of Hercules, I am reminded as the actor who played him for seven years in the hour-long action series, that not only did I act the role, but chose to do my own stunts, worked 12 to 14 hour days, and lifted weights for another hour and a half daily. Now what drives someone to work that hard, you might ask. For me, I don't know any other way to work. This gift was instilled in me by my father at a young age, who I will forever be grateful to.

My dad was an only child who grew up on a farm, and I remember him telling us, "Don't expect handouts. Don't expect people to help, and if they do, that's great, but always work hard." For me, that meant getting up at 4:30 am and delivering newspapers six days a week in the Minnesota winters. And the crazy part, rather than complain like some might, it fueled me with a sense of accomplishment and pride.

These core values would serve me well not only in Hollywood but as an athlete and businessman. One of my earliest jobs was to caddy at a private country club filled with very successful and wealthy people. As someone who was raised with a modest background, this was an ideal environment to not only make money but to get educated. I was fascinated to uncover how these men became so successful. So I asked. I asked all of them, and surprisingly, all of their answers were similar. They told me, "Oh, I failed, and I failed again, and then I failed again."

That powerful message of successful men embracing failure mixed with my drive and work ethic is what I attribute to my success as an actor and director. It even trickles into my personal life of how I am a father to my kids and a husband to my beautiful wife.

The truth is failure is a positive word, not a negative. I've picked up from experience that the more things that don't work out right in your life, the more you learn from it.

This was huge for me when I went out to LA to pursue my dream of an acting career. It was challenging venturing from a little town of about 7,000 people outside of Minneapolis, to the city of dreams, LA. I remember when I got there, I said to myself, "Here I am," and vowed not to take no for an answer from anyone.

Sadly everything in Hollywood is about rejection, and it destroys the spirit of so many innocent actors looking for their big break

And maybe this is where Hercules originated because I chose to let rejection fuel the fire in me. Rather than giving up, I worked harder, mentally, and physically. I got in the best acting classes, with the highest level acting coaches. I used every "no" as an opportunity to take a hard look at what I did wrong and strived to improve at every turn. After all, I had "burned all the boats" and made an unstoppable decision to work as a waiter or bartender, but to be a successful working actor, no matter what the odds.

Today, I count my blessings. From the day I got my all-important Screen Actors Guild card, I was a professional working actor. First, in Commercials for Best Buy, Target, 3m, Dairy Queen, and Pillsbury, I shot more than 150 of them. They allowed me to get residuals checks, earn a nice living, and the ability to invest in the best acting coaches who taught me to hone my craft.

My passion lies in the world of production, telling amazing stories, and inspiring people to live their best lives. Most importantly, though, the amount of work you put into something is what you will get out of it, so play hard, work hard, and strive for the stars because anything is possible with enough determination.

THE UN-HABIT: DON'T LET OTHERS SET YOUR LIMITATIONS

Why: Choosing to be all you can be, making decisions with strong follow-through, even when others think you can't, will determine your character and destiny. I believe this is the foundation of all personal and professional success. Too often, we believe those who reject us. In Hollywood, we see it all the time.

I remember on the set of Hercules how stunned the crew was that I did my stunts, and I also helped carry equipment up the hills when necessary, which is when I set out to direct. As an actor, you are often told that you should stay in your lane, but I don't believe or confine to limiting boundaries.

One of my surprise triumphs about overcoming limitations is the films I directed, Let There Be Light. Not only does it embrace my beliefs in a world where "feel good" movies are not wanted, I got to act and direct it with my wife and two sons. This movie went on to stay in theatres for four months! It can be hard to hear no, but always listen to your heart, because even though you might have been rejected... there is probably some bigger plan in store for you.

One of my best examples was when they were casting *Lois and Clark* for ABC Television. It got down to the last two guys. It was Dean Cain, who is a dear friend, and me. We tested with Teri Hatcher for this new series, and that night, I got a call from my agent, "You got the role. You're going to be Superman." Wow, this was huge for me.

The next day he called and said, "You're not going to believe this, but they canceled you, and they're going with Dean Cain."

My heart shattered. The lead and the chance to play Superman... gone in an instant. Three months later, I was cast as Hercules. I get to give my buddy Dean a hard time about this. I go, "Yeah, your show went three years and got canceled. Mine went seven and became the most-watched TV show in the world."

What I learned from all my experience is to be kind, work hard, and expect the best from yourself... you're liable to get it!

About Kevin: In 1993, Kevin emerged as a full-fledged international TV star when he was cast as the lead in the immensely popular series, Hercules: The Legendary Journeys. That was followed by the lead in the sci-fi series, Andromeda. He's guest-starred on numerous tv series including Dharma and Greg, Two and a Half Men, Cheers, Murder She Wrote, and Supergirl. To date, Kevin has shot over 60 movies.

Besides being a consummate actor, Kevin is also a producer and director and most proud of his feature, Let There Be Light.

Kevin authored the widely praised book, True Strength, that recounts the painful recovery from serious health setbacks that changed his life during his Hercules years.

Sorbo married actress Sam Jenkins, whom he met during her guest appearance on Hercules in 1998. They have three children together, Braeden, Shane and Octavia.

Besides his successful career in entertainment, is an avid golf enthusiast and has always devoted a hearty portion of his time to causes he believes in. In 2005 he was named successor to Arnold Schwarzenegger as the national spokesperson for The Afterschool Alliance, a non-profit working to ensure that all children have access to quality after school programs, and since '97 Kevin has donated his time as the spokesperson for the non-profit organization, A World Fit For Kids.

56

FOCUS ON YOUR HAPPINESS

DR.NITI SOLOMON

Why: Happiness is arguably the most important Habit to have as a human being because everything good is created from happiness. Don't you agree? Happiness creates positivity, which attracts and allows better outcomes manifested in life. Happiness is the core of who we are. As human beings, our natural state is being happy. Happiness is also a vital force toward vibrant health and well-being. Your vibrancy and vitality rely on a happiness Habit for maintaining and keeping your livelihood. When you are in a state of balance and appreciation, happiness, juice flows naturally. Doesn't that sound so awesome?

Don't you want to be your best self?

Of course, you do! What are the alternatives?

When you are less than happy, your mind, body, and spirit deflate, and you are less than you!!

The further you are from your great self—the more challenging to get back to YOU again. Then depression and all kinds of not so good emotions can sink you not to be the brilliant you. Once you practice happiness Habits, you can maintain your emotional state at a higher level.

Once you decide to make this the Habit, you are on track to your greatness and wonderful self plus feeling good and satisfied along the way.

What a price to pay!!

When you are happy, the joy you radiate can uplift others, and you are more creative and productive. Then... everyone benefits. The other way around is true as well. I realized a few years ago that happiness is a spillover effect. Unless you are filled to the brim and radiate outward happiness radiance, you do not have much to give. The wonderful effect returns to you multiple times. When your happiness positively impacts others, your world shifts to manifest vibrations of love and joy. Who does not want that??

We are all creators. Which state of being would you like to create, happy, or sad?

Remember, your happy life lies in your happiness Habits. You know you want this.

What are you waiting for...? Be happy. Be brilliant. Be YOU.

Buddha prayer

"May all beings have happiness and the causes of happiness;

May all be free from sorrow and the causes of sorrow;

May all never be separated from the sacred happiness which is sorrowless;

And may all live in equanimity, without too much attachment and too much aversion,

And live believing in the equality of all that lives."

THE UN-HABIT: COMPLAINING

Why: Complaining is a Habit that can diminish your POWER! When you complain, you are not in your power because complaining shifts your perspective to outside factors, often out of your control. Complaining unload responsibilities and creates blames and discord. True creators will find ways to enrich possibilities to change or own up to and accept the condition, perhaps at least until the new factors to better the circumstances are accessible. Either you can do something about that and change your situation or condition, or you accept. It is what it is. Verbally expressing negativity to others can bring other people's emotions down with you. Wouldn't you rather uplift someone? Yes, you do.

Poisoning the environment surrounding yourself by negative words does not help anyone, including YOU. The low vibration can only attract more of the same. Why would you want that?

We are all spiritual beings having human experiences. I truly believe that. Some days may be easier than others to keep your divine cool. However, the reward is HEAVEN on earth!! Sounds compelling? Start living your divine life TODAY!

The Journey can, of course, be unsmooth at times. Just remember that you must be alive to feel. Therefore, even feeling not so great is a good thing. Negative emotions are our guides to remind us to change our thinking or steer our course to smoother water. But let's face it, how boring life would be with the same old same old repeating like Groundhog days. Yes, that might be less challenging, would that be any fun or interesting though.

You are a powerful being, so own up to your power and power through. Things happen for a reason. By recognizing less than perfect conditions you do not enjoy, you may be a mover or shaker of our world-leading the way and paving the way for better tomorrow. You would be surprised about many conditions people are okay to live with that are less than optimum. Should you notice imperfections, take the opportunities to be an agent of change. When you know our planet is better off when you are participating lovingly, complaining, or constructing should not be challenging to choose. Especially, coming from the creator, YOU!!

ABOUT DR. NITI: To truly optimize your life and lifestyle, incorporate happiness as your best friend along your joyful journey, the AWE-some Life Program was created with happiness as an essential element for your wellbeing.

As a double board-certified medical doctor in both traditional and Integrative Holistic medicine who successfully overcame chronic diseases and after thorough studies, Dr. Niti has become an expert in Lifestyle Medicine and anti-aging. Her own experience led her to design an effective AWE-some Program, which drastically assisted hundreds of patients to well-being with ease. Her first book Project L.O.V.E. (Lifestyle Optimization Victoriously Established) is one of the most comprehensive guides for Lifestyle Optimization.

57

LOOK AT PROBLEMS AS OPPORTUNITIES
LYDIA LUKIC

W **hy:** Problems can feel overwhelming to the point of feeling like there is no way out. But I have good news for you – at your lowest point, just when you think that there is nothing more you can do, there is a powerful tool you can use to overcome this paralyzed feeling.

The answer to get you to feel empowered and unafraid to face problems may sound simple, but it is powerful: start viewing those problems as opportunities. Once you shift your mindset this way, your mind pivots into a problem-solving mode, like the amazing sophisticated computer it is. In such a state, your brain focuses on finding a solution – even while you sleep - and your creative juices start flowing to find a desired outcome.

For the brain in a creative zone, there is no room for limitations, playing a victim or feeling stuck; there is only room for growth and learning while searching for that solution. Seeing problems as opportunities also shifts your attitude into a positive space socially, because as you look for solutions, you naturally connect with other people who may be able to contribute to the solution you need. A symbiosis develops, as in return you may help others, building amazing new relationships. There is nothing more powerful than getting a group of like-minded individuals together on a problem-solving mission - it's a game-changer!

Focusing on *opportunities* rather than *problems* changes the very way you see the world. It pushes you out of static comfort zones where things are "always" done a certain way to discover new processes and learn new ways. It changes your journey. Perhaps the best part about viewing problems as opportunities is that once you do find a solution, the liberating feeling of success will push you to win even more and more in life!

The Un-Habit: Overthinking

Why: Overthinking: most of us do it from time to time - some of us more than others. We roll an idea around in our mind, poking it and prodding it, thinking of every angle how something went in the past, or how it could go in the future; of what someone meant by what they said or what they didn't say. Maybe overthinking has even kept you awake at night! It can be exhausting. It's definitely important to control this Habit or completely get rid of it. Take a minute and think of a time where you were overthinking. Was it a positive experience for you? How did it make you feel? I bet the answer to both questions falls into the category of "didn't feel so good." I doubt that anyone could have answered those two questions positively. That being said it's important to clarify that taking time to analyze pros and cons before making an intelligent decision is very different from overthinking.

Overthinking never leads to making decisions as it keeps you stuck in a vicious cycle of overanalyzing and never committing to anything. Overthinking often leads to self-doubt and loss of confidence. It never leads to taking action. It wastes time and energy that instead could be used toward a much more productive outcome. As nobody wants to feel powerless and stuck, it's important to stop overthinking in personal and professional life because wishful thinking never got anyone to achieve their goals and dreams. To stop this bad Habit in its tracks and develop confidence, start making decisions and start executing. Once you stop overthinking, and instead commit to an idea and make a decision, you allow yourself to take action and execute on your vision, goals or purpose. You must take action in order to build confidence and learn if a decision was a great move or not. There will be times where you make a decision and it doesn't turn out so great. But that's okay - you still get to learn from that experience. Even when you don't get your desired outcome, you learn to adjust and adapt when necessary. By not overthinking, and taking action instead, you develop personal power so that in the future you *can* get the desired results.

ABOUT LYDIA: As a little girl who grew up in a domestically abusive home, Lydia felt powerless. Watching her father control her mother, she lived in fear and carried this into adulthood.

Over the years, Lydia committed to investing in herself by working with top mentors, taking high-level courses and reading extensively on the power of mindset and coaching. Through this journey of self-discovery, Lydia regained her power, discovered her purpose and found her voice.

Today, as a Mindset Coach, she is an advocate for other women to find their voice through her personalized 1:1 online coaching. Lydia empowers women to shift their mindset by shattering limiting beliefs, creating healthy Habits and unleashing their own newly discovered power!

58

ADD VALUE EVERY DAY IN EVERY WAY

JILL WRIGHT

Why: I am sharing with you the one Habit responsible for 90% of my success in business and life. Always add value to every person and in every situation!

When you develop this Habit, you are guaranteed to succeed in all that you do!

If you want to stand out in the market, you need to become known for the value you bring consistently in all areas to see and feel the exceptional quality of your product or service over that of your competitors.

You can add value in many different ways.

For example, You could make life easier by simplifying things. Apple transformed the industry by simplifying the technical, often confusing computer processes and made them much more user friendly. The same is true for managing people, the clearer and simpler you can communicate, the more successful you can be.

You can also add value through having the best pricing for your market. Paying close attention to your costs and your quality can give you an edge that will build customer loyalty.

Another great way to build loyalty is in exceptional customer service. Taking the time to build solid relationships and add value to your staff and customers will pay huge dividends throughout your career.

Thinking creatively about how to offer greater convenience to your customers and your staff will also set you apart. Free delivery, work from home options, and childcare facilities on-site could also have a significant impact.

Recognition and appreciation are some of my most favorite ways to add value. Not only are they the most satisfying, but they pay the biggest dividends. Getting to know your staff and customers and understanding their unique preferences and rewarding them in special ways will create extraordinary loyalty that will guarantee success in any business.

When adding value and making impact becomes your Habit, you will have the Midas Touch in all you do!

THE UN-HABIT: JUDGEMENT

Why: Judgement stops all. Love! Need I say more? You are a unique gift to the world, and judging yourself and others shuts down innovation, creativity, and compassion. Judgment is oppressive low vibration energy that holds self-love hostage and stifles all growth. Judging and comparing yourself and your business to others is a ticking time bomb that will ultimately destroy you and your business if you let it.

However, we are all human and judgment a natural instinct. The goal is to become more self-aware and catch yourself before you do any permanent damage. Train yourself to respond instead of reacting.

I have witnessed judgment build walls between people because of the stories that people create in their minds about why and how things happened. It's important to be aware of these tricks that your ego and mind can play to protect themselves.

One solution to save you from the destruction of judgment is to build your capacity for compassion. It helps to ask yourself some questions to keep yourself in compassion and out of judgment. I try to ask myself, "Why not give them the benefit of the doubt? " Because in all honesty, we are all struggling with something. Some of us just hide it better than others. I find it helpful to ask myself, "Will this matter in five years? Or five hours?"

Remember that we are more alike than different, and often the things that you judge the most in others are things active within yourself. So consider the words of the Dalai Lama. People take different roads seeking fulfillment and happiness. Just because they are not on your road doesn't mean they have gotten lost.

I have seen first hand the damage judgment can cause in relationships, businesses, and organizations. You will live a much happier, more rewarding life if you develop an Un-Habit of Judging.

About Jill: Jill Wright is a Master Connector and Heart Centered Leader who has been recognized by both Forbes and Harvard Business Review. She is on a mission to share her 33 years of experience to mentor leaders to create connected, dedicated teams and has put together a new exciting course called Soul to Sole the Keys to Human Connection. Make sure you take advantage If you are ready to take your business to the next level.

59

DO IT AFRAID

SALLY LARKIN GREEN

Why: My gut tells me to go for it, but my head tells me I'm crazy. It happens all the time. A few years ago, I saw a Facebook post announcing a new woman's magazine. At the time, I had been writing a small weekly blog for my church and I had around 50 followers. I took a shot and sent the publisher a message telling her how wonderful I thought the idea for the magazine was and that I was writing a blog. I told her if she needed any content for the magazine, to let me know. I never thought she would respond. The next day I received a reply asking me to write an article for the magazine. That is when the fear set in and I almost said no. How many times have we let opportunities slip through our fingers because we were afraid?

All the negative thoughts and feelings can make us nervous. We get panicky at the thought of failing or succeeding. We say to ourselves, "What if this doesn't work and I disappoint my family" or "What if I'm successful and people start asking me to do things and I have no idea what I'm doing?"

I'm telling you today to DO IT AFRAID. Accept the fear, feel the emotions, realize that fear is meant to be overcome and jump in. Sometimes, when faced with a challenging decision or situation, the best way to deal with it is to embrace the opportunity.

You know what? Life is hard at times, and so many times it's not fair. We become familiar with sitting in darkness and being depressed that making an effort to change becomes a struggle. Some people are so focused on their sadness and troubles that fear, anxiety and worry becomes normal.

Life can knock you down hard, and those struggles can be used to keep you down or you can search for strength and continue to get up each time. If you stumble, steady your feet and try again. If you succeed and are afraid of all the added responsibilities, ask yourself, "Why not me?" When you choose to face your fears head-on, when you seize opportunities, you realize that no matter how wounded you are and no matter how dark it gets, you can always find a ray of hope or a glimmer of light that will pull you up and help you to live the life you were designed for.

THE UN-HABIT: STOP PUTTING JUNK IN YOUR BODY

Why: It felt like I was always taking care of everyone else, but I discovered it is equally important to put time aside to take care of me. Eating correctly and exercising didn't fit into my vocabulary. I had housework to do, a business to run, and a family to care for. I didn't have time for myself. I knew I was overweight; I knew I was tired all the time; I knew I should do something, but it was easier to keep doing what I always had done. And besides, I was too busy. I like to cook, and I enjoy food and stopping each morning for a coffee and doughnut made me happy.

My husband and I own a small cleaning company, and we had been working without a vacation for over four years. When the pandemic hit in March of 2020, we were without work for the first time ever. The first few days were nice, almost like the vacation we never had. But something happened. I was able to rest and get my head clear for the first time in a while. My daughter, husband, and I started walking every day. At first, it was less than a mile before I was out of breath. But we gradually began increasing the length of our walks. We are now walking over two miles a day. I started planning healthy meals, making grocery lists, researching recipes, and making salads. We cut out bread, alcohol, and sugary desserts. I began to notice something; I would wake up feeling refreshed. I had more energy, and I didn't have the brain fog anymore. I realized that garbage in, garbage out was a real thing.

I still have the occasional piece of chocolate, and my reward for losing 20 pounds was a glass of wine with my daughter. We have fallen off track, but the next day we get right back on. These new healthy recipes will now be part of our family for years to come. We are enjoying the hamburger salad and turkey tacos. I feel better, look better, and I am ready for my next adventure.

About Sally: What do you do when overwhelmed or stressed? Sally Larkin Green loves to paint. A gifted artist and storyteller, Sally teaches beginner paint and wine, coffee and canvas, and painting for anxiety and stress relief classes both in-person and online. She has written two bible studies and an inspirational book of poetry. Sally and her husband have owned a small cleaning and janitorial business for over 20 years.

60

LISTEN TO POSITIVE SELF-TALK DAILY

JIM ZACCARIA

Why: It's important to listen to positive self-talk regularly, because from the moment we were born, our brains have been inundated with and influenced by impressions of various sorts. For many of us, these impressions were Less than positive or favorable, and for some, they were downright Negative.

Sayings like "I'm not made of money," "We can't afford that", "Dirty Money", "Filthy Rich" are common negative statements that can leave an indelible mark on the psyche and, (not surprisingly), cause one to have various "Money issues" throughout their Lifetime.

The same holds true of assumptions we made as a child, about being "Bad", when being scolded. How often does one hear "No," (and at one time, delivered with a 'Smack'), when growing up? The marks, (in mind), are indelible and self-esteem suffers.

Often, overheard comments, like: "Oh, (so and so)... 'could Never wear something like that', 'is big-boned', 'eats too much', 'is skinny as a rail', 'is slow', is dumb as a rock' - ad-infinitum. Worse yet (and far Too

Often), Discouraging words are spoken *Directly* to children. i.e., "You'll never amount to anything," "How could you be so stupid?", "I wish you'd never been born," "You make me sick," "You're the reason for___.", and more, each leaving their unique marks. You likely have some 'marks' too, don't you? Everyone does. Consider the pervasiveness of marketing in our lives, telling us we are not "enough", be it, thin, pretty, smart, rich, etc. ad nauseam, unless we buy this or that.

There are not enough hours in the day for us to make enough affirmations or "Chants" to counteract the negative influences of a lifetime. And when we state an untruth as true, our subconscious-mind Knows we are Lying and will Never believe us again. Counter-productive, to say the least.

Good News! Neuroscientists have proven that Positive Self-Talk can effectively counteract ALL of that negative input, and all we need to do is "*Listen*". When we do, neural pathways are physically changed so that electrical impulses in our brain take a different route. Our brain is effectively re-wired for success. When we begin our day with positive self-talk, our day is bound to go better, and when we end our day with positive self-talk, we provide our sub-conscious mind tools to use to craft a path to whatever we desire, while we sleep.

HAB1T™

THE UN-HABIT: STOP SPEAKING ANY NEGATIVE WORD ABOUT YOURSELF

WHY: Self-Talk is the internal dialogue of an individual. It is important to NEVER speak negatively... Especially about ourselves (our "Self") Why? Because there is POWER in our words, and 'Why would you want to say bad things about yourself, when there are so many others who are more than

happy to do So?' Besides, '*Every*' time we do, we pick away at our self-esteem, (That is, the 'esteem' we have for ourselves).

Man and Woman are created to be creators. Most people create the wrong things by declaring how their body aches or that they're confused, etc. They focus on the problem and not the solution, or the Results they desire. They say things like 'How stupid can I be?'... instead of 'How can I do better?', 'I'll never be good at That', instead of 'I'm going to learn what successful people do, (for this situation), and then do that'. 'That's just the way I am', instead of 'I used to __, and Now I'm getting better every day'.

To change negative self-talk Habits, we must speak to the conscious mind, (ego), in a way that it will receive our message, without it realizing we are attempting to uproot it from its comfort zone, where it keeps us with it, to protect us, (which is the ego's job). For most, if we attempt things like hypnosis, it will be perceived as trickery, and will not last.

Though we must speak to the conscious mind, no conscious effort need be exerted to cause lasting, positive change and relinquish negative, limiting beliefs. Possibly hard to believe, but effectively, we can Do Less and Achieve More, by enlisting the power of our 'subconscious' mind.

By listening to and making positive self-talk an integral part of our lives, we can live happier, healthier, more successful, and potentially longer lives. And hopefully make a bigger, more positive, and impactful difference in the world. What is profound to consider, is that Self-Talk affects All aspects of us, Mentally, Physically, (even at a cell, level), Energetically, Emotionally and Spiritually, for all aspects are intertwined.

About Jim: I Empower People to Recognize, Restructure and Reprogram Negative Thoughts and Beliefs so that they can Get More of Whatever They Desire From Life. I do this by guiding them to follow simple D.I.Y. steps, or as we work together through a Proven, Done-With-You Program.

61

CHOOSE POSITIVE AFFIRMATION

LESLEY KLEIN

Why: Whenever negative thoughts like fear or depression come up for me, I immediately say, "Cancel! Cancel!" and replace the thought with a positive affirmation of what I want. My go to is, "All is well in my peaceful and prosperous world!" I repeat this aloud or in my head, depending on my location until I feel it. After repeating this affirmation thousands of times with feeling, over time, I "believed" them and manifested many dreams and goals.

This Habit of...

1) Being aware of any negative self-talk.

2) Saying, "Cancel! CANCEL"! Verbally.

3) Immediately replacing it with a positive affirmation of what you want, you cancel the negative and program your subconscious mind to work in your favor.

No matter what you believe, you are right, so it is important to believe things that serve you and align what you want to accomplish in life.

Practicing this Habit will change your life because everything starts with your mindset! You must be the captain of your ship and control where you are going. Otherwise, you will be tossed about with every emotional storm you encounter. This is a discipline, a practice, that you must commit to like you would working a muscle.

My entrepreneurial spirit from my Father, who immigrated to the US from Peru at age 17 with only his artistic talent. He believed in the American Dream, and he lived it. He was an inspiration to me and instilled the belief in me that anything was possible! "If there is a will, there is a way," he would say. That mindset enabled him to live the American Dream and inspired me to live my dreams!

Thank you, Papa!

THE UN-HABIT: NOT BEING AWARE OF YOUR THOUGHTS

Why: If you are not aware of your thoughts and are just living a reactionary life, you will be on that boat that gets tossed around during a stormy sea. The only way to get a handle of your "monkey mind" is first to be aware of what you are thinking, aka being mindful. Then, you have the opportunity to decide if that thought serves you. If it doesn't, then CHOOSE a better thought and change the trajectory of your life!

Another technique to cancel a negative thought is to wear a rubber band on your wrist and snap it whenever you notice the negative thought. Eventually, you will train yourself to stop the negative thought because you will finally get tired of the pain. This, I learned from T. Harv Eckert. I would recommend this technique if the verbal "cancel-cancel" one doesn't work or extra stubborn thought.

But you can't just cancel the thought and not replace it with something of your choosing. The Universe hates a void, and you will attract thoughts that resonate (match) your vibration. If you are vibrating from a place of fear, you will attract fearful thoughts. If you are vibrating from a place of anger, you will attract angry thoughts. If you vibrate from a place of love and gratitude, you will attract loving and grateful thoughts. Thoughts are things, and they are how you create your experience of the world.

A big part of this is self-responsibility, taking responsibility for your thoughts, which lead to your actions and, ultimately, your results. You must STOP the Habit of blaming others for your misfortunes. Your point of power is in the present moment where you take full responsibility for your life. You are the only one who thinks your thoughts. "You made me do it!" No one makes you do things. Ultimately, you choose to do them or not do them. Don't give away your power by blaming someone else for your negative circumstances or outcomes. Take the bull by the horns and own your life!

About Lesley: Lesley Klein has been an entrepreneur for over 25 years. Sixteen of those years, she created and operated an award-winning metaphysical bookstore in Florida. Her store specialized in personal growth and development, which helped her develop an eye for innovative products that up-level your life!

From Germany and new to the US market, the Healy is a wearable wellness device that uses frequency to balance & harmonize your four bodies (physical, mental, emotional, and spiritual). Her business is called Frequency Wellness Lifestyle. The other product is a fun, self-care product that raises your vibration differently... through beautiful DIY manicures and pedicures using Color Street nail strips! That business is called Nailcraft. She owned and operated a cafe/music venue called "The Witch's Brew" for 9 years, also in Palm Harbor, Florida.

62

CREATE YOUR VISION

MICHELLE DAVIS

Why: This Habit is important to me because everything in my life was so hard due to being fatherless. I needed to have a vision; my life could be better.

For me, it has taken a lifetime to recognize in myself or even appreciate my Habit of Vision. As I grew up in the Bronx projects, the standard of expectation was very low, especially in school. Growing up, we were very poor, but my mother made sure I knew two things about my life. She taught me how to pray, and she would tell me about my amazing birth story that empowered me my entire life.

After I was born, her nurse told her I was born to be rich and successful and gave her a silver dollar to hold on for me. The whole experience blessed my mom so much; she never forgot to pass on the silver coin and the affirmation. It made her so happy to share her story. She would remind me of my whole life, "Michelle, you were born to be rich and successful." After a while, I could tell she believed it too, and that's all I needed to hold on to my vision and live my dreams. Believing in myself led me to become the first college graduate. I want to encourage you to be strong and follow your dreams. Having vision changes your life for the better because it motivates you on the inside and exposes new opportunities and new people that will never appear without vision. Vision also makes suffering and disappointments bearable. Our world today desperately needs vision. I am also so glad my vision is not dependent on anything or anyone but me.

THE UN-HABIT: FEAR

Why: This Un-Habit of Fear is so important for me to break personally. I hate that fear creates stress, worry, or insecurity. This last week my fear stopped me from executing my daily goals. But then, miraculously, I was able to review my goals and push thru!

Some other ways my fear comes up - is when I hesitate to close the deal, making phone calls or pricing. I have to rely on my big vision continually, so I can turn my fear into the courage I need to be successful.

As an author, I can choose to have anxiety over the kids or parents liking my coloring book, or I can Believe in my book and Be bold.

So, I wanted to share some tools that help me - one is using motivating tapes from people like Les Brown, who says two things about fear 1)" you must find the place inside yourself where nothing is impossible."

2)" Fear does not have special power unless you empower it by submitting to it.

I love this because it's up to me to move from fear to Faith. This inspires me to work hard and fight for my dreams of building my Born to be Academy no matter what. I also de-stress by walking and meditating.

I know that I was born to do something amazing in my life. I also know I want to help my disabled daughter to have a home and live independently.

If you are like me, I cannot allow my thoughts and actions to prevent my fears from going all in. This Habit is too important not to change - I want to be successful and sell as many coloring books/crayons to kids worldwide. I also wish to start my" Born to Be" Academy to help kids have a dream space.

ABOUT MICHELLE: Michelle Marie Davis is an author, international speaker and coach. She is a bestselling 1 Habit author and Coloring Book Creator of Born to Be Affirmation/Activity. Beside with her writing, she has always had a gift for inspiring others and a love for helping people reach their potential, her life's journey led her to becoming a missionary. Michelle has coached and guided girls and women throughout the U.S., Africa, and the Caribbean, equipping them to discover their inner strength and follow their dreams. Along the way, she married Frank Davis, her husband of thirty-one years and gave birth to two beautiful daughters- Jacqueline and Kenya.

63

WAKING UP WITH THE SUN

AVA BOUDI

W hen I was 13 years old, I had a bicycle accident. I fell on my head, went to the hospital, and got stitches. I had Post-Concussion Syndrome. Headaches EVERY night. I learned how important sleep is and waking up when you have to be ready to be someplace.

I was a studious and good girl. But because of this, I was awake all night, missing morning classes. For three years, I had Math class first, and always missed it! I asked the school staff to reschedule for later, but they didn't. They didn't believe it was because I wasn't feeling well! I could have been a straight-A student if it was not for oversleeping.

This affected my teenage years until I was offered to learn about nightclub promotions. In NYC in the 1980's, parties didn't start until 11 pm! I became very successful. I had to be there "Early" to welcome entertainers, and nightclub or concert guests. I was never late! I stayed until after the venue closed. Then I was ready for bed, with good reason to sleep until noon!

Then I had a daytime job. It was not easy.. I was tired, unhappy, and unproductive.

When I had my daughter, I was up every 2 hours. Then finally regulated my sleep more normally. When she was a teenager, my grandmother moved in with us. She had dementia and couldn't walk alone. I had to sleep when she did..lightly... so I would wake up if she tried to get out of bed alone, again every 2 hours or so!

Since 2013 my husband has to wake at 5:30 am. I want to spend time with him before he leaves, hugging him goodbye. Do I go back to bed after?

NO! I force myself to stay awake and be productive. Having coffee (I have a book coming out about that!) listening to motivational videos while I have breakfast, and planning my day. This is much better than sleeping it away!

No more missing out on the sun, morning activities, early appointments.. getting work done, and on time! It takes time, but you can do it. If you're tired enough from waking early, you will sleep earlier.

Studies of successful entrepreneurs who wake up at five show they're more productive, have more energy, discipline, organized, less stressed, better-eating Habits, and have more control over our professional and personal time.

If I can do it, you can too!

THE UN-HABIT: NO MORE ALCOHOL

Why: For many entrepreneurs, they think it is "Normal," customary, or even expected to have a cocktail, a glass of wine, or any alcohol after a business meeting or while attending events and dinners.

But what they don't realize is how even small amounts of alcohol affects our minds immediately and our bodies over time.

Alcohol can change a person's emotions, perception, and thought process. It's a depressant, so alcohol can change your mood and inhibitions and make you ineffective at communication. Your speech slurs, and your body is unbalanced. Thirty seconds after you take a sip, alcohol goes to your brain cells. It affects your liver, kidneys, sleep, muscles, hormones, high blood pressure, digestive problems, and many other conditions all over your body.

It is important to stop drinking alcohol if you want to be happier and healthier and more successful. You can also save a lot of money by not buying alcohol, using it to invest in your business, learning new skills, and having great experiences.

I didn't have a glass of wine until I was 40. My reason for saying that is that it gave me a long time to observe other people who did have alcohol and knowing many alcoholics, I learned a lot about it. I'm not a doctor.

These days I think the more successful people are, the healthier they are and make health and happiness a priority.

To close with combining my two topics, alcohol also affects your sleep. Some people say wine is good with dinner, but it also causes headaches and makes you wake up in the middle of the night. Have some grapes instead! It's very difficult to wake up early in the morning, exercise, and be productive when you are suffering from a hangover.

About Ava: Ava of AvaHosting Internet Solutions is an Internet Marketing Consultant and Website Services provider, and the Editorial Director/Publisher of Busy-Mom.Com online magazine. Avahosting Internet Solutions has been a one stop shop for everything you need to get your business online and promoted since 2000.

64

PERSEVERANCE

MATTHEW GUMKE

Why: Most people will give up during the first few obstacles. Others will become successful then give up later when it becomes too difficult. An example of this is 2020. Many people I know had big plans for 2020 until their businesses were no longer allowed to operate.

I watched many young entrepreneurs give up or slow down at the most crucial time. They started wasting time and "hanging out" a lot because it became a lot more challenging to succeed.

Our water machine business in Spain wasn't allowed to operate for months and failed. I had to liquidate all my investments to pay for our staff, and I lost a lot of time, energy, and money during the most significant wealth transfer in history.

I returned to Scotland with nothing. I was disappointed because I gave so much and returned without money or opportunity. The worst part was, it wasn't the first time I'd ruined my life.

The first time I made a terrible investment, I couldn't pay my staff and lost all my clients. That time I couldn't blame anyone other than myself.

It's important to blame yourself even when it isn't technically your fault. Before lockdown, we were successful and making good money, and I don't believe there was much I could've done differently.

It would've been easy for me to return to Scotland, take handouts, and complain that business success is too difficult. That's not the person I want to be remembered as.

My family was concerned about my future and wanted me to give up being successful in business and go to university, join the army, or get a job. I never listened to their feedback.

I realized I was wasting so much time trying to make money from month to month. I realized I have an interesting personality and story. It was terrible that I wasn't going all-in on growing my personal brand, even if it meant short term financial sacrifice.

Everyone was at home on social media, and I started making YouTube videos all day, every day. My YouTube was tiny, but eventually, a video got suggested. Just one successful video helped me get monetized.

Since then, my channel has continued to grow. I'm in the initial stages of having a large, successful personal brand. By the end of 2020, I'll be making good money again with a higher future earning potential than ever before.

None of this would've happened if I gave up. That's why I believe perseverance is the most important Habit to change your life.

THE UN-HABIT: LISTENING TO FRIENDS AND FAMILY

Why: I always wanted to make a lot of money. As a young child, I would read a popular soccer magazine. I saw that the best players would make 10's of millions every year before their other businesses and sponsorships. This lit up my brain at the possibility of being rich and living an amazing life.

The only problem was, I was terrible at soccer. Every day after school, I would practice. All weekend I would practice. All the vacations I would practice. Eventually, I became quite good.

My mother hated soccer and told me I would never be successful, and I should focus on something realistic, like becoming a doctor or a lawyer instead. She said she wasn't paying my school fees for me to fail at becoming a soccer player.

I told her to let me drop out of private school and go to a normal school to play more. She told me I would end up in jail or on drugs at a normal school.

Eventually, I got what I wanted and ended up failing at soccer as I lost interest as a teenager. I became more interested in business and wanted to pursue that instead. I just didn't know how I would succeed.

Around this time, I remember my dad screaming that I would never become successful if I didn't go to university. My grades were so bad it wasn't even an option.

I decided university wasn't for me, and I dropped out of high school at 16. I realized none of my friends or family's advice could help me succeed at a high level.

The pressure kept getting ramped up to go back to school and go to university to become a doctor or lawyer. I felt that they didn't care about what would make me happy, only that we would look good to others.

I have a vision of a beautiful future. I won't feel happy under other circumstances, and happiness is the most important thing for me. When I'm happy, I can do anything. When I'm happy, I'm motivated and want to work every single day.

Ignore those telling you how to live. You can fail at doing something "realistic." Do what makes you happy. Do something "unrealistic." There's less competition. Trust your instincts. No one knows your hidden talents but you.

ABOUT MATTHEW: The best place to follow me for my most up to date content is on my YouTube channel MattyGTV. Here you can watch book summaries from some of the most successful authors in the present and throughout history. I believe that going through dozens of these summaries will prove to be a life changing experience as you'll gain knowledge from the world's brightest minds. We have almost 1000 summaries and we'll continue to grow to cement ourselves as the largest free online library. Your support will help me provide and improve this content over the next few years.

65

HEART-FOCUSED BREATHING

JANE HOGAN

Why: In our busy lifestyles, we go through much of life in a state of simmering stress. From my personal experience, I know chronic stress leads to inflammation and can be a precursor to many illnesses. Being in a stressed state also makes us more likely to make poor decisions, taking actions we later regret. We can easily lower stress levels with a simple technique: heart-focused breathing in as little as three minutes per day.

When we focus on breathing slowly and deeply into our heart, while feeling positive emotions like gratitude, compassion, excitement, joy, or love, we bring our hearts and brains into a state of coherence or harmony. When the brain and heart are in harmony, the stress response lowers, setting up positive physiological responses. We create positive vibrations.

A daily practice of heart-focused breathing creates harmony between the heart and brain and can be a game-changer!

Heart-focused breathing results in a higher heart-rate variability (HRV). HRV is the variation in the time between successive heartbeats. When a person is relaxed and breathing slowly, there is more variation between heartbeats resulting in higher HRV. In general, higher HRV is a sign of general health and fitness. When HRV is high, we release stress in our bodies.

Besides immediately lowering stress levels, heart-focused breathing improves the decision-making center of our brain. This results in better self-regulation so that a person is more likely to behave in a way that is best for them.

We all know instinctively that the heart is the feeling center in our body. When we focus on the heart, we are better able to tap into our innate intuition - literally, get answers from the heart! Once in a state of heart-brain coherence, you can ask your heart a question and wait for your intuition to answer.

Set aside just three minutes every day for heart-focused breathing and notice the magic happen. You will lower stress, create better health, make better decisions, and tap into your intuition. You can do this practice anytime, anywhere, and it's free. Sometimes the simplest Habits can be the most powerful!

THE UN-HABIT: PUTTING EVERYTHING ELSE AHEAD OF SELF-CARE

Why: So many of us, especially women, tend to put everything else ahead of self-care. We are busy trying to do it all, often setting impossible-to-achieve standards. With so much to do, self-care often falls at the bottom of our daily 'To Do' list, if it makes it there at all.

Why is this? There is a perception that self-care is selfish or a waste of time. Time spent on ourselves is time that could be spent doing more for other people or to get more done. This is a mental trap that ultimately is flawed.

Just like on a plane when we are told to put our mask on first before we help others, making our self-care a priority is HOW we can better serve ourselves and ultimately others too.

When we care for ourselves, we lower stress, which helps us both physically and emotionally. We are sending a signal to our mind and our body that we are worth it. The autonomic nervous system moves from a fight-or-flight response into the rest-digest response. In this state of rejuvenation, all systems in the body work better, including digestion, the immune system, endocrine, and cognitive functions.

For self-care to be genuinely beneficial, it can't be a once-in-a-while event. Self-care must become part of a daily routine.

Many people find that even if they have great intentions of adding self-care to their schedule, it rarely happens. The day slips away, and by the end of the day, there is no time or energy left for self-care. I was in this trap too, and ultimately I burnt out.

I have found that scheduling self-care as part of my morning routine has been the most successful way of making self-care a daily Habit. Cultivating a morning self-care Habit is best because it is more likely to happen. Starting each day off with a supporting self-care routine also sets a positive tone for the day, and each day is a mini-version of a life.

Try starting each day with self-care. You'll feel better, and you'll even be able to serve those around you better too.

About Jane: Jane Hogan, "The Wellness Engineer," combines 30 years of engineering problem-solving experience, energy healing, and neuroscience to help people release pain and inflammation naturally. In a perfect blend of science and spirituality, Jane designs personalized solutions to help people let go of inflammatory foods, thoughts, and feelings to regain freedom and become empowered creators of their health.

66

DECIDE TO GO LIGHT EACH DAY

HEATHER AARDEMA

Why: Life can get complicated fast.

Eat this way, no eat that way. Train for a marathon, no long-running distances is bad on the joints. Drink more water, but make sure you don't drink too much water at meals. Wake up early and make the most of the day, but also sleep in because exhaustion isn't good for you. Pause to smell the roses, but remember, if you aren't making the most of your time, you're wasting your time.

There are so many messages on how to do life, and on how to do it well. So how do you figure out what's right for you?

It's simple. Get in the Habit of going light. When you decide to do this, you'll make the right decisions for you.

This seems like such an obvious suggestion, but as humans, we're naturally drawn to the rich fabric of anything complicated, chaotic, and dramatic. This heaviness ends up distracting us from true peace, joy, and contentment. We're so overwhelmed by our clutter—all the physical, mental, and emotional stuff we're carrying around day-in and day-out that we miss the things that matter most.

So what does clutter look like? Physical clutter shows up as an uncomfortable amount of stuff stored in your house. Or foods with ingredients that you can't pronounce being put into your body. These things make life heavy.

Mental clutter is thoughts that you should be doing something or shouldn't be. Thoughts that you're not enough or that you're too much. Thoughts that you need to do it all to be lovable.

Emotional clutter is feelings that keep you trapped in a reality that you don't like.

So let's simplify things. When you go light, life feels easier. You find your flow. You uncover the things that matter most to you.

How do you know how to go light? Trust the deep knowing inside of you. Ask yourself, does thinking this thought, feeling this feeling, or taking this action feel light or heavy? And then pause and listen. Get quiet. And then when you're ready, go light.

With every decision, you have the choice between simplicity and complication. It's not always easy. At times you'll need to say 'no' to others so that you can say 'yes' to you. Regardless, if you have a big decision to make, go light. If you have a small decision to make, go light. And if you're hungry for health and happiness, and the best possible life, go light.

The Un-Habit: Stop overcomplicating things

Why: We unnecessarily overcomplicate things.

Why do we do this? It helps us delay decision making. And if we delay decision making, then we can't fail.

All of this creates massive mental and emotional clutter, making our internal lives much heavier.

So how do we overcomplicate things? We procrastinate. We worry about not knowing how to do things or about not knowing how to do them right. We wait for the perfect time knowing that there will never be a perfect time. We come up with excuses for why we are where we are and why we aren't where we want to be. We compare ourselves to others wasting time rationalizing why we aren't where they are. We welcome interruptions, and we hesitate by interpreting outside circumstances as roadblocks and reasons for why we can't or shouldn't move forward.

We're so afraid of the unknown that we unnecessarily overcomplicate things so that we don't have to move forward.

So how do we untangle ourselves from all the complications?

Joseph Campbell says, "the cave you fear to enter holds the treasure you seek."

Get curious about what it is you want in life. Face any fear you have with fascination, and in no time, that fear will lose the scary paralyzing grip it has on your life.

Life is as complicated as we make it.

Want to simplify your life? Stop hiding behind the complication. Get crystal clear on your dreams. Own them by knowing why they're so important to you. Figure out how you need to show up for them to come to fruition. Focus on the what, the why and the how, but don't forget who you need to become to create the magic you want to experience.

And then decide. Decide that life is not complicated and that you're going after your dreams no matter what. That failure isn't about the outcome. Instead, it's about whether or not you choose to move forward.

Once you commit to releasing the clutter and living a lighter life, you'll be able to truly commit to you, and all the good that wants to come to you.

Want a happier, more fulfilling, and lighter life? Start by un-complicating it.

About Heather: Heather Aardema helps women lose weight by releasing the clutter in their heads, hearts and homes. Combining tenants of minimalism, simplicity, positive psychology and functional nutrition she created a novel approach to weight-loss called "The Live Light Method." As a dedicated certified coach and aspiring minimalist, Heather has helped thousands of women transform their relationship with food, stop obsessing about their bodies, and finally release all of their mental, emotional and physical pounds for good — enabling them to focus on the things that matter most and live a lighter and brighter life.

67

EMBRACE YOUR "I AM" STATEMENT

LOREN LAHAV

Why: Embracing, owning and *living* one's **I AM** statements is a MUST, a non-negotiable because they are an absolute declaration of *WHO YOU ARE. Your essence...the very core of your being.* They are your commitment to *Yourself* to stay connected to the Truth of who you are and how you WILL show up in the world.

And it should start the moment you open your eyes *each and every day*. Your **I AM** statements are your high-octane fuel for your day and *for your life*. Many people get "physically" ready for their day but don't get *emotionally* ready. Use your **I AM** statements to get you emotionally amped by filling you up with what you need to *ignite YOU* for the day. Begin the moment you open your eyes! *I AM Alive! I AM Blessed! I AM Healthy!* And **celebrate who you are!** Imagine the feeling of celebration before you even get out of bed. Maintain that energy and momentum as you brush your teeth and put on that winning outfit for the day and present YOU to the world.

You'll soon discover that *this is happening because of your daily commitment to* **I AM...**

- You will feel *Unshakeable, Unflappable and Unapologetic!*
- You'll avoid *Stinkin' Thinkin'* and flow with whatever happens, instead of reacting.
- You'll be grounded and stay centered throughout the day, so you are always performing at your peak and from a place of love and gratitude.
- You will feel ready to *take on the world* when you remember *who you are, what you stand for, and what you will not tolerate in your life.* It will become your Rocket Fuel!

And remember... doing your **I AM statements** is not exclusive to the morning only. Do them *anytime* throughout the day. I do them before I jump on a call, have a meeting, do a coaching session, before I step on stage. They are a consistent reminder of: *"I got this. I know who I am. I am ready. It's my time."* Your **I Am statements are yours.** No one can ever take them from you UNLESS you give them permission to. *Because that is not who you are.*

Appreciate each and every moment. When you are aware and come from a place of love and gratitude, life becomes so much richer. Here are some **I AM Statements** that power me and my destiny...

- I AM **LOVE**
- I AM **PASSION**
- I AM **HUSTLE**
- I AM **HEART**
- I AM **COMPASSION**
- I AM THE **POWER** AND THE **PRESENCE OF G-D**
- I AM A **KICKASS MOM**
- I AM A **COMMITTED WIFE**
- I AM A **BILLIONAIRE BABE**
- I AM **HEALTHY**
- I AM **CREATIVE**
- I AM A **HEALER**
- I AM **PRESENT**
- I AM **REAL**
- I AM **SINCERE**
- I AM **GENEROUS**
- I AM A **VISIONARY**
- I AM **HONEST**
- I AM **SEXY**
- I AM **WISE**
- I AM **MAGICAL**
- I AM **FEMININE**
- I AM **SUCCESSFUL**
- I AM **THE REAL DEAL**
- I AM **AN AWESOME MOM**
- I AM **ALIVE**
- I AM **BLESSED**
- I AM **APPRECIATIVE**
- I AM **GRATEFUL**
- I AM **AUTHENTIC TO THE CORE**
- I AM **BADASS AND BEAUTIFUL.**

And so it is...!

The Un-Habit: GOYA!!! Get off your ass and just do it!

Why: Too often we wait for just that right moment... that ideal circumstance... that perfect situation to get something done. You get all worked up and then what happens? *Poof!* <u>NOTHING HAPPENS</u>. You talked your way out of it *again!* Your life goes on with a big long list of incompletions... things that are important to you, but you kept finding reasons not to take action. Not only are you left *unfulfilled*, you diminish your self-worth because you internalize and validate the fact that you are a person that doesn't follow-through or get sh—done, especially the things that are important in your life.

The Solution: GOYA! <u>G</u>et... <u>O</u>ff ...<u>Y</u>our... <u>A</u>ss *and Just Do It!* My approach is to *Fire! Ready! Aim!* Not get hung up on the details – just execute i.e., *FIRE!* and figure out the rest later. Done! √ ! *Next!*

About Loren: Loren Lahav is an international speaker, coach with over 30 years of experience in personal development. She loves to fire people up from the stage, wake them up and keep them awake. She is obsessed with helping people to get real create lasting change after the seminar is over and back to the daily grind. People love that she does practice what she teaches.

Needless to say, she is consistently switched on, especially when it comes to delivering her message to others from the front of the room, no matter the size of the audience. Classy, brassy and poised, Loren has shared the stage with notable and celebrated luminaries such as Barbara Walters, Tony Robbins, Gary Vaynerchuk, Mike Rowe, Kevin O'Leary, Barbara Corcoran, Erin Brockovich, Campbell Brown, Robert Herjavec, Bear Grylls and Jean Chatsky.

68

"I AM SO HAPPY AND GRATEFUL NOW THAT..."

SHERRY GIDEONS

W hy: In 1997, I had a near-death experience that awakened me to the realization of energy and what we are all capable of. What I learned within this experience was that we all create our reality. With a deep desire to create a better life for me and to help others, I learned how to apply universal principles and practices that would change my life. We are each living, breathing broadcasting system. We can all begin each day with a conscious choice to generate the power of gratitude. We are all that powerful! Most people do not know or realize is gratitude is a feeling, a vibration, or a frequency.

Everything in the universe is energy. Once you know about the role, energy vibrations play in shaping your life. It's possible to consciously raise your frequency by shifting the vibration you are within any present moment. Simply said, shift up to a higher vibration in the present. We can each make a decision that takes us forward and creates a life worth living. Have you ever thought about how highly successful people can create such extraordinary results in their lives? We can direct our day and set intentions with this daily Habit. This Habit sets the tone of the day and sets our biochemistry.

The state called being grateful is what is harmonious with abundance. Gratitude is a much higher vibration, a much deeper resonance. You see, it is the mindset, and the frequency that we operate from that generates and accelerates what shows up in our lives. When we feel from the feelings we would feel if something were already true; what we want shows up that much quicker. Living from gratitude has the power of transforming every area of our lives.

How do you get yourself to live from the Habit of gratitude every day? I learned this morning practice over 15 years ago. It's kind of like the practice of brushing your teeth; we have formed the Habit of brushing our teeth every morning because we know it serves us. This simple practice only takes writing 1-5 things we are grateful for FROM the place we would feel as if it were true now. It also sets our reticular activating system to notice things all day long we can be grateful for. When we develop this practice every day, what begins to show up is fascinating and amazing! The impact of what this practice generates changed my life forever.

THE UN-HABIT: SAYING I DON'T HAVE ENOUGH FREE TIME

Why: Why the Habit of I don't have enough free time is important to break? Everything is the universe is energy. Each of us is vibrating energy from emotion, a feeling, or an emotional charge. For example, we have a thought that I don't have enough free time. This belief creates a feeling, which creates an emotional charge, which becomes a memory, which then reflexively reproduces the emotion of the experience. If we keep thinking about the memory of, I don't have enough free time over and over, the thought, memory, and emotion merge and become one, and we memorize this emotion.

As we repeat this Habit and behavior enough times, the thought is the memory, which is the emotion. Therefore, this becomes a memorized emotion that is an operating program below our conscious awareness. It becomes a way of behaving for us on autopilot that continues to recreate the environment that reflects to us, "I don't have enough free time."

It takes baby steps each day to heal and release thoughts and behaviors that no longer serve us. Each person has similar and different programs running within them, but the more you are present in each day mindful and aware of what is presenting itself for you, you will notice over time how light and easy life is getting. How you feel aligned and one with an abundance of joy, peace, and beauty that is everywhere present in every moment.

Reflect Daily. At the beginning of and at the end of each day, take a minute to reflect on what has shown up today. I like to begin by making a statement: "It's going to be a great day!" In the end, ask yourself, how have you done with practicing being present in only today? In what areas have you struggled? Have you been using your tools that make it easier, like your mindfulness bells and setting intentions? What resistance has come up for you, what self-talk have you been using with yourself? Daily reflection is one of the most useful new Habits for practicing living in the moment.

About Sherry: Sherry Gideons has been a professional bodybuilder and fitness expert. As a Spiritual Teacher, and New Thought leader, she has achieved top honors in the fitness/wellness industry as a thriving coach and motivator. Her background includes more than thirty years of training in the health and wellness industry, as well as training in metaphysics and communications. Today she continues to lead hundreds of clients to do the same physically and mentally to grow their businesses and mindset and has a unique and powerful ability to address life issues from an integrated and comprehensive level. Sherry is also the host of "The High Vibe Nation" Live Show & Podcast".

69

SET YOURSELF APART

LORI A. MCNEIL

W hy: The truth? We are selfish by nature. When the majority of people inside our circles appear or are selfish, it juxtaposes an understanding that the majority of the people we come in contact with are most likely going to be selfish... whether or not they mean to be, or whether or not they realize it. Be different. Only those who regularly strive to be different, go the "extra mile," and do the unexpected is going to be those who set themselves apart.

There are so many benefits that maintaining this mindset and practice will allow us to serve as a ripple effect of positivity for all involved. You will feel good knowing that you have done your very best to achieve the desired results, as will the people you are involved with. You will also build a solid reputation as an entrepreneur as you build your brand, credibility, and thriving client base. People buy from people they like, know, and trust. Going the "extra mile" sets you apart and will push you toward the trust needed to attract the right clients, the perfect collaborations, and many opportunities to succeed.

When this is done with a generous and thankful heart, it will not feel manipulative on either side. Full integrity leads to massive success. A lack of integrity is nothing but more than building a house of cards. Your success will be capped more than you realize at some point, and your congruency will fall.

Never be afraid to put in the extra time, money, and resources needed. You will get your desired results and so much more for all involved... more than can be imagined. Actions are like a boomerang; you will get back what you throw out.

THE UN-HABIT: WATCHING TV DAILY

Why: Limiting your TV watching time is vital to your overall success in so many ways. Limiting and eliminating your TV watching allows for more time to be spent on healthy activities that will increase your quality of life and business productivity. If you want to keep growing and

moving your "Success Needle," you must stay focused on the things that get you closer to your goals, not distract you from them.

When I eliminated watching TV from my life over 25 years ago, I began to fill my time with reading more books and learning more specific ideas where I needed to grow personally & professionally. Additionally, I found that I had more time for research and, overall, more in-depth, more meaningful conversations.

More entrepreneurs need to focus on daily activities that produce the results they are after, not just get wrapped up in "being busy." Every minute of your day needs to be assigned a purpose. Truth is we need to control our time, or it will control us. Time is a precious resource you cannot get back. If you are not intentional with how you spend your time, you will end up wasting more than you realize. Collectively wasted minutes results in missed opportunities that keep you from being the most successful you that you can be.

Learning to incorporate a healthier lifestyle that does not involve watching TV also allows you to become more disciplined with the simple. If you fail to manage simple activities, you will not manage the bigger, more important ones. If you want to grow and become more successful, it must start with how you are managing your time - in easy, simple ways. Only then will you be ready to manage big levels of growth and success.

ABOUT LORI: Have you ever considered what your life or business would look like if you were continually thriving and consistently showing up? Are you? Do you? The results would be creating a legacy that outlives you all while living daily through you. This is my passion. I commit to showing up and helping you walk through whatever is holding you back to thrive and grow.

70

DO SOMETHING YOU LIKE/LOVE EVERYDAY

JOEL TAN

Why: My Mentor's Joel Bauer said to all of us: I had a wish, I wish I know the exact date, day, time to the second where I would depart from the world. So that I would know how to plan my entire life from there on.

No one will ever know how much time we have left on this Earth before we are called to God for coffee. We have statistics that shows that average lifespan of a person on Earth is about 80 odd years. Countless have gone before that. Countless leave after that. Statistics are just an aggregate. They are not exact. What if tomorrow you don't wake up? Isn't it important to start loving every moment of your life?

Whether it is good or bad. Embrace your life and start living it whole. It is important therefore, we have a little perk, a little motivation every single day to keep us motivated every single day.

Even when a bad day happens, we munch on a fat free cookie and think: Tomorrow will be better.

Tomorrow might not be better but we already feel better.

Everyone needs a little motivation to continue living, especially the World we are living is getting harsher and harsher.

Mean world brings out mean people and we do have to deal with people we don't like on a daily basis.

Hence, it is important to motivate yourself every day, with a little indulgence in what you love to do. That will make you feel better immediately, instantaneously and be prepared for a new day tomorrow.

Yes, we will face issues every day. Everyone has to face issues. And it is important when dealing with issues, we continue to motivate ourselves in life long journey.

So, putting things in another perspective. If tomorrow were our last day on Earth, what little indulgence will we want to do?

Life is Harsh, Life is Cruel, but there is no need to be depressed and all that. Life has to continue, while we munch on a little snacks that we like, or a Song that we love.

And Life will go on and on. So do remember to take a little break with a little indulgence.

THE UN-HABIT: STOP PROCRASTINATING

Why: We have a Nation of Procrastinators at hand. People who just procrastinate and do nothing with their life and wasting their precious Time on Earth.

We have about 80 years on Earth. Of which, 20 years will be spent sleeping. Another 20 years on traditional education or growing up.

We literally only have about 20 years or so to do what we like at our peak of our health. Before Mid-life crisis start taking over and we start having a lot of health issues and have to deal with it.

In short, in reality, we only have 20 years where we are at our peak and able to do what we want to do, love to do in the short period of time.

If I managed to jot you a little, I am so happy. Because I have not heard of anyone breaking down the time we have on Earth to such details yet. . .

Yes, let me summarize an average person life for you

- Year 0 – Year 20 --- Growing Up, Finding Directions
- Year 21 – Year 40 – Able to do what we want
- Year 40 – Year 60 – Midlife crisis takes over and we start having some health issues. But we learn to work smarter, not harder, with our life experiences.
- Year 61 – Year 80 – Most are too tired to go full steam at all, and have to adjust our pace of life.

And yes, in reality we have only about 20 years to live our life to our terms and there are tons of people wasting their lives by procrastinating. And before they know it, they are too old to do anything meaningful.

Yes, we do say that we can do anything we want at whatever age. But go and take a 70 year old grandmother to a mall and she will be so tired after that one trip. Imaging you trying to snow ski at the SWISS at age 70. It will be a different story than if you ski at age 20. Stop Procrastinating! Start Living! Start doing things you like today! Don't leave a big bucket list at the end of the day!

About Joel: Imagine, a mentally stronger version of you with potential spiritual upgrade. I would love, absolutely adore to help you build your own internal resilience through my proven process Rediscover the world from different point of view. Reborn with New Knowledge to face the world. One of my recent students Eyangz, is from the Philippines and was facing a cyber bullying. She thank me personally for helping her to resolve her issue.

71

DRESS FOR THE DAY YOU WANT

ASHLEY ARMSTRONG

Why: I think it is fair to say most of us want to be a top performer and increase our productivity, am I right, or am I right? A seemingly simple idea of getting dressed shouldn't be so powerful, but it is, especially if you work from home!

Multiple studies have shown that dressing well increases your performance and self-confidence and gives you the impression that you are better at your job. But how you feel when you wake up can affect your choice of outfit; knowing this, you will need to be intentional with your morning routines. If you purposely dress for the kind of day you want, you will increase your attitude, personality, mood, confidence, performance, and even the way you interact with others.

Those who work from home can easily get stuck in the rut of waking up just before you login online, where you start and end your day in your pajamas with unbrushed hair. This could hurt your sleep patterns, energy, productivity, and success at work. Create a morning routine and structure that you force yourself to stick to. Changing clothes to start your day will TRIGGER a change in your mindset, focus, and performance.

Dressing for the kind of success you want is not only mentally and emotionally beneficial for you to feel good about yourself but also make you achieve more! Scientific American highlights studies proving more formal outfits lead to higher complex thinking and efficiency. For example, wearing the color red encourages athletes to lift a heavier weight or wear a lab coat to make you focus better.

There's no denying it, what you wear matters and you should put effort into dressing for the kind of day you want whether you are in an office or work from home.

THE UN-HABIT: PAUSE YOUR FROWNING

Why: Bad days suck, they happen, and we all experience them, but what if you can change the feeling of a bad day in 60 seconds?

Let's put the idea out the window that a bad experience will ruin your whole day because frankly, that's nonsense. We may not always have control over what happens to us, but we can choose how we feel. I encourage you to think back to a time when something happened, and you allowed it to ruin the rest of your day. How often does that happen to you, and if you had a choice to change it, would you do something about it?

I assume you said yes, so let's do something about it by simply putting on a fake smile. I want you to legitimately reduce your stress and heart rate on purpose by cracking a smile. Smiling supercharges your mood, builds your immunity, lowers stress, and generates more positive emotions, allowing you to be more productive at work, and make more money.

Our bodies release cortisol and endorphins that provide numerous health benefits when we smile. Quickly shift your mood and stay more energized while avoiding burnout.

The brain doesn't know the difference if you are smiling because something made you happy or not; it just notices the trigger from the muscles. For a faster effect, smile at yourself in the mirror because our mirror neurons enable us to copy the behavior we see. Or hang out with children because, on average, they smile 400 times per day, whereas adults only smile 50 times a day.

Smiling is also contagious not just for its looks but also because of the intention and the feeling behind it. Studies show that people who smile appear more likable, which also boosts confidence.

I challenge you to put reminders in your phone, use post-it-notes, and whenever you are walking, feel stressed or anxious to put a smile on your face because you will feel the incredible benefits in 60 seconds. You will no longer need to fake it until you make it because you have created a happy Habit.

ABOUT ASHLEY: Ashley Armstrong aka 'The Hidden Rules Expert', E-Commerce Business Consultant and best-selling Author, helps established product companies successfully navigate the ins and outs of Amazon to scale their businesses to 8-figures and beyond. After building a 7-figure physical product business, Ashley went on to establish Amaz Authority, an eCommerce consulting firm that specialize in navigating Amazon's 'hidden rules' of engagement.

72

REVIEW YOUR PATTERNS WEEKLY

DR. JESSICA BORUSHOK

Why: It doesn't matter if you have one excellent day or one slip up. Accelerating your business, your brand, and yourself involves understanding your patterns; what you typically do both for success and for struggles. When we spend too much time focused on isolated events, we lose sight of the big picture, and we find ourselves lost, or worse, stuck.

Reflect on the last week: What thoughts and feelings held me back? What did I do in response that took me off track? When I'm on a roll, how is my day or environment set up to support me? And finally, who and what are important to me? What qualities or characteristics do I want to bring to every moment?

When we can step back and see the patterns instead of individual moments of procrastination, burnout, and doubt, we notice points where we can break this pattern and fine-tune our responses and skills to best support us. You may tend to react with leaving or dismissive language when you're feeling frustrated that derails productive conversations. The issue isn't this one conversation; it's the pattern of struggling to sit with frustration to decide for yourself the best next move.

Maybe you have a pattern of working nonstop only to have a forced recovery period due to burnout or getting sick. As soon as you are re-energized, you promise yourself you'll put more effort into self-care and then get right back to work. The problem isn't this one enormous project; the issue is a pattern of not paying attention to how much energy is in the tank and refilling it before it gets empty.

Or maybe you regularly talk down to yourself, obsess over what you "should" be doing, and beat yourself up over minor mistakes to the point where even if you succeed, it's difficult to celebrate without that mean mental bully chiming in. The concern isn't that one slip up; the issue is a pattern of believing negative self-talk is the best motivator (it isn't). When you can recognize this consistent pattern, you can begin to identify how to change it: "notice when I'm talking to myself like that and practice using self-compassion in its place."

Learning to see the patterns in my behavior that persist over days and weeks and months was the biggest game-changer in supercharging my progress. Instead of feeling stuck or obsessing over one specific scenario, it gave me the insight into knowing what needed to change.

The Un-Habit: Attempt to Fix Other People

Why: "If only he just did what I told him, we wouldn't be in this situation."

In my work with clients, I often notice an instinct to focus on what others are saying. We can spend an incredible amount of time and energy attempting to control factors outside of ourselves that frankly, we have no control over.

Why do we do this? Because it's easier to focus on others than ourselves.

Attempting to fix, correct, influence, or otherwise control other people is a fast trip to frustration and disappointment. We only have control over two things: what we say and what we do at this moment, right now. And even that isn't 100%. Sometimes thoughts or feelings overwhelm us, and we say something we shouldn't have or procrastinate on a task that needs to get done in favor of scrolling through social media.

If you can acknowledge that you can't control what others do, it can free you to focus your energy on what is within your control. Over time, you'll find that you are in a better physical, mental, and emotional state to adapt to whatever life throws your way. While letting go of fixing or managing others may initially appear like you have less control, it gives you more control in the long run.

When you aren't putting your precious hours towards a losing battle, you can speed up your progress. This happens because you are acknowledging your reality and adjusting accordingly.

Instead of pretending that if you find the right tool or way to describe a situation, others will naturally fall in line. You can direct that effort to yourself and use your time to improve your assertiveness skills, develop strategies for setting firmer boundaries, and noticing who provides value in your life.

These actions do help to nudge or influence others slightly. It's not an absolute win, but it increases your odds. So let go of the need to control everything because you can't and never will. Instead, stay focused on what you can do to transform your life.

About Dr. Jessica: Dr. Jessica Borushok, The Busy Mind Psychologist, helps busy minds get unstuck, out of their own way, and back to their best selves. An expert in Acceptance and Commitment Therapy (ACT), Dr, Jessica teaches productive procrastinators, overwhelmed high-achievers, recovering perfectionists, and self-proclaimed "control freaks" how to let go of perceived control to take back real power over their lives. Through her popular course, Busy Mind Reboot, she shares the mind-freeing formula to transform your relationship with your thoughts and optimize your world in 30 days.

73

WORK WHEN YOU DO YOUR BEST WORK

WHITNIE WILEY

Why: We live in a society that is continually telling us what we should do, be, and have. The never-ending pressure that comes from trying to meet other people's expectations can be damaging to our psyche and confidence, leading to a negative impact on our ability to do our best work.

Something that helps is knowing when to say no to requests or expectations that cause us to deliver less than our best. Saying no is not an excuse, nor is it the same as avoiding action in an attempt at perfection. Instead, this is about building the Habit of self-awareness about how and when we do our best work and to schedule our activities around that time frame.

I am best early in the day. I wake up early, follow my morning routine, set me up for success for the day, and then move into work mode. When I need to think analytically or creatively, I know those activities should be scheduled in the morning and early afternoon. If I am trying to do these things late in the day, I have a harder time focusing and bringing my "A" game.

Some people, however, are better working later in the day and into the evening. In the end, it doesn't matter. Morning person or a night owl, the key to success is knowing when you are at your best and do the work that matters most then. The bottom line is to make time during your prime times for the things you want and need to bring your best to.

While you cannot control the scheduling of every activity, those things you can control or manage make it a priority. One approach to help may include taking a power nap in the middle of the day to give yourself an extra boost to propel you through the evening and night hours.

As an entrepreneur who is in charge of your daily schedule think through when you are at your best, schedule those tasks that require your brainpower and creativity for the hours when you work best and put those things such as signing checks and deleting emails (if you haven't already delegated) to the time of day when you are not required to give everything you've got.

THE UN-HABIT: FITTING INTO SOMEONE ELSE'S MOLD

Why: Why did you become an entrepreneur? No doubt, it wasn't that you could play by other people's rules and meet their expectations. So why are you doing things the way other people are doing them? Looking at their rulebook for a play by play?

Don't get me wrong, I'm not saying don't learn from other people and model their success strategies, but when it comes to implementation, you are unique with your flavor and style. That means as you implement, speak, write, network, etc. you do you. Bring your authentic self to bear to every deal and interaction. You cannot be someone else, so don't try. It's one thing to use a strategy; it's a whole other thing to steal a personality.

If your clients and customers want to work with the other dude, they wouldn't be looking to work with you. As entrepreneurs, we spend lots of time thinking and talking through our ideal client avatars, value propositions, and the like. It would be a huge waste of time to figure all that out then serve up a poor replication of some other service provider.

If your ideal client is perfect for you, ask yourself if you are perfect for your ideal client? And if that is the case, then the only person who can provide for them the uniqueness you own is you.

Take the time to learn. Learn from the best. Analyze what they are saying and doing, then take what makes sense for you and implement it in the way only you can. Love your clients and customers as your authentic self, and you will begin to create the raving fans who would not settle for a second rate you.

Instead of copying others' style and flair, become the best you with the best product or service you can offer and watch how others will begin to imitate what you are doing. Each of our molds is broken the day we are born, so don't waste your time trying to fit into the busted mold of someone else.

About Whitnie: Whitnie Wiley is the founder and chief evolution officer (CEO) of Shifting Into Action (SIA), a coach, consultant, author, speaker and trainer.

As the premier next stage coach, Whitnie has over 25 years of experience coaching in the areas of dream and goal achieving, career management and transition, and leadership development. She helps new and aspiring leaders build and manage careers that feed their souls, use their talents and gifts, and finance the lives of their dreams through training programs and retreats, 1-on-1 and group coaching. Additionally, she provides consulting and coaching services to organizations relating to succession management, leadership development and training, human resources and talent development.

74

READ EVERY DAY

GARY LOCKWOOD

Why: I'm a prolific reader. I go to bed reading. I read on a tablet now, but I did read books for years.

I've been an avid reader since the time I was a child. I had a German uncle, who thought I was a smart kid and would bring me books all the time. I would not care about the subject matter, as long as it's a good read. I would read fantasy, fiction, drama, non-fiction, really anything. I read.

Today, I am blessed with a brilliant wife. I mean incredibly bright, who kind of picks my reading material for me, because she knows a lot about my personality.

Sometimes I'll read a book about sports. On occasion, I'll read fiction, and I'll read mystery.

Reading is so important because it exercises your mind while at the same time entertaining you. The payoff goes well beyond the exercise and entertainment. Being well-read opens up your creativity. It is a tool that lets you tap into you much more.

Lastly, being well-read has social benefits. A well-read person can speak to anyone because of the vast and diverse knowledge you have acquired. This is a priceless benefit.

THE UN-HABIT: USING DRUGS TO TRY TO FIND INSPIRATION AND HAPPINESS

Why: I can't even tell you why I started using drugs. It could be just the time I grew up in. It was the thing to do. It was a time where people were using drugs to expand their minds and creativity. But I think that was just an excuse. It's a bunch of bull sh@t.

When I quit, it was the happiest time of my life. I was around 50. So I'm 83, and drug-free. I don't even have one drink a week.

Being mentally bright and clear is the most beautiful thing in the world. Life is so beautiful, and I think we want to experiences all of it without the shade of some substance that alters its beautiful reality.

ABOUT GARY: Gary Lockwood is an American actor. He is known for his roles in the film 2001: A Space Odyssey, and in the Star Trek pilot episode "Where No Man Has Gone Before." Early films in his career include Splendor in the Grass with Natalie Wood and Warren Beatty, The Magic Sword with Basil Rathbone, two films with his friend Elvis Presley, Model Shop with Anouk Aimee, and R.P.M. with Anthony Quinn and Ann Margret. Television show appearances include The Lieutenant, Perry Mason, Gunsmoke, Night Gallery, Mission: Impossible, The Six Million Dollar Man, The Bionic Woman, Simon & Simon, and Murder, She Wrote.

75

WEARING FLOWERS

SAMANTHA LOCKWOOD

Why: While my Habit of wearing a flower may not be practical to all entrepreneurs. I suggest you stop and smell the roses as they say. I have found that we all get so caught up in the latest technologies, making more money, and forget the simple pleasures in life. My quest to keep that alive took me to Hawaii, where I have lived for many years.

As I learned from my mom and dad, entrepreneurship is more a state of mind, a curiosity that many people who "go to a job" never experience. It comes with risks, but so does a life well lived!

By nature, flowers are beautiful. Scientifically it is proven that flowers make us happier. They help us produce dopamine, serotonin, and other "happy good vibes" chemicals that stimulate us to be more positive, relaxed, and joyful. Further research has proven that wearing flowers "elicits positive emotions and fosters positive relationships" amongst people.

My grandmother suggested to me many years ago, when I was working as a waitress to wear a flower in my hair and crazy, my tips doubled... which helped as a struggling actress in LA. This little flower behind my ear became this talking piece, and it just worked.

But there was a slight problem, after 20-30 minutes, the flower in my hair wilted and died. So I came up with the idea that an earring made like a vase that contained water could keep my flower fresh for hours... and it worked. I created the company Fluerings. We are now sold around the world and have earrings AND necklaces. We hear from people everywhere that this is the best piece of jewelry they own, most versatile and ideal for women of ALL ages. So it turns out that now you can wear and enjoy fresh flowers all day long.

Flowers make me feel more feminine and empowered. The most exciting part is the reaction from others. It makes people's day and connects us with nature.

My vision is to see women and flowers, God's 2 most beautiful creations, together.

THE UN-HABIT: NOT BELIEVING IN YOURSELF

Why: As the daughter of 2 well-known actors, finding your own identity can be challenging. My parents have always been stars in their jobs, my father being a famous sci-fi icon Gary Lockwood and my mother, Denise DuBarry, being an actress turned infomercial mogul. It was hard to find my voice in any area because they were always right. Dad still has an opinion about what jobs I should take or not take, and my mom always had this competitive edge, which sometimes stifled me from even having my own opinion because "she was always right." I have struggled a lot to find my voice because I felt I had to fight to be heard.

It's also not easy on pretty girls in Hollywood because they don't want your opinion most of the time; it's just about "how hot is she." Having a voice is something I developed through painting, through my creations, and my life choices. My very way of life is my voice. I have chosen to live close to nature, close to friends who care. I realize that whatever the world thinks is their own opinion, and my voice doesn't need to be heard by everyone because, honestly, not everyone matters in my life. The people who care for me and who I care for are the ones who matter most. People in your famous fan club are not always going to care like the ones who are really in your life... those are the ones who matter most to me. The roles I choose, the relationships I choose ... my choices are my voice.

Everything is possible if you put your mind to it and decide to make it happen. When I first had the idea for my jewelry line, people didn't understand the concept, and some even ridiculed me.

Now I have managed to create gorgeous, functional, lightweight jewelry that keeps flowers fresh for hours and hours, and I've managed to create a successful business and ship them to customers or all over the world.

About Samantha: Actress Samantha Lockwood is the Designer & founder of Fleurings vase jewelry line that holds water and keeps flowers fresh. The "eco-fabulous must-have necklace" by GENLUX Magazine. Celebrity wedding gifts for the Bridal Party at Seth Rogen's and Lauren Miller Rogen's wedding and soul surfer Bethany Hamilton's wedding in Hawaii. Fleurings have been featured in press all over Japan, Milan, and the United States. She was first exposed to the arts by her parents – her father is the veteran actor sci-fi icon Gary Lockwood of '2001: A Space Odyssey'. Her mother is a successful actress and entrepreneur Denise DuBarry.

Recently, she played bad girl "Cindy Patterson" in Hawaii Five-o's Season 6 premiere episode. Many also may have seen her in the top 10 CMY music video, "Goodbyes Made You Mine," as J.T. Hodges' love interest.

76

LIVE IN YOUR PURPOSE EVERY DAY

DR. TRACIE HINES LASHLEY

Why: "We are what we repeatedly do. EXCELLENCE, then, is not an act but a Habit." ~Aristotle

Focus energy DAILY on your passion (what) to live in your purpose (why). God only gave your purpose to YOU. Do not try to live in someone else's purpose, because it is theirs, not yours. We should evaluate our alignment of daily activities with our purpose. When I was young, I had a passion for making a difference in other people's lives by inspiring, equipping, and growing them. I wanted my impact to reach millions of people around the world. If I had listened to other people or focused on being in their shadow, you would not be reading my words today. You see... I had a dream and vision to make a mountain out of a molehill even when people told me that I was crazy.

My purpose in life is to TRANSFORM LIVES. How could I do that if I sit and settle in my circumstance and not align my actions and goals within my purpose? When you walk in your purpose, everything that you do will seem easy. You may overthink things due to ease, but this could mean that you are walking in your purpose. Years of self-doubt and overthinking caused a delay in fulfilling my purpose. One of the first and hardest steps for me was to let go of attachments to past results. I had to stop keeping score against myself and start approaching goal achievement with a rear view mirror approach. My past results do not equal my future potential. I am aware that I have infinite potential, and I know that MY PAST WILL NEVER CONTROL MY FUTURE!!!

The first thing you must consider when seeking your purpose is to find out the things that make your heart sing. What are the reasons for this? What is your motivation? When you find them, think about the things that you love to do. Once you discover your "what," merge it with your "why" and move forward. There is no better place to be than working for yourself in a field where it does not feel like work. When I work on my business, time flies, and I feel like I can continue for hours and never get tired. That my friend is PASSION & PURPOSE living in HARMONY!!!

Do NOT die without the world witnessing your dreams coming true. If it DOES NOT align with your purpose, SAY NO. You owe it to yourself and your legacy.

THE UN-HABIT: KEEP DOING THINGS ALONE

Why: Don't allow negative and toxic energy to rent your space. Raise the rent and kick them out.

After you finalize your why (purpose), assess your immediate circle. Can the people around you help fulfill your vision (purpose + dreams)? Do the people around you support you in ways to elevate your growth and success? So many people believe that "I am the business." With this mindset, business owners fail within the first 2-5 years. No one is self-made or reaches success alone. You need a tribe around you to allow you to stop working "in the business" and work "on the business." What does this mean? Duties that do not align with your purpose and passion should be delegated or contracted out to others. When you calculate the time that it takes for you to do the smaller "minimum wage" job or tasks that will take you hours to complete (outside of your expertise), you are losing thousands or even millions of dollars. These functions take you away from developing programs or processes that are urgent for your business to thrive.

"Networking is an essential part of building wealth." ~ Armstrong Williams

Building a tribe can elevate your business to unimaginable heights. When you network with others, the energy in that space can change the dynamics of your team and business. Networking is a great way to build a team of excellence. The team you build should have expertise in various industries. When this happens, you can lean on individuals' skillsets and expertise. I remember when I first started on my entrepreneurial journey. I thought that I needed to be all things for every aspect of my business. Oh, was I wrong... The burnout was serious and draining. If you want the life sucked out of you, keep doing things alone. If you're going to get your life back, start building a network of people around to collaborate.

Get into the Habit of allowing others to shine in your purpose while elevating them simultaneously.

About Dr. Tracie: After being raised underprivileged and becoming a single mother of 2, Dr. Tracie Hines Lashley married an Army soldier who deployed to Afghanistan, Iraq, and Korea 11 times during his 20 years of service. She was forced to raise 3 of their 5 children essentially alone. As a working mother and college student for 10 years, she had to find a sense of balance while juggling her children's activities and not losing herself in the process. She now helps working mothers and women in leadership positions harmonize their life while creating dynamic and productive teams at home and work.

77

YOGA BEFORE BED

CALEB KOKE

Why: Yoga is a simple practice that allows self connection.

Most entrepreneurs feel their brain is always going full speed ahead, and I am no exception.

However, unlike most people I was diagnosed as a young child with SPD, Sensory Processing Disorder also known as Sensory Integration Dysfunction. This affects less than 5% of the population and is most commonly observed in children who are gifted, those with ADHD and those with Autism.

Bottom line, for me to "turn off" the thinking part of my brain is very challenging. BUT it can be done and that is where Yoga before bed comes in.

As wonderfully created human beings with multi-faceted dimensions, a yoga practice enables everyone at their own pace to explore different dimensions.

Although there are many dimensions, the 3 dimensions I want to focus on are:

1. Physical
2. Mental
3. Spiritual

Our bodies are physical marvels and a yoga practice gives your physical body a chance to rebalance. When I stretch my body, it signals any tightness or soreness. This is an indicator that tells me something was out of balance that day. Maybe I was sitting too long, or maybe I was leaning more to one side. Regardless it allows me to observe the imbalance and make a mental note, which leads us to the second dimension.

It is at this point, that I am also letting my mind wind down. I achieve this by focusing on my breath, and taking notes!...What?...Yes, you read that correctly: taking notes. This was a game-changer for me to form as part of this Habit. I keep a notepad within reach and any thought, idea, solution or question that comes up, I jot it down. I often end my note taking session with a prayer for someone in need, or a reminder to send a complimentary message to a friend, or journal a gratitude. This is where the mental cleansing occurs. I stretch until there is mental silence which leads us to the spiritual dimension...

When the body is relaxed and the mind is calm, your spirit is at peace. Sometimes answers and solutions will "appear" in this theta state. This is your spirit's dimension expressing itself, and that is my signal for bedtime.

Whether or not you have tried yoga before, I encourage you to make an effort to include yoga, or a form of it into your daily routine. There are many wonderful benefits to yoga and if you were to only experience one benefit I promise it will be worth it.

THE UN-HABIT: STOP SAYING "CAN'T" AND TAKE BACK YOUR POWER

Why: The word can't is rarely used accurately.

I would estimate that most of the time people improperly use the word "can't" in their communication.

For example, has your best friend ever asked you to catch a movie the night of and you replied, "I can't go."?

The truth is you CAN go to the movie, but you are choosing not too. But by using the word "can't" you are removing all the power of your choice.

Without the power of choice, your decision making ability appears weak on a subconscious level to your friend. This "catching a movie" scenario may only have minimal stakes, but in business when dealing with clients, contracts, services, products or experiences, the stakes are often higher because your professional reputation and brand is on the line.

Let's use another example with higher stakes; we'll use the question, "Will you be able to reduce your price?"

Because business is fluid and circumstances are always changing, this is a question that I don't think is asked enough, but when it is, I frequently hear or overhear the answer, "I can't".

The answer "I can't" is a powerless excuse. Both the seller and the buyer know it's possible to reduce the price, but now the seller sounds powerless.

Let's look at some alternative empowering responses the seller could use in the following examples.

Buyer: "Will you be able to reduce your price?"

Seller: "No, I won't be able to."

This response tells the listener, you can, but you are choosing not to. The buyer may not appreciate the answer, but the buyer will recognize and respect that you have the decision making ability. It may or may not be warranted to share the sellers reasons why they "won't be able to", however, this is a case by case basis. Let's look at another example:

Buyer: "Will you be able to reduce your price?"

Seller: "It's possible and this is how."

This response shows that the seller is open minded, creative and solution oriented.

I would encourage you to pay more attention to the language you use and replace "I can't" with powerful phrases based on truth.

It may be difficult in the beginning, but overtime you will become more aware of the words you use and the power, or lack of power, behind them.

About Caleb: If you want to improve how people perceive their experience with you, your organization and your business, then contact me for a custom user experience (UX) audit followed with one-on-one consulting.

As an entrepreneur who specializes in the details, my one-on-one consulting is designed to provide clients with a straightforward guide of customized action items to achieve success. With a satisfaction guarantee, why wait? (Additionally, 501(c)3 organizations may be eligible for services pro bono, please inquire.)

Today is the best time to begin improving how the world interprets you, your organization and your business.

78

MASTERING THE MUNDANE

JEFF MEADOR

Why: A number of years ago I attended a concert of one of my favorite guitar players on the planet. I was so excited and the anticipation grew every day as the concert grew closer. There was one song in particular that I was looking forward to hearing. It was hands down my favorite song he had ever recorded. His 1979 release had gone to No. 4 in the U.S. charts. The song was fun, had great lyrics and one of the best guitar solos ever recorded. The night of the concert came and thirty minutes into the concert the song started. The second he started playing the song I knew that intro and I knew my moment had come. He started singing the song and my heart dropped. What was he doing? This is NOT how the song had been recorded. The guitar solo was one of the greatest of all time and this was NOT it! This is NOT what I had paid good money to hear.

The fact is the artist lost sight the concert was not supposed to be about him. It was supposed to be about the fans. Give the fans what THEY want! Why did he change this GREAT song? The answer is very simple. After playing this song for over thirty years at countless concerts and different venues, he had become bored with it and was trying to make it interesting for himself.

This is a GREAT lesson for ALL entrepreneurs to learn. This is especially true in network marketing. When you are in business and have and/or find a system that works, stay with the system! In the words on one of my mentors who is one of the greatest network marketers of all time you have to MASTER THE MUNDANE! What does that mean? If you're in sales, for instance, then one of the things you are going to do is tell a story. It's important that you find one or two great stories that will create an emotion in your listeners that will in effect create a bond between you and them. When you find that story you want to stick with it for at least a year. The problem will then become that you will start to get bored of telling that same story over and over. I guarantee you will become tired of your story way before the people listening to it ever does.

If you are partnered with a network marketing company they have a system laid out to show you how to be successful with their product or service. IF you are going to be successful then you need to work the system. Day in and day out. The same thing over and over. Different people. Same thing. Different people. Same thing. Different people. Same thing. Once you understand that by sticking with the system, keeping your energy and enthusiasm up and doing the same things over and over you will see your business take off in ways you never imagined!

THE UN-HABIT: DON'T PROCRASTINATE

Why: Procrastination is the No. 1 reason why entrepreneurs fail! This is the No. 1 reason why network marketers fail! This is the No. 1 reason why anyone in business does not succeed. We put things off and we always have perfectly logical reasons for doing so. The reason I hear the most is that people are waiting until everything is perfect. They want everything to be ready to go. They are trying to make sure all systems are in place and when they launch it's going to take off like a rocket! The second reason and almost tied with the first is wanting to know everything about your product. Wanting to have the knowledge to be able to answer anyone and everyone's questions about your product or service. Wanting to be seen as the expert with all the confidence, with all the enthusiasm and with all the answers. My answer to that .... GET STARTED NOW! Don't wait another day.

As a very successful network marketer, I have learned that ACTIVITY FIXES EVERYTHING! You need to understand that you can't say the wrong thing to the right person no more than you can say the right thing to the wrong person. If someone has no interest in what you have to offer then nothing you say or do is going to result in a sale. If someone sees the value in what you have, then even if you "mess up" there is a good chance you'll still get them to make a purchase.

Make it a point every morning to ask yourself "What are the three things I'm going to do today that will move my business forward?" Write those things down on a notepad and show it to someone who will help to keep you accountable. THEN DO THE THINGS ON YOUR LIST! If you start with three things and become consistent at doing them, you will increase your business. It doesn't matter that everything is in place or that you know everything. If you're in a good network marketing company then you will have all the support and resources you need to be successful right at your fingertips. Do not hesitate. Do NOT procrastinate. Success is right around your corner!

About Jeff: Jeff Meador is an author, speaker, musician, singer/songwriter, world traveler, former youth pastor, father of three children and husband of Donna Sparaco Meador.

79

USE FEAR AS FRESH ENERGY

KRYSTYLLE RICHARDSON

Why: Can we just be honest for a moment? We all have fears even if it is at a minute level, we have them. I know that I do. The question is how will we deal with them on a daily basis. Another question might be how will they deal with us. This is where the word Habit comes in.

I sometimes find myself in a rut in my mind. I think that I'm on a path to do one thing and then it turns into something else. This does not always have to do with a lack of focus but more related to being open to be used by God based on his Divine will. Now I know everyone is not a Christian but the analogy and the realness of what I'm about to say still holds true. Most of us all have things that we've set out to do in life. We all have times where those things are interrupted. Right? We all have times where there's fear that creeps in due to us being overly anxious about the unknown or due to the fact that we know what is about the to come. Either way fear is something that is real that we all deal with. It is my hope that this chapter helps you find ways of repurposing your fear to help you versus block you. For some, being fearful has become a Habit. Is that you? Being an entrepreneur CAN be fearful it we allow it to be. It can also be exciting if we mandate it in our minds.

As entrepreneurs there's going to be things that continue to come up. Question is how are we going to deal with them. The other question is how are we going to define success. We should always have a definition of success. This helps to focus us and lessen the control of potential fear. Once we let fear control us, we have allowed it to take over our future, which means we will always continue to play small. So let's replace fear with my definition which is Fresh Energy Awaiting Reset. Let us reset our minds as entrepreneurs but also reset our definition of success without fear. Let us reset and JUMP into our greatness. Fear is a mind-chain. Don't let it hold onto you and don't hold onto it.

THE UN-HABIT: STOP GIVEN IN TO SELF HATE AND THUS SELF SABOTAGE

Why: Entrepreneurs, let's undo some patterns and thus undo some Habits.

As I thought about the word Habit, I also thought about the word routine and pattern. Here is my definition of all 3 and how they relate. A routine is something that you SET OUT to do. A Habit is something that you have actually DONE over and over. A pattern is something that is MANIFESTED based on our Habits and our routines.

So many times in our life we find ourselves doing the same things over and over even though we know it does not benefit our lives. Patterns emerge. This affects our success. Sometimes these patterns are carried down from generation to generation. In a study/survey I conducted, it was very clear that we all have different definitions of success. Our success is defined by our current circumstances and if we have had our basic needs met. Maslow's hierarchy of needs is real. When those needs are not met based on where we are in our lives one area may take higher precedence than another. So again our definition of success is affected by our needs, and yes our fears.

For instance with me, I had to come to a place in life where I used my definition and reaction to fear over and over again each day due to the PTSD of being bullied. I had to use it so that it became a Habit in my life to use fear as <u>F</u>resh <u>E</u>nergy <u>A</u>waiting <u>R</u>eset. As we think about the word "excitement" and the word "fear", our bodies basically handle both in the same way. Whether it is Serotonin, dopamine, oxytocin, and endorphins or maybe even adrenaline, there is a lot that is going on inside of our bodies AND with our emotions. What I do is find a way to <u>R</u>eset that energy to <u>make it</u> excitement instead. Sometimes that means I just need to go to my car or in any private place and just give myself a good talking to and go into prayer. All I am saying is that the more we accept ourselves and know how to develop good Habits and Un-Habits, the better life will be, the better our business will be, and the sooner we can be introduced to our successful future selves. Say I ACCEPT ME, Say NO FEAR, Say BETTER PATTERNS BETTER Habits BETTER LIFE.

About Krystylle: Krystylle loves seeing people become better versions of themselves mentally, physically, spiritually, financially, emotionally and more. She lives and breathes for this in her marriage, her children, friends, family, and clients. She is an International Speaker-the Global World Civility Ambassador of Innovation-Leadership and Mindset Accountability Coach-International Best-Selling Author-Radio Show Host-Red Carpet Interviewer-Philanthropist-Missionary-Wife and Mother of 2 young adult girls. Her radio show has been heard throughout almost 40 countries and she has taught and spoken in 25 countries and counting. She is hyper-focused on helping you be a better you! She believes that using our innovative minds, creativity, and self-expression, we then allow the world to experience our authentic selves. Krystylle believes that "Living out loud is non-negotiable."

80

MAKE SPACE FOR THE MAGIC TO HAPPEN!

MEL MASON

Why: We are all born connected to Source/Spirit, and we all come into this life with the same access to the Divine flow of abundance. If you can imagine it, there is a wide-open channel of Source energy flowing through us. Visualize a big water pipe that comes off the street and connects to your house.

That pipe is open and flowing when we are born, but what happens is as we grow up, we experience traumas and losses in our lives. As that occurs, because we don't know how to process those events, we begin to accumulate repressed emotions, resentments, fears, and limiting beliefs along the way. When we do that, those things act as sludge in the pipe and start to block the flow of abundance in our lives.

As the sludge accumulates and restricts access to the Divine flow of abundance, we experience it as a lack in our lives. Maybe we're not making the money we want to make. Perhaps we can't seem to feel happy. Perhaps we struggle with drug addiction or drinking too much alcohol. Maybe we keep attracting unhealthy partners that keep us small.

The repressed emotions, resentments, fears, and limiting beliefs only accumulate because we don't bring our attention to them. Quite frankly, we avoid them because they are uncomfortable!

But I have a secret for you. All you need to do is being willing to make space for the magic to happen, and your life will radically change! What I mean by that is this: The outside is a mirror of the inside. The Principle of Correspondence states, "As above, so below" or "As within, so without." So, all you need to do is change from the inside out for amazing things to start happening in your life.

> Be the change you wish to see
>
> — GANDHI

Making space for the magic to happen is learning to show up and bring your presence to your life. Take time each day to close your eyes and tune into what you're feeling in your body. When you do this, just be a witness to your experience. Don't try to change anything. Observe your experience without judgment.

When you can do this for even just a moment, you begin to make space for the magic to happen. You'll start to notice that you begin to experience more happiness and abundance in your life, and you'll let go of things that no longer serve you.

THE UN-HABIT: DON'T BITE OFF MORE THAN YOU CAN CHEW

Why: "The journey of a thousand miles begins with a single step." When we look at trying to walk a thousand miles all at once, it can feel overwhelming. So, can trying to tackle a project like decluttering the entire garage or your closet all in one sitting!

When we try to attack the whole project and do it all in one big bite, we often become paralyzed and frustrated. When that happens, we usually wind up starting the project, but really get nothing accomplished and then start beating ourselves up for failing to follow through and finish what we set out to do.

What we need to do is start small. Do it in bite-sized chunks. Take decluttering a garage as an example. Instead of looking at the whole garage, begin in one of the corners of the garage and work your way around dealing with one square foot at a time. Look at what's in that one square foot of space and only deal with that stuff. Make your decisions about what you are keeping and what you're letting go starting a pile for donation and a pile for keep. Once you've finished one square foot, move onto the next square foot and the next square foot, and before you know it, you've completed the entire garage and can park your car in there!

Tackling the project in bite-sized chunks begins to give you confidence and a sense of accomplishment because you were able to finish what you started. And that sense of accomplishment and confidence makes you want to do more. It also makes it easy to stop and come back later to finish without having a huge mess to deal with.

That's why it's so important not to bite off more than you can chew!

About Mel: Mel Mason is The Clutter Expert and she created a step-by-step program for getting free from clutter once and for all. Her system takes the stress and overwhelm out of getting organized and has been known to not only clear the clutter at the root but make the process fun and enjoyable. Her step-by-step method empowers you to start tackling the clutter that has accumulated over the years, one small chunk at a time and teaches you the secret to keeping it from coming back.

81

ALWAYS BE OPEN

AMY ZEAL

Why: The best Habit I could impart on someone is to always be open because the fact is you just never know. I never know where my next lead or client will come from. I never know where or how my next idea or project will develop. I never know who will become a potential partner or investor in something I am doing. So I have to stay open. This means being completely non judgmental about a person, place or thing. This means attending the networking event. This means taking the suggestion by a person more qualified than me even though I may not see the reason behind it. Being open of course though isn't the same as saying "Yes" to everything and everybody, That's a different story. You have to discriminate when it comes to saying yes and no. We do need boundaries and have to protect our time. But to be open is to be present and available to what the universe may bring into our world.

The opposite is being closed. Being closed doesn't give someone an opportunity to speak and share what they have to say. Being closed pre judges someone before they speak. Being closed will shut down the idea before they have all the details. Being closed doesn't take suggestions. Being closed won't attend the event. Being closed keeps our worlds and our minds very small. Being closed isn't inviting any goodness into the game and only hinders our progress.

Being open is saying yes to possibilities. Being open makes us available for expansion. Being open is saying yes to growth and positive change. If you really want to make it as an entrepreneur stay open and you will get much further faster than you ever thought possible.

THE UN-HABIT: NEGATIVE SELF-TALK

Why: Negative self-talk is poison, this is an absolute must not. We must speak positively to ourselves at all times. Our lives are created by what is between our ears. If there is one thing that should be done on a regular basis it's positive self-talk and regular self-development.

I had a lot of disempowering beliefs I had to get rid of. They were killing me, my productivity, my happiness, and my motivation. So how does someone get rid of them? What I did was first brought the limiting beliefs to light. I went to a seminar with a big time coach who did several processes to uncover what your limiting beliefs were. Our subconscious mind is extremely powerful. I discovered what three of my limiting beliefs were. We then did a new process to replace the old beliefs with the new ones. Was I fixed? Not yet because once is NEVER enough. Repetition is the mother of all skill. I needed to do something with these new beliefs I had. I was too nervous the old ones would come back.

So I created a new morning routine for myself. I would make my coffee, do some push ups, play some calming music and get my notebook out and start writing. I would write over and over again all the way down the entire page my new beliefs. I did this every day. This way I began to reprogram my subconscious mind to think in this new positive way so if the old beliefs came crawling back there was too much new energy now in the way to block the old thoughts.

I also began doing incantations. I would say out loud these new beliefs over and over again. This drowned out any old ideas and only left the new positive affirmations. Eventually over time I began feeling better and happier. I shifted my thinking from old to new and my life began to reflect the new positive affirmations I brought fourth.

What this will do for your life is you will become a new person. You will think differently. You will be stronger, happier and wiser. The quality of our life is the quality of our thoughts. Think positive and be positive and you will have a happy beautiful life.

ABOUT AMY: Amy Zeal is a professional health and fitness coach. She has been in the fitness and wellness industry for over two decades. She has competed in seven fitness competitions and won two, one being the 2016 Ms. Bikini America Classic division in Muscle Mania's Fitness Universe World Competition. Amy's mission is to help others understand the importance of health and fitness and guide them to become the best versions of themselves. Coming from a professional Broadway dancing background, Amy understands the pitfalls of always being under pressure to lose weight. She believes in teaching people to love themselves and strive for a happy and balanced lifestyle.

82

COMMIT TO COMMITMENT

SHAWNTE KINNEY

Why: What would you do to bring your dream to life? Whatever that action is, a commitment will be a significant contributing factor. But a commitment to what?

When you make the promise to marry, you stand before God and family and make vows. You make promises to be loyal, faithful, loving, and committed until death. After the joyful celebration and the fabulous honeymoon, you enter life together as one slaying any obstacles that you encounter and enduring any hardships because you took vows. You commit to honor those vows to one another and your family.

Marry yourself to your commitments

Commit yourself to your word and then commit to those commitments and let nothing stand between you and your vow.

Just like in marriage, situations will arise that may require you to pivot, which is ok. The goal may change, the vision may evolve, and the plan may need to be adjusted. But all of them are a part of you, so if you commit to you, the vision, the idea, and the goal will be the fruit of your dream and union to yourself. Be willing to make the necessary adjustments, but stay faithful to your commitment.

There will be days when it will be hard, and you will be tempted to quit. But remember the wedding and remember the emotion you had when you said yes. Remember your why. To see your dream come to life, you must cultivate the Habit of committing to the commitment that you made to build. You must develop the Habit of committing yourself to the process even when your expectations are not visible. When you cultivate this Habit of always keeping the promises you make to yourself, you build bridges of trust with yourself that span the gap of understanding.

The saddest thing in the world is to show up for everyone else and fail to show up for yourself. So, as you say yes to your dream to be an entrepreneur, remember to commit. And as with any relationship, success depends on you being committed to what you said you would do long after the mood you said it in has left.

The Un-Habit: Stop believing there is not enough time

Why: There is never enough time, such a trendy statement. Every person over the age of 13 at one point in their life has been guilty of declaring this. Interestingly, we have said it or heard it so often we have given life to this belief. But what if we are wrong? What if there is enough time to accomplish everything that we need to accomplish? What if the problem is not that there isn't enough time, but instead we spend our time giving attention to things that are not meant for that day or for that time?

I am sure you are familiar with Ecclesiastes and King Solomon's proclamation that there is a time for everything and every activity. If time was created for man, and the man was not created for a time, why is our enemy time? Because we spend time, wasting time. Every second is an investment, so our time is a primary key in determining if we are spending wisely. Prioritizing tasks is a necessary and deciding factor as you spend time. However, like life, it is easy to mismanage time. Spending countless hours on things that do not bring value or great benefit is wasted time. Then, you finally get focused enough to give attention to the necessary tasks, but the day is over. As a result, your actions provide truth to the statement that there is not enough time. But each day holds enough time to do what the day is meant to do. Trying to do more than what is necessary for the day is a wasted investment, and giving attention to what is not required for the day is a wasted investment.

As long as you give dedicated concentrated attention to a thing, it stays alive and continues in power; but if you stop watering it, it withers and dies. So, make a Habit of stop believing that there is not enough time to do what you need to do. Instead, be at work on things that will serve you, remembering you have been given enough time each day to do the tasks for that day. Make a Habit of not wasting your time.

About Shawnte: Shawnte Kinney is an Influencer who teaches women how to punch. Through her training and her transformation, she gives women the keys to empower themselves, embrace transition and make the changes necessary to transform and bear fruit in their lives.

83

USE WORDS THAT EMPOWER YOU

LIZA BOUBARI

Why: Words allow us to share our thoughts and build dreams. The skilled use of words can bring incredible power and shift patterns and wills to the whims of a single individual.

How much personal and professional power you generate depends on the flow of your communication. With the repetition of actions or thought processes, Habits are formed. Forming Habits is your gateway to your dreams. Your unconscious relies on the words you use.

Habits are useful because they allow you not to have to reprocess every bit of information that entered your brain. They enable you to make generalizations and expectations. If you believe that memory or Habit is fundamental to drive, then that becomes your truth, and subsequently, your actualized reality, and after you learn to drive, driving becomes automatic.

Speak about what you want to happen or create instead of "what you do not want."

Your subconscious mind does not compute the word "don't." So if you think "I don't want to get into debt," you'll get more of it. Think about making more money, and you'll get more of that.

Here are a few more examples.

- "I want to remain calm" vs. "I don't want to get angry."
- "I want to work in a healthy environment" vs. "I don't want to work in a toxic environment." "Hold that carefully" vs. "don't' drop that on the floor."

As you practice speaking and moving towards what you want, you'll form a new Habit of speaking more kindly and lovingly. Shift your words, and you'll shift your language. Shift your perception, and you'll create healthier Habits.

This helps us to be more aware of the choices we make in communicating.

1. Speak in the now.
2. Communicate what you want
3. Use because and now

As a clinical hypnotherapist, I now know the power of words. Words are powerful. Words consist of vibration and sound (tonality). Words are the creator, the creator of your universe, your lives, your reality. Without words, thought can never become an image or your new reality.

To be a good therapist, coach, mentor, and leader, I have learned that the words I use to speak and express a thought or emotion can have a significant impact, not only to my ears that hear but the souls who come to me to help heal.

Words are simple yet powerful. If you happen to have negative thought patterns and words that hurt you, then perhaps it is time for you to act as a change catalyst. What I know now is that transformation begins when you heal within. You can do so when you Evoke-what was (history), Embrace –what is (reality), and Evolve-to what will be (desired outcome) – because You Matter.

THE UN-HABIT: SAY "I CHOOSE VS. I SHOULD" DAILY

Why: "Should I" or "I can't make up my mind." I learned about the energetic meaning of Should while in hypnotherapy school. Words are powerful, and our subconscious, where records of words, behaviors, beliefs can translate words that can disempower the mind. How so?

"Should" can mean "I want to yet I can't make up my mind - so I ask you to decide for me." Suppose it turns out positive–awesome. If not, then it was you who decided, and it is your fault. In other words, "should" shift responsibility, and creates blame.

Indecisive statements like these reveal how years of conditioning can create mindsets that hinder your growth. They may seem "meaningless" or "just a thing you say", but the truth is these statements suggest a layer of self-doubt and false beliefs.

These beliefs were developed over a long period, every time an event happened in life that confirmed a belief, this belief became stronger.

To debunk self-doubt and limiting beliefs, you must make a choice. No matter what you choose – take ownership of choice. No matter good or bad, wrong or right – it is a choice. Once you own your choices, you empower yourself – for there are no wrong choices – perhaps the outcome may not turn to be exactly what you wanted or expected, yet again, it was your choice.

Once you realize this, you can choose something else – a different strategy with a new outlook. This creates a new Habit – making a decision, choosing, and standing by your word. You can meticulously, carefully, and consistently chip away these false beliefs and install new ones. Next time you want to do something and say "should I" – change it to "I choose." Remember, you always have a choice. Make one - Own it - Move On.

ABOUT LIZA: I can help you relieve stress and anxiety through hypnotherapy by tapping into your subconscious mind to shift emotions and alter certain Habits, behaviors, and beliefs. I treat you as a whole, not just your issues, by providing a safe environment for your journey towards a healthier you.

As a Certified Clinical Hypnotherapist and Stress Management Consultant practicing over 20 years, I have gone through massive transformation of my own. My mission is now to help you to debunk self-doubt, heal trauma, Stand Up for who you are, to Become the best version of You – because You Matter

84

PLAN FOR YOUR "BEST CASE" SCENARIO
MENDHI AUDLIN

Why: When I first hung my shingle as an entrepreneur, I was riddled with self-doubt. "What if I can't do this? What if it doesn't work? What if I fail?" I quickly learned that this kind of thinking spells doom to an entrepreneurial venture.

While it's not unusual for entrepreneurs to ponder the question: "What's the worst that could happen?" continually wallowing in your "Worst-Case Scenarios" can be mentally exhausting, robbing you of critical, creative energy and stifling your decision-making abilities.

Focusing on your "Best Case Scenarios" is an essential Habit if you want to survive and thrive as an entrepreneur!

Visualizing your "best-case scenarios" daily literally creates new neural connections that can change our behavior, open our eyes to new perspectives, and prepare us to step into exciting possibilities.

Like a football player who practices his celebratory end zone dance long before he scores the touchdown, as entrepreneurs, it's important to rehearse our highest vision of success mentally. What do you believe is possible? What is your best-case scenario in your marketing campaigns, your client-retention strategies, or your hiring practices? How will you celebrate achieving the benchmarks you seek to attain?

To do this, each morning, I begin my day by creating one positive "What if..." scenario. For example, I may write: "What if I close a big sale today?"

Once I've identified my intended "Best Case Scenario" for the day, I then extrapolate a game plan that aligns with my vision:

What (specifically) is the best-case outcome I want to achieve? (Signed contract for a full-price engagement.)

What thoughts do I need to affirm to align with this outcome? ("My program is exactly what this client needs to move forward on their journey!")

How will I feel when I am on track? (Confident, resourceful, and enthusiastic!)

What inspired actions do I need to take to put myself on a trajectory for this outcome? (Follow up on my proposal and offer to answer questions.)

When we repeatedly envision our best-case scenarios, it changes our outlook. It allows us to see opportunities that we otherwise may have missed. It helps us identify quickly when we are off course. It inspires and energizes us to show up day after day when the journey gets tough, and the end zone seems like a distant dream.

There is an exciting future that awaits you as an entrepreneur! Lock into your highest vision of what is possible, and live each day with hope and enthusiasm for the impact you can create with your business!

THE UN-HABIT: FOLLOW IN THE FOOTSTEPS OF YOUR COMPETITION

Why: When I started my business as a professional speaker almost 20 years ago, I wasn't sure where to begin. I looked online at websites of successful speakers and training companies, searching for inspiration to shorten my learning curve.

I tried to emulate companies that were already highly visible in the marketplace—big mistake.

I compared myself with those who had been in the field for years, trying to mimic their collateral materials and strategies.

This is the inherent problem with building a business based on the sparkle you might find in a Google search:

1. You don't necessarily know if the business you are emulating is revenue-producing. On more than one occasion, I found myself mirroring an unsuccessful competitor (with a great looking website!) as the basis for my marketing strategy.

2. If they are already successful, there's a good chance their budget is not a practical one for you to duplicate in the early

stages of your business. It's easy to look at your industry's superstars and think, "If I just do what they are doing, I'll have the same success they do." You pour time, money, and energy into strategies that likely take far more human resources and capital than you probably have as a start-up. Instead of comparing yourself to the competition, invest time in learning about how your industry's shining stars got started.

3. When you try to be like someone else, you will inevitably miss the opportunity to leverage the qualities and gifts that make you unique! Yes, it's great to surround yourself with people who can offer ideas, encouragement, and success tips. It is equally important to spend time looking within to realize your gifts, listen to your intuition, and bring a fresh perspective that only you can bring to the market.

To sum up: Make sure you know the track-record of the people that are giving you advice. Hold the big vision of where you want to go, start small, and expand what works as you go. Most of all, reach out to others for ideas and encouragement, but always check those ideas through your wisdom and experience. There's no need to do this on your own. But no one can know your calling as you do.

Invest in learning. Invest in mentors. Believe in yourself. And enjoy the ride!

ABOUT MENDHI: Mendhi Audlin is the founder and CEO of "The What If UP Club," inspiring people to initiate and sustain positive changes in their lives and in the world.

She is the author of "What If It All Goes RIGHT? Creating a New World of Peace, Prosperity & Possibility" and is the host of "The What If UP! Podcast with Mendhi Audlin."

85

NEVER GIVE UP AND FIND YOUR RESILIENCE

NANCY GORDON

Why: My sudden descent into the depths of disability after a car accident was a devastating turn in the road I never expected to happen to ME. It wasn't my intended path. But in an instant, when the metal of our two cars collided, my path was forever changed.

In the years following the accident, I struggled DAILY with the shattering impact that fibromyalgia and a mild traumatic brain injury imposed on every aspect of my life. This brought me to the doorstep of giving up on myself, on my return to my life's purpose, and in the darkest moments, on life itself.

Facing reality is imperative to learn some of the greatest lessons in our darkest moments that lead us to discover the treasure map to empower ourselves to find our courage to be resilient.

The resilience of the human spirit is infinite. But finding that resilience, and holding on to it, is not so easy. We are all in control of one thing, and that is our thoughts, our mindset that we whisper in our ears matters.

Sometimes, we don't even hear ourselves. The pattern of how we think is a Habit! It's something we often do unconsciously. We react instead of think. When we react negatively, we miss seeing possibilities and instead focus on our lack of confidence to make the situation any different. Again, giving up is born out of hopelessness.

Fortunately, we do have a choice of how we perceive and react. Awareness is the first step to shifting our thoughts and our reactions. If we focus on all that is wrong, we invite a sense of hopelessness, leading us down a path of negativity, from which our only option appears to be that we give up on our dreams, success, and ultimately we give up on ourselves.

Realizing we have a choice about what we think, how we perceive a situation to be negative or positive, is the antidote to that hopelessness.

THE UN-HABIT: SELF-DOUBT AND A NEGATIVE MINDSET

Why: "Nothing splendid has ever been achieved except by those who dared believe that something inside them was superior to circumstances." Bruce Barton

It may seem that life has a way of offering us a wide range of experiences, which can incite a wide range of responses. Yes, that means we have a choice. That means how you choose to perceive something determines how you choose to react. When we lack confidence and self-worth, we often pay attention to those experiences that we react most easily to with negativity, depression, anger, or lethargy.

When we don't believe in ourselves to be capable of handling adversity, obstacles, and challenges, our thoughts tend to spiral quickly into self-doubt, negative thoughts, limiting beliefs, and yes again, hopelessness.

Instead, suppose we can change our mindset to focus on the possibilities and positive outcomes of our strengths. In that case, we can succeed in changing those anticipated adverse outcomes to a positive outcome. We can choose to know that we will be ok. Sometimes in my most stressful and discouraging moments, I say to myself, "Well, I'm still standing." And I feel grateful for that thought and proud that I didn't give up.

The opposite of never giving up is having hope. With hopelessness, the only way to feel is down and depressed. With hope, the only way to feel is up and positive.

How do we get to this hope? Surrender. Let go. Trust. Surrender is a state of allowing. Surrendering...without giving up (Step 1 in the 7 Steps of Hope and Healing) allows us the grace to tap into our knowingness that all IS well. To know that surrender, that letting what is be what is, will enable us NOT to give up, and opens the door to a sense of worthiness, confidence, and hope.

Knowing we have a choice in what we think and perceive, which Habit would you instead practice- persevere, never give up, and have hope or give up and see life through a lens of pain, disappointment, and hopelessness?

Put that way, I vote for making your Habit right now be one that changes your mindset to uplift you and improve your self-confidence, which will ultimately bring you joy and success!

About Nancy: It's a shared human experience to encounter adversities and grief some time in our lives. When the metal of my car collided with another's, my life was forever changed. Combining my personal experience of disabling fibromyalgia and a mild traumatic brain injury, with my professional psychotherapist skills, I offer not only a unique perspective, but also expertise in my powerful transformational system "7 Steps of Hope and Healing."™ These steps inspire and teach anyone facing life-defining transitions, grief/loss (including pets), to find resilience and meaning in our challenges, which leads us to a path of transformational growth and evolution.

86

CELEBRATE YOU EVERYDAY

THOMESA LYDON

Why: Success begins in YOU. Therefore, YOU must always acknowledge YOURSELF and YOUR wins. Even YOUR smallest daily accomplishments are WINS and need recognition, especially by YOU! When YOU see YOU winning and being successful in YOUR own eyes, YOUR confidence will soar right before YOUR very eyes. The space between YOUR ears can be YOUR biggest critic. Celebrate daily all that YOU do and train 'that' space to dance with joy as YOUR confidence, consistency, and commitments to YOU begin to soar! You will be AMAZED at how rapidly YOU move forward in any endeavor YOU choose. I was notorious for 'beating myself up' and saying negative things to myself, about myself to the point of becoming my own worst enemy!

When I began to CELEBRATE ME, and every little thing I did, said, or thought is when my life changed for the better in every aspect. Many nay-sayers want to steal your joy; don't YOU be one of them! YOU can 'toot YOUR own horn' daily, even hourly, and FEEL the difference it creates in YOU! **Y**-You **O**-Offer **U**-Uniqueness. Respect it, Honor it and Celebrate it! YOU matter!

I grew up hearing how stupid, dumb, and ugly I was, and it took me decades to begin telling myself something different. My daily mantra became, "I am Smart, I am Sharp; I am Beautiful." And guess what? I am all of that and more because I celebrate ME. YOU can do the same. YOU just have to begin, and NOW could be the best time for YOU!

THE UN-HABIT: YOU CAN'T DO ANYTHING RIGHT!

Why: When we are young, comments such as, "Can't you do anything right?" can guide our lives, even unconsciously. Who knew? I certainly did not! But decades later, I had to figure out what was holding me back, and it turned out that it was ME! The phrases and comments I heard as a young girl were misleading me! Oh, how I wish I had known this information earlier on in my life, not just for me but for my kid's sake. I would have used different vocabulary to ensure they didn't move forward in life with similar inaccurate internal 'recordings' or beliefs that replay and replay. If this resonates with you, (no matter what the negative comment that is replaying and causing repeat patterns within your life), sooner rather than later would be the BEST time to break this un-Habit!

. . .

My Mom, who suffered for 14 years and died from Alzheimer's, worked to instill in me these three things to live by...

1. You only live once

2. If you want it, you can have it

3. You can't take it with you

Despite her efforts, I still needed to make "You can't do anything right," an UN-Habit! I encourage everyone to evaluate things that were said or done to you in the past and RE-FRAME what they may mean to you today with all the knowledge you now possess. We all have greatness, a uniqueness, a genius within, and NO ONE should get the right to steal that from us by words or deeds. Identify your greatness by writing down ALL things positive you know about yourself. Then ESPECIALLY note what others say about you that is positive but you have been unable to internalize because of your 'recordings' that have played a different message.

An AMAZING discovery will be unearthed that will change your life for the better, FOREVER! A simple list is golden to discovering your value, worth, greatness, and genius if you take a moment to make that list. Then verbalize that list OUT-LOUD, repeatedly until YOU believe in YOU!

ABOUT THOMESA: If it's not FUN, I am DONE! That has always been my motto. Watching my parents age in a large, high maintenance home that consumed their energy, time and extra money from a fixed income, it was apparent the FUN was disappearing from their vibrant lives. Consumed by the constant workload, an unsafe environment that no longer met their needs physically and the social decline that left them lonely as friends moved away, a 'crisis' occurred that put my Dad in his grave and landed my Mom in Memory Care. My mission is to educate and empower Baby Boomers & their parents to enjoy the next 'LIVING' chapter of their lives so no one has to endure the emotional, physical and financial drain that my family experienced. There is a strategy for a late-in-life move without overwhelm.

87

VISUALIZE EVERYTHING IN YOUR MIND FIRST

BRENDAN MCCAULEY

Why: "To bring anything into your life, imagine that it's already there." -Richard Bach

George Bernard Shaw said, "Imagination is the beginning of creation." There are endless stories of high school dropouts turned millionaires. They didn't have excellent schooling or wealthy parents. However, the one thing that they all had in common was a vision.

The truth is that everything around you that you desire to achieve is within your grasp. But first, you need to see it happening in your mind's eye. You need to see your future reality so clearly, almost as if it's currently being experienced.

Take, for example, the Sistine Chapel. Before Michelangelo picked up a paintbrush, he had a clear vision of what it would look like when it was done. Stephen Covey calls it "beginning with the end in mind."

440 | STEVEN SAMBLIS & FORBES RILEY

The target that you're headed towards is your Sistine Chapel. I'm asking that you create the vision and hold onto that before blindly taking action. You need to understand, however, that just thinking about it is not enough.

Understand that what you first see in your mind only turns into reality when you take massive action to turn your positive thoughts and visions into reality. The takeaway is that anything significant that has been created was formed first in the mind with a vision.

If you want to be a millionaire, you need to envision yourself with millions in the bank. If you're going to be a professional speaker, you need to envision yourself speaking on stage among the greats. The same concept goes for being a writer, losing weight, finding a spouse, and any other adventure worth working towards.

PLAN OF ACTION:

1. For one week, take between five to ten minutes to yourself away from others. Close your eyes, put on light transient music if you wish, and picture the perfect scenario of you accomplishing your goal.

2. Throughout the process, be as specific as you can. Envision yourself accomplishing your goal, and try to picture: What are you wearing? Where are you standing? Who's surrounding you? How do you feel at the moment?

3. Log these feelings in a journal and review them every morning. You'll find that you can always add to the journal as you go.

THE UN-HABIT: INABILITY TO REMAIN LASER FOCUSED

Why: FOCUS - Follow One Course Until Successful

With so many distractions, it can be easy to get thrown off your game. Although we start with the best intentions, life often gets in the way. We come out the gate strong, but sometimes find ourselves at crossroads, asking questions that hinder us rather than empower us.

Have you ever been working on a task and asked yourself questions like, "Why am I working so hard on this? What's the point? It's not going to work out for me anyhow, who was I kidding? I can't be like those guys." I know I've said that to myself before. While questions like this are normal, they can be hard to overcome at times.

What I can tell you is that you need to get your mindset right first and foremost if you plan on making it through the storm and safely to the other side. You need to gather a mental army of troops to help you remain consistent and push through hard times, even when you don't feel like it.

To be successful and create a laser-like focus, there are two things you must do.

- First, if you're experiencing paralysis by analysis, make a decision and run with it. If you can't decide which one of two (or more) options to pick, close your eyes, point to one, and make it happen. Yes, it is as simple as that. Burn the boats, leaving you no way to go back, and then attack your goal with 110% of your effort.
- Second, once you've decided which direction to go in,

you need to focus on the activity, not the result. If, for example, your goal is to lose weight, stop stepping on the scale and staring at yourself in the mirror after the first week of working out, getting upset because you don't look trimmer. Instead, pat yourself on the back and tell yourself what a Rockstar you are for pushing yourself in the right direction. Then stay consistent.

Regardless of your path to greatness, the journey is guaranteed to throw you curveballs. You most certainly will have questions, doubts, and insecurities along the way. The key is not to regret your decision and decide to make the most out of every experience with maximum effort.

ABOUT BRENDAN: Tired of wasting time and money trying to figure which tools to use in your coaching practice? Brendan created an all-in-one marketing platform that helps coaches stay organized and scale their business. With his system, you no longer need to duct tape together multiple systems to send contracts, email/text/message your clients, allow clients to book appointments, create landing pages, build a website, send surveys and forms, create courses, and most important track your numbers.

88

DO SOMETHING FOR YOUR FUTURE SELF

KELLY HOWARD

Why: It's so easy to always look for the "big win." That action that's going to make everything better. It's human nature. As entrepreneurs, I believe that we were even more enamored with the next big goal: win.

But, much like the Aesop fable of the Tortoise and the Hare, big spurts of action followed by inaction doesn't win a thing. It's small, consistent actions that create significant results. I'm betting everyone reading this book gets that, core level yes. Small, consistent actions = big results.

And still...we love a big win.

We're goal-setting machines, but we're not always goal hitting machines. Part of the problem with goals, desires, dreams are they are outside of us. They're something we're striving for instead of something that we are.

Stop for a moment and consider WHO you want to be. Who do you want to be in six months or a year? Can you get that feeling of what you are like in the future? What are you doing? What do you have and what do you want? When you can begin to embrace your future fully, everything shifts.

Think deep. Can you start to see, feel, understand who you would be, how you would be if you were the person who had reached your goals, your dreams. Who are you?

Once you can fully embrace the person you want to be (start with six months from this moment), anchor it. Truly embrace that future you.

Now, step back and look at your life today. The ONLY way you and your future are going to connect is if you take action. The future "you" depends on you 100% to do what needs to be done today to make it real.

Every day. Every action. Takes you closer or further away. They are cheering you on. You're either the one moving your life forward or holding it back.

Do something your future self will thank you for—every single day.

THE UN-HABIT: STOP THE EXCESSIVE SCREEN TIME

Why: Studies have shown that our ability to think drops markedly when your smartphone is in reach, even if it's silenced or powered down. Excessive screen time is teaching our brains to rewire, looking for outside stimuli from phones, not life. The release of dopamine your brain receives not only triggers your pleasure centers, but it can also trigger screen addiction. High levels of phone use have been tied directly to increased depression and stress and lowered productivity!

That might be good news. Studies show there is physical evidence of lower gray matter with screen over-use, much like has been seen in the past with drug use. Like Pavlov's salivating dog, notifications create instantaneous reactions and completely stop your ability to choose to be in the moment.

And that's just what's going on in your brain!

Greater screen use is consistently shown to lower our sleep and sleep quality and efficiency. We are taking away the regenerating health benefits of a good night's sleep.

Can we talk about relationships? People who bring their phone to the dinner table (even with it facedown or turned off) are less communicative. Conversations lag, and connections are lost. Many people report feeling more isolated and lonelier than ever in this over-connected world.

Think about everything you could improve by simply taking back a large portion of your life. You can grow your brain (and your business) by leaving the phone on your desk. Your relationship can flourish, and your community can grow through real connections. Your health will improve as your sleep improves.

All of this simply removing a bad Habit that wasn't even in our world twenty years ago. Don't think of it as losing friends on social media or less screen time; think of it as gaining your real life back. Look forward to a moment in time when "IRL" is just three letters that mean nothing because your real life is in front of you and being lived full out and in full color.

About Kelly: Kelly Howard, CEO of Fit is Freedom and the author of the Motivation Multiplier Method. The simple system that teaches small, quick shifts that lead to big wins. Apply it to your fitness, your health and especially your business. As a 4-time entrepreneur, Kelly knows a thing about making motivation happen. You don't need a 10-step process to make life work, you just need to apply the right multiplier where it matters the most for you. Never depend on willpower again!

89

UNITING YOUR INNER & OUTER BEAUTY

TOBEY ANN TERRY

Why: When you embrace your inner and outer beauty, you set yourself up for a successful day by being ready for the opportunities that can come your way instantly.

As entrepreneurs, we spend a lot of time and money learning how to market and grow our biz with copywriting, Facebook ads, posting on social media, email marketing, etc. but how much time do we spend on ourselves or learning the tools to look and feel like the CEO we truly are.

We're now on camera more than ever, and if you're not, you are leaving money on the table. But how are you showing up, and who are you showing up for? It's not just for your potential new client that's on the other side of the lens or your mastermind group or Interview appearances, but who you're showing up for is yourself.

When we truly stand in our sacred spotlight and show up with presence, not perfection, we tell the Universe...

Yes, I'm ready to receive and up-level my life and biz.

When you take the time and make an effort to show up looking your best, your Soul will shine through, and the people around you will respond. You know that moment when you're around someone that is so magnetic and vibrant that it makes you feel inspired? And in almost every case, there is something visual that amplifies their inner beauty like bright color, or an amazing dress, a statement piece of jewelry, a fun lip gloss, or a haircut to die for. They look the part, they feel the part, and we feel their energy!

When we choose to get ready for the day with intention, we are telling ourselves that we are successful, confident, powerful, and ready to serve. Ready to be of service to anyone that happens to contact you that day and is ready for a consult, ready to sign up, to buy your product, a collaboration opportunity, or even a last-minute once in a lifetime Interview spot.

You're telling the Universe that you are always ready for a moment that can move your business forward. Being a camera-ready or workday ready for success will help clear out any stagnant energy and help create a path for insights straight from the source because you are radiating from your inner beauty out.

HAB1T™

THE UN-HABIT: A SCHEDULE WITHOUT SELF-CARE

WHY: How are we supposed to serve anyone else when we're not truly serving ourselves? The number one mistake that entrepreneurs make, especially women and mothers, is not taking self-care time.

We go, go, go, and don't schedule in the time for ourselves, then we end up burned out, exhausted, unhealthy, and don't like what we see in the mirror. It doesn't have to be complicated or time-consuming, but it does need to be scheduled.

My three rules to follow for Transformational Self-Care is it needs to be consistent, it needs to resonate with your soul, and your self-care needs to be sprinkled with beauty.

I heavily leaned on spiritual self-care through my divorce to heal from the pain and guilt, so I know the power of these types of practices such as meditation, affirmations, yoga, journaling, and walking in nature. However, as a Beauty Professional for 25+ years, I know the power of practicing beauty has on a woman. When you allow yourself to enjoy beauty-related self-care, magic truly starts to happen. The nurturing of your physical body with your beauty and spirit is an alchemy of pure transformation that recharges you deep down on a cellular and soul level. This is a true formula for success as an entrepreneur.

Not taking the time to get a massage to relieve stress or pain, doing a home facial to nurture your skin, getting a fresh haircut, or taking yourself out in the most beautiful dress in your closet can prevent your true desires passions from coming through. Be the dynamic woman and entrepreneur you are meant to be!

Create the time for self-care in all the beautiful ways that it can be experienced. Take a stand for yourself and create beauty boundaries that won't be broken by the demands of life to celebrate the beauty of being you and all the beauty that life has to offer so you can renew your spirit and, ultimately, your business.

Take the time tonight by enjoying a candlelit evening in the bath with a facial mask while listening to your favorite meditation. If you feel inspired after your bath, then journal about how good you feel and see what else comes through your pen.

ABOUT TOBEY: Tobey Ann Terry created Live Camera Confidence, a signature system in her 1:1 and Group Coaching Programs that helps Women Entrepreneurs who struggle with using live video and interviews to show up looking vibrant, confident, and on point with their brand so they can gain visibility, grow influence, and attract their ideal client's attention.

90

DAYDREAM YOUR FUTURE

NICOLE WEBER

Why: If you can visualize your ultimate goal in a tangible way every day, then you can reverse engineer the steps to get there. Your day-to-day tasks then become more enjoyable because they are moving you closer to your passion. The "where" and what your life will look like can change, but you must combine this with the process of creating the milestones to achieve it.

How wonderful to wake up and immediately transport yourself to someplace amazing. Not only does it start your day on a positive note, but it also allows you that time of semi-consciousness when the brain is more open to access creative thoughts. That's often when breakthroughs come and why many famous authors and artists say that's when their best thoughts, writing, and inspirations come. You want to access your thoughts before your brain fully leaves its Alpha wave state. It doesn't work once your day is constantly interrupted.

And you have to break the Habit (if you have it) of reaching for your phone as your first action when you wake up!

And of course, this is only ultimately successful if you put in the work to get you there. Create goals and milestones so you have an outline of what it will take. Day-to-day is much easier to get through when you know why you're doing it and not just going through the motions.

Don't let life happen to you and see where you end up. That's fun on vacation but not for life. Like on a purposeful trip, decide on the destination, and create your roadmap to figure out what you need to do to get there. After all, there's a reason they describe life as a journey, and there are some great parallels to follow. I have been doing this Habit every morning for years; my best ideas come during this time.

THE UN-HABIT: STOP WITH THE SELF-DOUBT

Why: We all have the voice in our head that sometimes tells us "Don't say that - it's a dumb idea," or "I shouldn't put that in the email - someone's feelings might get hurt" or "Our company won't be selected so why should we bother?" I think this is especially true for women historically. Because we know some people confuse assertive with bitchy, we hold back. We devalue our opinions and let others lead. We hesitate to voice an alternative solution for fear of being dismissed.

It's easy to say "Be fearless" and much harder to put it into action. It takes practice to say to yourself, "My idea is valuable," "My contribution will be important," "I am qualified for this position."

I was shy as a little girl, and it took a lot to begin speaking up. I remember being so shy that I often went hungry because I wouldn't ask for someone to pass me the sandwiches plate at my preschool lunch table.

I was quiet all through school and into my first few jobs. I remember sitting around the conference table, silent unless someone were to ask me a direct question. Even then, my self-doubt sabotaged me, and most of my creative ideas were never heard.

My self-doubt lasted into my early 30's. It was during the dot com boom and bust that I stepped up my confidence. It made me sick to see how much waste and bad judgment happened during that time. I knew I could take my knowledge and run a better company than the previous ones I have been a part of.

It was a bold step for me to have the confidence to start my marketing firm, but that's exactly what I did 20 years ago. Not to say that self-doubt doesn't pop up every once in a while, but I know how to squash it pretty fast when it does!

ABOUT NICOLE: I have always loved design and advertising. When I started working in this industry, I noticed there were so many marketing options that it was really overwhelming to most businesses. Where to start? A website, social media, SEO, PPC, email? Not to mention the million apps out there! That's when I decided to start my own agency to help our clients navigate the marketing maze and focus on the top two-three things that will give them the best ROI. So, 20 years and hundreds of happy clients later, we're still going strong and loving it

91

GIVE YOUR CLIENTS EXTRAORDINARY CARE

MICHELE MARSHALL

Why: We are familiar with the adage "The Customer is Always Right". In my opinion, this statement is incomplete. For client retention and loyalty, I've reframed that statement to "The Customer should always be treated right."

Your client's experience is a vital building block for client retention, referrals, and your company's reputation. Imagine increasing your business from the referrals of your existing clients. Look at Zappos. In 2007 their gross sales increased by 40% based on repeat customer and customer referrals. How? It wasn't based on because of their products or pricing. It was due to their customer service. From unheard of return options to free overnight shipping; coupled with 24/7 access to a professional, kind, courteous phone support team. The word of mouth from satisfied customers helped Zappos grow into a Billon dollar company.

460 | STEVEN SAMBLIS & FORBES RILEY

The customer experience will make or break your business. You could have the best product or service on the market. However, fail to treat your customers with kindness and respect; your product or service isn't going to sell. Dell computers realized this lesson in 2005. They offered a quality product at a reasonable price point. However, Dell's client satisfaction rating dropped 6.3%, which translated into reduced sales. Why? It was their lack of customer service. Dissatisfied customers not only switched to Dell's competitors. They posted scathing reviews and told anyone who would listen. Don't buy from Dell; they have poor customer service. It was a harsh lesson for Dell. Fortunately, they adjusted their customer service protocols, which resulted in a boost in sales.

The common goal of every Entrepreneur is to grow their business. That growth rests on the client's experience after they have purchased a product or service. When you provide extraordinary care to your current clients, they will refer new clients. A strong Habit for success-give your clients an exceptional caring experience. In doing so, you will develop a client base that can serve as a partner in expanding your business.

"Here is a simple but powerful rule - always give people more than what they expect to get." - Nelson Boswell

THE UN-HABIT: DON'T LET YOUR EGO BLOCK YOUR LISTENING

Why: As an Entrepreneur, you're an expert in your field with years of experience — a self-made success story who has seen it all and done it all. You have a massive database of knowledge in your head to address just about any question thrown your way swiftly. In compiling this vast experience, knowledge, and success, it is natural to build up an ego. There is nothing wrong with having pride in your accomplishments. The un-Habit is to take care that this same ego doesn't inadvertently become a filter that blocks the opportunity to listen.

- Ego around your position could keep you from listening to your team's feedback; potentially stifling creativity amongst your team.
- Ego about your products or services could keep you from listening to your customers' needs and hence missing an opportunity to expand your reach and gain more customers.
- Ego around your expertise or how you run your company could keep you from listening to feedback from your hired business coach.
- Ego around your experience and knowledge could keep you from listening to potentially invaluable feedback from other entrepreneurs who have acquired equal or greater success, especially when ego skews that feedback and erroneously turns it into a personal attack.
- Ego around past mistakes, where you've removed your responsibility in those mistakes, keeps you from learning from those mistakes—therefore missing the opportunity to apply the learning toward course correction.

Breaking the Habit of filtering my listening based on my ego influences my two companies' success. The types of workshops offered at my company Authentic Voice are crafted based on our client's direct feedback of what they want, instead of what we thought they need. The expansion of PURE Client Services occurred when I removed my ego and listened to my mentor's recommendation.

"Ego is the enemy of what you want and what you have."

— RYAN HOLIDAY

About Michele: As a customer care expert for over 25 years, Michele Marshall has a keen knowledge of the life-changing value in treating people with kindness and respect. Her unique style of customer care has allowed her to excel in the industry. For a thriving business, product creation and customer acquisition are only the beginning. The lifeblood of every profitable business is its customers.

Michele understands retention and growth within a company comes from creating a patient, understanding, result-oriented customer experience. With her expertise, she guides companies on how to increase their revenue by putting systems in place to provide exceptional customer service.

92

TOUCH YOUR BUSINESS EVERYDAY

BLANEY TEAL

Why: As an entrepreneur, it's sometimes easy to get distracted or get caught up in the drama of "life." But to be a successful entrepreneur, you need to stay focused and have extreme commitment and passion to your ultimate vision. Your vision needs to bigger than the alternative. What will happen if you fail? What is the alternative? Are you going to flip burgers or drive Uber? For me, I know that I need to have my vision and work to that vision as there is no way I want the alternative for me.

Throughout the years, I have tried my hand at many opportunities. I started my 1st business at the age of 7, and it wasn't a lemonade stand! Some of my business ventures were super successful, and some not so much. But what I learned was that to be successful, you need to "touch your business "every day. It is much harder to start and stop working on and in your business. When you start and stop, you lose momentum.

Once you get in the Habit of conducting certain activities that you perform every day, each day will build on the last. You will see your business pick up and start to grow exponentially. If you work your business hard for 30 days and stop, so will your momentum. Then you have to start all over again, and that can be very exhausting.

Do this right now... grab a pencil, and I want you to tap the table with it and say, "touch my business every day, touch my business every day, and touch my business every day." Then make a list of activities that you can do every day to keep the momentum moving. It could make five calls to potential customers and make five calls to existing customers to ask for referrals; it could do a live stream or social media post every day. It doesn't matter how big or how small the activity is as long as it keeps you moving toward your vision. Just don't miss a day.... Do something small every day, and you will reach your goal!

The Un-Habit: Avoid shiny new objects!

Why: As entrepreneurs, it's easy to want to find a better way. It's easy to see others reaching success and wanted to be like them. It's easy to want to jump from one service or one system or one idea to be more successful. However, if it's not broke, don't fix it. Or at least right away! Resist the urge to need all the bells and whistles or the latest and greatest tech or the newest software. There is a time and place for upgrades and implementing new strategies. But if you try to make changes too fast, or too soon, it could have the opposite outcome than what you desire.

This is an UN-Habit that I had to learn the hard way. When you try to use or implement new systems into your business too soon or are not needed, it becomes a distraction. It takes extra time to learn or implement something new; this will distract you from your daily activities and cost you momentum.

So here is what I now ask myself before making any significant changes or purchasing new software, new system, etc.

Do I need this or do I want it?

Does this serve me now? If I buy it/invest in it now, will I implement and increase my bottom line or save me time or money?

If I know I will use it now and improve my business; I can justify it. Go for it!

If I may not use it or don't need it right now, I resist the "shiny new object," BUT I do put it in my list of potential ideas (my wish list) to implement when it is right, and I know I will use it.

I challenge you to ask yourself these questions before running off and buying a new piece of software or investing money in a strategy or idea.

This UN-Habit will help you be a more successful entrepreneur!

ABOUT BLANEY: Blaney Teal has a passion for helping entrepreneurs make more money doing what they love. Thus, why they call her The Passionpreneur Coach. Blaney founded the Next for Success Accelerator Academy for entrepreneurs to improve their mindset, skillset, and toolset, which will help entrepreneurs achieve their vision faster. The Academy focuses on implementing tools and systems to save entrepreneurs time and money and significantly shorten the learning curve without breaking the bank! You will find Blaney hosting networking & business events worldwide, bringing together entrepreneurs and small business owners at her MBX Events and Passionpreneur Summits. Just another way she helps business owners turn their passion into profits!

93

ASK FOR THE SALE!

JANE WARR / TRAINER JANE

Why: Whether you think you are in sales or not, if you are reading this book, you are in sales. The less comfortable you are with sales and the word selling, the less likely you are to ask for the sale at the end of a consultation or phone call.

When you were a kid, if you wanted something, you asked for it. You didn't pause and wonder how many different answers you might get. You didn't overthink it. Since then, someone must have told you it was wrong, or rude, or inappropriate. You don't want to be salesy; I get it. Salesy and asking for the sale are two very different things.

Salesy is being pushy and making the other person feel uncomfortable. In contrast, when you speak to someone, and it is flowing nicely, you are in rapport. Why break rapport and go silent when you get to "the money part"? If you are in business, a sale has to be made, to move forward with the other person, to have cash flow, and to grow your business. At some point, a payment needs to happen. You aren't going to give free samples and "share" your products, services, or opportunity, are you?

I challenge you to think of asking for the sale as just the next part of the sales process. Why would you have a meeting, discuss your product or service, features, and benefits, etc. and then stop there? It makes the other person feel uncomfortable if they then have to ask you what to do next if they are interested. Honor them by asking. If you have made it that far in a consultation, they have some interest, and it is only a question.

Change your mindset on this one part of the sales process, and your sales will skyrocket!

I have been an entrepreneur my whole life. I have transformed from shy and passive, to clear and confident. It was sales training and putting different lessons into practice that got me to where I am today.

If there was only one new Habit you instill in your sales profession, I advise you to ask for the sale EVERY time. The worst you can get is a no, and best case you get a Yes!, and your journey with that individual begins!

THE UN-HABIT: THINKING SELLING IS HARD

Why: Your thoughts lead to your emotions and feelings that lead to your actions or inaction, and thereby your results, or lack thereof!

Therefore every thought you have is important, often even critical!

If you think selling is hard, and you believe it, you will live as if so. It will stir up negative feelings, and you will likely talk yourself out of doing the activities that lead to success. You won't want to network or prospect, you won't go into sales presentations excitedly and confidently, you may show up late and unprepared, and your results will speak for themselves.

What if you changed your thinking? What if instead of telling yourself negative statements, you asked yourself questions and then answered them? Any question is followed by an answer in your mind. Try it right now!

Important: Phrase the questions with a positive and optimistic tone, with the goal of problem-solving.

Asking questions starting with "How" or "Where" or "What" is best. Let me explain. If you asked yourself, "How can I close more sales today?" you may come up with answers such as "by practicing my sales skills." or "by asking for the sale". If you asked yourself, "Where will I find customers?", you may answer with "at a networking event I will go to today" or "from an existing customer giving a referral". Our brains naturally answer questions. Ask great questions and get great answers!

We talk to ourselves all day. You are doing it right now! You have the option of good thoughts and poor thoughts. You can choose happy thoughts or sad thoughts. You can choose stress or ease. You can choose to stay the same or get out of your comfort zone, embrace something new, and get new results. You can instill new Habits with your thoughts.

About Jane: In a world where people make "selling" a bad word, we provide you with a safe environment to bring your products and services, to clearly and concisely introduce yourself, and ethically present your offers. This is how great business is done! Jane Warr, aka Trainer Jane, created a marketplace for you, the entrepreneur, business owner or sales professional, regardless of industry. Join us for fun virtual and in-person events, to find your niches and grow your riches. That is what we do at Selling on the Spot Marketplace.

94

BE CONFIDENT IN YOUR OWN WORTH

KATHERIN KOVIN - PACINO

Why: It's helped me grow as a personality and project my strengths. Self-confidence is a learned experience and one that is sadly lacking in most performers today. If I can help anyone feel secure inside in one's heartfelt projection of self, I have been hugely rewarded. Make love to the microphone; make love to your audience. People always remember those who "connect" and create "contact."

Go out, connect, meet people, make contacts, get pictures. Let people know in the industry that you are connecting with others. Contacts are everything! The guy or girl that's the extra today could easily, through circumstances, be the next casting director, producer, or director. You see this every day, so Rule #1 Be nice to everyone. Trust me. Out of experience, I've seen these things happen more often than one thinks!

Make a Habit of talking to people, connecting, collecting business cards, staying in touch, maybe inviting them over for lunch or dinner. Do a" get together." The key thing is to form a "relationship." You'll know when it's "right," as things will "flow!"

Habits of "inclusion" are so right, that is with the right people. If you are continually looking out for the other person, but it is not appreciated or exchanged, then you need to concentrate on people with a sense of "give and take." More than likely, you will feel what "right" is and what isn't "right," but then that's a whole other subject. Make sure you keep company with those who understand the laws of "give and take." There's a fine line of "give and take," "networking," and "using." Trust me; you will instinctively know!

Go out there. Look your best, and network, network, network! Be the best and most positive person you can be!

THE UN-HABIT: BEING CONTINUALLY LATE

Why: To be a good entrepreneur and have good entrepreneurial skills, one must be focused and enthusiastic, highly organized with a sense of true passion. He or she must WANT and feel that they DESERVE the success and see the light at the end of the tunnel, even in the most depressing days. He or she must be able to also lift those around them in the darkest of dark days. There's an old saying, "It's always darkest before the dawn."

I have a couple of friends, for instance, that are in the Bitcoin business. This takes mega entrepreneurial skills. "Why ?" you ask. In my personal opinion, though Bitcoin has been around for a couple of years, it's still relatively new to the average trader. One must understand the fluctuations, and one must have an inherent trust in the seller and the company they are investing with. Therefore, the entrepreneur, whether the investor OR the person one is investing WITH must be transparent, trustworthy, he or she must be on top of things, it is also important that people band together to find out what each other's strong points are. This also brings back the idea that one must be "clear-headed" and "responsive" to those he or she works with, who may have questions and need answers, and be on top of friends, investors, and clients' needs.

I do not believe in taking drugs. One must be in control of their actions and thinking. A glass or two of wine is usually permissible, depending on the person's metabolism. Moderation is everything. One must seek self-control to be trusted and respected with those they are doing business with. Clients want to feel safe. However, if one needs prescription drugs (such as blood thinning, heart, thyroid, etc.), this changes the whole synopsis.

I also believe in writing things down that makes us "click." Is this your favorite album? Is this gardening? Is this writing? Write down the things that bring you "passion." Commit to doing one of these things once a day, if not maybe once a week. Have a "Gratitude" jar. Think of all the positive things that are happening in your life. These things give you purpose, appreciation, and passion. These things play into "fulfillment," thus wanting YOU to empower a client's life, thus empowering oneself. This makes for a mega entrepreneur!

Be kind to others, be kind to yourself. Suppose one cannot be kind to oneself, nor fulfilled with oneself. In that case, it takes away from being the true, positive help for others, for they will look to acknowledge your clarity, positivity, and passion. It all comes into play. Be authentic! All these things combined will indeed create a successful entrepreneur.

One more thing. Eat right! Eat clean. Eat organic, if at all possible. Put fruits and veggies on your plate. Stay away and cut out completely red meat and refined sugars. Take supplements, such as Vitamin A, B12, C, D, E, Iodine, and Zinc. Drink plenty of water with lemon and put apple cider vinegar on your salads. All these things feed the pineal gland, which gives one clarity and raises one's energy level, thus emanating more energy toward one's client(s)

Be the best entrepreneur you can be. Build an empire!

About Katherin: Katherin Kovin- Pacino not only writes and acts, but enjoys mentoring actors, writers VOs, as well. She loves taking talent and setting them in the right direction as to "where to go for what" and" who and what to stay away from", so that they do not get scammed in the industry.

Katherin has worked in the beauty industry, and loves to consult actors, models, writers as to how to groom themselves, as well as how to glamorize via hair/makeup best wardrobe colors, best cosmetic/plastic surgeons, etc...

Katherin Kovin- Pacino acknowledges the importance of their own work, but the importance of empowering others, which in turn empowers her. Her and her husband received POWER COUPLE of the YEAR 2019 EZ Hall of Fame, and will be Presenters on Sept 26 2020 to the next Power Couple of the Year for 2020.

95

JOURNAL YOUR GRATEFUL

MARY SKUZA

Why: The Gratitude Habit is important to acquire because once you realize and accept what you already have in Gratefulness, the Universe or God lets you open up to more Blessings and Gifts in the future. It's also important to pause and meditate to feel the joy for each entry.

Many times we complain and are not aware of everything we have been given. We have places to live, a safe environment and loving families. We need to be thankful for what is, to get more.

No matter where you are in your life, you can be kind to others. Simple things to do is smile when you encounter people. Even if people can't see your face now due to wearing masks, people can see your smiling eyes. Make sure you tell loved ones often that you love them, it makes both of you feel happy and grateful.

Some ways to spread your gratitude are to support your favorite charities. There are so many worthy causes of helping people, especially to rescue children from sex trafficking, help feed your neighbors, and there are many charities near you that take a little money, and they have great buying power.

By sharing a little, your heart will be filled with gratefulness that you contributed.

By reaching out to people you know and telling them you love them, you spread it into their hearts. Take time and send a card or a handwritten note to people. You will be surprised as to how much the other person feel that. They will be talking about it and sharing the message for a long time. This is especially important for parents and grandparents, our older generation. I send cards to people all the time. I get a thank you, and I am grateful that I put a smile on their face.

Again, write in your journal ten things daily and meditate on them. Someday, maybe you can build a school like one of my friends did in Africa. Wow.

THE UN-HABIT: WHEN PROMPTED BY YOUR SPIRIT, MAKE SURE YOU FOLLOW THROUGH

Why: When you ignore the inner promptings that your spirit provides you with often, you will have regret that will follow you for decades.

An example I have is when my mother fell and hit her head. She was taken to the hospital and unbeknownst to us she had a brain bleed. I did visit her in the hospital. She was having trouble seeing, and we didn't know why. The blood was causing her to lose her sight. A vigilant nurse discovered the issue too late to save her life. She had the surgery to remove the blood clot, but unfortunately, we lost Mom. I have beaten myself up a lot for not being more alert to the gravity of the situation.

Before my father passed, I was blessed to be staying with him for four months before he died. One funny memory I have is I was able to work remotely from home to be with him. He couldn't figure out how I could work and be sitting with him in the living room. He fell at home overnight, and we took him to the hospital. He had pneumonia, but the hospital was having issues figuring out what kind. They finally took a biopsy of his lung and discovered it was a fungus type, which is why he wasn't recovering. He was getting better finally, but we were worried. Dad's final week in the hospital, he was so alert and talking, and we thought maybe he would pull through. That Friday, I HAD to drive into the office for work. Around noon I got a phone call to return, I didn't make it in time to say goodbye.

Okay, the reason for these two stories is that you DON'T know when you will see or be with your loved ones for the last time.

Make sure you always say "I Love You" and give hugs.

Also, make sure your Soul is right with your God or the Universe. I would hate for you to miss out on Eternal life.

About Mary: I am Mary Skuza, born and raised in central Minnesota on a dairy farm. I am the oldest of 6 children and helped my Dad in the fields from an early age. I loved the country life. I worked hard while attending school because I wanted to attend College when and if the opportunity presented itself.

I am so grateful that I always had an open mind to think outside the box when opportunities appeared. Besides working full time mainly in the computer industry, I attended a college in the High Desert in California and explored architectural design. I finally got my chance at College and graduated with a BSCS. I have been mentored by famous people such as Forbes, Jack Canfield, Bob Proctor. My passion is to awaken others to think outside the box and be open to opportunities.

96

DREAM BIGGER

ERIC RING

Why: Every person must form a Habit of learning how to dream bigger and outside the box. Too many people hold themselves back on a day to day basis, because they feel they can't dream large enough or that these things are not possible. And this limits their every day success.

Whatever goal you have, whatever dream you have, make sure it's much bigger than you ever thought possible. Constantly go over the numbers, constantly look at it. Pick up a notebook and write about it, figure out a way that it can be bigger, because there is a way. There is always a way. And when you can show yourself on paper and make yourself believe and limit the fear that surrounds that much bigger dream, reality sets in.

It's a form of setting an intention and manifesting great things. And when you set the intention and create a form of vision board through notes and mathematical equations and possibilities, before long, you start 100% believing in the possibility, and the possibility becomes reality with the intensity that you put into it. The story now is rewritten in your mind, that success can be much bigger than you originally thought.

I want to give you an example from my experience. I had very negative beliefs about the stock market that were ingrained in me as a child and throughout life. Throughout the pandemic I started playing with the stock market as a tool to keep me busy. And before long, I realized I was making a lot of money. My goal was to make $100,000 to pay off a bunch of bills. But every day hundreds of times a day I was doing math to figure out how that could get much bigger, how I can set the intention to go large. Five months later, I'm up over 1.1 million. This is the power of intention and of dreaming big. My new goal by the way is 1.6 million.

In this example, you see this is not just about setting an intention. The intention eliminates the fear, which gets you going towards your goal, but you have to put a lot of hard work into it. I spent countless hours concentrating, listening to news, reading articles to get where I am. But it all started with the first step. And it all started with getting rid of any fear based thoughts that I had around stocks.

THE UN-HABIT: SABOTAGING YOUR DREAMS

Why: The un-empowering Habit too many people on a day to day basis use as a crutch and as a tool to not accomplish their goals and to not take that first step is FEAR. When you allow fear to run your life, your life stays stagnant. You become complacent living paycheck to paycheck and not going on as many vacations or spending time with your family. The richest, the wealthiest, the most successful people in the world have more opportunities where fear is placed in front of them as a challenge every day. What separates them from the average person is that they've allowed themselves the opportunity to practice, over and over again, how to deal with that fear. It's how they handle the fear, not the fear itself. They identify the root cause of the challenge. What is the root cause that's causing fear? Analyze how to get around that obstacle. Fear is nothing more than an obstacle and every obstacle can be overcome. Definition of leadership: constantly adjust until you meet your desired outcome.

A leader, a successful person will analyze what their root cause is and they will come up with a solution. That makes sense. That's how they get to dream bigger, go larger and be successful in whatever it is they're doing. And this doesn't happen overnight. It may not happen for the first day or two, maybe the first week or two but the process is very simple. Write it down and revisit it over and over again throughout, however many days it takes to come up with a solution. I suggest using a notepad, I suggest writing down all of the things that are causing these emotions. And let's remember when your emotion goes up your intelligence goes down. So constantly step away from it. Have a cup of coffee, come back. Look at it again, and over and over again until you come up with a solution to eliminate that fear. Operating your life in this format will reduce stress and allow you to handle challenges with excitement, knowing success is a pen stroke away.

About Eric: Eric is a self-made multi-millionaire and a serial entrepreneur who owns several franchises, residential and commercial real estate and many other businesses. He is a master trainer and designer for leadership and personal growth programs. He has created and facilitated hundreds of customized programs for multi-million dollar companies and organizations like Success Resources and Fordham University.

Eric is a retired police officer with over 23 years of experience. He has worked undercover narcotics and is also a certified FBI fire arm instructor. His ability to interact with all cultures and personalities, allows him to have the insight to develop such amazing programs.

97

TAKE ACTION BEFORE YOU ARE READY

DAN "NITRO" CLARK

Why: You ever feel that flash of inspiration to do something, to be something more than you are now? But then it hits you. You realize you're not quite ready to start. Then you put off starting until you feel ready and motivated, until it's a perfect time. You tell yourself you'll do it tomorrow.

Tomorrow slowly turns into next week, which turns into next month. You keep punting your dreams and ambitions from one day's calendar to the next.

Soon that little voice that piped up inside of you is gone. You tell yourself that book you wanted to write, that diet you wanted to start, that career you wanted to pursue, was a dumb idea.

Each time you do this, a part of who you could be and what you could do in the world dies. Then you're besieged by an uneasiness, an emptiness. A feeling that you aren't living up to your potential. You know you could be more and do more if you could get yourself to START.

I'm going to be straightforward with you. You may not want to hear this.

But there will never be a perfect time to start. All the successes I've had in my life, and the successes of the people I've coached, worked with, and interviewed pro athletes, Celebrities, Olympic gold medal winners, millionaires, and billionaires, comes down to one simple Habit. The Habit of starting before you are ready.

The people who have the success you want aren't smarter than you or better than you; they have been able to get themselves to start and take action when:

- They are tired.
- They are afraid.
- They don't feel like it.
- They aren't motivated.

The good news is if you can master this one Habit of taking action when you don't want to or feel like it, or when you are afraid, you can completely transform your life one right-action step at a time.

The next time you feel yourself hesitating, the next time you feel yourself waiting to feel motivated to start, remember this Habit.

To succeed, you must start before you are ready. This one simple Habit of taking action, regardless if you feel motivated or not, will completely change your life one right step at a time towards the best version of your future self.

What are you waiting for? Gladiator Ready? 3-2-1 Go!

THE UN-HABIT: DON'T TRUST THAT VOICE IN YOUR HEAD. IT'S A LIAR

Why: If you're reading this now, I bet you've got two voices in your head.

You know that voice in your head. That one that's talking to you now as you read this.

You ever notice that sometimes it's a sinner and sometimes it's a saint?

There are times it's your greatest ally. That voice pumps you up. Tells you that you can do it. To go and take that risk. That everything is going to work out.

Other times it tells you – you are going to fail. That no one cares. That you aren't worthy. That you will fail. That it's not worth trying. That they will laugh at you. We've all got both voices.

But I want to make a very clear distinction for you. This distinction could change your life. It changed mine when I realized it. Your success depends on what voice you listen to most. Your success depends on which voice you let run the show and your life.

The biggest mistake is to think that successful people don't have that negative voice. Everyone does. Successful people learn not to listen to that negative voice.

Famous retired NFL quarterback, Joe Namath, who almost died from alcoholism, fended off drinking by naming the temptation that continually consumed him. He called that urge "Slick." "Now and then, 'Slick' whispers, but having a name for him makes me listen to him differently."

Instead, you learn to listen to what I call your "Gladiator voice."

Your Gladiator voice has all the traits and attributes you aspire to be when you're operating at your best. It's the voice that tells you, "Yes, you can." It whispers in your ear, "Let's go! You got this."

If you can learn to not listen to your version of "Slick" and instead listen to your Gladiator voice, you can tap into your courage, strength, passion, and bust through the limiting beliefs holding you back.

But remember, it's not a one-time battle. The gladiator must not only face the dragon, but defeat him each day.

ABOUT DAN: I am a TV Host, Speaker, Mindset Coach, Former American Gladiator, NFL player, #1 Bestselling Author of GLADIATOR and F DYING. Host of The Gladiator Way Podcast, and TEDx Speaker. (My TEDx Speech was watched over 500,000 times.)

98

MORNING MIRROR TALK

CARLA GITTO

Why: One night after school, I went to the doctor with my mother, only to have the doctor lean over his desk looking into my eyes saying little girl your mommy is going die soon, yes you heard me she will be gone soon, she was sick when you were born, you should NOT be here nor should she! My mother jumped up out of the chair grabbed my hand rushed me outside, Just as the door closed behind her she re-entering his room saying," I WILL Live to see my daughters sweet 16". "I am going to just fine." Every morning I would go downstairs watching her in the Mirror saying I will LIVE to see Carla's sweet 16, I declare, I AM well. At the Funeral talking to my cousin Vinny, he said Carla, you will need to be strong, learn how to love yourself, it is going to be hard. I thought I had been living in a bad dream. How much worst can it get when your mother dies in your arms. I listened intently to Vinny, deciding at that moment I will do what he said. HE shared his Habit. Mirror talk, talking to yourself every day looking into your eyes and declaring I AM _____. I Will_____. Eyes opened wide.

Every morning since the morning after receiving the horrific news. The decision was firmly made in mind I will do whatever he said; after all, I watched my mother. He looked at me, smiled, said it works as it did for two years.

The catch ONLY says good things and things you want, while you look into your eyes. For example, I AM Strong; I AM Love I will be successful. As I grew along my spiritual journey, spirit guided me to study with some of the greatest spiritual teachers. I learned more about the Power Of the Spoken Word, Spoken Word, Power of THE "I AM PRESENCE".

Morning Mirror Talk is a must ritual, not easy at first. As you build this new practice into your daily life wonderfully, you will build a new kind of strength and vision. I will tell you it will change your life! You will unlock your truth co-creating a new powerful you; you will become the deliberate creator of your life, life will happen for you and not to you! The power of the spoken word is outstanding!

THE UN-HABIT: BEING UNAWARE OF THE POWER OF YOUR WORDS SPOKEN AND UNSPOKEN

Why: Let's face it, aren't you sick and tired of disempowering yourself by saying both out loud and silently. Can WE agree it does not feel good, right? It drains you of life force energy. Making you irritated and quick to react. Life is dead and boring. Is that what you want? Indeed not that is why you have chosen to pick up this #1 NY Times Best Seller You are sick and tired of being sick and tired. You are tired of sabotaging your life. You NOW know you have no choice but to break the Habit of unconsciously speaking death and dis-ease over life.

When you make the conscious decision to break the Habit of negatively commanding your "I Am" and your "I" by the power of the spoken word, Then you are willing to conquer life and develop and new and deeper relationship with the power of the word, break this old Habit applying a new one will propel your life to new levels of success.

Let me explain the "I" is God "AM" is the Command, What you are speaking is God is, for example, I am tired you are saying God in me is tired. I am unworthy equals God in me is unworthy. I won't equal God in you won't. I Will equal God in you will. What are you declaring and speaking over your life? You are ready to be the co-creator of your life, living happy and joyously. Break this Habit will unlock your inner wisdom. There is simply no choice but to break the Habit of unconsciously speaking death and dis-ease into your life experience.

Imagine how amazing life will be or who's life you can save by the awareness of your spoken word to yourself, and imaging the kind of environment you can create how you can not only speak life into your life, but you become so aware you will speak life into the lives of those around you.

Once you break this Habit and start to speak life over your life, you will be, do, and have all you desire to experience. You will flow with life. Creative ideas will emerge. Life will become fun and not problem-filled. You will create a better, more loving relationship with yourself, and all the relationships around you will change.

About Carla: Are you ready to rise, shine, and awaken? Are you ready to Thrive? Then you are in the right place as an Interfaith Minister, Intuitive, Energy worker, Reiki Master Teacher, Crystals Healer; for more than half my life, I have helped my clients gain a better perspective of life. They are achieving their goals while mastering self-control of both their physical world and the spiritual world. As a result, my clients have acquired the tools strategies to live in harmony with an open heart, experiencing freedom, unity, and oneness. They have awakened to their divine essence living in joy and peace.

99

LIVE DAILY WITH A HEART FULL OF GRATITUDE

STEFANI STEVENSON

Why: Growing up in Texas, horses were a part of my daily life. They were my happy place, and every time I was around them, my heart filled with love, peace, and gratitude. To this day, horses are still my source of joy, and their sweet whinny fills my heart with gratitude.

Gratitude is an essential state of mind and state of being. Many of us have heard the saying that like attracts like. Gratefulness is a positive attribute, and a positive mindset allows for more positivity to flow; it opens new doors and brings a happier state of being.

How many times have we woken up in the morning and not wanted to get out of bed? You get up in a rather grouchy mood, stub your toe, and goes downhill from there. Or, imagine waking up in the morning still tired and not ready to face the day. This time, however, you turn over and see a picture on your nightstand. The happy memories flood in as your heart fills with gratitude. Lie there for few moments and soak in all there is to be grateful for; the sunlight filtering through the curtains, the sound of birds singing their song, or maybe it's the sound of a busy street, people out and about, and life brimming with possibilities! The day continues with more and more to be grateful for.

What we focus on sets the stage for our entire day. If gratitude for even the tiniest things, events, or circumstances becomes our focus, we open the door for even more to be grateful for entering. We change our perception and the way we view life.

One of the most important Habits is starting the day with three things to be grateful for. It can be as simple as the sun is out or a cup of freshly brewed coffee. Just about every person out there has a happy place, an event, item, memory, hobby, or thing that never fails to bring a smile.

When things get rough or seem to be falling apart, go back to that happy place and let the joy and gratitude fill your heart. Bask in that feeling and take a deep breath. Then look and find even one small thing that you are grateful for. Then think of another, and then watch as things turn around and more to be grateful for starts to show up! When we focus on gratitude, we make room for more to be grateful for.

THE UN-HABIT: EXPECTING THE WORST

Why: What's the worst that can happen? This is a common phrase majority of us have either heard or said.

How many times have we had that dreaded phone call to make and think, "well, what's the worst that can happen." The phone call goes pretty bad, as one expected.

Words and thoughts have such an impact on our reality, more so than we give credit. When we think or say the phrase "what's the worst that can happen," we set the worst-case scenario's expectation. It is as if we are asking for a negative outcome! It's all too common, and one of those phrases that is often said without realizing the implications. By using this phrase, it puts in our minds to expect the worst. We often get what we expect, whether it be good or bad.

So how do we break this Habit? We change one word! What is the BEST that can happen? By changing one word, you have successfully made a negative expectation of becoming hopeful and full of possibilities. This phrase is now positive and sets the expectation to one of a good outcome.

Get into the Habit of saying "what is the best that can happen" and watch how it changes your mindset. Instead of dreading the call, now the feeling is one of hope and positivity. It goes from this is going to be terrible to this is going to be great! The expectation of a negative experience has been replaced with the expectation of a positive experience. When we go into a situation with positive expectations, our whole demeanor changes. The energy we give off is lighter, happier, eager, and one of openness. Others felt that energy, and it is contagious!

Say you get a phone call from someone asking for a favor, and they are deadpan, negative, or sheepish, almost begging. This doesn't make you look forward to lending a hand. If the same person is hopeful, bright, and confident when they ask, not only would you be more willing to oblige, but you may even be looking forward to it!

Making it a Habit to approach situations with the thought "what's the best thing that can happen" will change your expectations from that of dread or negative results to an eagerness and positive results. We get what we expect in life, so why not expect the best!

About Stefani: After working in healthcare for over two decades, one of the most common stressors patients said was their living arrangements. They were constantly moving due to rent increases, or dealing with difficult landlords, or just struggling to afford rent. Sometimes their rent was more than some people's house payment! I would hear things like "I just want my own place" or "I wish I had my own house that no one can take from me". Specializing in pediatrics I often heard children say how badly they wanted their own room where they could run to when they were feeling scared. That's where I come in as a mortgage loan originator, helping make these dreams a reality by securing financing for all different credit and financial scenarios. Home ownership isn't an exclusive club and doesn't have to be an impossible dream.

100

REPLACE LIMITING BELIEFS

KALA KRISH

Why: Growing up, I have always had others telling me that I was not smart or good enough. I did not fit the requisites of my academic driven family. I was told I should do things that I am good at and not attempt things that would make me look 'dumb.'

There were many times I would go into periods of self-doubt questioning what I would do in life. That led to me being a lost soul even when I reached my 30s'. I had not figured out what I wanted to do with my life. I loved being a wife and mother but was not sure what else I was good at until I became an entrepreneur.

I loved it, but then again, there were days I would feel that I was not good enough at certain things. This one powerful Habit helped me to get things done and move forward. I learned how to install the word YET as my empowering belief, every-time I had negative beliefs on what I cannot do.

When I work with clients, I often hear them say, ' I don't know how to use social media or all this technology,' and I always add the word YET to finish off their sentence. So now the sentence reads, ' I don't know how to use social media or all these technologies, YET!'.

You see, this reframes the entire context of ones' thought pattern. By flipping your thought pattern with adding this simple one-word YET, you immediately believe that you CAN achieve what you thought was difficult or impossible with time and effort. You become solution-focused and confident instead of being in fear.

Most people grow up in environments where limiting thoughts get enforced—some more than others. What I have mastered or at least deliberately stayed aware of is that we all have the innate ability to change what our future looks like. Sounds cliché? But it's the truth. It starts with being aware that you have limiting thoughts and need to replace them with empowering beliefs. You can unlearn, relearn, and time is not of essence at all. We can flip our thoughts in seconds.

Whenever you find yourself in a space where you feel that you are not good enough or incompetent, know that you have not learned the skill or what it takes to achieve that thing YET! The next step, of course, is to take action and get the job done consciously.

THE UN-HABIT: EXCUSES

Why: Why do you do what you do? A very important question one needs to ask when embarking on this journey called

Entrepreneurship. Often, most start with the reason to make some money, maybe as a side hustle. Yes? And the question is, why do you want to make that extra money?

Have a better lifestyle or give the kids a better future or give back to the community or maybe more time with loved ones.

These 'whys' are great but are missing the bigger picture. You want to ask yourself why these reasons are important to you in the first place. Are they non-negotiable?

What I have seen most people do over time is continually using the very reasons they started as excuses not to take action to achieve.

' Can't wait for the kids to go back to school so that I can focus on the business.'

or maybe this,

'I can't put in the time needed for my business because my kids/ grandkids take up my time'?

This is guilt-tripping your loved ones.

You see how wanting to start to give the kids and family a better life has now become the very reason not to take action to commit to the business. This becomes a comfortable excuse to make one feel less guilty for not doing.

As a mum myself, I always want to give the best to my girl. I am setting an example. I take her to my events, meetings..whatever it took to get things done but never an excuse.

Many operate from a space of fear - The fear of failure or success.

While we are familiar with the fear of failure, the fear of success is very real. This is, in most cases, not fearing the success itself but rather the consequences of success. And these often stem from past influences where one could be taught not to 'show off' or celebrating success, not to have too much confidence, only to suffer from failures, etc

I challenge everyone to operate from a state of awareness and being present.

Understand that your 'why's' are more significant than your excuses, where your fears are originating from and face them,

Surrender to being the best YOU.

" You will either do it or keep finding excuses."

— STEVE JOBS

About Kala: Kala Krish is a Digital Lifestyle Influencer, an International Speaker, Branding & Leads Expert, and named the TOP 50 Inspiring Migrant Women UK. Described by mentors as the Zero to Hero Star - Kala is a passionate serial entrepreneur. In the last eight years, she has started up companies in various industries and raised six-figure investments.

Kala empowers and inspires thousands of entrepreneurs all around the world. Her heart-driven knowledge for marketing and sales, whether online or in-person has been a blueprint that allowed her to stand out in a crowded market. Her mission is to Inspire, Impact & Empower everyone to use their voice-tell their story to the world & in the process become a Digital Influencer adding value to others.

101

PERSEVERE THROUGH ANYTHING AND EVERYTHING

ANGIE MANSON

Why: People think that addiction happens to someone, but this isn't true. Addiction affects people of all backgrounds. Ultimately, though, people who suffer from addiction actively made choices that led them down that road. Once they find themselves trapped by addiction, perseverance is the Habit that will free them.

No magic pill or silver bullet will replace the personal work that must be done to change your Habits. Similar to losing weight, which also requires work and changing Habits, addiction is treated the same. Losing weight and quitting drugs or alcohol is a great comparison because it's easy to put on unhealthy weight by making poor food choices; however, taking that weight off requires a lot more effort.

> Determination and willingness to push through tough times when your mind or environment tells you to give in.

The same is true of substance abuse. Yes, a person may have mental health issues. Yes, a person may have a physical and psychological dependence on drugs or alcohol. Yes, a person may be trying to mask the pain or trauma from past experiences. All of these may be true, but these don't change what needs to be done. Like losing weight, there could be a million reasons why someone is overweight, but that doesn't change that the way out is the same. Addiction may be on a different scale, but the concept is the same. Overcoming addiction takes work and time. Learning the tools and rewiring the neural pathways with new routines leads to forming healthy daily Habits. In other words, overcoming addiction takes perseverance.

Perseverance is the way out. When your mind is giving in because feelings or situations are too difficult to confront, you must persevere. Likewise, and often overlooked, when things are going well, you can't let off the gas and celebrate with a substance. Both lead back to the same place, and that is a downward spiral spinning faster every time. For this reason, perseverance is key.

If you give up after a couple of months of sobriety, you won't reap the rewards you don't realize are just ahead of you. You really can achieve your true potential and the life you want by overcoming addiction. However, every day you must persevere with good Habits, especially when you aren't motivated. Eventually, sobriety itself becomes the Habit and a better life is the reward.

HAB1T™

The Un-Habit: Negative self-talk

Why: Negative self-talk is the #1 Habit that will make the difference between whether someone will be successful in recovery or not. Coincidentally (or perhaps not), it's also the #1 thing that will stop someone from doing anything they want in life.

Negative self-talk perpetuates addiction as it feeds the individual with thoughts of blame, shame, unworthiness, and paints a picture of failure in anything they want to do or achieve. Negative self-talk is the inner dialogue you have with yourself that limits your ability to have confidence and reach your potential. It leads you to believe that you are a victim of circumstance and not the master of your own destiny.

Even after someone gets sober, negative self-talk creeps in over and over with even the slightest bump in the road or minor pitfall. Negative self-talk is insidious and can affect anyone at any time. It is important to retrain the brain to recognize the good in things and not focus on all of the bad or set oneself up for failure because that is what has happened in the past.

Utilizing Positive Psychology, an individual can start focusing on the positive experiences and attributes instead of only seeing the negative. This isn't something we say or do once, and it is now a part of us, it takes conscious effort to change the negative to positive. We can practice optimism by seeing the glass as half full, we can look for the silver lining by finding the good in a bad situation, and we can practice gratitude by being thankful for what we have or what we've been through and acknowledging this is what makes us who we are. For someone who's addicted, this positive outlook is not a natural behavior, and so it must be practiced consistently so that the Habit is enforced and becomes part of who they are. Using these tools will build well-being, self-confidence, compassion, hope, and happiness. Sobriety doesn't have to be a somber condition; sobriety should be celebrated and joyful. And we need to have the ability to live that.

Negative self-talk must be eliminated and replaced with positive psychology for anyone getting sober or trying to improve their lives as it focuses the individual on their strengths, not their weaknesses, and builds self-esteem which has been ravaged by life or drugs or alcohol.

ABOUT ANGIE: The reason I am here and why I do what I do is because I've personally overcome immense obstacles through perseverance and have experienced real recovery. I was lucky enough to find my passion and purpose, which is to help people who were once like me to find happiness and success in life. Nothing makes me happier than seeing someone who had no hope get their confidence and self-esteem back and go on to live a happy and healthy life. I naturally root for the underdog and have seen so many people change their lives for the better and in turn, positively change the lives of those around them. Many people are like diamonds in the rough, they just need to be picked up, polished, shown that they are valuable and given the belief that they are tough and beautiful like diamonds and anything is possible.

102

GET COMFORTABLE ON VIDEO

NAOMI BAREKET AND RAMI BAREKET

Why: People want to know who is the person behind the service or product. They want to feel the real you. People buy with emotions and justify with logic, and through a video, you can share feelings and share your values. You can let your ideal customers get to know you and feel connected to you.

Years ago, when we started talking on video about mission-driven business, someone who felt numb and sick said that watching the video gave her the strength to chose life again and create her passionate business. She became our faithful client and a great source of word of mouth.

Since then, not only have we continued to do engaging videos, and get new clients, we also taught our clients to use our method, and the clients have been continually reporting amazing results.

The thing is that in the beginning, everyone feels awkward to speak to a camera. We tend to be afraid of how we look and sound and what people will say.

The more you do it, the more you become comfortable, more natural, and authentic despite being uncomfortable at first. And the more confident you become on the video, the more your ideal clients feel confident about you too.

Because...

✔ Video allows you to talk from your heart directly to the heart of your ideal client. It combines visual and auditory impact.... Prospect get to see you, hear you, and feel connected to you, and willing to learn more from you. Therefore showing up on video is memorable and influencing.

✔ It's easier for clients to decide to buy when they see the human behind the product or service. They know that you are a credible source.

✔ Prospects might not know or doubt that there's a solution to their problem, or perhaps they know of a few options of solutions, but they don't know about yours yet. So they need to see that you are confident in the video, and with what you convey, so they can feel confident that your solution is possible and best for them.

As an entrepreneur, you can't avoid doing videos, and the more comfortable you are, the more confident you will show up on video, stand out, and the more you attract new clients, serving your mission.

THE UN-HABIT: SHOWING UP UNPREPARED ON VIDEO (WHEN YOU GET TOO COMFORTABLE.)

Why: Prospects today more than ever want to get value for their time.

Time is precious, and the noise outside on social media is louder than ever. Prospects are more selective, and they lose interest very quickly.

I mean, think about it, how many times you signed out of a video because it was boring, or because you felt like you had no idea about what they were talking about.

As much as we love to be spontaneous, there's nothing like having a clear thought behind what you say on video. You can be prepared and still be natural and authentic.

It is better to prepare your thoughts, because...

⬤ If you are unprepared and you go around and around, prospects might get bored, signed out, and unfollow you.

⬤ Things that you say impulsively may trigger your clients. You might unintentionally say something offensive. My client told me about a video she saw, and she was very upset at the presenter because she felt he was disrespectful to people with disabilities. She said she would never listen to him again. And now she tells everyone that they shouldn't listen to him either.

⬤ As much as some of us love being spontaneous on video, sometimes it can distract you from your path or the message you want to convey.

When you are prepared and organized, you can be clear on your message. Specifically, when you try to sell something, a confused client will say no.

Even when you are spontaneous, organizing your thoughts before you speak makes your prospects feel that you value their time and will be more engaged and build stronger relationships with you.

It's ok to share moments from your private life, yet you should be prepared when it comes to your business, being respectful to your prospects' time, so your videos are efficient, valuable, and engaging.

Remember, it is not about you but about the value you give them.

About Naomi & Rami: Naomi Bareket and Rami Bareket help entrepreneurs monetize their passion by creating with them engaging and converting videos, courses, lead magnets, funnels, books, and more. So they can stand out, build their credibility, and attract more clients.

The Bareket believes that a mission-driven business is the only way to keep you motivated and thrive. They believe that no one has the same mission and purpose as you. Therefore, they are passionate about helping you to reveal your unique superpower so that you can shine it on the world. Their proven breakthrough method combines business with spiritual work to maximize your influence and turn it into affluence.

Their clients say, "The awesome scripts and videos learned from the Barekets, have converted more prospects into clients than we've ever experienced before."

103

TRANSFORM YOUR DREAM INTO A GOAL

CATHERINE HICKLAND

Why: As an actress (Knight Rider, One Life to Live) who now performs worldwide as a stage hypnotist and owns a cosmetic company, I am the epitome of turning dreams into reality.

I don't just dream. I set goals. This is how you turn your dreams into reality.

A dream is something that is just floating out in the ethereal, but a goal is something you can make a viable plan for. To turn your dreams into a goal, you have to see it like you're watching it in a movie on a 40-foot movie screen.

To continually be manifesting your goals is vital. You need to see it becoming a reality, full of color. Imagine you're sitting in the back of a theater, and every day you do something towards that goal, just one step at a time. You move one row up in the theater of life; you get closer and closer until you're part of the film.

Now the big question is, "What dreams do I strive for." My technique is first to turn my dreams into goals and then rank them in order of importance. This way, you get organized in a way that will allow you to move forward with an action plan.

To structure my goals, I'm a big fan of writing things down and getting it out of my head. Rather than just thinking about it, I act on it. Writing your goals down also stops you from being distracted by the next bright, shiny objects. You have to stay focused.

To achieve the success you desire, you have to devote every day to doing something that moves you closer to your goals. Remember, let NOTHING stop you.

THE UN-HABIT: STOP DOUBTING YOURSELF.

Why: It's too easy in this life to doubt yourself. Many of us get scared by things that keep us from living our best life. This fear-based thought process eventually turns into a fear-based Habit that will stop you from being successful in every aspect of your life.

Stop self-sabotaging yourself because someone told you you weren't good enough. A saying I love is that the best parts of life are on the other side of fear. If you can stop getting in your own way, nothing can hold you back.

One thing that never made sense to me was "The fear of success." It is honestly the stupidest thing I've ever heard. I don't buy it.

Your self-doubt is the most significant deterrent to reaching your goals and dreams. I need you to decide right now that you will no longer allow "you" to be the thing that holds you back ever again!

I recently found this quote that just resonated with me. "Some people are holding grudges for things they did to you."

I made a decision when I was very young... that when I grew up, I would be independent and never let anyone raise their voice to me like my parents did when I was little.

You need to remember that when self-doubt creeps in, it is the actions of another that are causing this in you. Are you going to let them dictate your life and your success? I don't think so.

In my case, a family doctor had molested me when I was young. I tried to speak about it, but no one believed me. When everyone calls you a liar or doesn't listen, it can make you feel quite ugly inside. For many years I didn't have a vehicle to express this because I confined myself to being the perfect actress on tv and trying to achieve that lifestyle. Gratefully, I did find an outlet in 2005. I did an Off-Broadway show that was wildly successful in NY, called "Pieces of Ass." It was about how being pretty affected your life, the good, bad, and the ugly. I got to talk about being violated and feeling helpless. It was the first time I realized that your experiences in life don't define who you are. One of the shining, most cherished moments of my life was when outside the theatre, there were lines of girls who wanted to share their stories to heal.

Today I have used these lessons in my life to transition to something I love doing, hypnosis and mentalism. The power of your mind is fascinating. If you get anything out of this, please do one thing for me... don't let the doubts creep in, you are better than that, stronger than that, and more powerful than you know. It is time for you to live out your dreams by understanding you define your life, no one else.

About Catherine: Catherine Hickland is an actress, best known for her starring roles on Daytime TV, most in the award-winning role of "Lindsay Rappaport" on ABC 's One Life to Live (1968). Fascinated by the mind and how it works, Catherine Hickland was first exposed to hypnosis, as a young girl watching Pat Collins, "The Hip Hypnotist" on television. During her final two years on "One Life", Catherine diligently studied the art of hypnosis. After becoming a certified hypnotherapist, and having spent her life in front of the camera and onstage, she took the art and science of hypnosis into entertainment.

She is a world class keynote speaker and the author of "The 30 Day Heartbreak Cure, a Guide to Getting Over Him and Back Out There One Month From Today" and in 2001, Catherine created and remains CEO of "Cat Cosmetics", a very successful line of color cosmetics

In 2013, Catherine opened a training facility in Las Vegas for people who want to learn self-hypnosis, as well as training hypnotists who want to learn the art of stage hypnosis. She plans to take hypnosis into the mainstream in a way that has never been done before.

She is married to the multi-talented Todd Fisher and loves her chickens!

104

TURN NEGATIVES INTO POSITIVES

FRANK SHANKWITZ

Why: I was ten years old when Juan Delgadillo, my mentor, taught me an important life lesson. I lived in the little town of Seligman, Arizona, population 500, in the mid-1950s. We were so poor, poor people in town were helping us. When I started the 7th grade, my mother left me again. She said, "You're on your own." I went to Juan, and I said, "I don't know what to do." He said, "Again, learn how to turn those negatives into positives." I said, "What do you mean? My mother just left me?" Juan was teaching me, no matter your circumstances, always turn the negatives into positives. He said, "I've arranged for you to live with the widow Sanchez."

You'll make $26 a week as a dishwasher (I'm 12 years old), and she's only going to charge you $20 a week room and board. The positives were something else for the first time in my life; I'm going to have my own bedroom. I never had indoor plumbing before; we had to go to the station master house to shower and use the bathroom, with all the male kids in town. Now, I've got my own bedroom, indoor plumbing, and she's the best cook in town, all of these are positives. Not only that, but she also had the first television set in Seligman, Arizona. So in all of those negatives of my mom leaving me, I found all of these positives (with Juan's help). Because of this, I started to change from a boy to a man. These years taught me self-survival and made me realize; you can find positives in any negative situation if you look.

So when you have a great idea and share it with others, people will say, repeatedly, "Oh, I've never heard of this, it's not going to work." Find the ways to make it work to turn those negatives into the positives. Don't give up on your mission you've got to do something with your great idea no matter what others say to you. You've got an idea, stick to it. Make it work.

THE UN-HABIT: NEGATIVITY

Why: Look for the positive in life, in people, and everything else. We've all met those negative people, and know what they are like to be around, they complain. You could have the best steak in the world, but they will say, "Oh, that's a rotten steak, they didn't do that right." It's all in your mindset. It isn't automatically within. It takes guidance and training; it's your mindset. Like I've said before, hang around with positive people and lose the negativity. The positive people, they're going to reinforce you all the time with positive thoughts. You hang around negative people, guess what? It's like in school; I heard this example before going into high school; if you hang around with the smokers and the dopers, that's what you're going to be. If you hang around with the jocks and the smart people, that's what you're going to be. Choose the people you're going to hang around with and choose the people who will reinforce your thoughts and ideas. Turn Negatives into Positives and Stick with Them!

About Frank: Frank Shankwitz is best known as the Creator, Co-Founder & first President/CEO of the Make - A - Wish Foundation, an extraordinary charity that grants the wishes to children with life-threatening illnesses. From humble beginnings, the Make-A-Wish Foundation is now a global organization that grants a child's wish somewhere in the world on an average of every 28 minutes. Frank is a U.S. Air Force veteran and has a long and distinguished career in law enforcement.

105

WRITE DOWN YOUR GOALS

JOE THEISMANN

Why: I mean, really writing it down. I can't tell you how important it is to write down the things that you want to do. It becomes a Habit, not just in the business world, but it becomes a Habit in your life, which really has to transition.

I mean, the book I wrote, How To Be A Champion Every Day, okay, basically touches the world of business, the world of sports, and our own lives. I try and draw the analogies between the three to show you that what you do in your personal life, what we do in the world of athletics, and what you do in the business world are all foundations of the same thing.

And one of the most important parts of it is to be able to write down what you want to do. Write down your accomplishments. You can check them off. But it also keeps you a little bit more focused, and keeps you between the lines a little bit more, because as you start to stray away, you can glance back and say, "This is what I needed to do today."

And so for me, I would say that the 1 Habit that I've developed, and I have now, and I think, and I attribute it to part of the success that I've been able to enjoy, is a simple fact that you identify it, you write it down, and then it gives you a guideline. It's like a contract with yourself.

Instead of being a rudderless ship, okay? I wake up in the morning, well, I'm going to cut the grass, I do this, I do that. You have a plan. I'll give you an example. In the book, I talk about me being on my Ranch. I get on my tractor one day, and I'm going to cut the grass. And I get up near a fence, and I look at one of the fence posts, and it's leaning. So I got about half the grass done.

So, I get off the tractor. I go, and I start to work on the fence post. I start taking the post out, digging a hole. And as I look down the fence, what do I see? I see a bush over the fence. So, now I stopped digging the hole. I mosey on down to the bush, and it gets dark. And what have I accomplished in this day? I've cut half the grass. I've got a hole dug in the ground, and I've got a pile of bushes that I have to pick up the next day.

So what I did was, is I got half of everything done, and before I can ever move forward, I have to clean up what I didn't do. And that's why I say if you write down what you want to do, you have to focus on completing it. A good friend of mine just told me that she doesn't feel like she's very focused, and I disagree— completely 100%. But I believe that writing down what you want to do is very, very important.

Instead of just saying, "These are the things I want to do." And get them done, and now you're not playing catch up. Now it's a clean sheet. It's, you get inspired a little bit more, you get more energy. How many of us wake up in the morning and go, "Oh, geez, I forgot to do that yesterday." Before I ever start my day today, I've got to clean up yesterday's mess, or I've got to go back and finish the project that I know I could have finished, but I didn't take the time to do it. This little Habit is a huge game-changer.

The Un-Habit: Being around the wrong people at the wrong place at the wrong time

Why: I have had the privilege to be associated with many elite individuals. Not just athletes, but business people, and everybody else that has made it to the very top. I always ask the question to them. Was it just talent? There was discipline. But what is the special sauce that makes an elite champion?

And I think one of the best phrases I heard came from Tom Brady. "It's the right place, the right time, with the right people." The right place, the right time, and the right people.

Now, sometimes that people part of it might be your family. Having that right unit around you to get it done. The right place. You want to be in an organization, or you want to be someplace where that opportunity is there.

Opportunity is my favorite word. And the thing is, is if that opportunity presents itself, if you're in that place, at the right time when they're transitioning maybe to another quarterback, or maybe a new coach, or whatever you might have that opportunity to present yourself to a different set of eyes. Someone that won't prejudge you, someone that didn't prejudge you. And then all of a sudden, it's the people around you.

And really, and I've repeated this time and time, the quarterback is the single most dependent position on a field in the world of football. And when you think about it, executives in a company are the same way. And that's why you have to be very respectful and understanding of the people that work with you. Notice I didn't say, "For you." But the people that work with you, that allow you to lead, that allow you to grow. That will enable you to think.

These are all things that are so vitally important when it comes to, I think, being able to try and be successful. And like I said, it took me five years to write the book, and just thinking back over the influences that I've had, people have had in my life. Little things like Joe Walton, who was my second offensive coordinator. We had a game against the Kansas City Chiefs, and after every game, Joe and I would meet personally, on Monday, our day off, and there would be five pages of corrections.

And so finally, we played the chiefs. I'm like, 22 for 27, 300 yards, two touchdowns, just a great day, and I went home, and I'm thinking, "Man, this is it. What can he do? How many corrections can he do?" Five pages. I sat there, and I had my shoulders slumped down. And he looked at me. He said, "Joe, look, the reason I'm doing this is because that team's not a very good football team. Both those touchdown passes probably should have been interceptions against a good football team."

He said, "I want to prepare you to be able to compete against the greatest. Not just think that you're good, or great against an average opponent." And that's always stayed with me. And so, it's been a driving force in my life. Why not compete to be the greatest? Why wake up in the morning and be average?

Joe was the right person to be in my life. I was in the right place at the right time. You have to pay attention and see where you are. If it is right, stay. If it is wrong, fix it.

Joe Theismann
Winning Quarterback
Entrepreneur
1 Habit Contributor

About Joe: Joe Theismann is a World Champion Quarterback and Entrepreneur. He spent 12 seasons with the Washington Redskins, where he was a two-time Pro Bowler and helped the team to two consecutive Super Bowl appearances, winning Super Bowl XVII over the Miami Dolphins

106

MEDITATE EVERY MORNING
BRIAN SMITH

Why: When I first came to America in 1979, some 40 plus years ago, I was 28 years old, invulnerable, ready to set the world on fire and looking for a new business. I rented a little house in Venice, Los Angeles, and all my friends told me not to go there because it was like a barrio (ghetto). But I was from Australia; they'll love me. So I rented this tiny house, and it was in a compound, and it didn't strike me at the time, but all the windows had bars on them. I moved in, bought a water bed, filled it up in the unusual sunken bedroom then I bought a pizza and a big candle. I stuck the candle on the wooden shelf in the living room, lit it and happy ate pizza and enjoyed a bottle of wine on my first night in the house.

The next morning, I woke up, sat up, and everything went black. "Oh, shit, the house is on fire!" There was a one foot pocket of air along the floor so I crawled up to the front door, and I was fumbling with the doorknob and couldn't get it to open. I just thought and almost said it out loud. "Oh shit, I'm going to die!" Then there was this voice, it wasn't in my eardrums and I wasn't thinking it, it was just this voice that said calmly and slowly, "Brian, you haven't done enough with your life yet." I listened and said "Shit, you're right!" I stood up, used the walls to lead me to the windows and started smashing out the glass first one then the next. Breathing was difficult so I kept ducking back into the sunken bedroom because there was about three feet of air left in the bottom. I thank God for that sunken bedroom. I smashed all the glass out and I got my head up against the iron bars, screaming for help. Eventually my calls for help were answered by some workmen who got the bars off the window and pulled me out.

This experience confirmed to me that there is an intelligence inside of us beyond our usual understanding of thinking and doing. Now usually, it only comes out in moments of absolute necessity like it did with me and most people probably never hear it but I believe it is there. I believe because I had that experience, it was so real, so true and so loving, I mean, there was no panic, like there was no fire, just some kind of inner intelligence guidance. It was just this loving voice stating the immediate point, Brian, get up and get out of there! So in my heart and conscious mind I've always known that there is another part of my life, of my being, an inner intelligence that I try and tune back into it every time I meditate.

I meditate every morning, not to go out into space and find peace or anything, but to try and connect with the spirit, that inner intelligence that's already in me. We all have some fragment of God or spirit or whatever in us and it's only when you try to truly connect to that part of you that you get a perspective on life and the other shit that's going on daily. So meditating is very grounding, and very, very strengthening, so no matter what comes up in the day, I can handle it.

I used to sit there on the carpet to meditate. As I got older I sat on chairs now years later I still, believe it or not I sit on a little stool with my back up against the window and listen with my eyes closed. I have a very spiritual book that I read or listen to in the morning while I make a coffee and prepare for my day. There are all sorts of forms of meditation; you don't have to be a guru with your legs crossed and your thumbs together, as long as you sincerely try to connect with that spark of God within you, that's meditation.

Sometimes it works and it's very powerful although most times, it's like, "Oh, well, 30 minutes better get up and start the day". Often, you'll have perplexing problems going on with your home life or your work or relationships and just by calming down and meditating quite often you'll get clarity, especially if there's been anger or fear involved. When you settle into yourself, being calm, you can think about the logic of the situation without the emotions and then things automatically fall into place.

So meditating just helps you figure out the easy path through all of the stuff that you're navigating whether it is relationships, work or any combination other things. I have had several instances where I'm so strong and powerful because I've experienced it to an extraordinary level.

The reason this is so important is very simple. If there was more love in the world, we wouldn't be fighting each other like this. Right? We wouldn't be intolerant with each other and the only way you can love somebody is if you love yourself first. You have to get yourself right first and realize that people aren't a threat to you; they're just other humans on their path trying to figure life out too. They're affected by everything they've read, seen and done. If you can get to understand somebody else's motivation, you can then sort of feel more relaxed that you can feel an affinity to them and then you can approach them on a different level with a new perspective. The more you do that and you get to know more about who they are and what motivates them, what their stresses are from family life to business, the more you can love them. As soon as you love people more, you'll find your life going along a lot better. When the love is real you can do social activities together. The trick is how do you branch out of your little circle and get to love one more person every day? Because that's the only way this will change the world is when we all try and love each other. Even if it's one more person a day, eventually it will overtake, and everybody will stop all this bullshit fighting, shaming, antagonizing and war. Just because they're in Asia or the Middle East, there're still humans. The person with a gun has still got a sister at home who's getting married in two weeks, and they want to be there for the wedding. Real-life goes on everywhere, all across the world. And we see him as a man with a gun, but that's where we do not understand where they're coming from. And if we could do that more often, it would be a much safer and better world.

The Un-Habit: Stop judging

Why: Stop judging and start understanding.

If you can disarm them because you get to know them and understand where they're coming from a great story could unfold. Imagine a snarling little half animal with a club, its spewing hate and fury out. You'd get a sense that this is a dangerous animal right? But then you expand your vision and begin to understand and see its world, this animal is standing in front of a saber tooth tiger and behind him is a wife and two children. See how the image just shifted, you have a better understanding now. Right? The animal described is mankind, at first you saw him as a threat in a horrible vision, then you come and see the noble, true strength of the person willing to give his life for his family. It's the same person in both situations, but when you expand your view and understand where he's coming from you have a different perception and the more you're open and willing to love that person. So it's really about our fearfulness of everyone. We've been taught to be afraid for our own protection a survival instinct. When I was a little kid, I was able to roam the streets until dark. Now my kids are never let out. They've got to be chaperoned and everything. We've been in the process of fear for as long as I've been alive. If we could get back to that period where there is love and safety and happiness, wow, what a great world it would be.

I think about 40 years ago. I mean, right when I got to America, I was intrigued by my roommate and a friend talking about the Lucifer Rebellion. I asked, "What the hell are you talking about?

Where'd you get this?" And they said it's in a book called the Urantia Book. And I said, "Hey, do you have one? Can I borrow it?" And it's 2000 pages, and it's a channel book. And I've used that as the basis of me getting good; it's a complete correlation of science, religion, and philosophy. The cosmos, the way we live, and the evolution of this planet. And it's just a fantastic overview of life and the evolution of where we are. It's compatible with creation and evolution if you can believe that. Absolutely compatible..

About Brian: At 29, Brian decided that a life in Public Accounting was not for him! He quit his job and went to California to look for a new business idea and to surf all the legendary breaks such as Rincon, Malibu, Dana Point and Windansea. He soon noticed that there were no sheepskin boots in California, so he and a friend brought six pairs from Australia to test and so, "UGG" was born and over the next seventeen years Brian built it into a national brand and solidified himself as a business expert.

107

FOCUSING ON THE ACTUAL AGENDA
PRESCOTT ELLISON

Why: Justin Timberlake, Christina Aguilera, Earth, Wind & Fire. Stevie Wonder, Brian McKnight, Sin Banderas, Lupe Fiasco, Kanye West, Smokey Robinson. The one thing that all of these artists have in common is I play the drums for all of them. That's ultimately, what my career is about.

I'm playing drums for artists that are playing a concert or recording something in the studio. My ability to listen, and because I don't read music, I'm a self-taught drummer, I don't have the luxury of getting a chart sent to me or reading on site. Some musicians don't know the song, they'll get to the gig, and they get the chart, and read it and play it.

I, fortunately, didn't pursue that path to become a musician. I learned everything by ear. And then it's funny because I had a conversation with Stevie wonder who cannot see, and he can't read music, but he plays everything by feel and by memory and everything.

So I had to figure out some method on how I would not only articulate but assimilate and remember. Store all this data in my brain, so when I'm sitting there on a stage and getting ready to perform in front of thousands of people, my memory retention has to be at its peak.

With that being said, studying, practicing, and focusing on what I was doing. I listened to the songs, wrote little short notes, and then got to the point where I could play without referring to my notes and then actually not remembering the song, but knowing the song. Those are two things there. Those are two things that whether you're an athlete or a surgeon or a musician or whatever walk of life, even if you're a keynote speaker, you can remember a speech or know what you're talking about.

People who try to remember things often forget what they're remembering, but if you know what you're doing, know your craft, master the craft, you will perform at the highest level of expertise. This all starts by knowing what your agenda is and focusing on it.

THE UN-HABIT: EATING OUT OF CONVENIENCE

Why: The one primary un-Habit that I would say, or the thing that I would say regarding the un-Habit of eating out of convenience, is to replace that convenient drive-through, pick up at the restaurant items, with things that you can primarily meal prep. Some carrots, some vegetables, broccoli, fruits, nuts, grains, smoothies. These are things that are much more convenient. It takes less time to go to the grocery store once a week and buy fresh fruits, fresh vegetables, chia seeds, flax seeds, sesame seeds, wheat germ, oatmeal, protein powder, celery, cucumber, broccoli. These are things, and you buy all that stuff.

Then you bring it to the kitchen, and you separate it, and you make it into seven days worth of it. And you pull that one container out. You put it in the blender. You either add aloe Vera juice or coconut milk or whatever your choice is, as far as the liquid. You blend it, you drink it. My blender, I have a Ninja blender, some people use the Vitamix, but my blender, the full capacity of it is probably, I don't know how many ounces it is, but when I pour it out, it makes like four Mason jars of blended drinks. And I just put the cap on the Mason jar. I drink one; I put the other three in the refrigerator. I drink them.

It is easy not to eat out of convenience, but it takes a little time to make it a Habit.

ABOUT PRESCOTT: Prescott Ellison is a Grammy Award Winning drummer, composer, author, and inventor-turned entrepreneur. He is the recipient of the Barack Obama Presidential Lifetime Achievement Award.

He has toured, recorded, and performed worldwide for 25 years with recording artists that include Brian Mcknight, Stevie Wonder, Sade, Justin Timberlake, and Christina Aguilera. Over the past decade, Prescott pursued his passion for nutrition, fitness, and education. He is the author of "Fit to Travel: A Travelers Guide to Nutrition and Fitness" and five children's books. He then created the SuperFood Friends who are over 100 fruit and vegetable characters, each with their own unique individual skill sets to help educate, inspire, and engage children about the importance of nutrition, fitness, and living a healthy lifestyle.

108

BE OPEN

ROB ANGEL

Why: This is what has guided me my entire life long before Pictionary. I'm open to experiences I'm open to new things. I don't judge opportunities or people or things when they come my way. And that's when for me, the magic happens.

Instead of I don't like this person or nowadays, the discourse that's going on will at least be open to the conversation. You don't have to like it. You don't have to agree with it. But you got to try it on. And then you can say yes or no. But being open for me is my whole life.

I love to travel. I love to meet new people. And if I'm not open, what's the point. It just kind of shuts the whole process down. And so I'm always curious. Being open is just about being curious.

I play a game called Left, Right, Center. And what I do is I will walk to the middle of the street, on the sidewalk, excuse me. I'll close my eyes, and I'll tilt my head back. And the first word that comes to my mind, I will do. Left, right, center, forward, back, or stay. And it's just a little trick I play on myself to be more open and be present and do whatever's around me at that moment.

And so it's a little Habit that I can do when I just let go. Because it's not thinking. Being open is really about not thinking. So if I'm overthinking being open, I'm not open. And I'm talking about myself. I mean, this is me as well. This isn't just people that I'm talking to. Some of the greatest stuff that's happened, some of my adventures happened when I was open.

You can do this anywhere. It doesn't have to be the best adventure in the world.

People that know me, they play a game. And when I'm not in Seattle or wherever and they're together, and they'll put a dollar in the table, and they all guess where in the world I am and who's ever closest gets the money.

Lastly, being open is important for creativity. It's important to keep your mind, and your heart open. It's important for experiences to happen because you don't know where those experiences will lead. Instead of just being focused on one thing, you've got to be focused on everything. And again, you don't have to like everything, but when you're open, that's when these different inputs come.

You're going to walk down a lot of different paths. And you will find your greatest passion in the process. A friend of mine once said, my passion

THE UN-HABIT: NOT TO BE IN MY ELECTRONICS WHEN I GO TO BED

Why: I'm actively working on this one right now. I'm going to pat myself on the back when I can do it. Two nights in a row now, I had not turned on my phone when I went to bed. This is new to me because I like reading the newspaper in bed.

There's nothing I'm going to learn at 11:00, midnight on the phone that I couldn't learn in the morning.

I want to look at it differently; electronics and things that aren't serving me easily are fixable. Meaning the phone in my hand isn't that complicated. I don't have to un-Habit eating, drinking, or breathing. It's keeping me awake at night.

The consequences of that phone is not the main point, but that Habit is taking time away from my sleep. That Habit is getting my mind racing when it shouldn't be. That Habit of that phone is now taking me away from what I should be doing. And that's primarily sleeping.

ABOUT ROB: Robert Angel invented the popular word guessing game Pictionary, which was self-published in his tiny apartment in 1985._Since selling Pictionary, he has gone on to invent board games and products. Most of his life is spent drawing fruit and surfing the Pacific Angel currently lives in Seattle and is involved in multiple non-profit companies.

109

LEARN TO TRUST THE PROCESS

BRIAN VANDER MEULEN

W hy: The ability to push through difficult situations will go a long way toward determining how successful you will be in your life and career. For example, before my current career, I was an automotive service manager and built a side career in real estate. My dream was to be an entrepreneur and to create my destiny. However, my boss was more interested in having me build his business, which is understandable since I was working for him. He decided that I wasn't loyal enough to him, so he gave me two weeks of severance pay and let me go.

Now I was faced with my first major lesson in perseverance. Not only had I just lost my job, but my wife and I had just purchased a house, and we had a 3-year-old and a 2.5-month old to provide for—and no steady income.

When things become difficult, it's important not to give in to overwhelm. I needed to take action to fix my situation quickly.

We decided to use a credit line on our home to buy investment properties to create rental income that we could live on.

The important thing to remember is that there is always an answer. The key is to assess your current situation correctly and then come up with an action plan. Then implement it as soon as possible. When you do these two things, you won't have time to worry about what could happen because you are now focused on the future instead of the past. All great champions think this way.

Even though we develop a great plan of action, things can still go wrong. When the real estate market crash happened in 2008, we lost our investment properties and had to pivot again, hence the second lesson of perseverance.

Losing my investment properties caused me to make another pivot without guarantee of success. When I moved into commercial real estate, I built a portfolio and then eventually became an author and speaker, which is where I am today.

However, I wouldn't have any of this had I chosen to give up. It's always a choice.

Never give up, and trust the process along the way.

THE UN-HABIT: SETTLING FOR THE STATUS QUO

Why: Most people find that they live an unfulfilling life. Often, that's because they are busy planning their lives around their career. After all, that's how they provide for their families. But the tricky part about that is they sacrifice their freedom to live the life they truly want. It's not their fault; they don't know any different.

For many, this is the status quo that they were socialized to believe in.

I choose differently for myself and my family.

Instead of planning my life around my business, I choose to plan my business around my life. This gives me the freedom to do what I enjoy, such as spending time with my family and planning vacations when I want to take them instead of when I am told I can.

Being an entrepreneur allows me to make these kinds of choices. I work when I want to while in the service of my clients. Also, I work with who I want to work with, not who I have to.

That gives me tremendous freedom.

As Charlie "Tremendous," Jones famously said, "You will be the same person in five years as you are today except for the people you meet and the books you read." Choosing the input, you receive from the world gives you an amazing level of power.

When you refuse to live by the status quo, you have the opportunity to reap great rewards if you are excellent at what you do and provide a customer experience that is second to none.

I am not here to live an ordinary life, and neither are you. When you raise your standards and believe in what's possible, the rewards are greater. Choose to impact the world around you within the context of the gifts God has given you.

I promise you will never regret making that choice.

About Brian: Brian has risen above the darkest of times and continued to push for his dreams. Brian is a husband to his wife Cathy of 22 years, father to 3 children, Nick (19), Nathan, (16), and his "special" little girl, Sarah (11). As a successful real estate investor/agent, Brian knows the real estate investing world's ins & outs, both personally and as a coach and mentor. Brian specializes in creative commercial transactions, speaking, and training where he helps counsel his clients and mentees in ways that will minimize the risks and therefore maximize their returns. Brian's experiences in life and business have taught him the importance of teamwork, the power that comes from pushing through life's many struggles, learning to trust the process, and finally having faith and knowing that God Is Good and Always provides.

110

ASSASSINATE THE GOLDEN RULE

JEANIE HOLZBACHER

Why: Many of us have been taught the golden rule, "Do unto others as you would have others do unto you."

However, it's somewhat narcissistic as it keeps you at the center of the throne. And it prevents you from making deep, quality connections as fast as you otherwise could.

The platinum rule says, "Do unto others as THEY would have you do."

Let's say my best sales guy, Bob landed another account through some real savvy effort. I decide to send an extra thanks for a job well done and the bonus he receives. I send him my favorite European chocolates. After all, I would certainly love that gift. Bob is not a fan of chocolate. (Isn't that wrong on so many levels?) He is allergic to it. I did not know because I measured the World through my reference frame and didn't spend much time getting to know him.

But what if I found out Bob loves hockey and I got him two tickets to the hockey game? How much more would he appreciate it and feel valued?

It's the difference between showing up in the room and saying, "Hello World! Here I am!" and entering with the attitude of, "Ah, there you are!"

This requires being intentional about valuing people. But it can revolutionize your life in two ways:

- It places the other person in the center of the equation, allowing for him or her to feel genuinely appreciated as an individual.
- It requires you to set aside your ego and operate in a spirit of humility. Great for character-building and getting things done the right way!

Every day we are all one interaction, one conversation away from enhancing or sabotaging our results.

Make them conversations that count!

THE UN-HABIT: GIVE UP THE NEED TO BE RIGHT

Why: Give up the need to be right because your way may not be the only way, and it could be wrong.

For example, two women were fitness partners on a weight loss journey. Sue is a strong-willed, take charge kind of girl. Kim is an easygoing individual who prefers to avoid the spotlight. They are out on a walk when a red sports car pulls up and yells "PIG" loudly as he speeds past them.

Sue gets angry and wants to give him a knuckle sandwich and a piece of her mind. Kim internally beats herself up and retreats, thinking, "It's my fault!" They round the corner, and in the middle of the street is a 600 lb prize-winning pig on the loose.

Such is life. It turns out; neither was accurate in her response because each was seeing and experiencing life through her unique lens. We don't see the World as it is. We see it as we are. And we would do well sometimes to question the accuracy of our beliefs. The truth is not always in the appearance of things.

This can save a lot of hassle because we don't get caught up in the story we tend to add to each situation. It's usually the story we tell ourselves more than the facts that cause our real suffering. The next time you feel a strong emotional reaction to circumstance, try pausing force moment to reflect. Ask yourself to review the facts, separate them from the emotions, and hit pause.

Many emails that would have been better off not being sent, many harsh words designed to attack another could be avoided.

But we have to be willing to slow down and make white space in our World to think and reflect.

Is it more important to be right, or more important to attempt restoring the relationship? I have learned that I need to stand like a rock in a matter of principle, and in a matter of preference, I can defer to the other. But it requires me to set aside my ego for the greater good.

About Jeanie: Want to prevent your great ideas from dying a rapid death because they weren't communicated with impact? Join Jeanie Holzbacher in her Conversations That Count online courses and private Mastermind Groups to learn how to expand your influence with powerful impact.

Great ideas and amazing visions must be combined with maximum influence in order to move individuals and organizations to change the world. This is true whether you offer coaching one-on-one, facilitate a successful meeting with your team, or speak to a large group.

Learn how to connect the head and the heart in your message to create buy-in that revolutionizes results!

111

NEVER GIVING UP

CHRISTOPHER LANDANO

Why: Life and running a business are filled with obstacles, and sometimes roadblocks are continually getting in your way. It's easy to give up and follow the crowd, but if you choose not to give up and figure out ways to keep getting past these obstacles, you will accomplish anything life or business throws your way. As a first responder in New York City for over 20 years, I've encountered many obstacles while attempting to save someone's life or rescue from a dangerous condition whether, in a burning building, during a natural disaster, or during a medical emergency, myself and my partners have had to come up with lifesaving solutions with little to no warning as the dangerous environment or patient's condition changes for the worst.

But we take it one obstacle at a time and figure it out because if we don't figure it out or come up with a solution to the issue in front of us, someone can die. Also known as perseverance, never giving up is an essential trait that every first responder learns to master over time. It's a trait that every entrepreneur and business leader must also master. This is why I say anyone who has a first responder or a military background, who decides a path of business or entrepreneurship, greatly increases their chances of success due to their military and first responder experience. Fear and obstacles stop average people from starting a business or venture that is new to them. Especially fear doing something different out of their comfort zone—fear if they fail and what their friends and family will say. But as military and first responders, we GIVE FEAR THE FINGER and walk right thru it to overcome the obstacles in our way. We don't have time to be scared or even think for a second about the danger to ourselves. If you master this Habit, nothing or nobody can ever stop you from accomplishing your goals and dreams because you will figure it out, even if it means building a few roads of your own to reach the finish line.

THE UN-HABIT: THINKING THE WORLD IS DESIGNED FOR ONLY THE RICH TO BENEFIT

Why: It's true, we were taught as young children by our teachers that to have a good life, we needed to go to school for an education to get a good job with benefits and security. Because if you didn't go to school, you could end up as a sanitation worker. But what's crazy is that some sanitation workers do well financially, so our teachers were wrong about that career. I've come to learn that most middle-class families send their children to non-private schools, which mostly teach students to become employees.

Many parents who went to private themselves send their children to private schools where the class only had around 15 students instead of middle-class learning, which filled the class to the point where no more desks could fit. Private schools taught students more about real-life situations and higher education to prepare for the real world. I know this from talking to a few close friends who went to private school and are now sending their children to similar schools. You could say kids from higher-income families or families of means have an advantage handed to them.

That doesn't mean a child who goes to a non-private school can't accomplish more and live a better life than someone who went to an elite private school. Yes, it could absolutely give them an advantage over others. But I believe true greatness comes from within as you grow as an individual. I think children that come from families of wealth and means could be at a disadvantage depending on the person because life in many cases is handed to them, or just a simpler life as opposed to a kid who comes from a poor household or rough neighborhood and has lots of obstacles in their way to make it far enough to escape that household or neighborhood, and in most cases will need to do it alone with little to no help. But if they accomplish the escape or overcome whatever challenges they faced, that journey could help them realize they can accomplish anything.

In this new world we live in, the opportunity for you to create wealth has never been better. The opportunities are there, especially with the internet and online business opportunities. Coming from a poor or middle class household, to be rich or wealthy, you need to reprogram your brain and become financially literate. Having a mentor or coach could be very helpful if one can be found. Once you think like a wealthy person, that wealthy thinking will eventually drip cash into your pockets. Once you get over that excuse of being at a disadvantage over wealthy people, you can achieve whatever level of financial success necessary.

About Christopher: Since the age of 12, when I began doing community service helping senior citizens with basic chores, they could no longer do themselves. The satisfaction I received from helping them was something I enjoyed. I continued doing community service, which led me to volunteer with the local Volunteer Ambulance Corps at age 18. I became an emergency medical technician, where I started working on an ambulance responding to 911 emergencies. During those years, I had received lots of service awards for simply doing what I enjoyed - helping people in my community as a volunteer.

It was at that time in my life when I knew helping people was my calling and would be the career I followed. I later became an Auxiliary Police Officer for the New York City Police Department. In 2000 I was hired by the New York City Fire Department to work as an EMT on their ambulance and in 2003, promoted to firefighter. Today I have over 23 years as a first responder. I'm an inventor launching my product Trakbelt360 in 2021 and another business called Inventor Rescue, focused on educating inventors about scams that target them.

112

TOMORROW WILL BE BETTER THAN TODAY

HINDY ZEIFMAN STEGMAN

W hy: Both my parents were Holocaust Survivors, and this was my dad's daily mantra of how he survived. Growing up, he would say this to us every day at breakfast and asked us did we understand. I didn't get it as a kid. I would say yes, Dad, but these words have gotten me through life. As a mother, grandmother, spiritual teacher, and businesswoman, it has been my rock, my go-to. Life is like a seesaw; it has its ups and downs, but I know if I have trust and faith, all will be well maybe not always the way I would want it to be, but always for my highest and best good.

I was married at 17 and moved from Toronto to New York, then back to Toronto 6 years later and divorced at 50. I was the President of an international furniture manufacturing company. I fought the Union and won. Then I went bankrupt. Mantra kicked in, "Tomorrow will be better than today, and the next day will be better still." So I went back to get my college degree at 40 and used by creative side and graduated with a degree in Interior Decorating, became a Feng Shui & Space Clearing Consultant, sold indoor gemstone fountains for Feng Shui on Home Shopping Channel in Toronto, and had no idea what I was doing. Still, I had trust and faith. I created empowerment and forgiveness workshops for children of holocaust survivors; you bet I taught them my dad's mantra.

I could go on and on. Why did I tell you all this because no matter whether in various businesses or daily life, if you repeat this daily mantra of...

"Tomorrow will be better than today, and the next day will be better still. If you lose money, you've lost losing. If you loose your hope, you've lost everything."

With this, you will be able to handle the ups and downs of life.

THE UN-HABIT: I'M SO STUPID

Why: The Habit of saying I'm So Stupid becomes ingrained in one's consciousness. How many times in one day do you say I'm So Stupid or I'm Bad. It becomes an automatic reflex. Everything has energy. When you see someone laugh, you want to laugh when you see someone angry; you want to get out of their energy field, but what about when you laugh, and when you get angry or frustrated, how does this affect your energy? By repeating these negative statements repeatedly, you en-train your nervous system to believe you are so stupid or bad.

Have you heard of the "Silent Saboteur" well, start to pay attention. Have you ever gotten a great idea for a new project, and the excitement is building, and then oops, the "Silent

Saboteur" is there to hold you back energetically. You get this amazing inspiration to try something new, and you are all excited but slowly lose momentum; why? Could it be the message you have given yourself over and over "I'm So Stupid" or "I'm Bad"? We all know the little caboose's story that said, I think I can I think I can I think I can and guess what... success. So change your self-talk use empowering statement like "what a learning lesson" rather than "I'm So Stupid" or I'm Bad." The Universe always shows us how right we are. One way to stop the pattern is to put a rubber band on your wrist. Each time you say "I'm So Stupid or I'm Bad," pull the rubber bank back and let it go... Ouch, that hurts. If you pull the rubber band every time, eventually, you will realize the pain both physically and energetically of these dis-empowering words.

About Hindy: My name is Hindy, and it means Energy Healer. I am a master of the ancient art of Feng Shui and Energy Healing for over 25 years. I help people remotely transform their environments and their lives to be empowered and enjoy an unlimited flow of energy, health, wealth, and happiness. My no-nonsense style appeals to audiences, making me a successful speaker and TV and radio show guest.

113

BEGIN WITH GRATITUDE, COUNT YOUR BLESSINGS

MARTINA COOGAN

Why: When I moved the USA, I was young full of adventure, and also had a lot of apprehension as this world I was now living in was very different to where I had grown up in the West of Ireland, and I no longer had the security of safety in my life. It was very obvious I was alone, and I had to learn how to take care of myself on every level for the first time in my life. I was very fortunate to meet a very wise and affectionate elderly lady named Mary, who immigrated to the US some 60 years earlier. She introduced me to the Habit of every day waking up and first thing in the morning, giving thanks for everything I have in life for all the positives and for all the blessings and lessons one learns and all the opportunities. She called it counting your blessings, and to this day I can still hear her voice as she coached me and mentored me to crafting this Habit. I had no idea at the time this was such a powerful and positive daily Habit. As I did it and kept reminding me, I felt stronger, comforted, and I could see its power and impact in my life, so I continued.

Habits are important for us to create and practice each day as they give us a solid and strong foundation upon which we build our daily lives—giving thanks and counting one's blessings I discovered many years later generates positivity into the mental and emotional body and causes the aura the field that is around the human body to generate a positive attraction.

Studies I have read indicate that people who use positive affirmations have better physical and mental health with increased immune systems. As we create and build a Habit, it becomes a routine. We automatically do it, which gives us daily certainty and allows our brain to go into autopilot mode, giving us the freedom to have no thought allowing us to do other things. Over the years, I noticed that without thinking, I would automatically give thanks and count my blessing during the day when good things happen or when I saw where I could have gone off track or was saved from many negative happenings, which in turn kept me in a positive mindset and a flow of acceptance and continuous gratitude for the simple and major lessons life offers.

THE UN-HABIT: LOSE THE ATTACHMENT TO PEOPLE, PLACES, OR THINGS!

Why: As I practice detachment, my wish is one day I will truly master it! As I observe people, read studies on mental and emotional patterns, I continuously observe how life gets complicated, how hurt and pain and suffering can start, and exist for years because of attachments. When we as humans get attached to people, places, or things, we lock into that attachment, and we begin to carry it, and it consumes so much of our energies and shuts us down from living life. We loose time, opportunities we become suppressed, and often depressed. Pain, suffering, and victim mindset become a normal, acceptable way of living. The body then breaks down and creates disease, destroying our lives and our ability to live life to the fullest. Many clients presenting with such Habits have taken themselves out of life.

Life is precious full of opportunities, fun, adventure, and we are not meant to live with the Habit of attachment. It is not positive. It's negative and harmful. We must break and release attachment and monitor ourselves, so we do not create an attachment that prevents us from living a positive, fulfilling life. I have fallen into this trap with people as my attachment to them has caused me to stop living, and I am so grateful to those who have held the light and guided me out of these situations. I have been attached to things and overused my energy to keep them in my life this has directly hurt me and caused me personal pain. I am not at all saying it is easy to detach. Still, I have found that once I detached and let go, there is an overpowering sense of release and that which is meant to come back to you and stays with you giving you the freedom and even more power to attract and sustain what is real and genuinely yours to enjoy.

I invite you to detach as the less you have, the more room you have to be you and bring into your life the endless, infinite possibilities that each day offers; as we empty our cup daily, the abundant flow has the opportunity to come in.

About Martina: With over 20 years of teaching ancient lineage healings and tools of power that balance the human energy fields, mental and emotional bodies, I specialize in empowering people to achieve inner peace and self-mastery. Using the aura and chakra alignment system, which releases limiting beliefs and programming, people start to love themselves and feel alive every day.

My Mission is to help people clear negativity, release debilitating programming, and limiting beliefs so they can attain a happy, healthy, well-balanced lifestyle. What I love most about what I do is seeing people transform into living their best life every day. When I am not working, I enjoy long walks in London Parks and meeting up with friends.

114

SAY YES! BE LIMITLESS!

DANIELLA R. PLATT

Why: To be a high-level Entrepreneur, you need to look the part. Even though there may be no uniform, there is still an image you need to convey. This Habit will help you to portray the image that matches who you are inside.

What's in your closet that when you wear it, you light up the room? Perhaps, you would say, "I always wear my Gucci shoes to close deals!" Men, women, alike, will say they have one piece that gives them the confidence to walk on stage. Sign a big deal. Or even a reason to get out of bed. Must you have one thing? Could it be the shoes, a bag, a jacket, an accessory? **Life is too short to wear boring clothes.**

You see, fashion is essential. It lets people feel amazing, cope, and have fun. How you wear fashion is your style, the brand of YOU. Style is your words without a voice, 100% self-expression.

Fashion is also addictive and costly! And I was heading towards a financial problem if I didn't take control. Working in fashion, I'd overdose on purchasing. Clothes were piling up. Too much money was spent, and still nothing matched.

I had to start dressing like a VIP and create shopping ground rules for a functioning, fierce wardrobe to fix this situation. So, I created a plan. Here are five tips to Dress Like A VIP with a wardrobe you love.

1. **Invest in neutrals; earth-tones and red, white, and blue. Use seasonless pieces to layers like short-sleeve tops and blazers.** Your wardrobe will work together, year-round.

2. **Invest in tops.** As a mom and working from home, shirts are versatile. Not dresses.

3. **Museum pieces are keepers for life.** Think of your body as a museum to curate it with pieces you love. Fashion is art. Learn about the designers and brand missions. You will begin to value your purchases.

4. **Ask yourself, "Does it make me dance?"** Body positivity is crucial, whatever size of fabulous you are. A trend isn't hot or sexy if you feel like a sausage! Dress according to your body type. Don't let a sale seduce you.

5. Eye a piece for a few days. It's Shopping Cart Stalking! A price may fluctuate. And, in a few days, you'll know if it's true love or a toss.

Fashion is love. Yet, the fashion industry is gritty. I talk about this in my book *Looking Good*; a playbook teaches how anyone can turn an idea into a fashion business. You can find the book on Amazon. What is remarkable about fashion is how it can everyone feel like a VIP. When you feel great, you will be ready to conquer the world!

So next time you go shopping, keep these **five tips** in mind **and Dress like a VIP.**

THE UN-HABIT: STOP IMPULSE SHOPPING AND DRESS LIKE A VIP!

Why: HOW COME NO ONE TOLD ME? It took four decades to find out you can be and do anything – Just by saying YES., You don't even need to be revolutionary. That may sound eye-opening, but it's true. You need passion, desire, and to say a three-letter word – YES!

For four decades, I laid low. I stayed humble. Modest. And while I served with love and dedication, there was a perpetual drive for achievement. Maybe you can relate to what I am saying?

I'd hear, "Daniella, you're a Rockstar," and "Oh, D, you are so creative!"

Well, darling, you're genuinely welcome. Only the welcome quickly expires when you are hungry to shake – it – up! Who is responsible for your destiny beside you?

What if you take on this challenge? Imagine the possibilities when you let go of limitations and say YES to the unknown!

I did and will never look back. It took a car accident to take a forensic peek at my life from Long Island to becoming a mom at the age of 41 in Los Angeles. Therapy turned the spotlight on my decisions that were tethered to 'what will they think,' and 'what will they say' influences, never allowing myself to elevate.

After I had my 2nd baby at 43, four decades on this planet, I realized how valuable time is. And 'what they think' has nothing to do with me. I went on a journey to say YES, and manifest magic into my world. I also want my girls to know they, too, are limitless.

What happens when saying YES becomes a Habit?

Remember the Gravatron? The ride spins fast. The bottom falls out. You stick to the wall, wondering, you will make it out alive? As it stops, while feet and body reunite, you're giddy and ready for more! That's saying YES and enjoying the ride.

Saying YES may ignite you to create brilliant ideas.

I said YES to things I never thought possible. While coaching, I wrote a book called *Looking Good, Ten Commandments To Be A Sales Rockstar & Fashion start-up Playbook,* empowering creatives to be unstoppable; when I see the Amazon listing, my heart dances.

Say YES to mingle with like-minded joy-seekers who allow you to rise. Say YES to novelty and fun. As your YESes become achievements, friends may vanish, and relationships will shift. You may not know where you're going or when you've arrived. But in your heart, you know you this is so good.

SAY YES. Be LIMITLESS. Will you join me?

About Daniella: Daniella Platt is a multi-platform creative who guides people to take their idea from the kitchen table to the world and make it happen with a few easy steps! She also teaches creatives sophisticated selling to be profitable and unstoppable. She wrote the best-selling book called Looking Good, Ten Commandments To Be A Sales Rockstar & Fashion start-up Playbook to empower creatives to create and sell with specific tools to communicate to build long-run relationships. Daniella has also made 100s of campaigns at ad agencies and fashion magazines for brands that fill your life like Visa, Alternative, and Hugo Boss, and let you stretch. To be a high-level Entrepreneur, you need to look the part. Even though there may be no uniform, there is still an image you need to convey. This Habit will help you to portray the image that matches who you are inside.

115

DO WHAT YOU SAY, SAY WHAT YOU MEAN

LAUREN POWERS

Why: That is my mantra. I live by that. It has run my entire career because if I say something, my word is gold, and if I say something, that means you can consider it done. Our word is all we have. Otherwise, I don't say it. It's really simple.

I attribute my success in the fitness industry to the fact that many of these girls are so flaky that they don't show up for auditions. They don't show up for photoshoots. They're not prepared. They're not in shape. All of these things, I've been around a long time, Forbes, like yourself, I've got what, 30 years in this industry. And you'd be amazed at what happened. Just being prepared, being in shape, and ready to go at all times, I've never had the luxury in the last 20 years to get offseason. If you will, it's a term used in fitness that this offseason to me is a reason to get out of shape. Well, my agent would call, and he would say you have an audition tomorrow competition ready in a bikini. Boom. You got to go.

This has always been a part of who I am. I think I've had this since birth. If you follow my career, everything I set out to do, I do it to the max and follow through on this Habit to myself. I tell myself I am going to be the best I can, and I do just that. There's no moderation for me. It's either all or nothing. One or the other. I follow this motto in all areas of my life.

If I'm in school, I might as well get the best grades I can. If I'm in a sport, I might as well be number one. If I'm in a race, I have to win. Everything is just an inner drive I'm born with. And I've used it in every single area of my life. I don't go out for something not to get it. Same with the auditions. If I go out for a project, I'm getting it. It's a mindset as well. I set my mind to get what I want. I'm an only child and I am use to getting everything I want. And I know it's in every area of my life, literally.

THE UN-HABIT: GETTING OUTSIDE YOUR LANE

Why: I just did this giant online TV Show, for the first time. I was the host not the tech person. I don't want to be. That's not my lane. So I bring in people to help me with this. Building a team and having the people around you that are experts in their field is the answer. No more trying to do it all myself!

I want to stay where my expertise is like being in front of the camera, doing interviews, sharing my experience, strength, knowledge, encouraging others, inspiring others, and motivating others to be the best version of themselves.

This is my lane. So I've created a fitness community, body breakthrough club, and it's for women 40 50 plus. So it's not for the young it's for us professional women that want to put their health first. What I've found is by doing this for a while is that so many women burn out, put themselves last, take care of their family, their kids, their husbands, the house, everything else but themselves.

Because I attract women entrepreneurs, there's no time for themselves at the end of the day. So they start getting out of shape. They start looking in the mirror; they loathe some of their body parts. Usually, it's their stomach, thighs, what have you, the bat wings. We know the deal. Start in with their limiting beliefs and negative self-talk.

I want to focus on those women, and help them turn it around, switch their mindset, put themselves first. Now, my whole thing is "choose you" The word choose, make a choice, make a decision, and stick to that decision by putting yourself first and making health your top priority. Because if you don't, you're going to spend the rest of your life spending your wealth to get your health.

ABOUT LAUREN: **Lauren Powers** is a ten-time, heavyweight bodybuilding champion, international best-selling author, entrepreneur, actor, model, award-winning international speaker in cinema and media for the Women of Excellence Forum and the founder of Powers Fitness Events. She is the most publicized female fitness competitor in the world and has been featured in numerous feature films, documentaries, television productions, and more than a dozen popular music videos from some of the top artists in the world. Lauren is a teacher, mentor, and advocate for individual achievement and excellence.

116

FIGHT THE AGING PROCESS

DR. CHRISTOPHER ASANDRA

Why: Successful Entrepreneurs need to look the part. Too many people think that aging is something we surrender to. I'm talking about all aspects: Mental, Physical, and even Spiritual.

So, where does this start? We must keep moving. And I think in today's society, we've gotten lazier, as you know. Everything's a little more convenient for us now. But also, besides that part is understanding that you don't have to be on a bunch of medications. If you can do the preventative part

The questions I always get is about understanding your hormones. What is the deal there? Do we naturally lose them? Can we replace them? Should we be replacing them?

We lose them over time. After the age of 30, we start to decline. Let's start with men. Men begin to decline after the age of 30; their testosterone starts going down. That's why we see them begin to gain weight, lack of libido, erectile dysfunction, lack of concentration. They lose muscle mass.

This is even more empowering for women. When women go through menopause, they notice things change. Their body changes. They have hot flashes, irritability, dryness, lack of intimacy, et cetera. And the body changes from there.

But once we can replace that safely and effectively, we are almost not only stopping the aging process, we're practically reversing it. And we're able to add more muscle mass to decrease the fat and make them feel better. That's where women feel more empowered with the whole thing.

This is not a new technology. It's been around since the early 1900s. It's a matter of how we've advanced in it in terms of doing it more safely, more effectively, and having a different type of treatment for it, for men and women. For example, they used to use pig testicles back in the early days to replace hormones. Now we can synthesize it bio-identically. And we use the pellets that I implant under the skin, which is only done every three or four months, and you get a consistent level of hormones in your body.

The best part. This is not only for the ultra-rich. Anybody can do this. It's becoming more affordable these days. It's about budgeting too. If you spend on a gym membership, you should be able to do this.

Using this system, people become more productive. So what is the value of your wellbeing, your relationship with others, your happiness?

Other things to fight aging...

Staying out of the sun. The more you're exposed to ultraviolet rays, and the sun can age you prematurely and faster.

Avoiding alcohol and drugs. I think that tends to age people a little bit quicker too. I'm not talking just a glass of wine a day. I'm talking when it becomes excessive. I think that can accelerate the aging process.

Eat organic foods, healthy foods, fruits and vegetables, and antioxidants to slow down the aging process. I think drinking lots of water. Hydration is also essential. Those are some natural things we can do. Taking your vitamins as well, but also hormone replacement therapy. A lot of ladies tell me that their skin starts looking more plump and full again. As they lose it, when they age, they become gaunter, they become more wrinkled, they see more wrinkles. But once the hormones get back in, they notice it kind of fills out a little bit.

THE UN-HABIT: BLAMING OTHERS AND BLAMING EVERY... SELF-VICTIMIZATION

Why: I think that there comes the point where they blame every problem on everybody else. It's everybody at fault. Listen, you have a choice. You wake up every day, it's your choice to make the decisions you do. And self-motivation is important and saying, "I'm going to make a difference." Stop blaming everyone else for your weight gain, your irritability, et cetera. You can change that yourself. It's if you choose to live that healthier and that happier lifestyle.

A lot of my patients come in on antidepressants. They're very depressed, et cetera. And they're able to get off of it once they're on my treatment, once we optimize the hormones. I see people every day saying, "The reason I can't lose weight is because of this, because of that."

I had a patient come in, who swears that it was because of the foods. It was because of their job and their stress. And I said... Sometimes you got to give them a kick in the ass and say, "You know what? I'm going to empower you again. I'm going to give you the hormones to be motivated, but I can lead a horse to the water; I can't make you drink it, but I'll give you the tools you need to get motivated again. I'll do my part. You got to do yours." And then they start losing weight. Well, you know this, once they get motivated.

ABOUT DR. ASANDRA: A Kansas City native, Dr. Asandra received his combined BA/MD in 2003 from the University of Missouri at Kansas City, upon the completion of an intensive six-year medical program. He then continued his training at the University of Illinois at the Chicago College of Medicine, where he served as chief resident, gaining unparalleled experience and insight that would inspire the pursuit of a cutting-edge specialty. Expanding upon his acclaimed anti-aging treatments and bio-identical hormone therapies, Dr. Asandra now provides a vast lineup of cosmetic procedures, hormone replacement programs, and sexual dysfunction treatments, tailored to each patient's needs and desires. Asandra continues to precept doctors and healthcare providers worldwide, training them on the latest techniques and his signature procedures, cultivating the next generation of industry leaders.

117

KEEP THE MINDSET - THE HARDER YOU WORK, BETTER YOU GET

CHUCK LIDELL

Why: As a kid I had a hard time staying focused, I needed something and I got lucky with the style of martial arts I chose. The school I went to was old school karate; I thought I would learn magic moves right away but they'd show you how to do one move, one punch and tell you, "Okay, go over there and do that 500 times on each side." Really; if you're asking me to do 500 of anything I couldn't do it; but this I could do!

From the time I started fighting, I knew if I worked harder, I would learn faster and I would get better. Doing something 500 times wasn't really possible in the beginning, but because I knew if I did something enough times I would get it down right and the prize would be mine, a new move. I could get better at it was in my mind all the time, it stuck with me I would just keep pushing. I've always felt that if I can keep working and keep going, I would succeed. My Grandfather believed in me and gave me the confidence to know I can do this. "You can be anyone, have anything you want just work for it". Even if I got knocked out in the first round he would be proud of me because he knew I gave it my all, I gave it my best. This is a great sport that I enjoyed fighting my way to the top in and I truly love it. I never let my emotions cloud my judgements and I wasn't mad when I fought but I was trying to hurt them. I would read my opponent and hit them this way or that watching their reactions to set them up for what I wanted them to do, then get in there and hurt them. When the fight was over I hoped the guy was ok. I was there to win. I knew I could get better than other people just by learning and working harder to pass those ahead of me. That mindset stuck with me, I always had that confidence that if I keep pushing myself and I keep going, eventually I will figure it out. There are always challenges in life, people can be freaking out around me and I just say "I'll figure it out". "What do you mean?" "I don't know yet. I'll figure it out. We're going to get there. I'll get through it." And you know we did figure it out, I did because of my mindset. I am mentally tough, being mentally tough is not a sometimes thing, it is an all the time thing and the best way to build that toughness is with good Habits. I lead by example and have had a positive impression on others when they realized that these good Habits are what champions do!

THE UN-HABIT: NOT PAYING THE PIPER

Why: One of the things I always said is, "You have to pay the piper." If you're supposed to work out tomorrow you better work out tomorrow, but then that night you decide to go out and stay out until five in the morning. You still have to get up and work out. You have to pay the piper in the morning. The morning workout is harder than ever and you might not like your performance, but you do it because that'll keep you in line! No matter how beat up you feel, you have to give that work out your best in the morning. Like my wife would say I don't give up easy. Pay the piper. If you don't it's you that loses in the end. This applies to everything I do. When we go for a run I try to be first even if it seems impossible; I'm giving it my best shot. When we'd do conditioning I'd try to beat everybody's score and some of those guys are hard to beat. We pushed each other by trying to outdo each other's scores, no matter what I felt like when I wake up in the morning. No excuses I don't like losing to anything or anybody, anytime so I pay the piper. That, for me, was big.

About Chuck: Chuck "The Iceman" Liddell burst onto the MMA scene in 1998 during his UFC debut fight win against Noe Hernandez in UFC 17. His rise to UFC champion includes most notable TKO wins against Randy Couture (UFC 52 & 57), Tito Ortiz (UFC 47 & 66), Wanderlei Silva (UFC 79), and the KO win that catapulted him into UFC stardom at UFC 31 against Kevin Randleman. Chuck reigned as UFC World Light Heavyweight Champion for two years, defending his title five times. Because of Chuck's love for the sport he is now promoting it and becoming an action hero in the movies. Keep the Mindset - The Harder You Work, the Better You Get.

118

FIND YOUR WAY INTO THE LIFE YOU DESIRE

DON "THE DRAGON" WILSON

Why: Do you belong, do you listen to others, do others define you, lead you? To be who you want to be, you have to believe in yourself.

I grew up in Florida when black folks were finally being allowed into the schools with white folks. They started desegregation in the '50s, where I went to high school. I wanted to belong, but I didn't look like anybody else, not black, not white; I had no visual group to identify with and wanted to be accepted by both.

This became one of my many challenges in life. When I was young, I had to figure out how I could be accepted and learned that I had to be successful in sports. If I sank a 30-foot jump shot or caught an interception and ran it in for a touchdown, everyone loved me.

My desire to be accepted gave me the drive to push myself hard. I trained hard, I played hard, and I was winning. I became the Most Valuable Player in 2 very different sports, Basketball and Football. I didn't listen to anyone who said I couldn't do this or that, and I am very thankful for my Mother's support in all I did.

When I started into martial arts in the '70s, it was known as Full Contact Karate. I had to trim down my from middle linebacker bodyweight into a lean agile one. This took determination and willpower that comes from within. I remember my first fight in Orlando, Florida, I was so green in the beginning, and if things went wrong, I could be dead. If you got knocked out, you fell lifelessly to the floor, a concrete floor, and that 6-foot fall with my head hitting the concrete wasn't going to happen to me! So I trained.

Kickboxing, as it is now known, changed my life. I wasn't a partier even though I was closely involved with a very successful night club in the disco era. I was a professional athlete, and like everything else I did, I was obsessive, I trained, I cross-trained, and I trained with whomever I could. When I look back now, I realize I didn't need to spend six hours every day training for a 30-minute contest. I didn't need to run nine miles every day, but I did. I just trained, the weight training, the aerobics, jumped rope, hit the heavy bag, and sparring. I hit it all hard, it was my nature, my obsessive nature, and it served me well as I was able to excel in my chosen area.

I excelled because I believed in myself. My father disapproved of me walking away from college and an engineering degree. (although I don't recommend doing such things either) and he never came to see me fight. But I went on to win my first title in1980, which is a huge accomplishment in itself, but I then went on to win the world title (11) eleven times. This has put my name in the record book, yes, the Guinness Book of World Records

When you win the world title, you think, oh, now everything will be great. But no, once you win it, you have to defend it. You have to fight only the top contenders. Those like me train hard, and they want the number one spot. They are hungry, and they want my title. I continued to fight professionally for a total of 28 years, always believing in my abilities.

My skill, ability, and multiple wins caught the attention of Chuck Norris. During the late 70s, Chuck started coming out to watch my fights. Then he would announce them, and eventually, he worked my corner. We became friends, and he passed along some advice; when I retire from the ring, move to LA, he said, get an agent and try to get into martial arts films because it's a great second career. That's how the movie thing happened to me.

Chuck Norris was a disciplined fighter with strength from within, and Bruce Lee put him in one movie. After that, Chuck started doing his own thing creating discipline training for students and performing many films and a television series. I listened to Chuck and made my way into the movies, 30 plus movies, and I appreciate his pro advice to put myself out there and go for it.

The Un-Habit: listening to the naysayers

WHY: Everybody told me I wasn't going to be a world champion. They said, "What World Champion comes from Cocoa Beach. Unless you are talking about surfing champs, there were no martial arts, no boxers, and world champions.

So it's a Habit, Habit of not listening to the naysayers. Normally when somebody tells you something negative, you think, oh, he doesn't like me, or he doesn't want me to be successful. Those comments from naysayers are easy to ignore. Those from people closest to you, the people who love you, your parents, your brothers, and your best friend, they don't want you to fail, are the hardest to overlook. But they don't know how to help you succeed with the words they speak. Believe in yourself and your inner voice of yes; I can.

Excellence comes from the Habit of doing, no procrastination when it comes to your inner desire to succeed. Attitudes, patterns, and Habits must be changed; you must repeatedly keep doing what you are trying to develop to become excellent at them. During my training, I didn't just want a good right jab; I wanted the best right jab, amongst other attributes, so I trained until it became a Habit.

ABOUT DON: DON "THE DRAGON" Wilson is considered the greatest kick-boxing champion in the sport's history. A native of South Florida, Wilson began fighting in the late 1970s. In a career which spanned 4 decades, he won 11 world kick-boxing championships, among them the WKA, STAR, WKC, PKO Lightheavyweight World Championships, WKA, STAR, ISKA World Cruiserweight Titles, and the WKA and STAR Super-Lightheavyweight World Championships.

He posted a record of 72-5-2 with 47 wins by knockout. Wilson defeated such world champions as Dennis Alexio, Oaktree Edwards, and Dick Kimber. He retired from the sport in 1990, but launched a comeback on May 14, 1999. Since his return he has knocked-out Dick Kimber and defeated Dewey Cooper.

119

EXERCISE DAILY

DR. BIRGER BAASTRUP

Why: I know; we have all heard you should exercise every day, but what does that have to do with the entrepreneur, you might ask? Let's get straight to the point – motion equals life! As an entrepreneur, you have this high energy and enthusiasm for what you do or want to accomplish, which will require a proper exercise plan to be sustained. Entrepreneurs generally are motivated, flexible, optimistic, resourceful, hard-working, passionate, and creative type folks and need a lot of energy to achieve their dreams and goals. The best way to keep your body going with that higher amount of energy is to keep up a regular exercise program. Entrepreneurs tend to work long hours, and having the physical capacity for such dedication is essential.

Another wonderful effect of a regular exercise program is how it improves our mental health. As a third-degree black belt martial artist for over 15 years, I also see how exercise positively affects both the kids and adults in our dojo. It calms them down and aids them in creating better focus. The same goes for the entrepreneur. There will always be people and situations on the road to success that will test you to see how focused and determined you are. When you exercise, your body releases endorphins, the "feel-good" hormones that relax you and reduce stress.

When you shut down movement, you decrease your quality of life. The entrepreneur needs all the energy and movement available as the body works better with proper movement. Lots of research support this notion, and as a chiropractor of 35+ years, I have seen time and time again, the benefits of proper, consistent movement on my patient population. There is no easy road to take for the entrepreneur, and having an ample amount of energy is essential for keeping up with the long hours required.

Entrepreneurs spend a considerable amount of time sitting at a desk and in front of a computer. According to Dr. Joan Vernikos, former director of NASA's Life Sciences Division and author of the book *Sitting Kills, Moving Heals,* "We weren't designed to sit. The body is a perpetual motion machine." Regular exercise feeds that machine.

An entrepreneur needs stamina. An entrepreneur requires mental focus. Exercise provides both of these. A successful entrepreneur works long hours and is most likely to be sleep-deprived: exercise promotes deeper and more restful sleep.

You deserve to enjoy the fruits of your labor; exercise prolongs and enhances your quality of life so you can.

THE UN-HABIT: QUITTING WHEN THE GOING GETS TOUGH

Why: One cannot quit. It's not an option. You have to have the tenacity and perseverance to pursue your dreams. You have to keep the course, and yes, there will be lessons along the way, but it's how we pick ourselves up after the failure, bankruptcy, etc. that determines your character. There will be times when you feel at the end of your rope and feel like throwing in the towel would be the easiest solution out but don't ever make that an option. Look at Arnold Schwarzenegger and how far he came from dreams of coming to the US and being Mr. Universe and being in the movies. There must have been tons of times when he felt like quitting along the way. When a baby starts walking, does it give up after the first 100 falls? No, it keeps trying until the nervous system has figured out how to stay balanced and coordinate the muscles to work in a synchronized manner to have you stand upright and walk. What an amazing feat that is! Life is a constant learning experience, and the more we embrace it and run with it, the more we can get out of it.

Reaching your goals requires perseverance and keeping the dream intact. Quitting would be giving up on that dream, giving up on you.

A real-life example would be from my own life. Deciding to study chiropractic meant leaving the comfort of the country I grew up in and a language I was familiar with, leaving my family behind, leaving a free school system, and then traveling to another country unknown to me. Studying a four year plus program in a foreign language was going to be no easy task. My view on it was this. Once I started school, I was going to finish it. Quitting was not an option. It was never going to be an option. It wasn't even in my vocabulary.

About Dr. Baastrup: Dr. Baastrup grew up in Scandinavia and went on to study chiropractic in America after which he moved to Alaska and has practiced there ever since. Post graduate studies involved several certifications in disciplines within the chiropractic field. He has a love for helping others and has made it his life mission to help people through chiropractic care. Hobbies include being in the outdoors whether it is hiking, mountain biking, kayaking, sailing, skiing, scuba diving or photography as well as karate. He is a contributing author in a patient chiropractic pediatrics text and has promoted health and proper exercises for years.

120

DEVELOP AN OWNERSHIP MINDSET

CARI ROSNO

Why: Have you ever heard of manifesting? Ok, if not manifesting..goal setting? Manifesting is much the same. We have a desire for our business, a goal to be attained. This could be financial success, impact with our clients, or merely creating a shift in the company culture. We look at these things, line them out and make a plan of attack so that the odds of achieving them are greater than not. When the plan is made we work diligently to accomplish the goals. Some are achieved, many are not. And when they are not met we go back to the drawing board and work to create a new plan so that there is "better luck next time". What if I told you that not only do you have the ability to create everything that you desire but that you are already creating everything you have. Would you believe me?

Read on because this may be the most powerful mindset shift that you could ever make. Why? Because if you have the power to create something, wouldn't you also have the power to dis-create what you don't like and create something new? Think about it.

As I navigated ownership of a multi-million dollar company I didn't always have this mindset. I sat in the passenger seat most of the time. Yes, of course I drove the company, but life and circumstances outside of my control were ultimately driving me. That was until I began asking two very important questions. "Why did I create this?" and "How is this serving me?". You don't have to have a difficult vendor, client or employee. If you do then ask these questions. Perhaps you created a situation where you have a difficult vendor because conflict motivates you to find different solutions or to be creative. Maybe that employee doesn't follow through because you have had difficulty trusting people in the past to complete things the way you would like so it's just "easier if you do them yourself". Whatever the case may be, get curious, dive deeper. In this curiosity you will not only discover more about yourself, but you may just have the ability to change the circumstances around you. If you understand you no longer need the conflict, you will no longer draw it to you.

THE UN-HABIT: INABILITY TO TAKE RESPONSIBILITY FOR YOUR CIRCUMSTANCES

Why: I like to call those with this Habit the all powerful-powerless. We can all recall a time when a client gives you a "let's go". It's all high-fives and celebrations, look at what you have accomplished. A client decides to go a different direction and this has nothing to do with you but is simply because they....well, you fill in the blank. Imagine if we were to take the same initiative of understanding what our responsibility was in the no as we do the yes. Keep in mind when I say understanding I am not asking you to look at the action of you within that situation, sure you could have made another call, asked a different question, etc. I am asking you to look at you within the action. What if we asked the same two questions as before..."Why did I create this?" and "How is this serving me?" We can create the wins and just as easily create the bumps in the road, the failures so to speak. And by asking these questions we have the ability to learn at a deeper level, create an awareness and again develop a curiosity that will provide incredible value so as to avoid doing the same in the future. Everything and everybody is serving you in some way. Every experience, both positive and negative. By giving both sides of these situations the same attention you have the ability to turn every opportunity into a win.

ABOUT CARI: As a strong and blossoming President/CEO, Cari's survival of the Boston Marathon bombing challenged her to identify her own limiting beliefs and search for her own voice and truth...successfully peeling away years of fear and self-imposed, destructive identities.

Cari Rosno is now a Global Manifestation Coach and Truth Seeker who empowers driven women, leaders and action takers to overcome all obstacles and mental resistance by creating a truth seeking mindset and an authentic awareness of their true desires. Cari is the creator of the Truth Seeking JourneyTM and has worked with hundreds of entrepreneurs, social influencers, c-suite executives and pro-athletes, helping them harness their manifestation energy and unlock their innate ability to act in the pursuit of their dreams.

121

PRACTICE MINDFULNESS

DHOMONIQUE MURPHY

Why: Remember, you are the sum total of your thoughts. You are literally what you think about. Affirmations can be positive or negative. If you are constantly having internal dialogues about how you are not good enough, or how you will fail — if you are living in a state of victim-mentality, you are creating your reality. Change your thoughts, change your life. The key is to be aware of when those negative thoughts come into your mind and stop them before they grow arms and legs. Awareness gives you clarity, clarity gives you focus, focus gives you action, action gives you results, results provide you with momentum, and when you have all those ingredients in the dish, you will have everything you desire.

If you want to master mindset and master it fast, there's something I want you to do. I highly recommend it and use it with all of my clients. Take a notecard or a piece of paper and write down A.I.E. It is an acronym. A.I.E. stands for "Attitude is Everything." Tape this on your computer at your desk, or on your bathroom mirror at home, or carry it around in your wallet. It doesn't matter where you put it, keep it close to you for at least two weeks, and hopefully beyond. Whenever a negative thought creeps into your mind, look at the card. Whenever anyone gets under your skin – look at the card... whenever someone doesn't call you back – look at the card. Never forget that you have a choice, believe it or not, in every aspect of your life. You can choose to feel good, or you can choose to feel bad. There's power in that! Don't let people take your power. Keep it, protect it, nurture it. Attitude is everything.

Practicing mindfulness will change your life. Who wants to walk around feeling miserable, broke, tired, lonely, afraid, and depleted? Not YOU! Nobody wants to feel that way. If you're going to start living the life you want...and you literally can design the life you WANT, you have to start with your mind. It's time to wake up! We have to look around and be present – mentally.

Most of us go through life on auto-pilot. We drive the same way to work every day; we have the same routine every morning, we drink coffee out of the same cup at our office, on and on. But we miss the most obvious things. When you parked your car today, what color was the car next to it...? That cashier who checked you out at the grocery store – what color were his or her eyes? You were looking directly into them...but the majority of people can't accurately answer that question...because even though we are looking at someone, we are not present.

The first and most important step to master if you want to fully be in control of your mind if you're going to be in the driver's seat is awareness. Be present. What's going on right NOW? Get out of your head, and be present.

Here's a really simple challenge for you. The next time you get in your car, I want you to notice ten things on your drive (wherever you're going). Ten things. It can be anything: the person at the stoplight singing in their car (my personal favorite)... the young couple holding hands walking down the street, the beautiful golden retriever playing catch with its owner. It sounds so basic, yet most of us are so caught up with our complaints of life that we don't take time to be present. Go get 'em, tiger!

THE UN-HABIT: INABILITY TO TAKE RESPONSIBILITY FOR YOUR CIRCUMSTANCES

Why: If you want results. And who doesn't...you have to have the right mindset. Think of it this way. Think about your home. Your home is your safe space. It is a sacred space. It is the place you go and are most comfortable. It's the place you can truly be you when you step away from the day-to-day life activities. You're not putting on an act, you're not trying to impress anyone, you're not "ON" as I like to say, you can just be you, and it's a place of sheer mental peace. Now imagine someone comes over to your home and interrupts your peaceful state. They're negative, always complaining, always dumbing themself down, playing a victim, gossiping about other people, whining, self-sabotaging, and wondering why no one wants to help them. Imagine this... your sacred space is filled with this level of negativity. You wouldn't like it, you won't appreciate it, and you certainly wouldn't deal with it. You would most likely tell this person to leave your home, right? Of course, you would. So why do you do that yourself? Your mind is the most precious piece of real estate. Your body is your home. Take care of it, fill it will positive affirmations, treat it the way it deserves to be treated.

It all starts with YOU. Don't wait for someone to come along and make you feel better. You have to develop the capacity to make yourself feel better. You have to start by loving yourself. Fall in love with yourself. Do you know how amazing you are? How amazing is the human body? Serious. Stop and think about this amazing vessel we are living in. You are truly an amazing, amazing person.

About Dhomonique: My name is Dhomonique Murphy. I help people see their full potential. I am a 3x Emmy Award Winning Journalist, a highly sought after personal development expert, the CEO of two companies including The Right Method, Founder of the non-profit Readers2Leaders, Mrs. Virginia American 2020, a wife and mom. My purpose in life is to help YOU live a life that counts. My mission is to help you RESET your life so you can live a life of abundance. I can help you get there and give you all the secrets highly successful people use and master to achieve optimum success. I travelled the nation and was invited into the homes of the most notable thought-leaders to learn their secrets of success and how they did it. I want to share that knowledge with you. I have the tools you have been looking for to elevate your life.

122

ALWAYS EAT ON TIME

LESLIE LEBARON

Why: I've been a type 1 diabetic for 27 years now, and since I can remember, my father always taught me good health keeping Habits, but when I was diagnosed with diabetes, he was very insistent in my eating Habits he went on to explain all that I would gain from taking good care of myself and never skipping any meals, the reason why I understand perfectly, but back then it took a lot of effort and discipline to get it right.

Before I got this Habit formed, I use to go out to places where I sometimes did not have food available or had food that would spike my glucose levels, so it was tough for me to keep my sugar levels where they should have been. I would do my best to eat whatever and whenever, which is very stressful to my body and very unhealthy. I then began paying attention to my eating Habits. I realized that when I eat at the same time every day, three times a day and sometimes need a snack in between helps me keep my sugar levels in better numbers and allow me to work longer hours and manage my family a lot better. So keeping my sugar levels is key for being the best version of myself, especially because I've always been a very active woman, taking care of my business and my family is a very demanding job, so forming Habits that help me stay balanced with my diabetes has been of significant help. When I travel, I make sure and look up the places where I can have my breakfast, my lunch, and my dinner ahead of time and plan everything else around that schedule, when it's not possible to do that, I will bring something with me, like a granola bar, grains of some sort, fruit or something to keep my sugar levels under control and avoid hypoglycemia. Creating good Habits is one of the best things that I have ever done for me and my independence as a working woman and mother with diabetes. So I encourage you to do the same even if you don't have diabetes. Not skipping meals will keep you on top of your game and get you a long way. If I can do it, so can you; with a little discipline, anything is possible.

THE UN-HABIT: UNPUNCTUALITY WHEN MEETING SOMEONE

Why: Since a very early age, I can remember my mother teaching us this Habit of always being on time. She said it was rude to be unpunctual because you were disrespectful to people's time, she rose early every day and planned to try to avoid ever being late, so she taught me how important it is to be on time, do things on time, and never lose track of time for your sake and others.

Let me explain when your future boss is an important man and is going out of his busy schedule to listen to what you have to offer; you make sure you are early to that appointment because it shows your true interest in getting the job to begin with. I know many people in this town who are very unpunctual. I have gently tried to explain why it is important to be on time, not only for a meeting but in life in general, to your child's recital, to a family reunion, to a group gathering, it shows a lot of who you are and the respect you are giving others in their time value.

So breaking this bad Habit will change your life in a lot of ways; you will soon find out you have more free time to do something you love or be able to go for a run etc. breaking a bad Habit when being aware of this, you can create a new Habit such as always eating on times, or merely being always on time, small steps always brings to your life bigger opportunities, because people always notice this small gestures as being on time or being late. Have a little faith that everything is possible if you want it. And work hard for it, you'll be able to break any bad Habit if you try hard enough and strive for change.

ABOUT LESLIE: Leslie LeBaron is a small town woman who has managed to stay positive through her life regardless of the struggles I've always managed to inspire others to do better in their lives by example, always being a woman of integrity and values growing up in a large family had a lot of struggles, but I never let all those barriers get in the way of reaching my personal goals.

123

IMPROVE YOURSELF EVERY DAY

LES BROWN

Why: I am continually looking for ways in which I can improve myself. Every day I'm reading something or listening to something or journaling and seeking to discover more about myself. That's a Habit that I've maintained for years.

What drives me is the Habit of striving to reach higher and seeing what else is within me. There's an old saying, "You never find out how much you know until you find out how little you know." So, I have a passion for learning.

This passion came about because I was looking for ways in which I could be able to become independent and be able to take care of my mother, being adopted and wanting to pay back the love and the security that she gave me and my twin and my other five foster brothers and sisters.

So that became my hunger always to reach higher. Socrates says a man's reach is to supersede his grasp, or what are the heavens for?

The Un-Habit: The unwillingness to work on themselves

Why: People pay more attention to things that entertain them. Stress-relieving activity. The average person spends around $14.50 a year on their personal growth and development. So, most people die at age 25 and don't get buried until they're 65. All that they know now is all that they will know. Not to be willing to step out of just being entertained and looking for things that can empower them and expand their vision beyond their circumstances and mental conditioning, I don't understand that.

About Les: Les Brown is a motivational speaker, author, former radio DJ, and former television host. He was a member of the Ohio House of Representatives from 1976 to 1981. As a motivational speaker, he uses the catch phrase "it's possible!" to encourage people to follow their dreams.

124

CODIFY YOUR LIFE

RAYMOND HARLALL

Why: The great Jim Rohn said, "It is the set of the sails, not the direction of the wind that determines which way we will go." One of my favorite quotes, but people are not ships, and we don't have wings. After many years of 'Entrepreneurial roadblocks' (not failures), it came to a point where I was learning many lessons but not achieving my desired result. So I stopped and evaluated my approach.

I have spoken with several Billionaires, and the one thing they had in common that I was missing was their ability to Codify. This single Habit changed my life. From this point on, I did not have to reinvent the wheel every time I started a new project. I asked myself three questions.

1. What's the worst that can happen?

2. What's the best-case scenario?

3. What do I have to do to get 100%?

With these three simple directional questions, I was able to create a Success Machine.

What is Codify?

According to the dictionary:

cod-i-fy (verb = action work)

- arrange (laws or rules) into a systematic code.

- arrange according to a plan or system

How does this apply to me?

No one but you can create this for you. It applies to your personal life as well as your professional life. As a business owner, your body and mind must be ready for all the business cycle's challenges and successes. There will be wins and lessons learned (not losses) along the way. The only way to continue growing or to get back up is to have a system that you have custom made to work regardless of external circumstances -our ability to set your sail to achieve success.

The best way to implement this into your life is to create a list of "I will" or "I am" and repeat every day until it becomes your new program. This simple Habit will ensure you never go on 'autopilot' and risk being blown by the wind in any directions, with no known destination insight.

THE UN-HABIT: STOP SWIMMING **DOWNSTREAM**

Wнy: Going with the flow is so easy to do. But it cost the most resources, especially in time, energy, and financial resources.

Let us compare people and fishes for this analogy. Fishes are confined to the ocean while humans are given dominion over the earth, the air, seas, and its inHabitants.

Fishes in lakes, rivers, ocean, or streams are known to always swim against the tide. It is part of their basic survival instincts. The did not go to a fishing school to learn this. The only fish that you will find going with the flow of the tide is a Dead fish!

As humans, we have been taught from a young age to go against our instinct to be unique and develop our God-given gift and talents.

Robert Kiyosaki and Sharon Lechter wrote about this in the book "Rich Dad Poor Dad." Our current school system teaches us to learn what the teacher teaches and then compete individually to see who has repeated best what the teacher has taught with no room for outside of the box thinking.

Even as an adult, with free will, working at a job as an employee, the corporate culture will demand the status quo be maintained - go with the flow or get fired.

As an entrepreneur - 'a person who eats what you kill' means you are the visionary, the implementer, the marketer, the accountant, the salesperson, and your boss. A mindset of being the creator is needed to survive and strive.

Swimming downstream is for people that are weak and indecisive. It is like playing in someone else's game, which makes you an effect of someone else's creation. If you want to hide and play it safe, you should consider being an #Intrapreneur, not an #Entrepreneur.

If you are not willing to stand out from the competition, you will not win. I am not saying for you to go and live on an island by yourself. Then you will not need to communicate with others.

In closing, until you have a list of the things that you will not do in your business. And a blueprint with a clear direction of where you would like to go. You will only start seeing results when you codify your moves to achieve success—trailblazing yourself and others to follow.

About Raymond: Dr. Raymond Harlall is on a trajectory for massive success. At 31 years old, he is a husband and father, a World Civility Ambassador, representative to the United

Nations, and Founder of the iEmpower Entrepreneurs™ Global Movement, where he works with community leaders in developing countries to position, package, and promote their natural talent and resources for success.

Raymond is Canada's 2020 Civility Icon of the year and recipient of the Nelson Mandela Peace Award in 2019.

The "Dr. Raymond Harlall Entrepreneurship Award" was created in his name for merging the United Nations 17 Sustainable Development Goals with Entrepreneurship.

As a millennial immigrant who realized that to rise above the rat race in a capitalistic society, he had to invest in himself. In his book "The Handbook to Becoming the AUTHORity,™" Raymond covers 33 Principles to Go Pro as an Author, Speaker, and Mentor.

125

FILL UP YOUR OWN CUP FIRST

MARIBEL COLMENARES MARTINEZ

Why: Here is what I noticed. We tend to focus on everyone else, from our spouse to our kids, relatives, friends, employees, clients, co-workers, you name it. The point is, we never take time for ourselves, and as a result, our cup is empty because we poured out more than we poured in. Isn't it ironic that we focus on caring for everyone else except for ourselves?

When we are focused on pleasing everyone else, we miss the opportunity to know ourselves better and do what makes us happy. For most of us, making time for ourselves is not an easy task, especially if you are married with children. Alone time seems to boil down to when you are in the toilet or when taking a bath. Even if you do not have kids, unplugging from technological devices and to enjoy the moment with yourself can be a daunting task.

In reality, for others to get the best of ourselves, we need to spend time with ourselves to create our best possible selves. Speaking as a mother, I have understood that my kids do not need a perfect mother, which I am far from being, but rather a loving and happy one. Hence, I believe that self-love and filling our cup first is not a selfish act. We are simply saying, "Me too."

Let me share with you what I do every day to ensure that I prioritize spending time with myself to refill my cup and pour it into others'.

First of all, I respect and prioritize my sleep. Proper sleep allows my body to reset and feel well-rested when I wake up. Then, I mindfully acknowledge what I have with gratitude, dress up in my exercise clothes, and hydrate with a glass of water. I like to kick-start my day with a power beach walk early enough to enjoy the sunrise. Once I reach my favorite spot, I like to sit and meditate. Once my meditation is over, I like to stretch my body before I head back home. I feel that having this morning routine helps me start my day feeling that I already achieved something important and prioritize my body and health.

It sounds really simple, and the truth is, it is. Once you know what matters most to you, find ways to make your priorities a priority.

THE UN-HABIT: BELIEVE AN EMPTY CUP IS A BURDEN

Why: Many might think that having an empty cup could be a burden to themselves and others, as the feeling of exhaustion due to the never-ending demands of pleasing everyone else invades them. An empty cup, with the right attitude, can be the perfect gift.

The truth is that while our cup should be full so that we can 'pour ourselves' into others, one must be extremely careful regarding how we fill it up. If we are not diligent in filling our cup, it could prevent us from living the life we dream and truly deserve.

At times an empty cup can represent the perfect opportunity to remind ourselves that we are enough and that we set the tone for others to treat us depending on how we treat ourselves.

We must consciously work on ourselves to remove all those limiting thoughts and beliefs from our cups, all those expectations that are not aligned with our purpose.

Until our cup is empty from what holds us back, we will not be able to fill it up with all that matters. Once our cup is full of the right ingredients, we will be able to be the CEO of our lives and live our dream and a life of design.

Let us fill our cups with gratefulness and focus on what we have. Gratitude opens our eyes to the possibilities in life.

May our cups be full of faith, joy, purpose, health, peace, success, significance, love, and resilience.

Bruce Lee sums it up nicely: "Empty your cup so that it may be filled; become devoid to gain totality."

Remember, when things do not add up, it is time to subtract. Filling our cup with the right things equals self-care, which in itself is an act of self- love!

About Maribel: Maribel Colmenares Martinez is the CEO of Ashirel Business Solutions Pte Ltd. She is an international bestselling and has co-authored with Brian Tracy, and written alongside other world-renowned authors such as John Gray (author of Men Are from Mars, Women Are from Venus).

Born in Puebla, Mexico, and educated with a bachelor's degree in Foreign Trade and Logistics from UMAD and a master's degree in International Business at La Trobe University of Melbourne, Australia. Maribel is today considered an authority in partnerships, deal facilitation, sales, and consulting. She is fluent in Spanish, English, Portuguese, and French.

Maribel is also the Director of FalconCrest Limited, an advisory firm providing a wide range of services to family offices and ultra-high net worth individuals, focusing on real estate.

126

NEVER BREAK A GOOD HABIT

BAS RUTTEN

Why: Because Habits are relatively easy to acquire, but that also means that you can quickly lose them again.

If it isn't broken, why fix it?

But this shouldn't stop you from trying to make that good Habit even better.

Especially when it comes to yourself, you always have strived for excellence in yourself; this doesn't mean you have an ego because you put yourself first; this means; the better you take care of yourself, the better you can take care of the ones around you.

Needless to say, this is in the category "life lessons". Example: If you tell a person he should stop drinking too much alcohol, and you are drinking large amounts of alcohol every day yourself, that, of course, doesn't work, it starts with yourself.

If you want people to show up on time, you have to make sure that you are always on time.

If your Habit is not to drink alcohol the night before you have an important meeting (which is a really good Habit) and you break that Habit one time and completely mess up the important meeting, use that experience never to make that same mistake again. We are often too hard on ourselves when that happens, don't be, learn from it, write it down so you won't forget, that's what I do! Now, if the same thing happens again, THEN you can be hard on yourself and have to figure out why you do it. You might have an alcohol problem.

As soon as you break a Habit and suffer the consequences, learn from it, so hopefully, you don't break it again.

If your Habit was not to drink alcohol the day before an important meeting and you broke that Habit but the meeting went well, watch out because now you might believe it's OK to drink the evening before you have an important meeting the next day, don't fall into that trap!

THE UN-HABIT: DON'T BE LATE FOR AN APPOINTMENT

Why: Time is the only thing we can't have more of; if your time is up, it's up. In my book, showing up late is one of the most disrespectful things a person can do. It shows a lack of respect.

I am a trainer; when we schedule an appointment, and you come late, you get a warning, that warning will be: "Don't do be late again because I will stop training you".

That's it, one warning, they show up late again, and I stop. Now, of course, an "act of nature" can happen, that's not a problem. But if I can manage never to be late for an appointment, you should be able to do so as well?

In the past, people would tell me if I would set the "leave time" at 1 PM. "Please wait 5 minutes before you leave". My answer: "Why don't you leave 5 minutes earlier? It is so simple

You can't show up late for a flight or a court appearance because the consequences are not fun when you do.

This Habit starts with your alarm clock. I do talks every year to kids who leave high school to go to college or work. The first question I ask is: "How many of you woke up this morning from your alarm, hit the snooze button, 10 min later, hit the snooze button, etc., for like 5 or 6 times?"

The response is always overwhelming, meaning, minimum of 90%, always.

I tell them that it is a bad Habit and that they can break that Habit starting today.

I tell them to set their alarm 40 min later than usual, and before they go to sleep, they make a pact with themselves that when they hear the alarm, they turn it off, immediately sit up straight in bed and get out. This can be hard for a few days, but within a week, it's normal. Now you have a better night's sleep and created a good Habit.

Now, I am an excellent self-motivator. I did this since I was a kid. If I tell myself I am going to do something, I do it. Not half, no, when I commit, I commit. When I say yes or no, I don't say "maybe".

If I don't do what I told myself I was going to do that day, I can't look at myself in the mirror that evening while brushing my teeth, I am ashamed.

I have used that in my fighting career, acting, commentating, teaching, everything!

Of course, I am talking about "positive things", not: "Today I am going to drink two bottles of tequila".

About Bas: Bas Rutten (Sebastiaan) was born in the Netherlands with severe asthma and severe eczema (skin disease) when growing up. He was bullied daily from the age of 6 till 14. After watching a Bruce Lee movie, he learned how to fight. When he was 14 years old, he knocked out the biggest bully in his school, and the bullying stopped

Bas started training and competing in Thai Boxing when he was 20 years old. He started in Mixed Martial Arts in Japan in 1993, became the 3-time undefeated World Champion for the organization Pancrase. Bas began to compete for the Ultimate Fighting Championship in 1998 and became the first European UFC Champion. He was inducted into the UFC Hall Of Fame in 2015.

127

START A BUSINESS TO MAKE A DIFFERENCE

DR. GRACE MANKOWSKI

W hy: Social entrepreneurship is when a company utilizes business structures, innovation, and ideas to effect social change. It can be starting a non-profit organization for a social cause or creating a non-profit entity out of a for-profit company. When a successful entrepreneur accomplishes all of their dreams and goals, then what motivates them next? When entrepreneurs reach a level of success that they previously thought would make them happy, they find themselves unfulfilled. They have reached their business goals and benchmarks, yet find that the business does not bring them as much joy as it used to. This is because their why is not greater than themselves. When you have a big enough WHY for doing your business, it keeps you motivated and passionate. These entrepreneurs want to make a real and lasting impact on people's lives. Giving back in this way is much more rewarding than any personal business success I can think of.

When you come from the heart, are present for the people you serve, and listen to their needs, the money will automatically follow. The customer must find your brand to be trustworthy. By spending their money with your company, customers display a vote of confidence in your product and what you stand for. Sharing your story with customers as to why you are trying to make a difference, not just from a marketing standpoint but also from a real caring standpoint, will build trust, confidence, and loyalty with your brand.

An example of social entrepreneurship is that every time one of a company's products is sold, the company donates school supplies to disadvantaged neighborhoods, youth groups, physically challenged individuals, or low-income households. When you focus on positive things and give, tenfold will come back to you in terms of happiness, increased business, and an amazing image.

The Un-Habit: Not taking time for self-care will cause your business to fail

Why: We all know that working for ourselves is difficult, and that stress and burnout are real concerns. As entrepreneurs, we often have to deal with unusual working hours, time pressures, fluctuations in finances, and limited social interactions. In our culture, we celebrate the "hustle" and those who don't have the time to sleep as being committed and dedicated. After all, who has time to rest and relax when you have a successful business to build? However, this attitude will result in stress, burnout, insomnia, and poor mental clarity. How can you build a successful business when dealing with these health issues?

One of the most important things in a self-care routine is to get enough sleep, and this rule applies to EVERYONE. People don't realize how much their sleep affects their energy levels, productivity, creativity, and mental clarity. As an entrepreneur, your top priority should be getting at least 6 to 8 hours of sleep every day because this allows your mind to function at its best.

Monitoring my heart rate variability daily (HRV) is a vital part of my self-care routine. Heart rate variability, which is the physiological phenomenon of variation in the time intervals between heartbeats, can monitor burnout. You can easily monitor your HRV on your smartwatch or Fit bit. This is a quick way of using science to monitor your numbers and make sure you are not pushing yourself beyond your physiological limits.

If your HRV reading is in the 20-30 range, it is time to break from work and exercise immediately to prevent a possible heart attack. Readings below 70 HRV show the entrepreneur that they are stressed, and it is time for a day off. You will be ineffective at work; you will have poor workouts or suffer an injury because you're pushing your body too much. Readings between 80-100 HRV indicate your body is sufficiently recovered from your busy work schedule or workouts. This is a great time to have an amazing workout at the gym or complete tasks at work.

Research shows that taking breaks and practicing self-care improves productivity in the workplace. Stress is one of the biggest contributors to poor physical and mental health problems. The physiological, emotional, and physical effects of prolonged stress can be devastating, so taking time to prioritize your self-care is vital.

About Dr. Grace: In her global humanitarian work, Dr. Grace Mankowski has developed the program Civility Interruption Strategist that helps uproot destructive patterns in mankind, releasing one to live a free and joyous life. Dr. Grace Mankowski is an Author, Speaker, Scientist, and Doctor of Chiropractic. She was a professor at Seneca and Centennial College, where she taught Business and English for several years. Her specialties are designing nutritional, detoxification, and infertility programs. Currently, she has helped many abused women, as well as Indigenous people, with her Dr. Grace Mirror Method™. Her passion is to help those in need and those who are less fortunate.

128

THINK GLOBALLY AND PLAY BIG

ERIK "MR. AWESOME" SWANSON

Why: It's time to start thinking, acting, and being the global entrepreneur from now on! It's time to play as big as you possibly can play! The reason simple... because others are *not!* The world *needs* you to step up. The universe is asking you to step up. Even the butterflies in your stomach right this second are dancing and are trying to grab your attention to tell you 'it's time to STEP UP!' Most entrepreneurs play it safe out of fear. And that's one of their biggest downfalls as a new entrepreneur. If you look back in history, time and time again, you will see leaders who stepped out of the norm and were considered a bit crazy at the time. They were the ones who had the biggest and best results and were widely recognized as 'geniuses' after that. So, it's time for you to start thinking of ways to step up your game and play big from now on.

Here's a great example and technique I can share with you, one of our Habitude Warrior techniques. It's called *'THE 10 CITY DOMAIN'*. Here's how it works. All you have to do is take your main domain name and search and secure the same name but add ten different city's names to it. Those cities can be geographically around you if you would like. The point and goal are to start marketing yourself as an Expert in other cities as well. But, you will simply forward all of those domain names over to your main domain and website. For example... If one of your main sites is MotivationKing.com (yes, I just made that up. No, I don't know if it's taken yet.) Anyway, let's say that's your site, and let's say you primarily work in the San Diego, California area. Then, with The 10 City Domain technique, you would secure these other sites as well...

- DallasMotivationKing.com
- StLouisMotivationKing.com
- KansasCityMotivationKing.com

... and so on. With most domains costing only about $12 a year nowadays, this will only cost you about $120 for the year to solidify all 10 of those city's domains. Then, you have to do some targeted online marketing in each of those cities. You will soon be taking your competitions bread and butter and placing it into your hands. But, more importantly, you will be thinking more globally rather than locally. You will also inevitably start playing bigger as an entrepreneur. They say that perception is reality. I truly believe that. I believe it so much that you have to see it in your own eyes first before you can ever see the success in reality. So, start imaging your entrepreneur business as big and fruitful and powerful and successful as you possibly can...

and guess what, the universe will deliver what you can imagine!

THE UN-HABIT: BECOME A "LOSER"

Why: To become a successful entrepreneur, you must learn the Habitude Warrior secret of becoming a 'LOSER!' Make a list right now of 10 things you can get rid of or lose, Habits that are no longer serving you. Take that list and vow to lose these bad Habits out of your every day routine. The most successful entrepreneurs I know and coach all have a series of things that they got rid of to grow into the truly successful businessperson and entrepreneur they are today.

Here are three things I started with. I got rid of 3 main things to start my list. The three things were #1 coffee, #2 alcohol, and #3 negativity! Start making your list now and start growing by becoming a 'loser.'

ABOUT ERIK: As an award-winning International Keynote Speaker, #1 National Best- Selling Author in 5 different categories of success & a Habits & Behavioral Coach, Erik Swanson is in great demand around the world!

Speaking on average to more than one million people per year, and honored to be invited to speak to the Business and Entrepreneurial school of Harvard University as well as joining the Ted Talk Family with his latest Tedx speech called "A Dose of Awesome," Erik is both versatile in his approach and effective in a wide array of training topics.

You can easily find Erik sharing stages with some of the most talented and famous speakers of the world, such as Brian Tracy, Dr. Denis Waitley, Bob Proctor, Jack Canfield, John Assaraf, Loral Langemeier, Co-Author of 'Rich Dad Poor Dad' Sharon Lechter, Legendary Motivator Les Brown, among many others!

129

MAKE 10 CALLS A DAY

KERRY GORDY

Why: Coming from a celebrity family can be an asset and a liability. As the son of Motown's founder Berry Gordy, many people think you are privileged and can have anything you want. When I was younger, it was amazing to grow up around superstars like Michael Jackson, Stevie Wonder, Smokey Robinson, Prince and... yes, I met them all; went to concerts, parties, and dinners and had a blast. But that was as the son of a legend. As I became a man and started to walk my own life, it is sometimes hard for people to imagine that I don't have endless resources, and the worst part is an entrepreneur when I set up a project and look to raise capital... no one wants to give money to Berry Gordy's son, mistakenly thinking I have my dad's resources. I often say no one wants to give money to the idiot son of a lucky mogul.

My dad focused on us all, earning our way in the world, and I believe it truly helped build character. I have had to do everything from my bootstraps and not use other people's money to do what I needed to do.

So I developed Habits for success, and one of my key ones is to make ten calls a day. If you make ten calls a day towards something you want, you will get several calls back.

THE UN-HABIT: DOING THE EASY THING FIRST

Why: This one is very simple, but it has a massive impact on your life. The first thing you do should be the thing you want to do the least.

The reason this has so much impact is the effect that time has on those unwanted tasks. It can be as small as an email that you keep putting off. As each hour goes by, that email is sitting on the back of your mind, and the dread of dealing with it becomes greater and greater to the point that it ruins your entire day.

This is just one example. Think about all the thngs you put off that you are probably emotionally carried around on your back. Think about how much better you would feel to get it over with. Do that, and the dread goes away, your head is clear, and you will be more powerful and useful for the rest of the day.

ABOUT KERRY: Kerry Gordy was born in Detroit Michigan the same year that his father, Berry Gordy, started Motown Records. He grew up around all of the major stars, such as: Diana Ross, Stevie Wonder, Smokey Robinson, Marvin Gaye, Lionel Richie and Michael Jackson. He started in the mail room at Motown and worked in every division from A&R to Publishing and Marketing to Business Affairs. While at Motown, he oversaw, wrote and produced songs for The Temptations, The Four Tops and Billy Preston. The first hit he had as an executive with Motown was with his brother Rockwell's "Somebody's Watching Me." KG was also the leader of the 1980's teen Idol band, Apollo.

In the early 90's, KG and Al Bell teamed up at Bellmark Records and released Tag Team's "Whoomp! (There It Is)", KG ran Prince's company, Paisley Park Records and was awarded 9 platinum albums. He managed Rick James, who grossed $40 Million in concert sales.

He has monetized and overseen many Artists' and Writers' songs valued at over $80 million, including the entire Smokey Robinson, Rick James, Ashford and Simpson and Norman Whitfield Catalogues.

He is also producing The Last Dragon for Sony Pictures with John Davis, who has produced over 90 feature films that have earned over $4.8 Billion at the box office worldwide.

130

CULTIVATE FORTITUDE

DR. GAURAV BHALLA

Why: Margaret Mitchell, the author of Gone with the Wind, spoke to all of us when she advised, "Life's under no obligation to give us what we expect. We take what we get and are thankful it's no worse than it is."

Her counsel is especially valid for entrepreneurs. Just because an entrepreneur starts a business doesn't mean Life will reward the effort with unlimited and unfettered success. By definition, it's impossible to live an entrepreneur's life and not encounter setbacks and failures.

No matter how hard entrepreneurs cross their fingers, Life will serve them and their businesses their bowl of OATS.

O – OBSTACLES,

A – Adversity

T – Trials

S – several times over...again and again and again.

Thinking that any entrepreneur or enterprise will be spared is utterly delusional.

Clients will cancel contracts without explaining; competitors will steal valuable employees just when the business needs them most; the eleventh hour, urgent deadlines will upend plans, just as an entrepreneur is packing to leave for vacation. And this is just a sampling.

Open for business also means open to adversity, setbacks, and failures. Entrepreneurs don't have an option.

How then should entrepreneurs respond when Life serves them their bowl of OATS? When adversity strikes?

Get knocked down and stay down? No, definitely not; that's against the entrepreneurial code. As the old adage says, what's important is not how often one is knocked down; the most important thing is how quickly one gets back up, each time life knocks us down.

For that to occur, entrepreneurs must respond with Fortitude – a dynamic mixture of courage, wisdom, and action to overcome adversity and setbacks. They cannot afford setbacks and failures to fill them with fear, frustration, and hopelessness.

Fortitude requires entrepreneurs to continually act with the belief and perspective that nothing is permanent in humans or businesses' affairs, so avoid undue depression in adversity. This perspective states that every obstacle carries within it the seeds of its own solution. That impediments to actively promote new and more effective action through learning and innovation.

Fortitude is as tangible as any asset an entrepreneur or a business has. I can't think of a single asset that produces a higher ROI for an entrepreneur than Fortitude. It's the ultimate differentiator between entrepreneurs who conquer adversity and achieve success and those who fall short.

THE UN-HABIT: STOP SAYING, "I KNOW"

Why: R.D. Laing, the world-renowned British psychiatrist, had an extremely provocative way of making people aware of the true nature of the problems confronting them. He would ask, "Do you have a problem, or are you the problem?"

Entrepreneurs should reflect on that question with undiluted sincerity. They are frequently the problem, especially when their egos promote the false belief concerning knowing and problem-solving. This belief manifests itself in two parts. The part that is verbalized, "I know." And the part that's implied, but not verbalized, "...and hence there is no problem I can't solve."

This false belief debilitates decision making in virtually all businesses. Because in today's VUCA world – Volatile, Uncertain, Complex, Ambiguous – it's impossible for a single person, no matter how brilliant, to know everything and solve all problems confronting a business. Consequently, I urge entrepreneurs to abandon the predisposition to say, "I know," and replace it instead with, "I am listening, help me learn, help me understand."

An entrepreneur's job isn't being the repository of all relevant knowledge in business. Entrepreneurs should be looking to unearth, nurture, and promote the best thinking, the best expertise, and hence the best decision-making in the business. This can only be achieved if diverse voices, favoring different perspectives, representing a spectrum of expertise domains are unleashed, and their recommendations integrated into a portfolio of decision options, not a single, one-best decision.

"I know," instead of unleashing and promoting diverse voices, stifles them. The moment a person says, "I know," they have effectively signaled that they aren't interested in listening, because they already "know" what the person will say. To make matters worse, whatever the person talking had to contribute is lost to the business. And replaced instead by one-person's ideas and point-of-view of what should be done.

Consequently, if entrepreneurs and business owners want to genuinely improve the quality of decision-making and increase their businesses' future well-being and prosperity, they would be well advised to abandon an "I Know" mindset. It may gratify the entrepreneur's ego, but at the expense of making the business increasingly vulnerable to the future and changing environmental and competitive threats—a high price to pay indeed.

About Dr. Bhalla: Dr. Gaurav Bhalla is a globally acclaimed leadership and marketing strategy specialist. Developer of the school of Soulful LeadershipTM, his purpose and passion is to inspire organizations, teams, and individuals to achieve greater professional success and personal fulfillment by leading with their humanity, not just their executive brilliance.

He helps companies and individuals achieve transformational success through entertaining and insightful keynote speeches, thought-provoking workshops, and human-centric coaching.

Published in both business and literature, his leading-edge thinking is reflected in his newest book, "Awakening A Leader's Soul: Learnings Through Immortal Poems," a 21st-century visionary manifesto on Soulful Leadership^{TM}. In 2016, he won a global award, "Executive Education Specialist of the Year."

131

TAKE TIME TO DEFINE YOUR BUSINESS

LEONA THOMAS

Why: Let me expand on this... Take the time to define what your business does, what it will do, and how you're going to get there.

It seems like common sense. Take the time to figure out what your business does today, what you want to do in the future, and how you will get there. And yet, I'm amazed at how many people and companies don't do this.

Almost every time I start this conversation about an organization's next steps, their focus is almost exclusively on sales, new offerings, new product features, and new markets.

Many companies don't take the time to create a comprehensive execution plan that turns that new vision, that new strategy, into an achievable reality.

There is often little thought on the impacts and the changes needed for the rest of your organization, partners, and service providers to function successfully and help you grow into the next steps.

Over the years, I have developed several strategies and frameworks for defining the business capabilities needed across an organization that can be tailored for a given point in time in a businesses' lifecycle. These start with defining and constantly re-evaluating your company's purpose and market and then span defining your company's business capabilities needed in:

- Building, Delivering and Supporting your products and services.
- Pricing, Selling, and Processing sales transactions for your products and services.
- Acquiring customers who want your products and services.
- Funding your company operations and resources needed to build, sell, market, deliver, and support your company.
- Managing, Leading, and Keeping control of your company.
- Ensuring your back office and support teams such as legal, finance, HR, IT, business continuity, and security can support and protect your business.

While defining how to successfully tailor these as your company continues to change and evolve at different points within their lifecycle. While I can't teach you all of the techniques I've learned over the years, I can tell you that companies who recognize when it's time to move from doing their books to hiring a professional or that selling into a new market means needing to expand their supply chains and sales messaging are ten steps in front of their competition. Companies who do this type of ongoing analysis across their organization are typically part of that 45% that make it to year five and are genuinely poised for real, sustainable growth!

Want a perfect example? Check out Google's growth before and after they hired Eric Schmidt as Chairman and CEO. Even two of the most brilliant inventors in the world needed to ensure their internal operations worked!

The Un-Habit: Building It Won't Necessarily Make Them Come

Why: All too often, the first thing someone says to me when they want to start a new business is, "I have to build my website." They will even tell me they can't start working on their business or start selling until they have their website up – and all too often, they are entirely wrong. I've seen too many new founders and business owners throw themselves, their time, and their resources into building that new website and then get little to nothing out of it. Why? ... Because they didn't take the time to build their business first and they assumed if they made it, people would just come.

Unless your website is a core part of delivering your products and services, you should wait.... Yes, you read that correctly – UNLESS YOU NEED YOUR WEBSITE TO RUN YOUR BUSINESS, YOU SHOULD WAIT TO BUILD YOUR WEBSITE.

You should wait until you have defined:

- Who you are and what products and services your selling.
- How you're going to sell and deliver those products and services.
- Who your target market is.
- What is your business's messaging.
- What you are using your website for –marketing, branding, eCommerce, product delivery, or just validation if someone wants to see who you are.

Even if you need your website to run your business, you should take the time to define all of these before building it. Don't waste time, money, and effort churning through multiple versions of who you are and what you do for anyone in the world to see.

And most importantly, don't fall into the trap that your website should be your first step in marketing your company... your friends, family, associates, and their referrals should be. These are people who can provide you warm introductions and friendly places to sell into. And then NETWORK, NETWORK, NETWORK. These are WARM LEADS. Anyone who finds you through your website is a COLD LEAD.

Who would you rather sell to – someone you know or someone you've never even talked to? To me, that answer is easy. If you feel you HAVE to have a presence on the web, build your LinkedIn profile or put up a basic information page. But, don't waste your time, money, and effort with internet marketing before you've built your company and your community first!

About Leona: Leona Thomas is President & Founder of Enabling Investments, LLC providing Strategic Management and Business Advisory Services. Leona is a Business Transformation Expert with over 25 years in building and reshaping organizations. Leona has led and advised companies from start-ups to Global Fortune 500 corporations. Leona has BSE in Electrical and Computer Engineering and an Executive MBA from Drexel University and is a member of Beta Gamma Sigma.

Leona has always committed to serving her community. She is a member of SIM Women's Executive Leadership Council and long-standing Board Member and Strategic Planning Chairperson for the William Way Community Center - Philadelphia's LGBTQA Community Center, directly serving over 60,000 people a year.

132

STAY CONFIDENT IN THE CHAOS

KELLY BYRNES

Why: Entrepreneurs expect chaos, competition, and uncertainty. A lot of people might tell you to expect it and roll with the punches. Settling for rolling along is what leads to failure by one-third of entrepreneurs within the first two years. My father was an entrepreneur for most of his career, and he taught me not to roll along but to have discipline.

It takes discipline to establish a company and to lead one (or many). There are three key areas to be disciplined about: strategy, money, and mental fortitude.

1) The strategic plan is key. My company's strategic plan fits on three pages, a far cry from the binders full I learned in my corporate jobs twenty years ago. Operating without deliberate strategic thought is inefficient and irresponsible, especially if you have a team. Schedule it quarterly and keep it fluid so you can respond to customer and market changes. If you don't have

a plan, you are reacting instead of responding. Reacting is always more costly in dollars and time.

2) Always know where the money is, comes from, and goes. Get monthly updates from the team that handles it and ensure oversights are in place at levels you trust. Write your checks for amounts over anything you would be uncomfortable losing. Be disciplined about the money, so you do not have to judge the people you hire. It's the way business is done, not a judgment.

3) Do what you need to do every day to be at your best. Do not risk being mentally slow because that's when you could get taken advantage of or make a bad decision. There is not much time for entrepreneurs to sulk, whine, or pity themselves. If/when you have a bad day, set a timer and wallow for minutes, not hours. Be mature enough to figure out systems to get yourself back where you need to be mentally. Have a morning routine that sets your day up right every single day. The routine brings in discipline immediately and sets the tone for your day.

Being disciplined will help you stay confident when things do not go as planned, which you can expect most days in the beginning. It also will help you stay confident when your competitors freak out over changes in the marketplace. If you are disciplined, you will remain confident and unafraid when outcomes are uncertain. That may even be part of why you became an entrepreneur in the first place: no fear. Discipline is the antidote to fear.

THE UN-HABIT: BREAK THE HABIT OF LISTENING TO ADVICE FROM TOO MANY PEOPLE

WHY: People love to give entrepreneurs advice! Launching a company is scary, so we entrepreneurs love seeking advice from lots of people too. The key is to SEEK advice from lots of people but be discerning about the advice you LISTEN to.

One mistake I made when moving my first company from Chicago back to my hometown of Kansas City was not having a plan for learning about the market. I was from KC and took that for granted. It led to so many random meetings, frequent changes to my services and approaches, chasing shiny objects, and a year of inefficient use of time.

I was networking without a purpose, guessing that random meetings would lead somewhere good. I needed to identify what was required, seek input for relevant experts, then make decisions based on MY company. Being open to ideas is admirable unless openness stems from a lack of strategy and discipline.

The wake-up call came when preparing my taxes that year. I needed a new approach to learning. Now, I keep seven lists. These are lists of people you may want to seek advice from in the next year.

1) Anticipate the stages your company will go through this year; the first list is of people worth seeking out during each stage.

2) A customer expert list of those who know everything about your target customers and could introduce you.

3) A marketing list who knows how to reach and attract your target customers.

4) Financial experts who serve your industry providers and customers.

5) Suppliers to your industry. This might need to be broken further, depending on your business.

6) An employee list of people you want to work with you or people who know them.

7) A general list of people you want advice from, but they don't fit the other lists.

Plan to attend events to meet people on those lists, connect with them on LinkedIn, sign up for their emails, and invite them to your events. Request a personal meeting over a cup of coffee. Most will take your meeting because people want to help entrepreneurs.

Seek input and ideas from people you intentionally want to meet, and always remember the decisions and choices are yours. Your company is being run by you—not by a committee of the seven lists.

ABOUT KELLY: Kelly Byrnes is the founder of Voyage Consulting Group where she helps purpose-driven leaders build companies that make their people and grandparents proud.

A sought-after leadership and company culture expert, Kelly also serves as an adjunct MBA professor, contributor to Forbes.com, best-selling author, and award-winning national speaker. Her career includes leading on three corporate executive teams and collaborating across operations, marketing, strategic planning, and Human Resources.

Kelly has had the privilege to serve a variety of organizations as an employee or consultant including: MRIGlobal, Sprint, TargetCom, Schlage, Honda, DaimlerChrysler, Mercedes, Bank of America, Bayer Animal Health, Honeywell, Kauffman Foun

133

EMBODY THE "I AM SHARPER!" MINDSET

RAQUEL SHARPER

Why: To say "I am Sharper" means to be better today than you were yesterday.

"I am" is the most powerful phrase you can say to yourself. Whatever follows will speak life and action into your subconscious.

" Whatever your mind can conceive and believe, the mind can achieve" – Napoleon Hill

To become the best, you must approach every day with the "I am Sharper" mindset. To STAY the best, you must approach every day with the "I am Sharper" mindset.

When you are dressed up, people will say, "You look sharp!" That is just for the moment. When you are the best, people say, "You are the Sharpest!" That is just for the moment.

If you strive to be 1% better every day, does that mean you are 100% better in 100 days? Well, the answer to that is yes and no. Yes, you are 100% better than you were yesterday. Being 100% better doesn't mean you are done.

No, because there is no ceiling to improving your greatness on becoming the best version of yourself. Remember, you are always a work in process. There is always room to be better and Sharper!

Now let's get started with your "I am Sharper!" mindset

Create your I AMs list! Think big! Your I AMs are you claiming who you are and who you want to be. Remember, Muhammad Ali said, "I am the greatest!" way before he was the greatest! That's why he became the greatest! What can you create? Be sure your I AM list has each area of your life from health, relationships, and career/business. You can start this list by saying, "I am SHARPER!" Because you are!

Start every day and say, "I am Sharper!" Take these three actions daily:

1. Start with your gratitudes - What are you grateful for in life? Starting the day with positive thoughts will have your mind looking for positive thoughts and outcomes. Positive brings more positive.
2. Do your I AMs! - Claim it and speak it into existence.
3. Take Action – Find one action you can do daily to improve for each of your I AMs. You will be amazed at who you will become tomorrow with the action you take today!

You are Sharper! We are Sharper! I am Sharper!

THE UN-HABIT: STOP MISUSING, "I CAN'T!"

Why: I can't is the most misused phrase. Most use the phrase I can't remove accountability. I can't means it's impossible to do when in actuality, it is "I won't"!

"Whether you think you can, or you think you can't – you're right," - Henry Ford

I Can't vs. I Won't vs. I Can

Let me show you the proper use of I can't.

I can't fly! This is a true statement! If you start flapping your arms and running, you can't fly. No one can fly. This is impossible. You can get on a plane and fly, but you can't fly personally.

Why do we misuse the phrase I can't. We misuse the phrase I can't because we want to remove personal accountability and ownership.

Nothing is ever created or sourced from an "I can't" mindset. Let me show you some examples of the misuse of the word I can't.

- I can't write a book!
- I can't cook!
- I can't exercise!
- I can't make money!
- I can't go......
- I can't be......
- I can't do......

What if you changed all of the above to "I won't"? Changes the ownership and accountability. If you used, I won't; you probably would feel uncomfortable using this phrase in a conversation. Why does it feel uncomfortable? IF it feels uncomfortable to use "I won't," this means you probably CAN DO your CAN'T list!

What if you changed all of the above to I can? I can write a book! If you never wrote a book saying, "I can't" cuts off all possibilities of you even trying. Saying you won't write a book means you won't even try. Saying I can write a book means you start taking action on figuring out what you can do to write a book.

What if you stopped using the phrase "I can't," where could you be? Carefully examine your I CAN'Ts see that they are your I WON'Ts! This opens up you turning your CAN'Ts into CANs!

About Raquel: Raquel Sharper is an international self-empowerment speaker. She is Transforming Dreamers into Life Stylers "The Sharper Way"!

Raquel began as an IT Consultant for fortune 500 companies for over ten years. She cultivated her corporate skills into a business and entrepreneurial skills to create a better life for her daughter as a single parent.

Raquel has worked with:

- Tony Robbins organization
- Robert Kiyosaki's (Rich Dad) organizations
- Kevin Harrington from ABC's hit show Shark Tank.

Raquel is a highly sought after due to her passion as an influencer. Raquel's charismatic delivery allows her to connect and impact audiences worldwide while providing inspiration and empowering the individual to take action on their passion by discovering their untapped talents and infinite potential.

As she says, "She teaches people to work smarter because that's The Sharper Way!"

134

LOOK IN THE MIRROR, AND SAY I LOVE YOU

EMMANUEL KELLY

Why: You would think that would be easy enough. Especially after your appearance singing John Lennon's "Imagine" on X-Factor was seen and loved by millions and you had record deal offers, got to work with David Foster, Snoop Dog, and Coldplay's Chris Martin and have over one billion views collectively online.

... but it wasn't.

After my first brush with fame, I got swept up in the fast lane only to crash. To realize that even though I could sing like a bird, I couldn't fly. Couldn't soar above the fact that I'm Iraqi born and there's a fear among people that mid-Easterners are terrorists. I couldn't forget that I had no birth certificate, no idea how truly old I am, and no clear connection to my birth parents.

And finally couldn't pretend that when people looked at me, they focused on my different physical appearance and felt a sense of pity.

All of this led to a spiral toward self-loathing even though I had already defied ALL the odds. My brother and I had been rescued from 7 years of living in Baghdad orphanage subjected to nearby bombs and public executions, always fearing we would be next. In spite of the fact that an angel, a former actress and humanitarian named Moira Kelly, would adopt my brother and me and whisk us to freedom and safety in Australia. She granted me eight life-altering surgeries and taught us how to walk, dress, feed ourselves, and even drive a car. She instilled in me a sense of endless possibility... yet one day, I forgot it all.

It's sad how we let ourselves succumb to others' lack of belief or judgment about us. How even though we have greatness all around us, one rejection or bullying moment can shatter that.

I am here as proof that you must stand strong and believe in who you are. Fight to find your purpose and meaning on this planet and serve others with your gifts.

I have found that the daily Habit of just looking in the mirror, being grateful, and saying I love puts it all back into perspective. And as they say, if I can do it... anyone can!

THE UN-HABIT: NOT REALIZING WE ALL HAVE GIFTS TO SHARE

Why: Have you ever thought, what if?

What if the Beatles never got together and wrote the music they did

What if Thomas Edison had stopped just short of inventing the lightbulb

What if Jesus had stayed being just a carpenter.

I often wonder, what if my Mom hadn't come to get my brother and I. The world would have been robbed of a differently-abled rockstar, for the very first. It would have been nice to have had a normal body, a normal upbringing, and normal family... but if all that HAD happened, I wouldn't be able to make the impact I am having on the world. It seems my story crosses all borders, all cultures, all races. People of every walk of life face physical challenges, and as music is universal, it seems I was destined for this path.

Too many times, people play small and deny the world of THEIR gifts because they're afraid. So whether it is performing, writing, coaching, starting a new business, or supporting those who do, my suggestion is to make it a Habit to face your fears and go for your dreams no matter what.

I firmly believe we all have unique gifts. And when we focus on what we can contribute to serve others, perhaps, we can begin to experience a bit of world peace.

About Emmanuel: Emmanuel Kelly has defied all odds! He has entertained close to 1 billion people worldwide after his rendition of the song *"Imagine"* by John Lennon on the Australian X-Factor show went viral. From there, he has gone on to perform at other iconic platforms such as the United Nations.

"I've gone from Iraq and being in a box in a park to seeing executions in war to now being here in the U.S. where I get to perform and show people life is great."

Emmanuel has Toured with Coldplay as a special guest, opened for Snoop Dogg, and performed with David Foster. His music video,"**Never Alone,**" features many "A-List" celebrities and social impact Influencers joining him to advocate global mental health and encourage people to virtually embrace and authentically connect. From Demi Lovato, Chris Martin,

Emmanuel's two-time Para Olympian and World Champ Gold medalist brother Ahmed Kelly, Terrance Howard, JK Simmons, Elizabeth Moss, Jean Claude Van Dame, Brian Grazer and his wife Veronica, and many more. They share encouraging and inspirational 30-second cameos of raw, unfiltered, and heartfelt words telling the camera what they do to gain strength when they feel alone and building a community that is so crucial for everyone.

135

STOP SELLING AND START CONNECTING

PAUL ANDRÉS TRUDEL-PAYNE

Why: I started my first business in 2014 in real estate. I met my very first clients during my very first open house and thought I was the man. It was a husband and wife, and both were friendly but not too forthcoming. They asked me how I got into this career, and instead of reciting a canned answer I had heard from numerous agents before, I told them the truth. I loved all things home, and creating spaces where people can feel love and make memories, is all I ever wanted to do because I didn't have that for most of my life growing up.

They left the open house, and 1 hour later, called me to ask if I would be their Agent. I said yes, and the next day I showed them three homes. They decided to write up an offer that same evening, and I ran to my office, printed the sales contract, asked someone how to fill out the sales contract, and then met them at a coffee shop soon after. Once everything was signed, I placed the contract into a folder, we hugged, and both drove away. Not even 2 mins after I left the parking lot, I heard loud honking and in my rear view mirror saw their car approaching fast behind me. I pulled over, and they pulled up beside, rolled down the window, and handed me a folder. Their folder. The folder I put their signed contract in before leaving. The folder I had placed on my car's roof while I dug in my bag looking for my keys. The folder that fell off the roof of my car and into the street right in front of them as they followed me out of the lot. I couldn't stop apologizing while they couldn't stop laughing. I submitted their offer, and we won. Over the next four years, they purchased three other properties with me.

I have told the story of my first clients to every consultation since. And more times than I can remember, it is this story that clients say helped them decide to use me as their Agent. Taking a transaction from an exchange of money to an exchange of emotional connection is how you create loyal clients. And a repetition of authenticity and connection will cultivate a dedicated following of raving fans. The kind that helps you withstand anything the market throws at you and allows you to build a referral-based business.

The Un-Habit: Keep the Work you and the Personal you, separate at all times

Why: Gone are the days of the salesperson. No one wants to be "sold to" because, for many consumers, the ends no longer justify the means. More than any other time in history, consumers are mission-driven, socially aware, and feel empowered to ask questions. Because of this, consumers are increasingly making choices based on emotions and ideology vs. deliverables or results.

Why you do what you do and how you do it are the important questions every entrepreneur should be prepared to answer. Consumers are determined to put their dollar where their heart is, meaning the transaction is shifting from money-focused to emotionally charged. Allowing the consumer to support businesses that align with their values but put more pressure on entrepreneurs and their companies to be more forthcoming with who they are on a deeper level. Connecting with the clients at this level is increasingly becoming more imperative to the success of new businesses and even shifting the popularity of many well-established companies.

This is where we say goodbye to splitting ourselves into a professional and personal side, and instead be fully who we are. And when it comes to being our whole self, authenticity is key. While some see this as invasive and unnecessary, the truth is that every entrepreneur, in every sector of business, has seen a shift in sales due to consumer priorities.

The personal you is equally, if not more important to consumers than the professional you. And the businesses that do not adapt to this new expected connection between business and consumers are quickly seeing their clients leave to spend their money with companies they better align with. Companies that are sharing behind the scenes stories, struggles, growth, and even social and political stances. Welcome to the new era of conscious business.

About Paul: Paul Andrés Trudel-Payne is a Home & Lifestyle expert, having opened numerous home-focused companies since 2014. He also is the creator of one of the Top 20 LGBT Parenting Blogs, The Dada Diary, and host of the new video podcast, In your Mind. Recently Paul sold his first and largest company, after achieving roughly 75 million in sales, developing a 90 day universal sales training to cultivate a referral-based business, creating corporate partnerships with global giants like Microsoft or Costco, and crafting a 4 hour, 3 day work week. Much to the demand of others, Paul is now sharing his experience and best practices for following your passion while maintaining work/life balance. Transitioning from service provider to industry consultant, Paul now helps industry professionals and other creatives design the life they deserve at work and home.

136

USE THE TOOL BOX

RUTH YOUNG-LOAEZA

Why: Since I started this entrepreneurial journey, I have had to change my mindset. I was cleaning houses for twenty-three years, and I was successful in my cleaning business, but now I had become an inventor with ideas that have changed my life, and needed to ensure that I will succeed in my new start-up business.

The "Tool Box," what is it, and why I created it. By God's grace, I started implementing a Habit in my life every time I was struggling, and to this day, I practice this Habit. I created a 'Tool Box," where I've been storing positive memories, inspirational quotes, Bible verses, other helpful tools that I can use to seek a brighter future when my reality is cloudy.

I write positive messages and place them where I can read them constantly. I write my goals on cardboard and put it on the ceiling above my bed, or in front of my desk. Seeing positive messages helps me stay strong and focus. Going from cleaning houses to becoming an inventor was less challenging because of this Habit. Using these tools I have put together has taken me from a limited mentality to seeing endless possibilities.

As an inventor, innovator, and creator, I use tools to fix things, so I logically apply this same principle to my physical, spiritual, and mental peace of mind.

As I grow older, I continue updating and adding vibrant and sophisticated new tools to my 'Tool Box." Life is becoming increasingly fast and advanced, so I need to do the same in my life. Now with the click of a button, I can be listening to amazing messages or hearing audiobooks that will help me succeed in my plans if I practice the good I learn.

Daily, I prepare for the ups and downs of life. I listen to Psalms, Proverbs, and the book of Job constantly. I also listen to the titans of faith that instill faith within my soul. Magic happens when I use my "Tool Box." The trick is to practice the Habit of surrounding myself with positive things, such as books, messages, music, and people too.

I carry this "Tool Box" within my heart and mind, but if I forget to practice this Habit, it is a sure recipe for a day full of frustration and regrets. My constant reminder is that it only works when I open it, and I wisely utilize the tools available

inside!

THE UN-HABIT: STOP NEGLECTING YOURSELF

Why: Every single one of us has a purpose in this world for their life. I asked God the same question several times, 'What is my purpose in this world?" but I wasn't paying attention to hear an answer yet.

I was too busy working overtime, having three jobs, and working seven days a week. My time was fully committed to volunteering in my community, fully committed to serving in my church, fully committed to my children's school, and fully committed to everything except myself.

For the longest time, I only weighed 90 lbs. I was neglecting myself, and I was sleep-deprived to the point that I rather slept instead of eating. We all know that to be healthy, we need to eat healthy food and have enough sleep daily.

After an accident I suffered while I was on my way to work, I realized that I was dangerously neglecting myself. Not sleeping or eating healthy had become a horrible Habit, and I knew I needed to get rid of it as soon as possible because I started suffering the consequences.

I knew that enough was enough, and I realized I wasn't ready to die. The decision was immediate; I quit one of my jobs, and decreased the amount of time I volunteered and worked. I implemented good healthy Habits to make sure that I stayed healthy and strong to take care of myself and my children; I was finally investing in myself.

The change was pleasant to my life and health. I started feeding my soul by truly listening to the word of God. I also started taking care of my body by riding my bike every day. I made sure I ate at least three full meals and slept at least six hours daily. I included healthy snacks in my eating Habits too.

The reality is that it is up to us to love ourselves and recognize that this body we have needs nurturing. The Bible says that it is our temple, and we only get one body. If you have dreams and want to fulfill them, I'd say you need to stay healthy, physically, spiritually, and mentally You are obstructing the purpose of your life by neglecting yourself, so stop neglecting yourself while you are living in this amazing world.

About Ruth: Ruth Young-Loaeza is an innovative thinker and the inventor of NEET Sheets. NEET Sheets are bed linen that addresses the stressful and difficult task of bed making.

The clever and doubled patented design allows the bedsheets to be applied to the mattress easier and 47% faster than the conventional bedsheets.

No more ripped corners, no more struggle to fit the bedsheet on the mattress, and no more bedsheets popping from the corner of your mattress.

The idea was born due to Young-Loaeza's experienced after making the beds over twenty thousand times.

A recent study conducted by CSUSM found that there is a possibility to decrease musculoskeletal injuries because the lifting of the mattress gets reduced from sixteen times VS only four times lifting the mattress with NEET Sheets.

With NEET, Sheets don't cut corners, cut time!

137

BE TENACIOUS

JERRY DUNN

Why: Throughout one's life, there will continuously be roadblocks, be they physical, mental, etc.

From the time that I was a young boy, there were many, many times when I was told no, where I was told you were not good enough, for many, many reasons, Jerry is not artistic enough, he's not smart enough, he's not athletic enough, he's not tough enough, he doesn't have a killer instinct, he's not deep enough, he's not attractive enough, on and on and on. Several times whether they were from a teacher, an athletic coach, A mentor, a peer, an authority figure, a panel of my experts, etc., I was told that I could not be a certain thing because of my lack. At age 61, and a very successful freelance career in Hollywood, California, I looked back at all of these different times of my life. I realize who these people were, And I know that without the Habit of tenacity, where I would have been and what my life has been like had I not had tenacity.

Tenacity, paraphrased from the dictionary, is a quality of being very determined, very persistent, no matter the odds.

Without tenacity, I would've given up a long, long time ago, taking a safe and secure job they gave me a touch of prestige, and I would've only been using a tiny percentage of my abilities.

Tenacity is important to create to build up the muscle needed never to quit, no matter what the circumstances, nothing keeps going.

Tenacity will change your life because every roadblock that you meet or challenge that you have you will know deep in your soul to keep plugging away if new talents are needed, develop them, if new skills are needed to learn them, keep going, don't stop

The answer no to anything. It's just showing up to give you something else to strengthen the muscle.

The Un-Habit: Stop being timid. Period.

Why: If one is timid, they may never know what the possibilities could have been in their lives. The catchphrase of living to your full potential is always a bit squirrelly. Being timid can hold you back in every single area of your life. The project at school you never took on, the athletic venture that you stopped for one reason or another, the song you never sang, The language you never tried to learn, the relationship that you could've had all pop up due to being timid. Timidity should be banned from your brain. No successful person ever has gotten to where they are no matter what the field, etc. by being timid; it serves no one least of all you. I always wonder how many fabulous famous, talented, amazing people that we've never met or never seen are out there because they took on being timid as a way of being. Never let anyone tell you that you can't do anything.

About Jerry: Emmy® and Art Director's Guild-nominated Production Designer Jerry Dunn is best known for his multi-camera situation comedy TV work on some of the biggest international hits in Television history. His portfolio includes thousands of sets for *The Cosby Show* for the legendary Carsey-Werner Company, Anger Management, and decorated numerous sets for the Witt/Thomas/Harris Company and The

Carsey Werner on *The Golden Girls, Blossom,* Roseanne. His career includes designing some of the most prestigious international stages ranging from the swanky Miss Universe Pageants in Taiwan and Bangkok to luxury looks for the Academy Awards telecast in Los Angeles. Following his time in variety television, Jerry has designed some of Disney Channel's biggest hits, including *Hannah Montana, Hannah Montana Forever, That's So Raven, Cory In The House, The Suite Life of Zack and Cody,* and *The Suite Life on Deck.* Most recently, he designed Fuller House for Netflix, a re-mount of the iconic Full House series. Currently, Jerry has gotten the opportunity to re-visit his work on Roseanne by being part of the Art Department for ABC's top-rated The Conners.

138

HAVE UNWAVERING COMMITMENT

RYAN ANDERTON

Why: All successful people have one thing in common: persisting without exception. I can speak to this from direct experience. I grew up in a neighborhood where a lot of people either end up in a body bag, addicted, or in jail. I found myself being on a similar path, drifting through life; not living, merely surviving. At one point, after falling into a downward spiral of addiction, I recall looking in the mirror and not recognizing my own reflection. It was at this moment that I felt a push to do more, to BE more.

This was a key moment in my life whereupon I severed all ties to my old life and enrolled in the military, where I learned discipline, leadership, commitment and integrity. From there, I pursued a path of sales and business excellence with a foundation of personal and professional development.

I have committed to a life whereupon I constantly strive, learn, improve and, most importantly, IMPLEMENT. I went from filling my being with toxins to filling my being with hope in a brighter tomorrow. I started investing in myself rather than weapons of mass distraction. This investment has been the best investment I could have ever chosen, leading me to build multiple businesses that have generated tens of millions of dollars in sales. I have learned how to amass wealth and nurture my health. I have committed to making it my mission to meet new people every single day, to continuously expand my network and help as many people as I can. This is the key to success. Even in the midst of hopelessness and despair, if you dig deep, you can find a reason, a spark...a purpose larger than yourself.

But don't take my word for it...the world is ripe with examples of people pushing through despite the odds. Take the King of Rock and Roll, for example. After failing countless auditions to join bands, being rejected after auditioning for a national televised talent show, and being told by the manager of the Grand Ole Opry

"You ain't going nowhere, son. You ought to go back to driving a truck", Elvis Presley rose to the top. His life was testament to the idea that we must believe to achieve. And let's not forget Thomas Edison's 1000 failed attempts to invent a product that forever changed the world, the light in a time of darkness. Let this light never dim as within you is the key to greatness. It just takes unwavering belief and a commitment to excellence.

THE UN-HABIT: STOP NEGLECTING YOURSELF

Why: Overnight success is mostly a myth. Most overnight success has been years in the making. After mentoring and coaching thousands of entrepreneurs over the years, I have come to realize that one of the most common obstacles to becoming successful is the unconscious wish for having it all and acquiring overnight success without putting in the hours and paying the price with work ethic. This can lead to capriciousness, impatience and shortcut-oriented behavior. What I have found is that people who cut corners run in circles, leading to devastating impacts on performance and judgement. Debunking this myth is crucial.

When I consult people on this matter, I often hear them tell me that they have "given up" that "there is no point", however, nothing could be farther from the truth. No matter the entrepreneur that has made it, a part of the journey is facing failure and rising above.

Walt Disney was confronted with countless reasons to give up. Fired by a newspaper editor before because he "lacked imagination and had no good ideas," it would have been easy for him to quit. Had he done so, however, he never would have received the success he has to date...and Disney would never have come to be.

These examples serve to show the power of persistence beyond exception and not being a chicken when it comes to following your dreams. On the other side of fear is success and, unlike the belief of many, failure is not the opposite of success, it is a part of it. In short, if I have learned one thing in life it is this: never throw in the towel...use it to wipe off the sweat and keep going!

About Ryan: Known by most as the Enlightened Wealth Warrior and the "Fill Your Live Events Guy" Ryan Anderton is highly skilled at Global Joint Ventures, is a Profit Specialist and an international best-selling author. Often accused of being a marketing genius, he excels at guerrilla marketing and business strategies. Also a Mentor, Coach, Consultant, & Speaker with a proven track record in speaking with crowds upwards of 15,000+, he loves transforming organizations and lives. With multiple streams of income, and a willingness to teach the classes to the masses, if you are seeking to learn while you earn, consult with him today!

139

FOCUS ON CUSTOMER EXPERIENCE
ANDREW HINKELMAN

Why: As an entrepreneur, you're focused on building a business and bringing in revenue. You have talent, passion, and vision.

But what is it like for a customer or client to work with you? Of course, you deliver a world-class product or service, but what about everything else? As a customer, what is like initiating an engagement with you, scheduling a call, executing contracts, the meetings, follow-through... the full end-to-end process?

Is it a smooth, efficient, and seamless customer experience (CX) interacting with your company? Or do they have to print, sign, scan, and email you the contract? Are you "just" a little late to their meetings? Do they have to pay by snail-mailing you a paper check?

Everything that a customer experiences when interacting with you and your business reflects—positively or negatively—on your service and brand.

I recently purchased a wireless mouse from a company that prides itself on usability and design. The messaging and photos were clear and helpful. It arrived quickly in minimal, recyclable packaging and worked seamlessly. No charging, no drivers to install, and not only is it beautiful (for a mouse), it's quiet, sturdy, and well-made. I will definitely leave positive reviews and purchase more from this company based on that experience.

It's time to start seeing your end-to-end business and customer journey in terms of CX and not just promotions, programs, followers, and price-points. You can develop awareness for customer experience by merely noticing and being curious about what's happening around you. This means seeing how YOU experience products, services, brands, and their marketing. How well did their end-to-end purchase lifecycle work for you?

Once you see the world as a creative place, full of different brand experiences, you'll see limitless opportunities for assessing and improving the customer experience with your own company and brand. More feedback is easy to come by... just ask your customers about different aspects of their experience.

Ultimately, you'll need to engage a CX firm to provide a thorough, objective review of your customer's journey, including usability testing. This used to be the domain of large tech companies but can now be achieved online/remote and is surprisingly inexpensive. Still, spend some time researching the ROI of investing in CX and be sure it makes sense for your business or niche.

Putting others first--the essence of strong customer experience--is the best long-term strategy for getting people to genuinely love your brand and want to work with you again and again.

THE UN-HABIT: STOP MISSING THE BIGGER PICTURE

Why: Let's go back in time for a moment.

Most of us learned a specific skill, often in college, that formed our professional foundation. Maybe it was in business or engineering or biology. We then became more employable by learning additional skills or gaining more experience. We were, and still are, technicians in a certain field.

At some point, you were inspired to take that foundation and build a business.

Being an entrepreneur requires you to continually add new skills like business development, personal branding, public speaking, marketing, etc. You now have an even stronger foundation and level of expertise built with your courage, passion, and a growth mindset. You've worked hard to build a life that few people will have the bravery or confidence to consider building for themselves.

Well, great news: you're not done yet.

You're not done because the world needs you to be even more: to be an entrepreneur AND a leader. To build your business AND make a positive impact in the world. You have a unique and rare opportunity to use your skills, education, drive, and compassion to inspire and lead people. To be an amazing employer. To be a generous and caring member of your community.

This means you need to be adept at promoting your business AND communicating your vision of the future. It means carrying your business on your shoulders every day AND motivating people to engage with that vision in a genuine, authentic way.

On a tactical level, being an entrepreneur and a leader go hand-in-hand when you:

- Over-communicate with your employees, partners, and customers
- Influence behavior by modeling the leadership, ethics, and empathy you expect in others
- Recognize and praise your team's efforts
- Slow down, see people, and build rapport with the individuals around you

Yes, you still need to build your business. But having a purpose and listening to others has the potential to create true, long-lasting growth and success for you and your business while you inspire others to grow alongside you.

The world is ready for you to BE even more.

About Andrew: Andrew Hinkelman is the CEO of Priority-1 Group, a Leadership Coaching and Consulting organization focused on guiding driven, ambitious executives to optimize their teams while building their own personal definition of success.

Andrew has more than 25 years of experience in the Technology and Financial Services industries across roles in IT, Product Management, and Business Intelligence, along with consulting and advisory roles. As a former Chief Technology Officer, his expertise is in solving complex, company-wide challenges and driving strategic goals while leading teams through periods of steep growth and disruptive change.

140

WALK INTO EVERY ROOM WITH AN OPEN MIND

LYNDA SUNSHINE WEST

Why: Have you ever heard the phrase, "A closed mind never learns"? In 2005, the National Science Foundation published an article summarizing research on human thoughts per day. According to their article, the average person has anywhere from 12,000 to 60,000 thoughts every day. Of those thoughts, 80% were negative, and 95% were the same repetitive thoughts as the day before.

WOW! Incredible, right? Whoever thought we had so many thoughts? There are only 86,400 seconds every day, so that means we're thinking a new thought almost every second. Fathom that. Of course, most of our ideas are subconscious, but, still, when seeing the words in print, it's pretty darn amazing how many thoughts we have every day.

Now that we have that out of the way, I'm going to shed some light on your brilliance.

If you go by the National Science Foundation study, 5% of your thoughts EV-ER-Y DAY are NEW thoughts. In 20 days, you will have 100% new thoughts. Let's not stop there. After 200 days, you will have increased your thoughts by 1,000%. That's incredible. That's not even one year. NOW let's take that one day of 5% new thoughts and insert ourselves into a room filled with people you've never met before. This 5% is about to be blown out of the water. With every interaction you have with another human being, there is what's referred to as 1 + 1 = 11. Why? Think about it.

Let's say you're having a conversation with me. I say something that "sparks" an idea in your mind. You then start sharing your newly sparked idea with me, which, in turn, "sparks" an idea in my head. Next thing you know, we are exploring a completely new idea between the two of us. The one idea has blossomed into something new.

But let's say you entered the room with a closed mind. I started having the same conversation with you, and you just shut me out. That conversation just ended. No new ideas. No new thoughts to explore with each other. No exciting theories being thrown around. When you enter a room with an open mind and an open heart, you never know what will happen. This one Habit of opening your mind and heart will change your whole perspective of what's available to you.

THE UN-HABIT: BE YOUR OWN BEST CHEERLEADER, NOT YOUR OWN WORST ENEMY

Why: I don't know how many times I've heard people say, "I'm my own worst enemy" (including me). Why is that? Why are we so critical of ourselves? Were we born with it? Is it something we learned as children? Did we learn it from our parents, grandparents, teachers, fellow students? Did we learn it from our friends, co-workers, spouse?

Wherever we learned the negative self-talk, it's time to change it. Words are our greatest weapon. We can use them for good or for bad. When saying negative words to ourselves, we start to believe them. What we believe is how we behave and how we behave is who we become.

At the ripe old age of 51, I hired a life coach. She helped me see that I WAS my own worst enemy. What I loved about learning this was that once I became aware of my Habit of beating myself up verbally, I now focused on changing it. This awareness became my first step in changing my beliefs about myself.

Now that I became aware, I was able to apply this new awareness to my self-talk. With my new and improved self-talk, I started seeing changes in who I was being, and, for the first time in my life, I started loving myself for who I am, rather than beating myself up.

Success comes from being the best you, and you can't be the best you if you are busy being your own worst enemy. Start today by listening to your self-talk. What are you saying to yourself? What names are you calling yourself? What attitude are you taking on with yourself? If you notice negativity, it's time to change one thing this week, then another next week, and so on until you have become your own BEST cheerleader. The beauty of being your own best cheerleader is you no longer need others to pump you up. You got YOU!!

About Lynda: I help women entrepreneurs become more visible with my Women Action Takers Collaboration Books, Podcast and Video Interviews, Summits, and Magazine. As a Collaboration Strategist, Speaker, Bestselling Author, Executive Film Producer, Red Carpet Interviewer, and Philanthropist, I am passionate about sharing YOUR voice with the world.

Why am I so passionate about this? Well, I grew up in a volatile, abusive alcoholic household, and that left me becoming a people-pleaser and with so many fears that I was scared to talk to people. In 2015 I faced one fear every day. In doing so, I gained an exorbitant amount of confidence, and I use that confidence today to make a difference on the planet. I know how sharing YOUR story will change your life for the better and am here to make the process quick, painless, and easy.

141

IN SERVICE TO HUMANITY REMEMBER TO BE HUMAN

JACQUELINE BUCKLEY

Why: As a single parent serving in the Canadian Armed Forces, I was often referred to as "the machine." I was viewed as dedicated, committed, and someone who could get the job done efficiently at any cost.

However, in my efforts to be perfect in all aspects of my life, I failed to be human. My connection to others and family faded and while I appeared to have it all together on the outside, what was not apparent was the damage I was creating on the inside.

I became emotionless and showed very little compassion to others. I forgot what it was like to be human, and at all costs, I placed everyone and everything before myself to prove to others that I was an achiever. In having no healthy boundaries, I taught people how to treat me, and the only emotion I connected with was anger.

Like all machines, they eventually break down and need repair. And, like all machines...so did I. In 2009, I was diagnosed with Post Traumatic Stress Disorder, brought on after participating as a member of the dental forensic team tasked in identifying those who died aboard Swissair 111 in September of 1998.

For over 11 years, I strived for perfection to hide my human side at a cost to my family and myself.

Today, in my journey to entrepreneurship, I realize that we need to be human to achieve balanced success. We need to place ourselves at the top of our to-do list. We need to have compassion for ourselves when we don't get everything done as planned in a day. We need to be human while serving humanity. Otherwise, we become a machine and machines cannot form real human connections.

THE UN-HABIT: STOP PREDICTING THE FUTURE

Why: "The afternoon knows what the morning never suspected" ~Swedish Proverb

In today's society, we are flooded with individuals suffering from anxiety. Even my own experience with anxiety can speak to how debilitating it can become.

In my life today and working as a mental health counselor, I often receive referrals for individuals suffering from anxiety. When I ask them what they are anxious about, most of the time, it is thoughts they have created about the future. However, we cannot predict the future, nor do we know what it holds. Yet, we spend most of our waking time either trying to live in the future of what if...or struggling in the past.

What I have learned over my time in treatment for PTSD and during my Masters education journey is that if one wants to succeed in business or anything in life, it serves no purpose to dwell on things of the past or worry about a future that has not yet arrived. By spending time focused on what has past or what has not yet arrived, we waste valuable time to create or cherish what is in our present.

Focusing on and trying to predict and worry about circumstances that may or may not happen drains us of valuable emotional energy. The energy needed to thrive in business. When we live in negative emotions such as worry and that worry creates anxiety, we cannot access the part of our brain used for making rational decisions. As an entrepreneur, that could be costly for business.

Accepting that we cannot control or predict the future and practicing healthy coping strategies to prepare for uncertain times will be more advantageous to our health and long term success.

Spending time worrying and predicting in a future that has not arrived could lead to a missed opportunity within the present.

ABOUT JACQUELINE: Jacqueline Marie is a published author, motivational speaker, and veteran who personally understands how burnout and stress can impact family, self, and the ability to lead others. As the sole proprietor of Blue Alliance 10-33 Consulting, a business that delivers resiliency programs to first responders with compassion, trust, and hope.

As a volunteer with the Memory Project, she has been called upon to speak at various events. She has been featured in several media publications, television, and radio interviews on her PTSD experience after working as a first responder within the Canadian Forces Dental Services as part of the dental forensic team during Operation Persistence.

142

READ 10 PAGES OF A BOOK EVERY DAY
DENISE KOZLOWSKI

Why: If you're not growing, you're dying. The best ways to grow are through your own experiences, or other people's experiences, given to us through books. We read to stretch the imagination, gain knowledge, and better ourselves, and it is imperative that this is a daily Habit. Books teach us to relate with each other, see different points of views and share experiences together, without having to physically be with each other. They put us into a creative state and foster new ideas and connections. Reading just 10 pages a day is surmountable for even the busiest person, yet long enough to drop us into another world, a healthy escape from the stress and chaos we face on a daily basis.

You will be amazed at how quickly you finish books by building this Habit. While audio books are great tools, that is not what I am talking about here. Reading physical books is a different experience. It requires our full attention. And there is an energy that resides in books, an energy of wisdom from another time and space that is passed from author to reader, from creator to receiver. It is an energy that deserves reverence. Wayne Dyer would surround himself by books whenever he wrote, because he believed all of the knowledge around him would influence the depth of his texts. Phil Knight has a room in his home full of books, and whenever he enters, he takes off his shoes out of respect for the energy, the weight, the gravitas those books hold.

You may find that you enjoy reading several books at a time. I do this. I am usually reading at least five books, so I can pick up the one I want to read based on my mood or interest at that given time. I have built quite a library this way. Books titles are great to swap with friends and colleagues and give you endless topics for discussion. Once, I even met someone who happened to be reading the same book at the same time as me. We are still great friends to this day. Reading must be a foundational Habit for any successful entrepreneur, so keep reading, you still have nine pages left to go today.

The Un-Habit: Preparation Paralysis

Why: We have all done it. We obsess about the details of the perfect pitch, the flawless presentation, the properly styled video or the impeccable look, all to avoid actually putting our work out into the world. If we could get one more opinion first, or if we change a few more lines, or just take one more class, then we'll be ready, right?

Do you ever notice how the men and women who have three or four credentials after their name seem to be stuck in low-paying or mid-level careers, while entrepreneurs with no college education like Richard Branson, Steve Jobs and Oprah Winfrey became billionaires?

I once met a man who had been an aviation engineer in the air force, had an MBA, and had been a financial analyst for one of the largest firms in the world, but he was financially depleted and struggling to get a job, so he spent an additional $5,000 to get another certification. I was baffled. Qualifications were not his problem!

It is not another skill that you need, it's ingenuity. As entrepreneurs it is easy to get stuck in the minutia of the planning, the statistics and the data. And while those things can be important and can enhance your bottom line, without the novel idea, viral video, press stunt or killer catch phrase your impact will always fall flat. What's the best way to create buzz? In the marketing world we call it AB Testing, but what does it really mean? Trial and error! The only way to get feedback is by actually taking the action! So, make sure you are spending only the essential amount of time preparing, and then get out there! What you don't know you will figure out along the way. And if things don't work, don't get stuck, pivot! After all the definition of an entrepreneur is a master problem solver, so if you can embody that above all else, you are guaranteed to find the success you desire.

About Denise: Denise Kozlowski is a Financial Professional and Business and Life Coach with a Master's Degree in Spiritual Psychology, who focuses on helping others grow personally and financially. She is a serial entrepreneur and marketing expert with 17 years of marketing, fund-raising, sales and entertainment experience, gained while studying conscious leadership and communication. She has run results-driven influencer and experiential marketing campaigns for top consumer brands including AllSaints Spitalfields, Diesel, MTV, Red Bull, TOMS and others. She is known for creating data-driven, strategic campaigns measured using KPIs, focused on ROI. Her undergraduate Humanities studies have also influenced her passion for non-profit and volunteer work locally and abroad in countries including China, Cuba and Kenya.

143

SET UP A NATURAL HEALTH ROUTINE TO OPTIMIZE YOUR DAY

BRADLEY HANSELMAN

Why: We need to be able to function optimally mentally and physically to take on our daily business procedures. Before we are mentally assaulted with calls, texts, emails, production, etc., we can be more prepared to handle every day as it comes by making a routine of natural health supplements, essential oils, and mindwork.

In our daily grind, we are always striving to improve in one aspect or another. Supporting proper Habits using essential oils is a positive-feedback loop to our body to keep using them regularly. As with anything worth doing, true results and profound health benefits will come from daily use of small amounts, rather than pouring one bottle on a scar (physical or mental) and hoping for the best. For example, getting up in the morning and turning on our diffuser with a citrus essential oil like lemon or wild orange will create mood-boosting effects.

While we are praying, meditating (mindset framing for the day), and doing physical activity, we can subconsciously program the good mood smell of citrus with the positive emotions we feel from the mentioned mental and physical exercises. This will keep us coming back for more and create a foundational approach to taking on the day with minimum stress, which means more time smashing your goals and aspirations!

Gut health is another key area we lack focus on. We are discovering more about the GBA, the gut-brain-axis. What we eat and how we structure our meals will affect our mood, meaning stress control and hormones being balanced.

Now you've made progress in an area of your entrepreneurial life. It builds confidence that you can overcome this challenge and the ones that follow. You may find out other things about your body, as when you're using natural medicine, you are working with products that naturally work with the body instead of forcing an effect and merely masking a symptom of what's truly going on. You're more inclined to look deeper, improve your health, and build a stronger foundation through good Habits of using your essential oils throughout the day.

The Un-Habit: Stop you from thinking you can't incorporate a natural health protocol into your business life

Why: It's important to think of your own body as continually striving to become better, whether you are conscious of it or not. Whether you feel like you're too old, too sick, or just will never become the more successful version of yourself you've always wanted, the truth is that you will always have time and resources available to make yourself healthier naturally. Think of the little weed you've seen growing in the most random crack, with no water, hardly any sun, and seemingly no way of surviving. Our universe, our living creatures (including you!), will always strive to survive. Everything is a defense mechanism in the body. When we have a disease, it's exactly what the body tells you that it is at dis-ease with itself. You must figure what it's missing, or what needs to be removed, to let the self-healing mechanisms take over and nourish itself.

Healing, true healing, comes from within. It comes in 2 halves, the physical and the mental. Modern healthcare only treats physical symptoms. Even though the mental aspects are rarely targeted with modern treatments, they are almost unanimously forgotten about with the speed at which modern medicine flies today. Stress alone blocks mechanisms and pathways in the body that are crucial for healing. Daily, which is far too often, I see people go through their business day, and it leads them straight into the modern health system, from appointments to specialists to diagnostic testing and bloodwork, etc. It only leads to you being a repeat customer of some other person's business (instead of your own), and I'm here to tell you, that's precisely what you don't want! You don't want external interventions to be the first line of defense for your health. If you're in business, you need to both feel and BE in control of your day. Being in control of your health first ensures your empowerment, which will positively affect your business and life that surrounds it. Diet, lifestyle, and deep nutrition are the root cause of 9 out of 10 problems I see in the hospital setting. And we can't fix health problems that were caused by these metrics. The dis-ease we experience has to be approached with the same diet, lifestyle, and nutritional choices we made originally. We may mask the symptoms of the problems, whatever the body is telling us is wrong (digestive discomfort, headaches, joint pains, skin problems, lack of energy, mood irritability), but those are expressions of the body of what is truly happening. What is causing these issues to occur? What is causing those symptoms in the first place? That is what we need to address. More commonplace than ever is a hormone imbalance caused by fake, processed foods that make us addicted to the on-the-go lifestyle most people assume during business hours. They trade health in exchange for money. When you get to be older, you'll want to enjoy the fruits of your labor and the mental bandwidth to know you did it right, by making a natural health routine upfront. If you did this, you would certainly live more abundantly and save tons of money and self-detriment!

ABOUT BRADLEY: Bradley is ambitious to change the views of how the world sees healthcare. Studying radiologic technology and natural medicine simultaneously, he discovered the two halves rarely, if ever meet, and made it a mission to bridge these two halves. He consults with clientele, on the natural ways to remedy health problems that would otherwise be subject to less effective measures that the current medical system provides. Bradley has turned one area of major concern and rising incidence rates, hormone imbalance, into a digital course that is easily digestible to help restart, rebuild, and take back your health naturally. An in-depth approach to deep purging of our cleansing organs over 30 days gives the body it needs with a course content + natural medicine approach. He has successfully helped dozens to restore their hormone imbalance and return to their vibrant, youthful selves.

144

LEARN TO SAY NO

ANDREA HEUSTON

Why: I was recently looking through one of my old notebooks. I write daily, weekly, and monthly to-do lists, and I take copious handwritten notes during meetings and presentations. If I write something down, it gets done or remembered about 50% more often than if I do not.

In the middle of a random page in the notebook, I wrote, "Very successful people say no to almost everything." I was attending a conference and listening to Sean Stephenson speak to a group of successful entrepreneurs. The quote, "Very successful people say no to almost everything," is a well-known quote by Warren Buffett. The actual quote is a bit longer, "The difference between successful people and very successful people is that very successful people say no to almost everything." Whether Buffett meant saying no in the context of investing is not that important. What is important is that his advice can apply to any entrepreneur who is tasked with making small or large decisions on an ongoing basis.

But how do we say no to that next commitment or opportunity so that we can keep saying yes to that which is most vital? That's when it's important to focus and simplify. It means saying no again and again to all of the extraneous things each day to remain focused on saying yes to the few things that really matter in our lives.

To be more successful, more productive, more relevant, and more passionate about what I do, I had to learn to say, "no." Now I say no to things that detract from my purpose, things that I may do well but dislike doing, things that do nothing to add to my intention for growth and creativity. Doing so has freed me up to say yes to the things that create real value in my life and business. When I say no to the unimportant things in life, it makes way for me to say yes to those things that feed my soul and create value in my business.

THE UN-HABIT: STOP PUTTING TOO MUCH VALUE ON WHAT OTHERS THINK

Why: "What other people think of you is none of your business." – Jack Canfield

As social creatures, we are concerned with how the people around us perceive us. We worry about whether or not we are appreciated and respected. We try to behave cordially, make the correct remark, not say anything to offend, all for the sake of winning over others. The approval of others becomes a top priority and dictates many of our actions.

It took me years, but I've learned it's a good thing if there are some people who don't accept or agree with me. In business or the community, there are excellent reasons to be okay with not being liked. I'm not suggesting we should be rude, inconsiderate, or disrespectful. But as entrepreneurs, we are even more exposed to people's preconceived notions about who we should be and how we should act. But when we stay true to our beliefs and ourselves, we are more authentic leaders.

Being disliked by people is truly a sign that you're doing something worthwhile. Here's why I think it's good to not be everyone's cup of tea:

1. You become less critical of others. The act of judging others reflects your intolerance. When you're more comfortable in your skin, you become more comfortable with others.
2. Being disliked means you stand for something. Being courageous enough to stand by your values and live your lifestyle (even if it isn't popular) is empowering because you develop a strong identity.
3. It gives you the power to say NO. When you're willing to risk being disliked, you're able to say no when you need to.
4. Your candor can help others. Those who have the least popular opinions and are willing to stand by them often strike the deepest chord in us. Be unpopular when necessary; it can push yourself and others to do their best.

There's no way to please everyone all of the time. It's an utter impossibility. The more you're okay with not being liked all of the time, the more comfortable you'll be as a leader and entrepreneur. By realizing that the only approval you need is yourself, you free yourself up to create a clear path to success.

About Andrea: Andrea Heuston, founder, and CEO of Artitudes Design, has been in the tech industry for 30 years. The company is a creative service and experiential design firm specializing in providing high-level speaking and design support to top executives. Andrea is a respected business leader and entrepreneur who is sought after as a board member and a Keynote speaker. She also hosts the Lead Like a Woman Show podcast, empowering women leaders to empower others through topical discussions and interviews with female leaders.

145

AGREE ON TIMING WHEN MAKING A COMMITMENT

SHARÓN LYNN WYETH

Why: Clear Communications and Agreements Make Great Relationships

The Assistant Superintendent handed me yet another assignment. I was swamped and had resorted to only sleeping four hours a night to get the ever-increasing workload done. Continually working these long hours creates burnout and a cascade of internal raging stress that needed to be incinerated. This could not continue indefinitely as much as I was driven to be excellent in my career, for I had advanced in my school district to being a Director. There was one Superintendent, four Assistant Superintendents, then eight Directors, followed by the principals and other school staff in our District. The pressure was high, the work never stopped, and the expectations were unreasonable. Unreasonable, that is, until I acquired one incredible Habit.

My boss, one of the Assistant Superintendents, would continually pass me other people's work simply because he wanted it done, even though it didn't fall into my preview. It's always challenging to say no to a boss, so instead, this is what I learned to do and invite you to do the same.

When my boss dumped more work on me, I would say, I won't be able to start on that assignment until..., and then I'd give him a date in the future. Starting on that date, you can expect to have this completed by..., and I'd give him another date after the start date. Thus, he wouldn't expect this to get done quickly, and it would be clear when he could expect it. Occasionally he'd inform me that he needed this assignment before the dates that I gave to him. When that happened, I would get out my current list of assignments and ask him which of these items could have a later finish date so that there would be time to do the new assignment. He would often remove any assignment from me that wasn't technically mine so that I'd have the time to do my job. Miraculous! This was also a way of educating my boss on how long an assignment would reasonably take. Plus, he was the one making the decisions on task priorities so he couldn't be upset with me.

I had a working paper calendar to assist me in managing my tasks, written in pencil so that my boss could readily see how I planned my time to accomplish my work. This made it easy for him to see when I would be starting any new assignment and trading out one that already existed. Creating time on our calendar to accomplish our tasks also reduces stress since stress is always time-related.

THE UN-HABIT: STOP USING FILLER WORDS WHEN SPEAKING

WHY: You wish people to hear what you have say.

The words we utilize cause someone to listen more intently to us, or the opposite, to tune us out. Words that cause us to listen more intently fall into one of two categories. They either evoke our emotions, or we heard our name or the name of someone we know. Sharing a short story and to the point keeps our attention, whereas dragging a story on ad infinitum bores us to tears, and we consequently tune out.

There are also phrases and miscellaneous words that, when repeated, because they add nothing to the story, cause the best stories to bore us. These redundant phrases buy the speaker time to think but are nothing short of irritating to the listener.

Some of these phrases are: You know, um, so, like, and you know what I mean? The worst of these repetitive statements is the 'You know what I mean?' phrase because it doesn't require an answer, and it insults the listener at the same time. Are we too stupid to know what you mean? If that is the case, why are you telling us what you are?

Here are two examples, one with the irritants and one without. Which would you prefer to hear out loud?

Example: I am, um, Sharón Lynn Wyeth, creator of you know Neimology® Science, the study of the placement of the um letters in a name, um, that reveals one's personality predispositions. Do you know what I mean? Like the Myers Briggs, like astrology, like face reading, and like handwriting analysis, give clues to you know one's personality, so does Neimology® Science. Do you know what I mean?

About Sharón: Sharón Lynn Wyeth is an internationally recognized name expert. She can determine one's strengths, challenges and the purpose of one's life by deciphering a person's name. Sharón created Neimology® Science, the study of the placement of the letters in a name, after 15 years of research. Sharón helps HR business departments narrow down candidates to be interviewed; she assists lawyers in presenting cases to judges and helps couples and families communicate better. Sharón also creates names for new business, new products, and when people wish to change their name. She has written several bestselling books and is a frequent guest on radio and television.

146

CREATE SYSTEMS

ANDRU VERGARA

Why: Create a system for anything you repeatedly do. Something that can be accomplished by itself, and you gain at least ten more years of free time for yourself.

For example, with any bill, set it to auto-pay from your bank. Add an extra money cushion just in case to cover your monthly expense. Now you know you will never pay late fees and don't have to worry about the same accounts repeatedly.

Also, if you train staff, video record what you are doing to show your staff. They will feel like you are right next to them, showing them how to do it. The other advantage of this method is that they can pause and rewind as many times as they need until they master the task.

I use this method a lot for my Realtors; it's called BRW University. They can see step by step how to fill out contracts, upload new listings, how to use the MLS, how to make a sales comparable, etc. It's like replicating yourself so you can focus on more important things that need your direct attention.

THE UN-HABIT: USING THE WORD DON'T

Why: As humans beings, it is normal to always think of survival, and either consciously or unconsciously, we are always worried or stressed out for something. The problem with this is that as we worry about many things, even though we try to be positive either on a regular day or in the worst situation that we've never dealt with, our survival instinct is going to overcome our fears, and automatically we are going to think of what we don't want to happen to us.

When you are going to work, and you have an important meeting that you must attend or host, and you have to be early, automatically we think or say, "I hope there is NO traffic or I DON'T want to be late" The problem with the last phrases is that even though you are wishing or thinking for the opposite, you are thinking and imagining TRAFFIC and being LATE. It does not matter what you believe, either God, the universe, or energy; you are thinking of the opposite of what you would want to attract or to happen.

The Neurolinguistic study says we can program our conscious mind first so we can have a positive subconscious. In this case, we should think of a clear and smooth highway, a few cars on the way, parking the car near the building, walking inside the office, greeting everyone with a big smile, and looking at our watch and seeing that we are ten minutes earlier than the meeting.

Another example I often see is when people say, "I DON'T want to be poor" or "I don't want to get hurt." Automatically you are inviting scarcity and suffering. The second you mention those words automatically, you imagine someone without clothes and dirty face sleeping on the street, or if you are thinking in getting into a relationship, you imagine the other person cheating on you or stealing money from you even though you don't want that to happen to you. In this case, you should think of a lovely house with a pool with nice cars or a beautiful penthouse on the beach.

About Andru: I created a website that will pinpoint crucial financial subjects and explain to you in the most basic way, so it's easy to understand the main points of each subject. Depending on the subject, if after reviewing the information, you want to go forward and proceed, you can click the link that will take you to the next step, making it easy and convenient from wherever you are to reach your goal. If the subject you want more information on needs to be done in person or over the phone, you will be directed to the contact us section, and within the same day, someone will reach out to you.

147

STAYING OPEN BY NEVER SAYING NEVER

MARTINO CARTIER

Why: To live life to the fullest, we need hope. I live by the words "hope for the best, work for the rest, and whatever you do, never say never again." This Habit keeps you open to all life's possibilities.

I didn't know my birth parents growing up, and I had a deep burning wish to find my true blood family. In 1986 An American Tail came out, I connected with the song Somewhere Out There. This gave me hope to find my birth mother someday even though we lived worlds apart. That hope became a goal, and eventually, I found both parents. My father had a family, a lovely woman, and children who accepted and loved me. Hope led me, guided me to the opportunity, and provided me with 13 years with my father. So when I say "never say never," I mean it from the bottom of my heart. Against all the odds, I found my blood family; my childhood wish was granted all by having hope.

With hope, all things are possible. I believe that every woman should not only look amazing, but they should feel amazing too! I set out to empower women by creating an initiative with other salons to help women with hair loss from battling cancer. In 2011 this charity began. It is now a worldwide, and run by volunteers involving 100s of salons know as Wigs and Wishes by Martino Cartier. We provide hope and restore dignity to women by providing wigs at no charge to those battling cancer. A child battling cancer is given hope that their wish will come true. In 2012 I learned of a little girl named Kiki who deserved a wig, I made one for her, and a friendship began. Kiki had been battling cancer, and her dying wish was to meet Justin Bieber.

I did what I could to get her wish, and it just wasn't happening, but I still had hope. Then two special concert tickets became available. We arrived in style in a hot pink stretch limousine with front row tickets. Kiki sat on my shoulders throughout the concert, and she screamed like a little girl and thoroughly enjoyed herself. Kiki complained of a sore back later that evening, it worsened overnight, and within a week, my friend passed away. Kiki had a profound impact on my life by helping me define my life's purpose. We provide hope, and if you don't know how to give, you don't know how to live.

THE UN-HABIT: NOT LOVING WHAT YOU DO

Why: Why is it important to love where you're at? Is your Habit just living a mundane existence? Do you know the great feeling of leaving the salon looking like a million bucks? You are thinking good thoughts, and you feel great. Now think how you feel when you have been let down, or things don't go your way.

The difference is as big as night is to day in how you feel. If you hang around negative people, that is how you will feel. Every day we should try to make our Habits better Habits. When we are not happy or are just tired of something, it affects us and impacts others' lives. Being trapped in an unhappy situation is unhealthy for you and everyone around you. Find freedom in leaving the bad behind. It is important never to get tired of what you do and love what you do, but when you don't love it anymore, or just tire of it, stop doing it. Stop surrounding yourself with negative people.

A way to think about this is; if you always do what you've always done, you'll always get what you've always got, so break from those Habits.

When people see me, they say, "Who are you?", and "What do you do?", "Are you a singer in a band?". I once pulled up to a gas station in my Lamborghini, and a father and son asked me what I did for a living. I answered I cut hair. It was so empowering for them that you don't have to be this crazy doctor or brain surgeon to afford the car you want. But it also empowered me because people made fun of me going to hair school, saying you're never going to be able to make any money or have a lifestyle that you want. Never Say Never! I got here not by shooting for the moon; I plan on going to the universe that we haven't found yet. And to share a quote from a friend, "never be ordinary when you can be extraordinary."

ABOUT MARTINO: Martino Cartier is the founder of Wigs & Wishes by Martino Cartier and Friends by Your Side. A celebrity stylist, philanthropist, award-winning salon owner with over 50 stylists, educator, inspirational speaker, and television personality who has been named in W Magazine as a most sought after stylist and ranked in the top 20 U.S. salons by the beauty industry. Entertainer of the year at the HSN Awards (Home Shopping Network). He has partnered up with superstar Paula Abdul to bring out the amazing Forever Your Curl styling tool. He is the creator of signature products MARTINO by Martino Cartier. Martino Cartier and his salon have been featured on Bravo TV, Modern Salon Magazine, Vogue, Launch-pad, Behind the Chair, Salon Today, and The Golden Globes. International Artistic Director for Keratin Complex for six years, Global Artist Director for Hotheads for two years.

148

TODAY, I WILL BEGIN A NEW LIFE

JAMES DENTLEY

Why: Every day has a brand new life of its own. Each day you and I can begin with a renewed sense of clarity. The Bible says "Give us this day our daily bread". Why not ask for the entire week? Month? oh heck, why not just put in a request for the entire year? There's an old saying " by the yard its hard, but inch by inch, life's a chinch" Just focus on making each day the best day ever! When we make Monday a great day, Tuesday starts off fine. Every day begin with a new sense of fresh gratitude. Every day, love your life and the lives of the people dear to you with a fresh love. Like picking fresh roses from the garden. Every day, get in alignment with your goals, your dreams, and a renewed sense of purpose. Every day begin your new life, seeking new experiences, appreciating everything you have with a smile on your face and a song in your heart. Greet each day as the new day. Set yourself on path and purpose each day. Every day remember that you set the stage. This is your life and the only one you and I are going to get! With a renewed sense of clarity, you find more peace, more love, more joy, and you become more inter-directed and no longer outer-directed. When things go wrong, you won't go wrong with them. When life seems crazy you refuse to follow that path. When you approach life in this way, you can separate the feelings that would usually disrupt your happiness, and focus on what you know to be true. Every bit of adversity carries a seed when nourished has within it an equal and powerful advantage. Never forget, every day is a great day! Some are even better!

THE UN-HABIT: CHALLENGE THE POVERTY DRIVEN NEGATIVE THOUGHTS

Why: It is critical that we guard our thoughts. It has been said that we become what we continuously think about. In other words, what we think about, we bring about. Everything in life happens two times, the inner and then the outer, the mental and next the physical, the thought and then the thing. In the Bible, Job states" The things I have feared have come upon me"

We create our own reality, whatever we feed is what grows. When we dwell on our lack of money, joy, love, bad health we manifest more of that energy in our life. If negative thoughts can make you sick, then positive empowering thoughts can make you well! The brain doesn't hold two opposite thoughts at the same time. Our feeling begin with our thoughts, so think happy empowering thoughts. When you plant and water negativity, you are carrying that energy and attracting that same energy into your life. When you invest in negative and poverty driven thoughts, words and actions, it's like a vampire that sucks the life out of you, your dreams and your goals. Remember, a vampire can't come into your house without an invitation. It's also the company you keep. Negative people can't survive in a positive environment. You can't create and keep a life of abundance, bliss, and possibility with a negative mindset. Your thoughts influence your words, think before you speak! Your words influence your actions. Your repeated actions create your Habits, which are embedded in your subconscious. Did you know 95% of your live is driven by your subconscious. Your Habits describe your character. We define ourselves by what we do repeatedly. Your character creates your destiny, in life you don't always get what you want, but who you are. Guard and strengthen your heart and your mind by

reading books that empower and enlighten you. Spend your time with people that have a positive mindset and nature. When you show up with a positive mindset and spirit, watch the negative people in your life try to win you back to their side or flee. Decide to be positive, be the light in the room when you show up. Remember O.P.P. (only positive people)

ABOUT JAMES: James Dentley is the founder of Inspired2Speak, helping people and organizations achieve their goals through empowering purpose driven communication. We teach you the psychology and power in becoming a great communicator. Great communication comes from the inside-out. Our words and the energy behind those words come from where we are in that moment. I have spent over 40 years managing, directing and developing people in corporate America and in the home-based business industry. I am also a life-long learner and listener as well. The central key to creating success in your relationships, company culture, customer /employee experience and your own personal state of mind and spirit is founded in quality communication.

149

EACH MORNING, WRITE YOUR THOUGHTS FOR MAKING THE DAY POSITIVE, POWERFUL AND PRODUCTIVE

DR. KEN J. ROCHON

Why: Wake up as early as your mind allows, and write your intentions and thoughts for making the day positive, powerful, and productive.

This Habit will shift you going into your day as a participant, to being a leader who is proactively being powerful about how your day will create abundance, connection, positivity profitability with all you communicate and connect with.

It is important to note that a predecessor to this Habit would be to go to bed when your body and mind need rest and with a question on how to empower yourself the following day with either a specific outcome or problem to be solved.

Declaring your intention to the world through social media holds you to account. Enrolling another leader to be an accountability partner will certainly help you be more successful.

If you are an author or wish to be an author, this will be the optimal time to download your most creative thoughts. As a coach, leader, and speaker, it is equally valuable to command your day with an intention that solves your biggest challenge for that day/week/month.

Since we are given 24 hours a day ... 168 hours a week, after sleeping roughly 68 hours, we will have about 100 hours to utilize. The intention will shift the 100 hours to be valuable gifts to invest in ourselves.

One of the best measures I have found to qualify you are achieving your best day with your intentions is to measure your SPH (Smiles Per Hour). I have found the correlation of the amount of smiles you give yourself and inspire in others to enjoy will demonstrate your proportional success in creating the abundance and happiness you wanted that day.

Since the universe is in collusion to helping you achieve what you believe, it is important that you revisit your intention with gratitude and speaking your desire hourly if necessary.

Interviewing your heroes and learning their Habits is what this book is about; taking an extra step and finding out how they set their intention (mindset) for the day will reinforce you making this Habit a priority.

Finally, journaling your intentions will reinforce this Habit, especially if you include role models who have a similar mission or vision you would wish to accomplish. Ultimately, documenting your intention will allow you to revisit successes and prove most valuable in your pursuit of a life you love.

THE UN-HABIT: STOP SAYING, 'IT IS WHAT IT IS.'

Why: I did not choose 'I don't care', because you obviously care, or you wouldn't be reading this book.

However, this saying is almost as bad as saying 'I am too busy.' Therefore, the ultimate disempowering expression would be 'I am so busy saying: 'It is what it is". :)

Every word and expression has the meaning we give it and programming consequences.

All the above expressions disempower you to have control of owning your life and the time you have in your day.

If you want a better life, better relationship, better anything... know you control the power to empower yourself with the choice to create this aspect of your life and the result you are rewarded with.

Can you imagine any champion, disruptor, or innovator taking on this mindset philosophy? Gandhi, Mother Teresa, Sir Richard Branson, Steve Jobs, or the other thousands of leaders who changed the world because they knew 'It is what it is' is not empowering change, innovation, or progress.

Busy is a BS word... it means you have no control of your time. Or translated that you choose to do something you feel is more fun, valuable, etc. instead of what is being offered. Here is a test I do to help me be unbusy... I ask if I was paid $10K to do this would I have time... WOW! Almost every time I find I can make the time. Which is really what busy means you can't do. Being 'busy' is not powerful and reinforcing 'it is what it is' mentality.

So, care about your time, care about your words, and care about creating what it is you want. If 'it is what it is' could not be changed, then I suppose the expression would be accurate.

Choose to say 'It is what I create it to be'... or 'What would I wish to create it to be given what it is now?'

Ask better questions, and you will always get better answers and a better access to abundance and happiness.

Choose to live with creating a life you love and not one you react to because 'it is what it is.' You are never too 'busy' to shift your life to be in control and open to new possibilities. Care and dare to remove any expression that does not serve you as a leader.

About Ken: The Keep Smiling Movement is a non-profit set up to honor leaders who are creating community, inspiring hope and leading with their heart.

We do this with books and social proof campaigns.

If you are a leader with an inspirational story, we want to share it with the world as a D.O.S.E. (Dopamine, Oxytocin, Serotonin, and Endorphins) of Hope.

Your story is your journey that gave you a purpose and proof that your life creates abundance, solves problems and inspires hope.

We are committed to providing solutions to those with dental and mental health challenges.

We believe smiles are the best measure of one's abundance. The higher your Smiles Per Hour (SPH) are, the more abundance you will experiences and give to the world.

A smile is the universal expression for acceptance and love... so Keep Smiling!

150

FOLLOW UP, FOLLOW UP IS EVERYTHING!

THOMAS DUBOIS

Why: We have all heard it said, " The Fortune is in the Follow Up!" Well, I believe almost all of the business that is lost is because of following up! The Habit of always following through with clients and creating the opportunity to secure the business relationship or sale is super important. When accessing business relationships, we should honor them by always booking a meeting from a meeting, "BAMFAM," to get all their questions answered and create more opportunities for securing the business relationship. Most people get uncomfortable in the follow-up part of business, thinking they are bugging the client or being too pushy. Well, I believe that is just a fearful mindset and a fear of rejection. If there is no setup or proper follow-up, it tells me what kind of business I can expect out of that person or company in the future. We need to respect our client's time and resources by staying on top of our game! Asking for the Business is the part of follow up most people are afraid of and is the difference between getting business and not getting business. I can think of at least a few times just in the last month, that if a person wanting my business failed to follow up and more so failed to ask for the business and I am not doing business with them, period! One of those instances, I expressed that I was very interested and just wanted a day to pray about it, and one month later, I have still not heard from them. This tells me a lot about my importance in that situation, and I would refuse to do business in the future because of it! I like to call this Habit, always touching my client, making sure that they know I am available, there for them, and seriously want their business relationship. This can be done in so many ways, with even a text thanking them for their time. Many better ways make a bigger impact, and we can be really creative to show we care and even better that we listened to their needs in the previous meeting. For example, if I heard the client talk about their dog, I might include something about that in my follow up or in a gift of some sort. Creative follow up can be so rewarding to both parties. Believe in yourself and your business enough to make Follow Up a priority always!

The Un-Habit: Procrastination, Someday never comes!

Why: When the student is ready, the teacher will appear. When I was hungry for my first taste of success, I was a sponge for every teaching and personal growth I could find. I was at an event for the Network Marketing business I was in at the time, and a speaker said a real simple phrase, "Now and Next to Now!" This phrase has proven to be profoundly impacting upon my life. Build your business Now and next to Now! I love the fact that when the un-Habit of procrastination comes up, these words ring powerfully in my ear.

Procrastination is the opportunity killer, and it is always very sad to watch. I have squandered opportunities and have seen others do the same. Mostly procrastination is putting off something that could make a difference today, and in most cases, it builds up and becomes unrepairable for accomplishing anything of significance. When business is concerned, prioritizing is important, but not to be mistaken by procrastination. I believe procrastination is putting something off that is supposed to get done. I have heard it said, "Opportunities do not go away; they just go to someone else." I have witnessed this to be true in my own experiences. In the Network Marketing industry, we see some of these results in full color. I know of many times that I procrastinated, calling a person I wanted in business with me for whatever reason. That person ended up in someone else's business and flourishing with them and not me. Yuck, not a good feeling at all.

This is why I am so grateful that I heard those great words, "Now and Next to Now." Whenever I want to procrastinate, these great words change my mindset, and I take action on the task at hand. I strongly hope those words will help someone not miss an opportunity or fall behind. Un- Habit Procrastination and watch the Successes show up.

ABOUT THOMAS: As an adult I did not start out so well, making a lot of mistakes and developing as a businessman rather slowly. I went from shoveling manure to entrepreneur and through all the learning's, have became somewhat successful. Laura and I are now multiple business owners. We have a passion for helping people earn secondary streams of income in Network Marketing and I developed, Cutting Through the BS for the LOVE of Network Marketing! With all that experience under my belt, I am grateful to share a digital technology platform that all entrepreneur's need! We love offering our services and expertise through free strategy sessions or demos of the product.

151

PAYING ATTENTION TO SMALL DETAILS

BARB SWAN-WILSON

Why: The Smallest Details Can Open The Biggest Door

Why does paying attention to small details make a good Habit? It is like the saying 'paying attention to the dimes takes care of the dollars.' All the little things add up to the big things. We notice certain things based on our interests, and one simple request set the direction of my entire life. "Please match this bottle of purple nail polish." No paint chip was close, and I thought I could make this colour; I'd call her when I had it matched. Hear the positive tone in that statement? I had no notion that it couldn't be done. She left a very happy customer. I stood there thinking how nice it was that I could make someone that happy with a can of purple paint.

Turning point right there! I could make people happy with colour (and yes, colour has a "u" in it as I am Canadian, and that's how we do things up here. It's a lot about "u"). That can of purple paint created an entrepreneurial dream. I started paying attention to the smallest details, putting the plastic bag into the garbage can the most efficient way, to how to ask questions, so you knew what the customer's needs and wants were. When you pay attention to the small details, you catch little mistakes that can avoid big disasters. You have heard to cross your 'T's and dot your 'I's being careful with contracts. You can rest easy knowing you didn't skip over an important detail because your Habit is to do just that, pay attention to the small details. Before this, I hardly ever asked a question, but now I wanted to know how you do this and that, why this way or that. It became my own private thing. I don't think I ever told anyone about my dream. I set my sights on becoming an Interior Designer, but we never know what will come our way, and one day I was downsized out of a Director of Sales position and what shows up but an entrepreneurial business start-up course. All the little details over the years got me in the door by being the most prepared applicant. I launched my dream Strokes of Genius, and purple was my main logo colour! My Habit of paying attention and asking questions gave me the right of passage to my dream, to my raving fans, and to make people happy with colour.

THE UN-HABIT: THE END IS WORTH THE BEGINNING

Why: When you break this Habit, your reward is so much more than just more time. Think for a moment about how and why you do something; think about it because that was my key to success. I knew the when, how, and why of my Habit, and I also knew I had to stop it, but I liked my bad Habit, yep, I liked my lifelong buddy, my crutch, my cigarettes. I had set dates, made

New Year's resolutions year after year without much success as the cravings and desires still hung around when I did quit for a few days, weeks, or even months. It is very different this time as I don't think about them at all. I thank Bob Proctor and Sandy Gallagher for helping me through the process this time as I take one of their courses, I listen and read their messages over and over, and bits started to stick. I began to pick apart the when I smoked, how much I smoked, and why I smoked. I looked closely at when I chose to smoke: when I was lonely, sad, stressed, happy, hungry, or full, needing a break, drinking coffee or alcohol, driving, it was part of my social networking toolbox. It ruled my life and emptied my bank account. When I looked at how much time every day I needed that crutch, I thought for a few moments how weak I was. But I am not weak (as I roared to Helen Reddy's song). Bob popped into my head to tell me again, make the decision, and stick to it. So I set the date, and on that day, I made coffee, went outside, and had a break-up party with my cigarettes and coffee. It was Ash Wednesday, which has been my quit date for many years. Another thing I thought about that helped me get to the quitting was thinking about automatic body functions like breathing; what if I damage my lungs to the point that every breath I take, I needed to think about it. Now I want you to think about that and breathe freely; it feels great.

Habits are important because they put your brain on auto-pilot, just like your body is on auto-pilot when you breathe. You don't have to think about Habits; you do them, but that can be a double edged sword.

About Barb: Barb Swan-Wilson makes your memories count by putting them on a shareable treasure. Your special moments, sayings, and pictures are preserved on stainless steel, ceramic, cloth, and coins. Your child's artwork displayed, shared, and gifted will put a smile on a lot of faces. Barb is the Co-Founder of Healthy Mugs, and they have a purpose with you in mind; to keep you happy, healthy, and connected. Motivational mugs will inspire you, and healthy energy drinks will keep you focused and allow creativity to flow throughout the day. When you want personalized service from a creative mind, so your message or memory gets noticed, we'll get you there!

152

DON'T IMAGINE SUCCESS, LIVE IT

HEATHER HARDEN

W hy: Visualization is often marketed as a panacea — a way to fill holes in your life by imagining a better situation. Perhaps you have tried it before. You craft a vivid abstraction of where you want your life to be and beg the universe to supply the missing elements. You cling to the image in your mind, hoping that treasuring this picture will be enough to bring lasting change. At least, this is how I used to approach visualization.

For decades, I held the image of my father being present so tightly that it eventually became thread-bare and fell apart. The tattered shreds of my dream falling to a floor worn smooth from fretful pacing. More than anything, I longed to see my mother incandescent with the joy of finally having him home.

As the mirage I had created dissolved, I realized the beautiful images in my mind were not enough to create the corporeal reality I sought. While I could not, through imagination, bring my father home, I could embark on a mission to build the security for myself and my family that I associated with his presence. At this point, I realized an important truth: Only when bolstered with actions do dreams take form in the physical world.

The problem with my original approach — the same mistake many people make — is that it doesn't provide the structure necessary to make lasting change. The goal of visualization is not to create a magical but unattainable ideal in your mind; the objective is to introduce an image of completion and joy that your mind accepts as something that can happen now.

Out of these realizations, a fragile idea germinated into the company my brother and I started. For years we daydreamed about helping businesses tackle growth yet nothing happened. The day we filed our operating agreement, we decided to treat our business as if it was already flourishing. It wasn't until we stopped imagining success and started living it that we were able to make our dreams a reality.

Don't waste time envisioning what could be. Think instead of what Habits you would have if you had already achieved your goal and make those Habits real now. Don't wait for the future to come to you. Become the future now so as you step into it, you have the foundation laid to enjoy it. The secret is that in manifesting your ideal future now, you build the Habits that will carry you into the future you hope for.

THE UN-HABIT: CARRYING CHAINS FROM THE PAST

Why: No one gets through life without experiencing trauma. We've all carried pain and heartbreak. Eventually, we can become desensitized to this weight, and it can be easy to forget what it's like to live without heavy chains rusted from years of salty tears dragging behind you. The thing to remember is that these chains don't define you — they exist outside of you, and you can step away from them when you are ready. Indeed, it is essential to step away from the chains if you want to realize new growth in your life. Carrying link upon link of interconnected emotional baggage erodes your ability to evaluate situations and to express creatively. This erosion can prevent the successful adoption of new, healthy Habits, and attempting to force healthy Habits without first cutting off the corroded length often results in the subversion of these Habits into familiar, destructive patterns.

A return to destructive patterns is not unusual. As humans, we tend to gravitate toward accustomed practices. Achieving success, however, requires breaking free of these well-worn ruts and embarking on new ways of thinking and moving through the world. Continuing in the same routine day after day only ensures dragging monotony. Take, for example, Tom Hanks' character, Joe, from Joe Versus The Volcano (1990) — every day involved the same commute, the same headache, the same depression. It wasn't until he was shocked out of his daily tedium that he began his journey toward happiness and the fulfillment of his dreams.

Tremendous perseverance and fortitude are required to drop the chains of the past. Regardless of how heavy your chains have become, however, healing the wounds left by them is always possible. The choice is yours: continue to carry the burden of chains of the past or make a new Habit of severing each link and letting the weight fall away. I urge you to choose the latter; it is not an easy choice , but it will lay a steady foundation for every subsequent Habit you cultivate.

About Heather: Heather Harden sees every person as an essential and expressive individual: her passion is empowering others in bringing their dreams to fruition. It was this passion that drove her to start Nachat Consulting LLC with her brother, Joshua. Their mission: To help business owners revolutionize their customer support and prepare their business for periods of rapid growth through the use of scalable software solutions. No more worrying about what software to use — the friendly and knowledgeable team at Nachat Consulting will assist you in choosing the best software for your business needs and help you get it running smoothly!

153

REINFORCE A RED CARPET CONNECTION EVERY DAY.

DR. ANDREA ADAMS-MILLER

Why: Relational Capital is the most valuable asset acquired as a leader. The people you connect with, such as media sources, vendors, partners, peers, influencers, celebrities, entrepreneurs, non-profits, fans, followers, stakeholders, investors, peers, employers, sponsors, clients, and employees, fall under the commodity of Relational Capital. Yet, there is more to relationships besides **QUANTITY**.

Moreover, the value lies within the **QUALITY** of the relationships combined with the sum of the connections. Together these factors increase according to how you make people feel. If they feel loved, respected, and heard, the relationship equals a priceless intangible asset. Intangible assets like relationships affect how others view you and your business regarding reputation, brand, credibility, authority, integrity, emotional intelligence, and sense of self.

Fortunately, we have come into an age where business professionalism has moved to a wiser, deeper, more connected level. In contrast, business relationships used to be heeded as a need to 'stay professional,' keep people at arm's length. Nowadays, relationships without more profound connections take on an unfavored superficial vibe

The most forward-thinking and most successful movers and shakers of the world value real relationships, aka "**REALationships™.**" Becoming more vulnerable ourselves and spending more time getting to know others, we realize their purpose and passions. Therefore, this information integrates into a true 'listening' of others. As a result, there is a 'knowing' that allows you to serve them at a heart-centered level. This heart-to-heart connection generates loyalty that cannot be bought or sold, achieving "**REALationships™**" at the utmost level. These high-level connections are the most significant to your successes, personally and professionally.

To foster the utmost Relational Capital with the people in your life and generate that feel-good situation for others is to create **RED Carpet Connections**. A **RED Carpet Connection** puts the person you are connecting to within the theoretical spotlight, allowing them to shine in their greatness. Make it a practice to speak, act, and live RED: R --Relevance, E -- Enthusiasm, and D –Delivery. When you #**LiveRED**, you engage new and renewed connections to generate the relationships you dare to desire.

Therefore, **loyalty commences when you make RED Carpet Connections to build Relational Capital.** Loyalty increases engagement, retention, and growth of your business. Loyalty increases your ability to gain support in challenging situations and increases your chance of success as loyal people are vested in YOU. Furthermore, loyalty decreases self-sabotaging habits, vague plans, and limiting beliefs as your community will call you out on faulty thinking and push you to achieve higher successes than you might have wished for yourself.

The Un-Habit: Forget the Follow Up

Why: If you want to destroy your Relational Capital, the most valuable asset acquired as a leader, forget the follow-up. In blowing off the follow up with the new connect, you disconnect with the very people you desire to do business. Instead of having a partner, client, fan, follower, or investor, you have a name and phone number with no connection to that person. In other words, you have little capital at all, and in some cases, that equals NO capital. Having a Rolodex with no connection to the people holding the numbers means your **QUANTITY** of connections is useless.

Moreover, without connection, you have **NO QUALITY** vested in those relationships. The people you bothered to meet and collect data on are now are only data. They do not feel loved, respected, and heard, and the value they see in you is obsolete. You won't exist in their world. Sadly, how they will view you and your business, you will not even exist.

Talk about keeping people at arm's length; you have integrated the 100 ft pole. Nothing is sadder than being unknown. When you don't follow up, that is precisely what you create. You become nothing. Ouch.

If you want to be a forward-thinking, successful mover and shaker, you have to value real relationships, aka **"REALationships™."** You have to step out of your comfort zone; become more vulnerable. Follow up. Get to know others; ask them how they are, listen. Without it, you will never get the 'listening' of others. As a result, there is no 'knowing.' You will not connect heart-to-heart. This lack will leave you lonely, wondering why you can't get ahead. Unfortunately, this result is a reality for many entrepreneurs that won't get out of their way.

Therefore, without relationships, you never achieve the **loyalty of RED Carpet Connections nor build Relational Capital.** Without loyalty, you do not increase business engagement, retention, and growth. Without loyalty you do not have support as no one will be vested in your success. Furthermore, without allegiance, your self-doubt increases self-sabotaging habits and limiting beliefs. Without a community to call you out on faulty thinking, you are doomed for failure.

Although I am writing this information, I feel sick to my stomach, telling you the heart truth. As a professional consultant, and as a leader, I would be doing you a disservice by not telling you the truth. You want someone like me in your life, willing to love you enough to push you to greater heights than you are now. Seeing the havoc caused by not following up lends me to BEG you to change your bad habit. Take responsibility; FOLLOW UP! You have the POWER to change the gloomy future forecast into a positive one. #KeepSmiling

ABOUT DR. ANDREA: Dr. Andrea Adams-Miller helps dreamers implement actionable steps to achieve their dreams higher than they ever dreamed possible. As an Award-Winning International Publicist, Business Consultant, NLP Practitioner, and Hypnotherapist, she utilizes these tools to excel you further than you dared to dream. Just imagine the lives you will affect, possibly save, when your message, services, and products are known to the world. As the recipient of the Heart of Gold award, imagine how good it feels to have a team member who always has your back. Discover how she, a whirlwind of energy with high authority, credibility, & connections, puts you in the limelight, create JV's, set up sponsorships, and assists you with the management of your dreams so that dreams become a reality. Let's say, "Get ready to smile!" :)

154

HIRE A VA AND OUTSOURCE

LINDA NICOL

Why: Hiring a VA can be one of the most effective ways to scale your business quickly if done well. However, if done poorly can cause more issues than it solves.

A good VA is the difference between freeing up more of your time or being tied down even further.

As an entrepreneur, it's tempting to become one-person bands, trying to cover all business areas from marketing to bookkeeping and everything in between. This is where we come unstuck. Why do we suddenly think we have the skills to cover all these areas when we didn't have them previously?

If you weren't a marketer in your previous role, learning to do this is going to involve you undertaking a course followed by months of trial and error, probably resulting in a whole lot of tears as you watch many failed attempts of your hard work.

Hiring in professionals to help you is the quickest and easiest way to have this done well.

There are many excellent VA's out there. This may sound like an expensive exercise, but it's not. You can hire a VA for a few hours per week for as little as $10ph. You don't have to hire them full time. Alternatively, you can hire them for a particular project, such as creating your website.

It's important to be strategic when hiring outside help. There's much more to it than 'Oh, I need a VA.' If you do the hiring well, you can free up many hours to concentrate on your core skills, hire poorly, and you could be left untangling a mess.

When selecting a VA, you must be specific about the tasks that you need the VA to do. This will help you choose the correct VA that specializes in this area and not a generalist.

You must be clear about whether this hire is a permanent fixture or a particular project only. A trial period should be built into your contract. This way, if it isn't working out after a few weeks, you can cut the ties and find someone else; no harm is done.

When you're taking on a VA, it's worthwhile to have a process in place to hand over. It doesn't have to be flash, just something to start with. If they don't have anything to work from, it may be a bit hit and miss whether you are returned what you expected.

Treat them favorably just like you would with a permanent employee; your VA is a key member of your team; when you've found a good one, hang onto them. Think about what you can do to inspire them to want to stay with you.

Once you have had a great experience with a VA, you will become addicted; you will be looking to outsource everything. Your stress levels and overwhelm will be greatly reduced.

THE UN-HABIT: STOP CHASING SHINY OBJECTS

Why: Did you know that 'Shiny Object Syndrome' is a form of procrastination?

It's very common among business owners. We tend to jump from one thing to the next without concluding the project at hand. We somehow think that the next offering will give us the Holy Grail that we've been looking for. The next thing is going to provide us with the success that we desperately want.

I've been guilty of this on many occasions.

The reality is if you see the project that you're working on to the conclusion, you'll see the benefits. However, in this instant gratification world, we want the results right now, so we jump off to the next thing that is promising success.

The best example is the diet industry, so many people jump from diet to diet—each promising better results than the one before. If you stuck to any one of those diets for the recommended length of time, you'd probably get the results you are looking for.

The good news is that if you are a 'Shiny Object' person, you have two great traits working in your favor:

1. You're able to make decisions (usually quickly) as you move from one thing to the next; and

2. You can take action. You start each project with great enthusiasm.

If you turn those skills to the task/project at hand and decide to see it through to fruition, you will see the results.

Think about the extra profit you will be adding to your bottom line by stopping procrastinating and finish the project at hand. You will see the results come through quicker now that you are not wasting precious time getting up to speed with the next shiny object.

One great trick to deal with the Shiny Object is to write whatever you're considering in a notebook. That way, you can revisit the projects later and assess whether they are the right thing to do. You can make that decision when you are not in a heightened state of emotion. If you suffer from FOMO, it's worth noting that most 'can't miss this' offers usually do come back around in a similar format.

ABOUT LINDA: Linda Nicol is a Time Management & Productivity Coach who helps female business owners increase profits with productivity in their days, enabling them to grow their business and live the life they desire.

Before becoming a coach, Linda spent 15 years in the corporate world as an accountant, trainer, coach, mentor, managing, and leading global teams. Linda specialized in coaching her staff to further their careers and take on new challenges. Linda brings her skills in finance, processes & systems to help women increase their profits through productivity.

Since leaving the corporate world, Linda has gone from being an overwhelmed & stressed mum of triplet toddlers to running multiple thriving businesses while raising five small children. After almost a decade of establishing businesses while growing and raising her young family, she has figured out what needs to happen to get things done.

Linda's tools and systems have been described as "game-changer," and her clients are doing more in their days than they ever thought possible. Overwhelm and stress are a thing of the past.

Today, she empowers female business owners to control their time, enabling them to grow their business without sacrificing time with their children. They even have Guilt-Free Me Time. Linda is committed to empowering as many female business owners as possible because Women CAN have it ALL. Originally from Scotland, Linda know lives in Australia with her husband and five children.

155

BIOHACKING TIME AND SLEEP

HERSH SANDHOO

Why: Why do so many entrepreneurs endure grueling hours with little or no pay, risk relationships with loved ones, miss out on fun activities, and open themselves to the ridicule of family, friends, and keyboard warriors? Especially when over 96% of businesses fail, and less than 4% will ever even gross one million dollars. Rationally, it does not seem to make sense to most people.

If you are reading this book, I would wager you already said the answer out loud, or in your mind as soon I asked. Freedom. The desire to be in control of your destiny and life path. The ability to do what you want, with whom you want and when you want. This has been my obsession since I was 17 years old. What is the one master key that unlocks the path to true freedom?

The one master key that serves as a catalyst and unleashes my full potential; fills me with unlimited confidence and courage;

that allows me to foster amazing relationships with family, friends, and my children; that provides me financial success and abundance; that fills me with energy and vibrant health; that feeds my mind and soul; that allows me to give back and contribute to others; and enjoy life in the process.

After 25 years, I have discovered that the master key is a daily habit of biohacking time and sleep. Time is the greatest resource we all have equally, and the one constant holds true for all humankind. By learning to biohack time and sleep in a way that allows me to not only be full of energy and healthy sleeping just 4.5 hours a night but also get more focused work done in a shorter period of time, it has allowed me to achieve what many think is impossible:

1. Waking up at 12:30 a.m. every morning
2. Sleeping as little as 4.5 hours a night while becoming more healthy
3. Working 90 hours a week without burning out
4. Spending 9X more time with my family than the average father
5. Having over 2 hours a day for myself
6. Creating financial security for my family
7. Helping thousands of small business owners

All while becoming more fulfilled, happy, and purpose-driven. Excelling at virtually anything I put my mind too and never having to say "No" to something I want to do because of a lack of time or money. When time is used properly and expanded, you truly can have it all.

The Un-Habit: Consuming Media

Why: Technology is truly a blessing. The power we hold in our hands, the general quality of life, advances in health and medicine, and our near-instant access to virtually any topic of information would have been unfathomable even a few decades ago. Yet while technology empowers and brings opportunity, it also can consume and sabotage us.

News media, entertainment companies, businesses, social media networks, app developers, family, friends, and adorable cat videos all compete for our attention in a constant barrage of emails, text messages, alerts, comments, posts, notifications, and must watch "television." These platforms have been designed to alter our brain wave patterns, lure us into spending hours a day consuming useless information, promote negativity, and waste our most precious resource of time.

Therefore, we must develop the un-habit of consuming media to guard our minds, time, emotions, and physical well-being from anything that does not serve us, bring us joy or propel us toward achieving our goals. The best way to use technology to grow, connect, and contribute is to become a producer of content rather than a consumer to use technology in order to empower yourself and others. Develop the un-habit of consuming media by:

- Avoid reaching for your phone first thing in the morning
- Only check email 2 to 3 times a day at prescheduled times.

- Turn off all email alerts and app notifications except for your nuclear family and VIPs
- Create content and automatic post schedules with software to avoid having to log in directly to a social network
- Only check in to social media networks and news sites for 10-20 minutes a day after your main priorities have been accomplished
- Limit any binge-watching of shows until the weekend or after you have achieved your top 3 must action of the day

This un-habit of consuming media and shift to becoming a producer will save the average person five to six hours a day from social media, news programs, on-demand videos, gaming, television programs, and streaming. For context, that is up to 42 hours a week, or 2184 hours a year, which would allow you to gain a full extra 12 work months per year—giving you double the amount of time to focus on more important tasks, such as work, launching a new business, mastering new skills, spending more time with family, and taking care of yourself.

ABOUT HERSH: Hersh Sandhoo is one of the top experts in strategic communication, branding, and digital marketing for small business owners. As the Founder of Webmation, he has helped thousands of business owners generate hundreds of million dollars by automating their sales, marketing, and operations.

Nicknamed the "Dragon" for his insane work ethic, Hersh is most well-known for biohacking himself to sleep just four hours a night, 12:30 a.m. wake up time, personal transformation, and dedication to family while achieving business success. He founded Becoming Legendary to create a positive success-oriented community of small business owners dedicated to financial success and freedom without sacrificing their health, relationships or family.

Hersh has received praise from members of Congress, Navy Seals Leadership, Army Ranger Instructors, Grant Cardone, Forbes Riley, Dean Graziosi and the news media. He is a National Academy of Best-Selling Authors inductee and author of the *Becoming Legendary Codex* series

ACKNOWLEDGMENTS

We greatly appreciate the following contributors for offering their own 1 Habit™s to this book.

A

• Heather Aardema - Creator of The Live Light Method and Founder of Root of Wellbeing

• Dr. Andrea Adams-Miller - International Publicist & Keynote Speaker, The RED Carpet Connection, & Executive Director, The Keep Smiling Movement

• Louis Agius - Founder of RIZE Events, Digital Marketing Consultant

• Eleni Anastos - Business Strategist, Speaker, Prosperity Coach

• Ryan Anderton - Enlightened Wealth Warrior, Global Joint Venture Specialist, "Fill Your Live Events" Guy

- Rob Angel - Creator of Pictionary, Author, Speaker, Explorer

- Ashley Armstrong - best-selling Author, Business Consultant, eCommerce 'Hidden Rules Expert'

- Dr. Christopher Asandra - Celebrity, Anti-Aging Physician

- Mendhi Audlin, Author of "What If It All Goes RIGHT?" & Founder of The What If UP Club™

B

- Naomi Bareket and Rami Bareket, Co-creators of Virtual Influencer Academy, Video Content Experts, NLP Trainers, Authors, and Speakers

- Dr. Birger Baastrup - Chiropractic Sports Physician, Professional Photographer, Author

- Gaurav Bhalla, Ph.D. - Bestselling Author, Entrepreneur, Transformational Speaker, Training Specialist

- Dr. Manon Bolliger, Founder of Bowen College, Podcast Host of The Healer's Cafe"

- Dr. Jessica Borushok - The Busy Mind Psychologist

- Liza Boubari, CCHt – CSMc Author, Speaker and Founder of HealWithin, and The 3E Events

- Les Brown - Motivational Speaker, Author, Former Radio DJ, Former Television Host

- Jacqueline Buckley - Author , Veteran , CCC-Q , Owner Blue Alliance Consulting

• Kelly Tyler Byrnes - Founder and CEO of Voyage Consulting Group

C

• LaurieAnn Campbell - Masters Certified Handwriting Analyst and Author of Author of Make Up Not Required

• Paul Capozio - Diamond Ambassador, NewULife, whole body health

• Martino Cartier - Celebrity Stylist, Entrepreneur & Philanthropist

• Ashley Cheeks MBA - Founder of Written Success, Business Planning & Investor Pitching Expert

• Dan - "Nitro" Clark - Former American Gladiator, NFL Player, Bestselling Author

• Sonia Clark - Prosperity Entre-Leadership Creator, Founder of Sonic Lark for Entrepreneurs & Lead Business Education for Corporate Training, Podcast Host of Prosper with Sonia Clark, and Interviewer of Formidable Leaders

• Martina Coogan -Holistic Practitioner, Coach, International Trainer

• Albert Corey - Business Growth Specialist

• Dr. Cindy Cork - Holistic Optometrist, Health Advocate, Educator, CEO

• Teresa Cundiff - Professional Proof-reader, Co-Founder at Empower Her Power Facebook Group, Singer, Speaker, Actor

D

- Michelle Davis - Relationship Expert, Coloring Book Creator of "Born to Be", International Speaker

- James Dentley - International Keynote Speaker, Author, Success, Leadership and Productivity Sculptor

- Sherontelle Dirskell - Celebrity Publicist, Author, Motivational Speaker

- Thomas Dubois - Creator of "Cutting Through the BS for the LOVE of Network Marketing!"

- Jerry Dunn - Emmy® and Art Director's Guild-nominated Production Designer

E

- Jose Elizondo - Marketing Systems Expert

- Prescott Ellison - Grammy Award-winning drummer, patented inventor, published author, educator, animator

G

- Marla Gibbs - Actress, Singer, Writer. 5 time Emmy Nominee, Golden Globe Nominee. 2021 Hollywood Star Recipient.

- Sherry Gideons - Success Mentor, Spiritual Teacher, Transformational Speaker, Author, and Creator of The High Vibe Nation Movement

- Carla Gitto - Interfaith Minister, Reiki Master Teacher, Certified Crystal Healer. Founder of The Emerald Lotus, Healing Sanctuary

- Nancy Gordon - LCSW, CLC Creator of the 7 Steps of Hope and Healing"™ System for Transformation.

- Kerry Gordy - Multi-Platinum Music Producer

- Matthew Gumke - Star of MattyGTV, YouTuber

H

- Heather Harden - CEO of Nachat Consulting LLC

- Ambassador Dr. Raymond Harlall, Ph.D. (hon) - Representative to the United Nations, Activist for Sustainable Development, Author of 10 Books, Keynote Speaker & Consultant

- Bradley Hanselman – CAT Scan Technologist and Natural Health Advocate

- Cristian Hauser - Founder of Live Greatness

- Andrea Heuston - CEO of Artitudes Design, Author, Keynote Speaker and Host of the Lead Like a Woman podcast

- Catherine Hickland - Actress in Knight Rider and One Life to Live, Mentalist, Keynote Speaker, Entrepreneur

- Andrew Hinkelman - CEO of Priority-1 Group Leadership Coaching and Consulting

- Jane Hogan - Founder and CEO of Jane Hogan Health

- Jeanie Holzbacher, RN, BSN - Creator of Conversations That Count

- Kelly Howard - Motivation, Mindset & Adventure Coach

- Amanda Hudes - Event Planner and Coach, Founder of Smiling Through Chaos

J

- Jennifer Jerald - Healing Strategist, Coach & Entrepreneur

- Melody Johnson - Writer, Content Creator and CEO and Founder of Loving Literacy.

K

- Emmanuel Kelly - Upcoming Pop Music Icon

- Lesley Klein - Entrepreneur, Purveyor of Innovative Products that up-level your life

- Shawnte Kinney - Author, Speaker, Coach

- Edit B Kiss - Spiritual Healer and Life Coach

- Caleb Koke - Serial Entrepreneur

- Katherine Kovin-Pacino - Actress, Host, Radio Personality, Contributing Writer

- Denise Kozlowski - Founder and CEO of Particle Marketing Agency House of Fame

- Christina Kumar - Google for Entrepreneurs award-winning entrepreneur, featured journalist, and co-author

L

- Christopher Landano - First Responder & Entrepreneur

- Ann Landstrom - Award Winning Master Photographer

- Loren Lahav-International Speaker, CEO of True and Badass and Beautiful, Author, Executive Coach, Live and Virtual Emcee

- Sally Larkin Green - Faith Teacher and Artist

- Dr. Tracie Hines Lashley - Chief Elevation Officer (CEO), Leadership Expert, best-selling Author, International Business Radio Host

- Sharon Lechter - Author of Think and Grow Rich for Women, New York Times Bestselling Co-Author of Rich Dad Poor Dad, 14 other Rich Dad books, Three Feet From Gold, Outwitting the Devil and Success and Something Greater, International Speaker and featured as one of the World's Greatest Motivators.

- Sherri Leopold - Leader of the Stop Self-Bullying Movement, Author, Speaker

- Susan Levin - Creator of Personal Priorities Yoga and Wellness

- Jill Liberman - best-selling Author, Motivational Speaker, Founder of Choose Happy

- Chuck Liddell - Hall of Fame Mixed Martial Artist, Former UFC Light Heavyweight Champ, Actor / Action Hero

- Gary Lockwood - Star of 2001: A Space Odyssey, and in the Star Trek pilot episode

- Samantha Lockwood Actress - Founder of Fleurings the Original Vase Jewelry

- Paul Logan - Actor, Producer, Writer, Fitness Superstar

- Lisa Long - Influencer, Screenwriter, Producer and Intuitive Success Coach For Entertainment Professionals

- Lydia Lukic - Entrepreneur, Mindset Coach

- Thomesa Lydon - CEO of Lydon Senior Pathways, Real Estate Specialist for Seniors, ReSize Expert, Speaker and Author of 'SMART-LIVING for Seniors; How to Make the Best of the Rest'

M

- Michele Malo - Restoration Specialist

- Angie Manson - CEO Elevate Addiction Services, Crossfit EAS

- Dr. Grace Mankowski - Doctor of Chiropractic, Global Humanitarian, Founder of The Dr. Grace Mirror Method ™

- Michele Marshall - Creator of PURE Client Service

- Dr. Kim Martin - Creator of Health Solutions with Dr. Kim Podcast

- Brendan McCauley - MBA, CPC - Author of "13 Principles To Achieve Greatness", Organization & Automation Expert

- Lori A. McNeil, International Business Coach & Media Strategist

- Jeff Meador - Author, Speaker, Musician, Singer/Songwriter, Former Youth Pastor and Network Marketing Expert

- Julie Michelson - International Speaker, National Board Certified Functional Medicine Health Coach

- Denise Millett-Burkhardt - Meditate Daily for Inspiration, President eZWay Network TV

- Robert J Moore - Founder of Magnetic Entrepreneur Inc., Guinness World Record Holder, 5x International Award Bestselling Author / Speaker

- Amy J. Morrison - Founder of "Empower Her Power", Principle Owner of " Serving Hearts, LLC"

- Tsao-Lin Moy - Alternative and Chinese Medicine Expert

- Dhomonique Murphy - Creator of The Right Method, Celebrity TV Host, 3x Emmy Award Winning Journalist, Mrs. Virginia American, Philanthropist

N

- Linda Nicol - Founder of Women CAN have it ALL program

- Chineme Noke - Corporate Lawyer, Success Coach and International Award Winning, best-selling Author

P

- Daniella R. Platt Top Fashion & Lifestyle Industry Expert, Brand Strategist & Sales Coach, Author of Looking Good #1 Best Seller

- Lauren Powers - 10 Time Overall Heavyweight, Bodybuilding Champion, International best-selling Author, Celebrity Fitness Icon

R

- Krystylle Richardson - Speaker, Author, Jumpologist, World Civility Ambassador of Innovation

- Forbes Riley - Celebrity TV Host, "Queen of the Pitch" and Creator of SpinGym

- Makenna Riley- Award Winning Digital Marketer & Entrepreneur

- Ryker Riley- Entrepreneur Strategist

- Eric Ring - Serial Entrepreneur

- Mel Robertson - De-Clutter Expert & Coach

- Dr. Ken J. Rochon, Jr. - Co-Founder of The Keep Smiling Movement, Author & International Speaker

- Cari Rosno - best-selling Author, Speaker, Truth Seeker

- Bas Rutten - Retired professional Mixed Martial Artist, TV host, Sports commentator, Actor, Inventor

S

- Steven Samblis – Creator of 1 Habit, Celebrity Interviewer, Entrepreneur

- Hersh Sandhoo - Founder of Webmation and Becoming Legendary, best-selling Author

- Dr. Danté Sears - CHt, NLLC, RMP, TLLC, Metaphysician, Doctor of Divinity, Heartprenuer

- Joshua Self -Professional World Champion Bodybuilder, 3d Graphic Artist

- Frank Shankwitz – Founder of the Make–A–Wish Foundation

- Raquel Sharper - International Self-Empowerment Speaker and Coach

- Domingo Silvas III - Creator of Scale 8UP and Stimulus Summit

- Mary Skuza - Consultant

- Brian Smith - Founder of UGG Boots.

- Nora Lynch Smith - Success Coach, Realtor, Educator

- Dr.Niti Solomon - Board-certified physician and creator of Healthier Mastery Program

- Kevin Sorbo - Producer, Director, Lead Actor in Hercules, The Legendary Journeys

- Donna Sparaco Meador - Certified Women's Empowerment Coach

- Alec Stern - Serial Entrepreneur, "America's start-up Success Expert" Co-Founder of Constant Contact

- Stefani Stevenson - Mortgage loan Originator

- Eric Stuerken - Founder of the "One Minute Before" wellness program, All America sprinter and sports enthusiast

- Todd Su -Serial Entrepreneur,CEO of Advantage Homes and 8 other Multi-Million Dollar Businesses

- Barb Swan-Wilson – Co-Founder Healthy Mugs, Founder of Strokes of Genius, Award Winning Entrepreneur

- Erik Swanson - Author, Speaker, Success Coach

T

- Joel Tan - Founder, Joel Tan Online

- Blaney Teal - The Passionpreneur Coach, Founder of MBX Events & Next for Success

- Tobey Ann Terry - Beauty Industry Leader, Beauty & Confidence Coach, Founder of Naked Soul Beauty

- Joe Theismann - Winning Quarterback, Entrepreneur

- Leona Thomas - President and Founder, Enabling Investments, LLC.

- Evan Trad - Educator, Advocate, Visionary

- Paul Andrés Trudel-Payne — a Home & Lifestyle Expert, Creative Director of Casa Consult+Design, Business Solutions & Innovation Consultant, Strategy & Discovery Coach, #1 best-selling Author

- Angel Tuccy - Author, Speaker, Media Exposure Specialist

V

- Brian Vander Meulen - Commercial Real Estate Investor/Agent, Coach, Speaker, Author

W

- DK Warinner – Founder of The DK Method for Stress and Anxiety Elimination, Author, Consultant

- Jane Warr - aka "Trainer Jane" Founder & CEO of Selling on the Spot Marketplace, Communications and Sales Trainer, Collaboration Expert

- Nicole Weber - Founder/CEO Spot Color Marketing

- Steve "The Hurricane" Weiss - Speaker, Sales and Marketing Guru, Small Business Growth Expert, Child of God

- Lynda Sunshine West - Creator of Women Action Takers, Celebrity Interviewer

- Whitnie Wiley, Founder at Shifting Into Action; Creator of The SIMPLE Leadership Method

- Don "The Dragon" Wilson - Martial Arts Action Star, Guinness Book of World Records 11-time Professional Kickboxing World Champion,

- Jill Wright - CEO Executiveshine

- Sharón Lynn Wyeth - Creator of Neimology® Science, Bestselling Author, Speaker, Radio Host

Y

- Ruth Young-Loaeza - CEO & Founder, Genius On Development, NEET Sheets Inventor, Serial Entrepreneur, Small Business Owner, Innovator,   Visionary, Dreamer, Bestseller Author

Z

- Jim Zaccaria - Certified Self-Talk Trainer and Life Coach/Mentor

- CocoVinny Zaldivar- Creator of Coco Taps-Zero Waste Eco Inventor

- Amy Zeal - Expert Fitness and Wellness Coach

- Eric J. Zuley - CEO eZWay Broadcasting Network, Prepare Yourself For Take Off

ABOUT THE CREATOR OF THE 1 HABIT™ MOVEMENT

Steven Samblis is the creator of the 1 Habit book series.

He is the founder of 1 Habit Press. Before creating Samblis Press, Steven had a meteoric career in business that saw him go from being ranked among the top 50 rookie stockbrokers at Dean Witter, to speaking before 250,000 people for The Investors Institute. He has spoken before congress on shareholder's rights representing T Boone Pickens' "United Shares Holders Association."

In 1989 he founded "The Reason For My Success". which grew into one of the largest sellers of self-improvement programs in

North America. The Company expanded into production where Steve collaborated with Chicken Soup for the Soul co-creator Mark Victor Hansen on the audio program The program, called "The World's Greatest Marketing Tools".

As a consultant, Steve created a new name brand for a struggling gym in Dover New Hampshire called Coastal Fitness. He then created a $9.95 a month business model which helped to turn the single gym into one of the most successful fitness franchises in the world, Planet Fitness. In November of 2015 Planet Fitness went public with a 1.6 billion dollar market valuation.

For six years, before launching 1 Habit Press, Steve was the on-air host and Editor in chief for Cinema Buzz, a website and syndicated television show in North America and the UK. On the show, Steve has interviewed over 1000 of the biggest actors and directors in entertainment one on one on camera.

facebook.com/samblis

instagram.com/samblis

amazon.com/author/samblis

ABOUT CO-AUTHOR - FORBES RILEY

Starting her career as a Broadway, tv and film actress, Forbes gives new meaning to Renaissance women and striving for excellence in all that she pursues. Her doing stand-up led to a permanent hosting position at the Hollywood Laugh Factory working alongside Ellen DeGeneres, Jerry Seinfeld, Robin Williams and Wayan Bros. Her radio show career skyrocketed on Westwood One with the interview series Off The Record, getting raw and unscripted with Foreigner, Journey, Clapton, Steely Dan and more. When cable tv launched, her series ranged from the Dog Game Show Zig & Zig on Animal Planet, her own yearlong 2 women hosted talk show, Essentials on TLC, shows on Discovery, ABC Family, helping to create and launch the X-Games for ESPN (for 5 years) AND the launch-pad for selling fitness products on TV - the Hit 24 hour network with Body by Jake, called Fit-TV that eventually sold to Fox for $500 million dollars.

As an actress she has starred on Broadway with Christopher Reeve and starred in Lily Tomlin's Comedy, Search for Signs. Forbes appeared a variety of favorite Soap Operas, TV (24, Boy Meets World, The Practice) and more than a dozen films including her debut (Splatter University)

And as if that isn't enough career for several people, she pioneered the world of infomercials, alongside Shark Tank's Kevin Harrington, hosting and producing more than 200 of them and ultimately grossing more than $2.5 Billion dollars. A familiar face on late night tv, she won the hearts of America co-hosting alongside Jack Lalanne, Montel Williams, Mario Lopez, Bruce Jenner, Kim Kardashian, Tony Little, Betty White and P90x's Tony Horton to name a few.

When home shopping launched she worked for 28 years, not only QVC and HSN but globally at channels in Canada, Great Britain, Italy, France and Germany. Her key to success is her quick wit and mastery of the verbal art of communication and pitching. She now owns the Communication Arts Institute coaching and training entrepreneurs of all levels to perfect their pitch and monetize their messages both on and offline.

But wait, there's more. May sound cliché to some, but it's truly words that Forbes Riley lives by. In 2009, she elevated her game to a whole new level. After being inducted into the National Fitness Hall of Fame, she set out to create what many have called, the greatest fitness product on the planet. Her portable SpinGym is not only compact and portable so you get a resistance and cardio workout in anywhere and anytime but versatile enough to be used by bodybuilders and fitness competitors but people bound to wheelchairs, seniors, amputee, stroke victims and more. Her Dream Makers Foundation aids entrepreneurs from education to start-up funds and works with business on all levels to rise to their fullest potential.

www.Forbes360.com

www.PitchSecretsMasterClass.com

.

The Book That Started a Movement. 1 Habit™

You know the joy you feel when you are so passionate about your "why" that you can't wait to wake up and jump right into life? That motivation will get you started, but to be able to follow through, you need the Habits that will help you place one foot in front of the other when things get tough.

Author, Steve Samblis spent years searching the world for the most successful people on the planet. He got to know them and asked them each "What was the one most crucial Habit in your life that has made the most significant impact on your success." He then took these 100 Habits and put them into a book called 1 Habit.

Not only does the 1 Habit contain the Habits, but it also teaches you how to make a Habit part of who you are. Make it part of your being. Once instilled in you, the Habits becomes something you just automatically now do, and that automates your pathway to success.

Bottom line, you could spend 20 years of trial and error trying to find these Habits for yourself, or you can read 1 Habit and learn from others that have already done the work for you. 1 Habit compresses decades into days.

Lastly, the knowledge you will find in 1 Habit is not power. Execution is power. If you don't put these Habits into your life, what you have in your heart, your desires will honestly only be a dream. And, the last thing we want is for you to be 90 years old and you look back and say... "Wow, that was a nice dream." When it could be your reality if you start adopting these Habits into your life right today.

Get your copy at 1Habit.com/product/1-Habit/

STEVEN SAMBLIS & DEBBIE ROSEMONT

FOR A THRIVING HOME OFFICE

KILLER HABITS OF THE MOST SUCCESSFUL
HOME-BASED BUSINESS
PEOPLE ON THE PLANET

1 Habit For a Thriving Home Office ™

1 Habit For a Thriving Home Office is for anyone running a business at home, people who work for a company, and telecommute and for companies that are transitioning more of their employees to a work-from-home force.

The book can help you take the giant leap to exit the cubicle farm and take your life back while making more money, saving more money, and having an impact beyond your own life.

Look at these stats...

* The US alone would save over $650 billion by changing to Home Based Business or Telecommute work models.

* Oil consumption would be reduced by 280 million barrels a year.

* Greenhouse Gas Emissions would be reduced by the equivalent of 9 million cars a year.

Most people will save

* $1500.00 a year on gas.

* $3000 a year on lunch, dinner, and coffee

* $4-7k a year on child care.

* $1700 a year on wardrobe.

* Gain 12 weeks a year by not sitting in your car every day, in traffic going to and from the cubicle farm.

Get your copy at https://www.1Habit.com/product/1-Habit-for-a-thriving-home-office

STEVEN SAMBLIS & LYNDA SUNSHINE WEST

HAB1T

FOR WOMEN ACTION TAKERS

amazon.com
BEST
SELLING
BOOK

LIFE-CHANGING HABITS FROM
50 OF THE HAPPIEST ACHIEVING WOMEN ON THE PLANET

1 Habit for Women Action Takers ™

Habits Shape Who We Are.

The cool thing, though, is we can instill in ourselves good Habits. Even better, we can change bad Habits (aka un-Habits) into good Habits.

In this book, you will find stories from women action takers who are on a mission to make a significant impact on this planet by sharing their Habits and un-Habits to help you place one foot in front of the other when you need it most.

No matter how much you wish, hope, pray, desire, want, or manifest, nothing happens without action. You can see an opportunity staring you in the face, but if your Habit is to ignore that opportunity and turn the other way, that opportunity is lost forever.

1 Habit will challenge you to take an action step into the unknown. If you have a desire to be more, but don't know where to start, this is the book for you. 1 Habit For Women Action Takers offers small impactful steps that will help you create the life you have always dreamed of.

Get your copy at www.1Habit.com/product/wat

STEVEN SAMBLIS & CORT DAVIES

HAB1T

TO BEAT CANCER

FORWARDS BY
BRIAN TRACY & KATHLEEN O'KEEFE-KANAVOS

SECRETS FROM THE HAPPIEST CANCER THRIVERS ON THE PLANET

1 Habit to Beat Cancer™

Helping Cancer Suck Less: Daily Habits that Helped Incredible Cancer Thrivers Survive and Enjoy Life

1 Habit To Beat Cancer is a simple, easily digestible book that shares the new Habits that inspired these people to overcome their cancer as well as the bad Habits they did away with on their journey.

This book will teach you ways to overcome stress, feelings of despair, and overwhelm to feel instead determined and empowered to live your greatest life, and often, it takes JUST 1 Habit to change your life.

Get your copy at https://www.1Habit.com/product/1-Habit-to-beat-cancer

HAB1T

FOR SUCCESS

Created & Compiled by
STEVEN SAMBLIS
Co-Author **LEA WOODFORD**
FORWARD BY: LISA GUERRERO

SMARTFEM SUMMIT SPECIAL EDITION

1 Habit For Success - SmartFem Summit Special Edition

Imagine being mentored by some of the most respected people in the world. You are who you hang with, why not level up and learn from some of the most accomplished people of our time. This book will allow you to get an insider's look at the Habits of people who are on top of their game in all areas of these lives.

https://www.1Habit.com/product/success/

CREATED AND COMPILED BY STEVEN SAMBLIS

HAB1T

FOR CHRONIC DISORGANIZATION

CO-AUTHOR - REGINA F. LARK, PH.D.

LIFE-CHANGING HABITS TO END PHYSICAL & MENTAL DISORGANIZATION

There are common themes among the chronically disorganized that center around confusion and bewilderment about how effortless it seems for some people to get and stay organized, and how really, really hard it is for others.

This is how people start conversations with me about their disorganized and cluttered spaces:

- It's always been this way.
- I can't remember a time when…
- I've always been ashamed of this.

And chronically disorganized people tend to have a really lousy relationship with time, as in:

- I have no time
- I'm out of time
- There is no time

And there are consequences – minor ones (I forgot to buy the eggs!) and catastrophes (I'm late filing taxes again!). And all the consequences in between:

- High stress
- Everyone thinks you waste time
- Lose sight of personal/professional goals

1 Habit for Chronic Disorganization will give you the space to explore the chronic nature of this condition and how it lands in your life, and then help you unpack and dismantle its effects.

STEVEN SAMBLIS & KRYSTYLLE RICHARDSON

HAB1T

TO END BULLYING

IF YOU HAVE BEEN
BULLIED OR HAVE

BULLIED

THIS BOOK CAN
CHANGE YOUR LIFE

TOGETHER WE CREATE A BETTER WORLD

1 Habit to End Bullying

Bullying knows no barriers.

The dictionary states that the definition of resilience is the capacity to recover quickly from difficulties; toughness or the ability of a substance or object to spring back into shape; elasticity.

Resilience is needed in the case of bullying. It is true that bullying does not care whether you are a business executive, vice president of the United States, a diplomat of a foreign country, the cashier at a checkout counter, a high school baseball coach, Junior High School student or homeless person. There are people across all walks of life that have been affected by this poison.

https://www.1Habit.com/product/1-Habit-to-end-bullying/

ARE YOU A HAPPY ACHIEVER?

For years, my life was focused on being a high achiever. Success was all I could think about. And success meant one thing and one thing only, how much money I made.

Throughout my journey, I would go out of my way to meet respected leaders in business, culture, and social change to learn their secrets and apply them to my success.

But, as I set out to create 1 Habit, I learned something even more amazing. It turns out, my desire to achieve was on target, but I measured it all wrong—in dollars and cents.

I realized, no matter how much money I made, I wasn't as happy as I thought I'd be; there was always going to be someone making more.

One day it dawned on me, I needed to redefine what success meant to me. Money was not the right measurement of success.

Money may be how others measure my success. Why should I give them this power?

I soon realized that happiness is how I wanted to measure my success. My happiness is something I am in control of. The way to reach happiness is to perform at your highest level in all plains of existence. The people that came together as contributors for 1 Habit all did this. These amazing people were all operating at the highest levels, Emotionally, Spiritual, their physical character, the way they live, and of course, financially. Happiness through the balance of performing and living at your peak in all those areas of their lives.

From that day forward, I would keep score based on the time I spent with my family, my friends, my hobbies, exploring the world, and realizing my passions and dreams.

I knew what I wanted to do now but did not know what to call this new category of a person that achieved highly at all levels and, as a result, were some of the happiest people on the planet.

Ask, and you shall receive

Whenever I have a question or a problem, I put it out there, and the universe always seems to give me the answers when I need them.

I was sitting with a friend who started out creating marketing campaigns for companies like ATT. He moved from there to head up a company that produces the marketing campaign for all the major Hollywood studios. If you saw a movie in the last 20 years, there is a high likelihood that Mike Tankel was part of the reason you walked into that theater.

I told Mike about my new way of keeping score in life with happiness, not money. I no longer wanted to be a singular high achiever. I was something more. This thing was "the" more.

With little effort, it rolled off Mike's tongue. "You don't want to be a High Achiever. You want to be a Happy Achiever". And there we have it. A "Happy Achiever."

So now I ask you, my dear reader. How do you keep score in life? More importantly, how do you *want* to keep score in life?

I hope you will join us and live your life to the fullest on all planes of existence. I hope you, too, will become a Happy Achiever!

Steven Samblis

Creator of 1 Habit™

Get Forbes Riley's
<u>BEST PITCH</u>
Secrets for Success!

Get your <u>FREE</u> in-depth Training Videos
on how to PITCH <u>your</u> product, service or idea
to attract more opportunities, get more YESes
and create Financial Freedom.

www.**FreeGift**from**Forbes**.com

Manufactured by Amazon.ca
Bolton, ON